by Gavin Wright and Ben Williams

Cycling For Dummies®

Published by:
John Wiley & Sons, Ltd.,
The Atrium, Southern Gate,
Chichester,
www.wiley.com

This edition first published 2013

© 2013 John Wiley & Sons, Ltd, Chichester, West Sussex.

John Wiley & Sons Ltd, The Atrium, Southern Gate, Chichester, West Sussex, PO19 8SQ, United Kingdom

For details of our global editorial offices, for customer services and for information about how to apply for permission to reuse the copyright material in this book please see our website at www.wiley.com.

Wiley publishes in a variety of print and electronic formats and by print-on-demand. Some material included with standard print versions of this book may not be included in e-books or in print-on-demand. If this book refers to media such as a CD or DVD that is not included in the version you purchased, you may download this material at http://booksupport.wiley.com. For more information about Wiley products, visit www.wiley.com.

Designations used by companies to distinguish their products are often claimed as trademarks. All brand names and product names used in this book are trade names, service marks, trademarks or registered trademarks of their respective owners. The publisher is not associated with any product or vendor mentioned in this book.

For general information on our other products and services, please contact our Customer Care Department within the U.S. at 877-762-2974, outside the U.S. at (001) 317-572-3993, or fax 317-572-4002. For technical support, please visit www.wiley.com/techsupport.

For technical support, please visit www.wiley.com/techsupport.

A catalogue record for this book is available from the British Library.

ISBN 978-1-118-36435-2 (pbk), ISBN 978-1-118-36437-6 (ebk), ISBN 978-1-118-36438-3 (ebk), ISBN 978-1-118-36436-9 (ebk)

Printed in Great Britain by Bell & Bain Ltd, Glasgow

10 9 8 7 6 5 4 3 2 1

Contents at a Glance

Table of Contents

Introduction

. . . .

*A*nnual surveys have shown for years that cycling is one of the most popular physical activities, along with swimming, fishing and walking. Cycling, though, is *so* much better than all of those things put together (at least, we think so). Bike sales in all forms of cycling have been increasing year on year, leaving car sales trailing.

Governments have recognised the advantages of having more people riding rather than driving, and traffic planners have learned that after cycling infrastructure – such as bike lanes, bike paths and real help for bicycles through junctions – is put in place, cyclists come pouring onto roads by the thousand. Campaigns and better facilities have seen some commuter cycling corridors increase their use twentyfold over the last 20 years.

More people are riding bicycles as each day goes by. Some of them are brand new to the world of bikes, some of them have just been away and some people are making the decision to cycle more. Wherever you are in this picture, no doubt you feel you need to know more in some area of cycling. You're in luck, then, because cycling is definitely the topic of this book.

About This Book

This book, like all *For Dummies* books, is designed to be as easy as possible to use and read. Although we've included tonnes of information, it should be the simplest and best cycling book ever to sit on the bookshop shelf.

All the information in this book is easy to find. Whether you want to get to grips with everything about one aspect of cycling by reading the whole chapter on that aspect, or target one specific point in a chapter, you can locate your subject in no time and focus on precisely what you want to find out.

The information is also easy to understand. We don't assume you'll read the whole book and we don't use any jargon, just plain English. You'll come across names to learn as you find out about different parts of your bike, or even various parts of your body, but no overly technical talk is used that would build a barrier between you and what you need to know.

You can often use alternative methods to what we show you to achieve the same result. In this book, however, we don't show you lots of ways of doing things – we just show you the easiest or most effective method. After all, you only really have to have one technique up your sleeve to be able to get the job done.

We've written this book to try to answer most of your questions – anything from, 'Okay, which is the front end?' to, 'How can I shift my lactate threshold?'. If you want to ride a bike – or ride a bike more – this book is both a comprehensive reference, with everything you need to know, and an engaging read you'll enjoy and keep for years.

This book gives you the power, in small, simple stages, to take control of all aspects of your cycling. You can make the decisions, but then this book helps you carry them through. Whatever you want to get out of your bicycle, this book shows you the way.

Conventions Used in This Book

We've presented important bits of information in special ways to make sure you notice them right away:

- **Bulleted lists:** Bulleted lists (just like this one) indicate things you can do in any order or group related bits of information, such as what spare parts to take when you cycle over mountains.

- **Currency:** Every cost that we mention, such as the price of a tyre, is a rough guide and is given in pounds.

- **New terms:** We put any new words or terms in italics and either closely precede or follow them by a simple definition.

- **Numbered lists:** When you see a numbered list, follow the steps in number order to get a job, such as fixing a puncture, done.

- **Sidebars:** Text enclosed in a shaded grey box is always interesting information, but you don't absolutely have to read it to understand the topic.

- **Web addresses:** When we write about a website of interest we include the web address in a special typeface like this: www.bikesaregreat.co.uk.

  Web addresses do change from time to time, so if the website's not there – sorry – try doing an online search. Also, when this book was printed, some web addresses may have been broken across two lines of text. If that happened, rest assured that we haven't put in any extra characters (such as hyphens) to indicate the break and there won't be any spaces. So, when using one of these web addresses, just type in exactly what you see in this book, pretending the line break doesn't exist.

Foolish Assumptions

To write this book we had to make assumptions about you that may not be true. Because we've aimed this book primarily at beginners, but also at people who want to learn more, we've assumed all the way through that you don't know anything about the topic at hand.

We do understand that some people picking up this book already know quite a bit about bikes. Those readers might find some of our explanations overly simple and some of the instructions we've included painfully obvious. If you find yourself reading through one of those spots, just tell yourself, 'Too easy!' and skip to a section that covers an area you need to know more about.

How This Book Is Organised

We've divided this book into five parts.

Part 1: Getting Started with Cycling

This part prepares you for cycling, with lots of information about all sorts of different bikes, other things you can buy to go with bikes, how to make sure your bike is set up right and ideas about riding and feeling good about riding. These are things to help you get the best bike to suit your needs and get the most out of cycling, with all sorts of suggestions about shopping and how to look for the best way to go now you're on a bicycle.

Part 11: Freewheeling Away: The Fundamentals

From the very basic first lessons in sitting on a saddle and pedalling off to dealing with difficult junctions, this part gives you the lowdown on riding and roads. Along the way, I cover safety and the rules for cycling in the UK. Find out where you can safely leave your bike, what the dangers are to cyclists, and how best to tackle them.

Part III: Rolling beyond the Basics

In this part, we go a little further into cycling. We provide ideas and strategies for getting better at your cycling, whether on- or off-road, and cover the physiological side as well as all other aspects of training. We've included a chapter on touring and what you need to take, and a chapter on everything about children and bikes.

Part IV: Maintaining Your Bike and Yourself

In this part, you can read about the aches and pains you might get and how to fix them, as well as what you should be eating (your essential fuel) to give yourself the right energy for cycling. You can then move on to fixing your bike, starting with the very basic jobs of fixing a flat and oiling your chain, then tackling a few more complicated maintenance tasks to put yourself more in control.

Part V: The Part of Tens

This part gives you four cycling super-lists: A list of cycling do's and don'ts, ten of the best rides around the UK, ten of the most awesome races and tours around the world and ten great things about cycling.

Icons Used in This Book

Throughout *Cycling For Dummies,* you encounter little icons in the left margin of the pages, which alert you to specific types of information in the text. Here's what the icons mean:

This little icon points you to stories from our cycling experiences around the world and our meetings with other cyclists. They all contain some little piece of wisdom and are there to illustrate the subject we're explaining.

When you see this icon, you know a little piece of wisdom is coming your way. Not something to worry you, just a point to bear in mind. Your cycling will go smoother if you don't forget these points.

Here and there in this book we've felt it important to explain exactly how things work, what they're made of or how they're put together. For some people this will satisfy a need to understand why they have to do what needs to be done. Other people don't want to be bothered with that. If you see this icon, it indicates some good stuff, but reading those paragraphs isn't essential.

Tips are little bits of know-how we've picked up as we've cycled or that we've picked up from other cyclists over the years – little tricks for making your cycling, training or repairing easier, and ways of doing things better or quicker. You'll pick up tips from other cyclists too — this icon just helps to speed things up for you.

Danger ahead: don't do it, don't go there. This icon alerts you to possible dire consequences if you don't heed the advice we give. We don't want you to suffer as a cyclist, so pay close attention when you see this sign.

Where to Go from Here

Reading this book should be like riding your bike: it's the Freedom Machine and you can go where you like. Stop and take in the view here, sit in the shade for a snack there. You can steer your way through these pages, avoiding parts that are irrelevant to your needs like potholes on a wet bend, but you always have an easy downhill dash to the bit you need to read.

If you're a cycling newbie, the first points about getting on your bike should be a big help and should get you launched on a tour of discovery, good health and long-lasting pleasure. You can leave the pages on interval training until a time when you feel you need to know about it – they'll keep.

If all the simple stuff is old hat (or maybe helmet) to you, the more involved sections of this book should get you fired up and pedalling fast towards achieving your goals and fulfilling your dreams.

And hopefully we'll see you out there on your bike sometime.

Part I
Getting Started with Cycling

For Dummies can help you get started with lots of subjects. Visit www.dummies.com to learn more and do more with *For Dummies*.

In this part . . .

✔ Dazzle yourself with the range of bikes available and pick the type that best suits your needs.

✔ Twiddle your bike's adjustable parts to ensure that you always have a comfortable – and safe – ride.

✔ Bolt, clamp, strap and clip any number of accessories to your bike – and yourself.

✔ Making space in your weekly schedule to incorporate cycling into your lifestyle.

Chapter 1

Getting into Cycling

Deciding to ride a bicycle, or to ride a bike more, is a move you won't regret. You may have worked out that it's better for the environment, better for traffic congestion and your community and, perhaps most of all, better for your health. When you start riding, you'll kick yourself that you didn't do it earlier.

Riding a bike is fun – it starts that way and it doesn't stop. Every time we rest our feet on the pedals and speed off down the road, we get a feeling of great pleasure, just as we did as kids when we first took off on bikes with a spirit of freedom and adventure.

But getting into cycling isn't as simple as just going to the shop, buying a bike and riding off down the street. You don't need to know a great deal initially – you can go on learning about bikes forever – but you need to start with an awareness of the basics.

Get the wrong bike and your relationship could become rocky and eventually fall apart. Get the right one and it'll be a marriage made on the perfect bike path. And from there, the richness of your developing affair with your bike will have you dreaming of all the possible things the two of you could do together.

This chapter covers the basics to get you started (or back) on the bike and on the right path to a long life together.

Meeting Your Bike

When looking for your bike, play it cool and get it right. A key point in searching for any new relationship is to be self-aware, and that's true for cycling as well. Know your own needs and be positive about them. Focus on the many positive aspects a bicycle can provide, rather than what it can't give you.

Stay in control and don't let your feelings be dominated by any past experiences. If you're coming back to cycling after a break of many years, keep in mind that bikes are different these days. Your perfect bike is out there waiting for you – one that will be kind to you and that you will love.

Riding for the first time

If cycling is a whole new world for you, then welcome. We guarantee you're going to enjoy it, but we also know you have to take a couple of big steps before you're waking up in the morning with that big I'm-a-cyclist smile on your face.

The biggest decision you have to make is what kind of bicycle to buy. You might have studied those racy-looking figures in Lycra and decided that's the gear for you, but you first need to think about the type of cycling you're going to be doing. Ask yourself what you want the bike for. If you're going to train, race and win, you're absolutely right – you need a road bike. But most people's requirements are a little less intense and bike makers spend a great deal of time crafting machines to suit the most specific of needs. If you want a bike to use when you go shopping, to ride on bike paths or to cycle into the hills on unsurfaced roads, you can be sure that someone has designed and built a bike with precisely you in mind.

If you want to speed up and down rocky paths in the wild, a mountain bike is what you need. If you've decided to commute, a road bike might be best, but you could be more comfortable on a flat-bar road bike, a hybrid or a touring bike. If you're thinking about riding instead of driving when you want to visit friends or pop to the supermarket (good for you), a great-looking retro bike or even an electric bike might be the best idea.

Have a look at Chapter 2 for plenty of information on different kinds of bikes. Then have a chat with the people down at the bike shop – tell them what your plans are and get some advice. They don't expect you to buy straight-away, so don't feel you're under any pressure.

You might not yet know how to ride a bike. Riding a bike always used to be taught with an adult running along hanging on to the learner's saddle. If you don't have anyone available for that, don't worry – see Chapter 14 for a method that's much easier and less stressful and is good for children or adults.

Even getting on and off your new bike can be a headache. The best way to start on a bike is to straddle it, put one foot on a raised pedal, push forward, then sit in the saddle and get the other foot on the other pedal. This way you don't have to swing a leg through the air while you're rolling along. For more about this and some tips on steering, pedalling and gears, see Chapter 6.

Getting back on the bike: It's been a long time

If years have gone by since you last rode a bicycle, don't worry. Think of going cycling again as like an elephant riding a bike – the elephant never forgets. You're in for some pleasant surprises. Bike manufacturers constantly work to improve their products. Frames get lighter and stronger, gears get smoother and more reliable, and the whole process of riding is made easier and more comfortable.

A big range of different styles is available in bike shops now and sometimes even slight changes to, say, the length of the frame or the angle of the handlebars can make a big difference to how you feel on a particular bike. Check out a few different bikes in the store and take a selection for a test ride.

If, however, you're dusting off an old pedaller you've had for years, you'll find that you'll be the envy of the cycling crowd. Old steel road bikes are on every racer's wish list these days and anything with an extravagant curve turns heads like only curves can.

You need to run through a number of checks if you're resurrecting an old flame. Assessing tyres and brakes is important every time you take out any bike, but bringing an old bike out of the shed you need to be a lot more thorough. You need to investigate and test gears, steering and any funny noises. Chapters 17 and 18 walk you through doing this, dealing with some basic and then slightly more in-depth maintenance procedures.

Starting again on your old bike is a good idea, but think back: was there a reason you stopped riding this bicycle? Maybe it was the wrong size or you weren't comfortable in the position it gave you. It could be the time to invest in a new one. We both remember so clearly the feeling of excitement we had as kids when we got new bikes. We still get that feeling now every time it happens. Why not treat yourself to that wonderful feeling.

If you're getting back on a bike after a break, you might just be doing so with the aim of getting a bit fitter. An excellent reason, but do have a think about some other possible benefits. Some people feel a bit flat riding around on their own, but get a great deal of enjoyment from riding in a group of like-minded cyclists.

Get in touch with your local cycle club or council to find out if any people meet locally for the kind of cycling you want to do. This could be anything from a ride around the park to a long-distance sprint to an off-road mudfest, but if other people are doing it you could join in. Before you know it, you might be exploring distant lands on a bike with your new-found friends.

Check out Chapter 13 for tips on cycling with other people, including details of some great longer rides put on by cycling organisations across the UK.

Wanting to do that little bit more

If you've already got a bike and know how to ride it, but are thinking about making cycling a bigger part of your life, you can put in place a number of very practical strategies.

Bicycle commuting is one of the best decisions anyone could make – when you've tried it out, you won't believe you ever took the car or public transport to work. Some people aren't lucky enough to be able to ride the whole way, but if you don't need to drive as part of your job and don't live too far away from work, starting to commute by bike is a move you won't regret. You won't have to find the time or money for the gym, your petrol bills or public transport costs will evaporate and you'll probably get to work quicker and certainly feeling better.

If you've just got a vague idea about riding more because you know cycling is good for you, but want to start slowly, then get a bit more structured. Think about when you ride now – for example, perhaps it's Mondays, Wednesdays and sometimes Fridays. Write down a plan and commit to riding on each of these days for a set distance. Then give yourself a goal, such as riding your set distance within a certain time. How big your goal is doesn't matter – if you reach it, you have succeeded and deserve a great big pat on the back.

See Chapter 5 for more tips on making time to ride and increasing your commitment.

Building a Relationship with Your Bike

When you've found your perfect bicycle, the fun doesn't end there – you then get to start building a strong, long-term relationship with your bike.

You can work out where your bike is going to live. (A bike can somehow seem relatively small until you realise you've got nowhere to put one.) Then you can spend time getting to know all your bike's different parts, learning names of bits you never knew existed. So the bottom bracket won't seem so base. You'll get to grips with handlebars. You'll get your teeth into forks. You can kit your bike out with various accessories and presents, and introduce it to family and friends – and perhaps you can even get them involved in your trips out with your bike. To ensure you and your bike both look the part, you can work out the most appropriate attire for the kind of cycling you do together. And further down the track, you may even consider taking your loved one on a well-earned trip away. (You could even check if family or friends want to go along too.)

Finding a space for your bike

Owning a bike is a marvellous thing, but before you walk away from the shop wheeling your brand new friend, you have to give some thought to where you're going to put it. If you've got a big shed or garage with plenty of space, you certainly don't have to think about it very long. That's where it'll live.

Even if you have space for your bike in a shed or garage, think about whether this space is secure. Will you lock your bike away? If you've spent a lot of money on a bike (and sometimes even regardless of cost), it'll be an awful shame if it goes missing. Also check whether your home insurance covers theft of your bicycle from your home. You often need to add your bike as an extra to your policy, so contact your insurers to confirm what you're already covered for and what you might need to change. Also check whether your insurers cover the full cost of replacement.

Unless insurance representatives are cyclists themselves, they often have no idea how expensive bikes can be, so be quite specific with the representative you talk to and don't settle for any such answers as, 'I should think so'.

If the only secure place you can leave your bike means that you'll be sharing your living space with it, you have to give placement much more thought. Squeezing past bikes in confined places can be difficult, and they can fall over quite easily.

Freedom machines: Bicycle history

The bicycle as we know it first appeared in the 1880s, coming along soon after penny-farthings, which were generally only used by reckless young men because of the dangers involved. If anything, such as a rock or hole in the road, stopped the front wheel, the rider and the bike would fly over the top and land on the road. The big development that constituted the 'safety bicycle' was the chain running to the back wheel, which meant that by altering the ratio of the cogs on the front and the back chainwheels you could make the bicycle go very fast without having to have a huge wheel. Bicycles became something most people could consider riding, and were soon widely known as *freedom machines*.

Early in the history of bikes, brakes and gears appeared, although racing cyclists weren't allowed to use *dérailleur gears* (the system where a bar shifts the chain from one cogwheel to another of a different size) until the 1930s. Birmingham Small Arms (BSA, the motorcycle manufacturer) first produced folding bikes for British paratroopers in the Second World War and the US military still use similar bikes for fast, undetectable paratrooper infiltration. BMX bikes have been around since the early 1970s and the first mountain bikes came on the market in 1981.

Bicycles have been on the roads about 20 years longer than cars, and currently about one billion of them are in use worldwide, making them twice as common as cars. In many places in the world, cycling is the main form of transport for ordinary people.

 Gavin used to know a man who worked for a cycling group who told him that before he got into a personal relationship and started a family he slept with his bicycle on the other side of his double bed. Obviously, his situation had changed, but as he related the story Gavin could see an almost wistful look in his eye.

 If you've got the tools and the strength, attaching brackets fairly high up on a wall to hold your top bike tube gets the wide part of the bike (the handlebars) out of the way, but you have to be sure you can lift the bike that far. Hooks in the ceiling are also handy, but you must make sure you anchor them into a joist and that you can get the front wheel up that high. Alternatively, bike lift pulley systems are a great idea if you want to keep your bike up high. They're secure, easy and, because of the way pulleys work, you only lift a fraction of the weight of your bike. You can use these systems in a house or apartment but, again, you have to be very sure that you fix the system to a really solid surface.

Balconies are a favourite spot for people who live in apartments, but bikes stored here might need extra protection from the elements. Bike covers offer this protection while also hiding the bike from the view of anyone who might try to climb up and steal it. (Although locking the bike up is still a good idea.)

Recognising your bike's features: Knowing which bit is which

I hope you already know which part on the bike is the saddle and which parts are the pedals and the handlebars. Wheels too. But obviously lots of other parts make up a bike and they all have names. Some of them have several names. You don't need to know them all, but learning a few helps you in a conversation about your new pastime and friend.

Figure 1-1 shows you the most important parts of a bike to know. (***Note:*** In Figure 1-1, the bottom bracket is hidden. This part of the bike runs through the frame behind the chainring, connecting the cranks.)

Knowing the names of parts helps you if anything goes wrong. You won't find yourself down at the bike shop pointing to the busted component and saying simply, 'Broken'. Also, I have found there's no end to the enjoyment you can have with good friends chatting about such things as rear dropouts and bottom brackets.

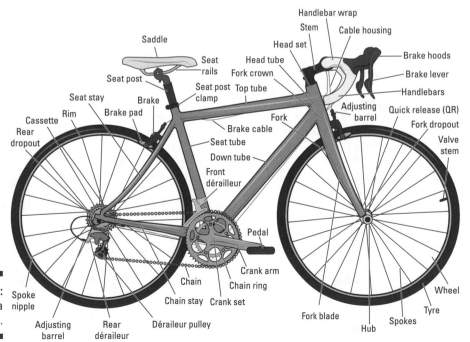

Figure 1-1: Parts of a bicycle.

For the love of cycling

Pierre-Auguste Renoir, the famous impressionist painter, loved his bicycle – even though in 1897 he fell off his bike and broke his arm. Marcel Duchamp, the great Dadaist, used a bicycle wheel and fork for the first of his famous and controversial 'readymades' in 1917, saying, 'I liked the idea of having a bicycle wheel in my studio. I enjoyed looking at it just as I enjoy looking at the flames dancing in a fireplace. It was like having a fireplace in my studio, the movement of the wheel reminded me of the movement of the flames.' And in 1943, Pablo Picasso hung a bike saddle on the wall with some handlebars curving upwards to create the powerful *Bull's Head*.

The performance of 'Do-Re-Mi' in *The Sound of Music* wouldn't be as good if Julie Andrews and the others playing the Von Trapp family weren't singing at least part of it on bikes. Paul Newman as Butch Cassidy melted an awful lot of hearts when he cycled round an orchard to the tune of 'Raindrops Keep Fallin' on my Head', wearing a bowler hat, and with Katharine Ross on his handlebars. And ET would never have been able to phone home without those brave kids on BMX bikes.

But quite possibly our favourite picture from bicycling history is of Albert Einstein riding a bike in Santa Barbara, cornering precariously with a big smile on his face. Einstein was a vociferous supporter of cycling, claiming that great thoughts came to him while riding. Indeed, in this picture Einstein could well be saying, 'By George, I've got it!'

Adorning your bike with accessories

Some bits and pieces to go with a new bike are very important. You need a pump, and lights – front and back – are essential for riding after dark or in poor light. You also won't be riding long before you need to carry something, so working out where you're going to put it is important. Backpacks and courier-style bags can be fine, but having suitable baskets, bags and racks attached to your bike makes riding far more comfortable.

As well as pumps, lights and carriers, other, more standard items you can shop for include bells, mudguards, mirrors and bar-ends, but many more intriguing things you can bolt to your bike are available. Just spend some time at your local bike shop marvelling at the huge range of attachable inventions.

See Chapter 3 for more on choosing the right accessories for your bike.

Discovering hidden talents: Uses you never thought of

You may have bought your bike for a certain purpose – for example, riding with the family – but no doubt you'll soon be hopping in the saddle for other reasons as well, such as popping down to the shops. Using your bike is often quicker and you can park up right outside. Visits to the library, chip shop or cinema are all more satisfying journeys on a bicycle.

Maybe you've started to commute and found you can keep up with, or pass, most other cyclists on your route. If you really are a fast pedaller, try a visit to your local cycling club at the weekend. These clubs organise racing in different levels so that you compete against people who are roughly in the same class. Check out Chapter 13 for information about cycling clubs and racing.

Cycling is such an enjoyable thing to do you'll soon find yourself reaching more and more for your helmet rather than your car keys. For some people cycling becomes a way of life. The more you pedal, the healthier and happier you become, so the more ways you find of using your bicycle, the better life becomes for you.

Planning for a child

Children and bikes go hand in hand. If you're used to riding and want to bring your tiny offspring along, a few different ways of carrying them are available, including the following:

- ✔ **Handlebar seats:** These are good for very small children and the position of the seat means you can interact well with the child.

- ✔ **Rear seats:** These are stronger than handlebar seats and take a child up to four years old, or even older if they're little. Because of the height of the seat, children get a good view of everything as you carry them along and you still have the comfort of knowing they're with you.

- ✔ **Trailers:** These come with one or two seats and are covered, which protects little VIPs from the weather. Children are strapped in, but have a bit of space around them for soft toys. An added bonus is that many trailers convert to a stroller when not attached to your bike.

- ✔ **Tag-Alongs/Trail-a-Bikes:** These suit riders aged from around five upwards. Instead of a front wheel, they have a bar that clamps onto the seat post of your bike. So, while your child gets the full experience of pedalling and riding with you, the steering is left entirely to you. They are a great way of introducing young ones to riding longer distances (they can just stop pedalling and get a tow if they get tired) and to places with other traffic, so they can learn from you.

Children of any age or size should wear helmets when they're being carried or towed by a bicycle.

You can first put a youngster on a bicycle of their own at about two-and-a-half years old. Children this young may need training wheels, but by four years old you should be able to take off the trainers.

Cycling is all about balance and you don't learn any of that with training wheels, so starting off with a *balance bike* (a bike with no pedals where children move forward by pushing with their feet), a standard child's bike without training wheels or getting rid of the training wheels early is best.

Riding with your child or family is often a great way to bolster your personal team. It also teaches your kids that a bike isn't just a child's toy – a bike is also something that smart adults enjoy and use for transport. Small minds often set their sights on such things as little red Corvettes, but you can show the young people in your life that whatever choices they make they don't ever have to give up riding a bicycle.

See Chapter 14 for tips on choosing either the right method of transporting your child on your bike or your child's first bike, as well as a simple, quick and painless method of teaching a child to ride a bike.

Dressing up: Finding the right clothing

Experts have invented fabrics especially for cycling and you can fill a whole wardrobe with clothes designed specifically for riding a bike. Seamless cycling shorts are designed to give you frictionless pedalling and jerseys are built to draw away your perspiration before you even know it's there.

If you're after the look of Mark Cavendish, say, your bike shop is a good place to start dressing yourself up for riding, but you can find the perfect jersey in many other places as well. Sometimes you can get them by joining a club or doing a big, organised ride, but you can always find a huge assortment online. As well as jerseys and cycling shorts, you can also find cycling gloves, socks, tights, arm warmers, jackets and plenty more clothes made solely with cyclists in mind.

You don't have to wear specialist clothing to ride a bike. If you visit any of the great cycling nations of the world – China, India, Colombia, the Netherlands, Vietnam, Germany and Denmark spring to mind – you rarely see any riders togged up for a tour.

As long as you follow a few sensible guidelines to prevent your ordinary clothes getting ruined by contact with grease or moving parts, and to ensure your clothes help you stay at a comfortable temperature, you're free to wear anything you like. In fact, if you have a close look at what riders are wearing in Amsterdam or Copenhagen, you might feel a strong urge to visit the boutique rather than the bike shop.

Travelling with your loved one

When riding a bicycle has become a happy part of your life, you're going to start seeing opportunities to improve the quality of your other activities by simply taking along your bike. You'll want it with you any time you go to the countryside, the big city or on holiday.

Several ways to travel with a bike are possible. Folding bikes are allowed pretty much everywhere, but full-size bikes are restricted. Buses are out and so are coaches and trams. However, bikes are allowed on most trains (sometimes under certain conditions), and a boxed or bagged bike is generally an acceptable piece of luggage on an aeroplane (although you may have to check in early and pay extra).

Carrying your bike in or on your car is very handy for all sorts of reasons. For example, you might be taking your bike with you so you can:

- ✔ Cycle only part of your commuting journey
- ✔ Have your bike with you on holiday
- ✔ Use your bike at an event or on a trail

When taking your bike in or on your car, making sure that it arrives safe and sound is obviously important. If you can't fit the bike on the back seat, you can fit roof racks or rear racks to your car. You can carry up to four bikes on rear racks and sometimes more on the roof. You can also get special racks that fit to the rear of a caravan or motorhome.

Check out Chapter 12 for more details on travelling near and far with your bike.

Loving Your Bike Forever

When you become a regular cyclist, you start to enjoy the long-term benefits to your health, and you start being able to pick up on the signs that something might be amiss with your bike's health. The more you ride socially or in groups, the more likely you are to meet people you get along with really well and who end up being close personal friends. And when you've been riding a little while, you might also start to realise that distances you once thought colossal are now quite ordinary – and you might feel ready to take on a programme of training, or even move into racing or touring the world.

Growing old together: Staying healthy and living longer

Riding a bicycle is good for your health in many ways. Consider the following:

- ✔ Cycling strengthens your heart and makes it work more efficiently. As you ride your bike, your heart pumps more blood with every contraction and so needs to beat less when you're resting. Regular exercise also reduces your blood pressure to a healthy low level and helps maintain good cholesterol levels. All these factors reduce the risk of heart disease, one of the biggest killers in the UK.

- ✔ Cycling improves your circulation and breathing. It conditions muscles all over your body (not just your legs) and tunes the rest of your system to supply them with energy.

- ✔ Riding a bike helps get rid of or prevent excess bodyweight. Unfortunately, obesity is very common in Britain today, the product of a sedentary lifestyle and poor food choices. The prevalence of type 2 diabetes has grown to epidemic proportions largely due to this sad fact.

- ✔ Cycling helps your sense of wellbeing by leading your body to produce endorphins. *Endorphins* are produced by the pituitary gland and released during medium- to high-intensity aerobic exercise (exercise that gets the heart rate up). They make you feel less pain and less stress and boost your immune system. Basically, they make you feel better, and it's partly these chemicals that make you feel happy and give you that sense of wellbeing after a bike ride. This simple consequence is a highly effective tool to improve mental health and tackle depression.

With all these health benefits, you can see that if you ride a bike you're likely to live and stay in good health much longer. And people who've been cycling for years tend to look far younger than many of their non-bike-riding contemporaries. The simple act of sitting on a saddle, holding on to handlebars and pedalling can substantially improve the quality and length of your life.

Cycling is a form of exercise that doesn't involve a high level of skill and that you can practise at anything from very low to very high intensity. Cycling isn't an expensive activity to take up and even saves money if it replaces car or public transport journeys. Riding a bike is one of the easiest and most efficient ways for people to get back to a better shape and better health.

Riding a bicycle is not an inherently dangerous thing to do. Very few people fall off, so if you're in a safe environment you're quite secure on a bike. Ben's wife enjoyed riding bikes almost all the way through pregnancy. No reason exists for a cyclist to give up riding unless some misfortune makes it impossible.

Making your bike better when it's not well: In sickness and in health

A few basic bike maintenance skills are required of all cyclists. Punctured tyres happen to the best of us. Little bits of glass, nails or devilishly sharp pieces of plant matter slide through the material of your tyre and inner tube and leave you with that flat feeling at the side of the road. If this happens to you, you'll almost certainly have to fix it on the spot. This can either mean repairing the puncture or fitting a new inner tube. Both procedures require you to remove one side of the tyre from the wheel and fitting an inner tube requires you to take the wheel off.

The other most elementary task for a bike owner is knowing how to thoroughly clean your bike. This includes sprucing up the chain and giving it a liberal dose of lubrication. See Chapter 17 for help with these basic skills.

Being able to perform a few other maintenance jobs and alterations is also extremely useful. Getting your saddle to the right height might take a bit of working out, so being able to do it yourself saves a lot of time and frustration. Knowing how to adjust your own gears and brakes can be very satisfying, not least because you don't have to worry about the mechanic not getting it quite right – you can just jump off and fix them straightaway. Likewise, looking after your suspension, if you have it, and getting to grips with your chain when it needs replacing are both processes that can be very empowering.

Chapter 18 covers all you need to know about these more advanced (although still very easy to master) maintenance and repair jobs.

Meeting new people: Making bicycle friends

We've talked to cyclists from every walk of life. We've ridden in company we would otherwise have thought incompatible, even alien. And we've asked many riders, from couriers to CEOs, anarchists to architects, the same thing: 'Do you have something in common with someone else just because he or she rides a bicycle?' And the answer has invariably been an immediate and resounding, 'Yes!'

Cycling isn't like driving a car – you rarely see any rage on the bike path. Healthy humans, feeling great to be out exercising, are always more likely to be pleasant and welcoming. If you meet someone on a bike, that person is already halfway to being a friend.

So if you join a cycling group that has something else in common – a love of racing, a devotion to forest trails, a fondness for farmers' markets or a passion for visiting country pubs, for example – you're likely to make some very good, long-term friends.

You can become more than friends with a cycling companion. Gavin has known romance of the most profound kind kindled and inflamed when lonely eyes met across firmly gripped handlebars.

See Chapter 13 for more on cycling with other people and joining an organised group.

Discovering new things about each other: Setting up a training programme

When you start riding a bike, you might reach a point where you don't appear to be improving, or your improvement seems to be haphazard and slow. Perhaps you want to be faster than anyone else on the road, get strong enough to tackle any of the tough slopes on your local hills, or just be able to cycle for a very long way.

If you want to get better you should think about setting yourself some goals and working out a schedule of riding that will help you to achieve them.

Writing down your schedule and having someone to report your progress to are excellent tools for solid improvement. If you're training with a club or team, you'll probably find the structure of your cycling lends itself well to discipline, reporting and achievement. If you're out there on your own it can be harder, but write it all down and see if you can find someone who takes an interest and gives support.

Always set realistic goals without huge jumps up in performance. Setting your sights too high makes you more likely to give up or over-train and knock yourself out. Instead, a series of minor goals leading up to a major event or challenge motivates you and gives you a ladder of easy steps to success.

See Chapter 5 for more on increasing the time you spend cycling, and check out Chapter 11 for tips on training and improving your cycling fitness.

Looking for adventure: Winning the Tour or touring the world

If you really are good at this cycling thing, anything's possible. From the ranks of local cycling clubs, Britain's Olympic and Grand Tour champions have emerged. Every one of those super-cyclists you see pounding away at their pedals in the Tour de France started racing at their local club. They've practised a lot since then, of course, but they were all green young hopefuls once.

If you find the urge to win gives power to your legs, you're capable of changing your lifestyle to suit your body's training requirements and you enjoy spending many hours putting in the hard graft on your bike, then nothing is stopping you from aiming for the top. You could be riding in that mighty, magic tour one day. Go for it! (Chapter 11 contains loads more tips on increasing your training and building fitness.)

However, if it's travel and adventure that thrills you to the bone, a bicycle's the perfect vehicle for it. Get yourself fit and strong and the world is your oyster – and, in many ways, your bicycle is better than any other vehicle to help you experience the land you travel through, whatever the conditions.

Gavin once pulled his atlas off the shelf with the sole intention of finding the hardest road for a bicycle in the world. He ended up on a route that took him right over the high Andes and far out into the Amazon jungle. It was the journey of a lifetime.

People have now been almost everywhere on bikes – almost, but not quite. Why not take this as a challenge? When you've made your way through this book, if you train hard, do your research and gather together a lot of money, you could be the first person to ride a bicycle from London to the South Pole. How cool would that be?

Chapter 2

Picking the Right Bike

• •

In This Chapter

▶ Working out your cycling needs

▶ Revealing road bikes

▶ Mastering mountain bikes

▶ Cutting through categories with a bike blend

▶ Focusing in on specialist bikes

• •

Deciding to buy a bike is a great first step to taking up cycling – you can't do much without one. But you can't just rock up at your local bicycle shop and say you want to buy a bike. The good people there will ask you lots of questions and, chances are, you won't have the answers. You've got to have some idea what kind of bike you want or you'll come away with nothing. Or worse, you'll come away confused and further from buying a bike than when you started. Worse still, you might come away with the wrong bike.

Naturally, buying a bike is best not hurried, unless you already know exactly what you want. A bike is an investment and something that will hopefully become close to you and stay with you for a long time. Don't buy the first one you see: bicycles are as complicated as your feelings and needs are, and taking the time to think out your purchase is a smart idea.

If you do know exactly what you want, and you want a bicycle for just one thing – for example, for racing, riding to work, or delivering pizza in a university city – and you don't have any strong style preferences, then this chapter is bound to make clear what you need. In fact, you can just go to the bike shop and they'll show you the right bikes straightaway. From there, you can just pick the one you like.

In this chapter, we discuss what the various types of bicycles were designed for and what they're good for (and how many piggy banks you'll need to fill up to pay for one.). If you're not yet sure what bike you want, this information will help you take a giant leap forward in working out exactly which bike is right for you. Your ideal bike is out there, but you're the one who has to find it.

Defining Your Needs

Before you can choose a bicycle, you do need to have some idea about what kind of riding you intend to do. The more precise you can be, the easier you'll find choosing the type of bike to buy. If you already know you're going to be commuting to work in style (and still beating the train there), or joining your mates on weekend runs with the *peloton* (a group of cyclists riding in a pack) or following them on singletrack mountain bike adventures, then that's great – you're halfway there.

Asking the tough questions

Bikes are very good for lots of things. You might have made the decision to start riding to work – good for you! – but then realise that not only is it quicker to get to work on a bike, but it's also much quicker to get to the shops. So you need a bike that's fast on tarmac, but that you can also load up with some purchases and that doesn't stand out as having cost a royal ransom – so you can happily leave it tethered on the street or outside the shops.

Maybe you're after a bike to take on holiday (which is a very good idea) or for daytrips. If so, then you might well be riding on both roads and trails, and you'll want to be sure you've got one that is comfortable and can handle these different conditions.

If any of this sounds familiar and, like many people, you want your bike for a few different kinds of riding, you'll have to look at what's on offer. It might help if you ask yourself some of these questions:

- Do I need a bike that goes fast?
- Do I need to be able to put both feet on the ground when I'm sitting on my bike?
- Do I want my bike to be a particular colour?
- How do I feel about leaning forward when I sit on a bike?
- How much am I willing to spend?
- Will I be riding off-road?
- Will I ride to work?
- Will I travel (by car, train or some other form of transport) with my bike?
- Will I want to leave my bike chained up in a public space?

In the end, it may be that after much consideration you find you have bicycle needs that are actually incompatible – you're going to ride in the Tour de France, but you also need to ride out taking the dog with you on forest trails. You're obviously well worth meeting, but you really need two different bikes. While you can take your top-end road bike through mud and over tree roots, doing so isn't going to be very comfortable or easy (and you really shouldn't treat racers that way).

Having more than one bicycle is okay, but if you can merge your needs to start off with, we're sure you'll be very happy with just one bike – and you'll certainly spend less. Bear in mind that your routines and needs might change. Lower-priced bikes are fine for starting out on and it might be a good idea to invest less at first, just to see how you go. Then, if you find you need to spend more on a different kind of bike, you won't feel you've overspent on the first one.

Knowing where you're going

So you've decided you're going to ride to work. Excellent! You won't regret it. But what route do you take? While you may know the way very well in a car – and you can almost certainly cycle the same way – this route isn't necessarily the best way.

Online and hard-copy maps are excellent tools for finding alternative cycling routes: off-road pathways, trails or just plain short cuts. These can lessen the distance and are often much safer, because you're not mixing with motor traffic. You can also head off at the weekend and just explore – definitely a great way to spend your spare time.

The point is, even though you may be travelling to the same place that you used to go in the car, bus or tram, on a bike you may well not be doing it all on-road, and your choice of bicycle needs to reflect this.

So, the bicycle you choose should be a good match for the places you'll be riding in. If you're planning a holiday cycling over some mountains, for example – and many people do – then a mountain bike might sound like the right vehicle for the job. But you need to know a little bit more about what makes up different kinds of bikes and what these parts are good for. In this case, if you happen to be on a road the whole time, then although your mountain bike may be comfortable, its knobbly tyres and suspension will give you an inefficient, slow ride to the top. You may be on a mountain, but mountain bikes aren't built for roads. The wide, knobbly tyres (see the sidebar 'Choosing your tread and TPI' for more on tyres) on mountain bikes are good for dealing with loose gravel, sand and wet surfaces – the kinds of things you're likely to encounter on a mountain.

Choosing your tread and TPI

When choosing the type of tyres your bike will need, two things are important: tread and threads per inch (TPI).

On a surfaced road you don't need any tread at all. The rubber on the outside of a tyre is a very good material for holding and sticking to tarmac without slipping. Road bike tyres are only a few centimetres wide and have very little tread, yet they fly round sharp corners at high speed and at steep angles. As long as the rider doesn't lean too far, they keep a perfect grip on the road. If you're riding over surfaces that are loose, sandy or wet, however, you need a tyre that's wider and has more bumps. The bumps on the tyres grip the terrain surface and the width covers a greater ground area for more traction.

Another aspect to look at is the *TPI*. Most bicycle tyres are made of two *beads,* the metal or Kevlar rings that hook onto the rim of the wheel; cloth fabric that's woven between the two beads; and rubber, which protects the structure from damage. The TPI is the density of the strands that make up the fabric part: the higher the TPI, the less the rolling resistance and the better the performance of the bike. Tyres used on racing bikes have a high TPI. The trouble is, high TPI tyres are also much more vulnerable to wear and damage. They may puncture more easily and if you take them out on all your long training rides on the road they simply won't last very long.

This figure shows three different tyre treads: A mountain bike, which is thick and knobbly; a medium tyre, thinner with some tread; and a racing tyre, narrow with no tread on the contact surface and just a little on the sides.

Most bikes in between mountain and road will have medium-width tyres with some tread. This should give you confidence and grip for almost all riding situations.

You need to decide what the majority of your cycling will be, what surface or surfaces you will be riding over, and how far you want to go. If you might ride on difficult terrain now and then, you'll need a bike that will be able to cope.

Feeling comfortable

During your first visit to a cycle shop, your eyes may fall upon what you think is the perfect bicycle. Your heart leaps. You can see that bike is just what you always wanted. But then you sit on it and find your head is terrifyingly close to your knees and you haven't felt less in control since you last went on the Big Dipper at Blackpool. Not so perfect, after all.

You don't want to be rolling along a country road or trail in a position that you're not absolutely happy with. You don't want to be going faster – or slower – than you're comfortable with. That's no fun. And you don't want to fork out far more than you need to for the right bicycle for you. Instead, you want to be looking good and enjoying every minute of an activity that's good for you, your community and your environment.

Don't buy a bike on which you feel uncomfortable thinking, 'It's okay, I'll get used to it'. Chances are you won't. You'll continue to feel uncomfortable and the bike will end up unused and gathering dust in your shed. You need to look for a bike that you feel comfortable on right from the start.

Raiding the piggy bank

A bicycle is a great financial investment. Bicycles don't need much maintenance and you can do most of what is required yourself. Because you're the human who powers the bicycle, its fuel bills are zero, and if the bike rides you plan will replace a regular car or public transport journey that you make, you'll save a lot of money.

If you manage to save £20 a week in petrol or travel costs, that's £1,000 per year and you may very well spend less than the first year's savings on the purchase price of your bike. As you continue to save on travel costs, you shouldn't have to worry about replacing the occasional inner tube or tyre, or even paying someone else to give your bike a service now and again.

In the following sections, we give you a general summary of how much you might spend for the most common types of bicycle. (For the costs of specific types of bikes, flick to the sections that cover different kinds of bikes later in this chapter. For more on the typical costs of kids' bikes (as well as all other aspects of children and cycling) check out Chapter 14.)

Figuring out what the bike is worth

Bicycles range in price from about £100 to £10,000, and as you climb up the price ladder of bicycles, they get better and better. Components start being made out of exotic-sounding materials in space-age, technological processes. Imagine how good a bicycle that costs £3,000 would be. Then think about the one that costs £10,000: how much better can it be?

If you won't use a bicycle very often, there's hardly any point in investing heavily. However, if you want to ride a lot, then the bicycle and all its components will tend to last longer if you fork out more. How much to spend is entirely up to you – generally, the more you pay, the better the quality, but you don't need an expensive bicycle just for the sake of it. Less expensive bikes are made with cheaper components and often put together in a hurry, but if you get one that works, there's no particular reason why it won't carry on working.

Deciding where to shop

If you decide to buy your new bike at a supermarket or department store that's part of a big chain, you'll spend less than you would at a bike shop – and possibly not much more than £100. For a long time, these shops only sold mountain bikes, but now they're beginning to wake up to the fact that some people like other kinds of bicycles and an assortment is now appearing.

Although it may be the cheap option, buying a bike at these places does have some disadvantages:

- ✔ The bikes might work okay, but they're definitely not top quality.
- ✔ Shop staff are unlikely to actually know anything about the bikes and/or be able to answer your questions.
- ✔ If the bike needs repairing, it won't be fixed in-store – and getting a bike fixed by someone you never get to speak to is a slow process.

On the other hand, these shops do make getting your money back very easy if you're not satisfied.

Prices at specialist bike shops are higher, and generally start at about £250. For this amount, these stores might have basic mountain bikes or other upright bikes on sale. Specialist bike shops also have a wide range of bikes under £500, including most of their hybrids, city bikes and flat-bar road bikes. (See the sections later in this chapter for more on these specific kinds of bikes.)

These shops also offer bikes above the £500 price point – and sometimes substantially above, particularly if you're looking in the full-suspension mountain bike, touring and racing bike categories, because some of these types of bikes have very good quality components and are built for a high performance level. If you want a bike with a really light frame (meaning that the frame needs to be made of carbon fibre; see the sidebar 'Getting inside the frame: Bicycle frame materials' for more information about this product), expect to have to shell out to the tune of £1,500, or more.

Looking at the bike, not the price

If the bike shop has one bike you like at £400 and another at £600, try them both out. Different bikes perform in very different ways and the experience of riding them can be poles apart. Bike shops are usually happy for you to try out bikes by riding them round the block, so take advantage of this.

When trying out the bike you like, check the following:

- ✔ Can you reach the brakes? You want to be able to apply the brakes almost automatically, not to have to scramble to reach them every time you need to slow down or stop.

- ✔ Do the gears change smoothly and are you happy with the variation between each gear? Try changing through all the gears if you can, and check you're happy with the number of options provided.

- ✔ How comfortable are you on the bike? You need to be happy with the seating position to ensure you continue to use your bike.

If you can't detect any difference between the £400 and the £600 bikes, you probably don't need the more expensive one.

If you want to change any parts on your bike once you've bought it, you could be in for some serious spending. The sum of a bicycle's components, if bought separately, is always far greater than the price of purchasing such components in a group as a ready-made bike.

Ask about making substitutions for components on your bike before you buy it, as many specialist bike stores give discounts on the extra components if you purchase them at the same time as purchasing the bike, especially if you offer to leave the components you'll be replacing with the store. And they might do the fitting for free, too.

Stating your style

Getting the right bike is definitely not just about practical matters and finance. You're putting yourself in the public arena on your new machine and whether you like it or not it will be an expression of yourself and an extension of your personality.

Are you the fast chick in Lycra? Or the slow gent sitting upright with his trousers tucked into his socks? Maybe you're an iron-clad terminator shooting out over a cliff in a muddy forest? If you're any of these, we can tell you straightaway the kind of bike you should get: a road bike, an upright hybrid bike (or even a penny farthing) and a downhill racing mountain bike, respectively. Easy.

These examples are excellent stereotypes, but most likely you're a little less easy to read. You may well be deeper, made of more complicated fabric or just less ostentatious than these people, but you still need to think about how your style might influence your choice of bike. You can't meditate for hours and come up with 'BMX' if you actually need a bike for a 15-mile (24-kilometre) journey to work. That's not what BMXs are built for. Similarly, you wouldn't go for a speedy road bike if you prefer to take your time on your journey and like to be able to wear practically any style of outfit while you cycle.

You have to make your style statement choosing from the range of bikes that fits your practical needs.

Planning for the future

When trying to decide on the kind of bike that's right for you, you need to think ahead. Say you live in the city but in a couple of years you plan to move to the country or somewhere close to a rail trail or major cycling track. In this situation, you almost certainly want a bike that can handle different surface conditions, even if all you'll be using it for now is road cycling.

Are there any plans to build a fabulous recreational trail near your home? (If not, then perhaps you should speak to your local politician.) Will the children be riding bikes soon – and want you to ride with them in the park?

You want your bike to last you at least a few years, so try to think about what changes your lifestyle might go through over that time.

Racing Onto a Road Bike

If you watched Bradley Wiggins win the Tour and you're now sure you have the required skills to beat him, there's no stopping you: you just need a road bike (see Figure 2-1).

Road bikes are all about fun, efficiency and speed. Good road bikes are so light that you can pick them up with one finger. And give a front wheel a spin – you'll be standing all day before you see it slow down. The gears are so smooth you won't at first even notice a change. Few people who switch from any other kind of bike to a road bike ever turn back.

Massive amounts of money are channelled into the research and production of these amazing bikes. They get lighter, stronger and faster every year. Improvements made for professional teams in Grand Tours (such as the Tour de France) filter down annually into bikes for sale to everyone. These bikes are designed to place your body in a position that allows the muscles to work most efficiently, with minimal wind resistance. They're built so that very little of the energy you expend gets wasted on bending and flexing the frame. And all of their very expensive parts are created to run smoothly and swiftly against each other and the road.

Figure 2-1:
The classic
silhouette of
a road bike.

Gavin had been riding a mountain bike for years when he finally bought a road bike. He took it on a ride to show it off to some friends and one of them commented, wryly, 'So you've gone over to the Dark Side'. And he was right; Gavin had been seduced by a power greater than good and it was many months before he glanced once again at his mountain bike.

If you're buying a road bike to commute or for rides at weekends and you haven't ridden one before, you'll be amazed at how these bikes just take off. Put pressure on the pedals and you'll feel the skin on your face forced back with the pressure of acceleration. Just head off on your own or with friends and you'll enjoy smooth, efficient, fast riding everywhere you go.

If you're thinking about racing, you'll need to get the best bike you can afford, because the more you pay, the faster it will be. Undoubtedly, bike shop assistants and even peers put a lot of pressure on road bike riders to spend large amounts of money, and a major slice of the competition among riders relates to who has the best bike. If you ever do get to ride with Bradley, you'll likely have to be on a top-end machine to have a chance of keeping up. It certainly is a great feeling to own a bicycle that's worth more than most second-hand cars (and can go faster than some of them, too), but be aware of what you're getting into.

Building the fastest bike on the road

For some people, a road bike is too fast or too flash for commuting, but if you want to train and ride with a fast pack, it's perfect – although you need to get a good one. As you clock up the thousands (of pounds) on your way up the road bike hierarchy, the frames and other components get better and better.

Not by much sometimes, but once you get into serious road racing, any discernible difference is worth paying for.

One of the big differences in road bikes is whether they have two or three chainwheels at the front. Having three chainwheels gives you a greater range of gears to choose from, typically making it easier to climb long hills. The downside to this is the slight increase in weight (which slows you down). (To see a diagram of a basic bike, refer to Chapter 1.)

Frame material is an important factor in how fast a road bike is (see the sidebar 'Getting inside the frame: Bicycle frame materials' for more), but so is frame geometry. Frame geometry is all about the shape of the frame, where the different tubes meet and the angles at the joints. The more a frame is bunched up, with the wheels closer together, the faster it will be and the more your body will be in the most energy-efficient position, but this doesn't make it more comfortable to ride.

You're likely to want to stay on the bike longer if you're in a comfortable position and feel a bit more relaxed. You can find many top-end road bikes with geometry that provides this (look for Audax or Sportive bikes which are designed with more comfort in mind).

The makeup of the *groupset* is another important factor in building a road bike. Groupset is a term for most of the other bits that make up your bicycle – the brakes, shifters, dérailleurs, rear cassette, bottom bracket, chain, cranks and possibly the headset, seatpost and hubs. These components are all lumped together because bicycle manufacturers buy them as a group from one supplier to ease their process of building your bike.

The most important components from the groupset, in terms of how fast your road bike is, are the gears. If you're looking at a road bike in a shop, you can check out the name of the manufacturer of the particular gearing system on the gear/brake shifters and on the rear dérailleur body. All manufacturers offer a range of systems, and going one level up in the range means better materials and better design, making a big difference to the performance and quality of the bike – and to the price.

You need to do your homework and consider the build of the bikes you're looking at when buying a good road bike. With each brand of bike, a step up in frame material often means a step down in the quality of the groupset, including the gears, for the same price. Expect a significant jump in price to reach the better frame material combined with a higher-grade component such as gears. Look at a number of different combinations of better quality frames and components and decide what's important for you and what you can afford.

Getting inside the frame: Bicycle frame materials

When it comes to the frame of your bike, strength, stiffness and weight are the crucial factors, and these factors are affected by what material is used. Bike frames can be made out of the following materials:

- **Aluminium:** In bicycle frames, this metal is actually an *alloy* (a metal mixture) of aluminium and silicon or, more expensively, of aluminium, zinc, magnesium and some traces of other elements. Aluminium frames first appeared in the 1970s and became very popular because they're so light. Aluminium tubes aren't very strong compared to steel ones, though, so they have to be made thicker. Although thicker, they're still significantly lighter than steel, but the thickness makes them very rigid by comparison, giving a harsh ride. Aluminium does fatigue (become weaker due to stress) over time.

- **Carbon fibre:** These frames are really made of plastic: A polymer resin is poured into a mould with layers of carbon-fibre mesh that give the resin great strength. The strength of a carbon-fibre frame is designed so that the wasteful sideways flexing during acceleration is minimised, but also so that the frame can absorb vibration from the road, much like a steel one. Only a few years ago, bikes with carbon-fibre frames were quite rare and very expensive. Now, they're coming down in price very fast and a huge surge in their popularity has meant they're also a common sight. All professional road bike racing is done on carbon-fibre framed bicycles.

- **Combinations:** Bikes are often made with a combination of different materials – for example, they may have carbon-fibre forks or stays, with the rest of the frame made from one of the other materials listed here, usually aluminium. Aluminium frames are cheaper, but including carbon fibre in some parts helps reduce overall rigidity.

- **Steel:** This metal is an alloy of mostly iron and some carbon. For a long time, all bikes were made of steel tubing, but today, it is the heaviest of commonly used materials. Despite this, steel tubing is back in fashion, although now more commonly as *chromoly:* a high-carbon steel with little bits of chromium and molybdenum added. The extra bits make it stronger and so the walls of the tubes used can be thinner and therefore lighter. Steel tubes are stronger than aluminium tubes and because the tubes can be made thinner than they can with aluminium, they are far less stiff, which makes a big difference to how the bike feels on a bumpy road.

- **Titanium:** This metal is the most difficult of all the major frame materials. It has to be worked in an environment that doesn't include oxygen by technicians in space suits. Titanium is almost as light as aluminium, but stronger and because the tubing can be made thinner, frames are less rigid – again, much like steel. Bikes made of titanium are meant to last forever.

- **Other materials:** Bikes can be made out of a variety of materials, including wood or bamboo. Try an online image search and have a look. Bikes made out of wood or bamboo can actually be ridden – and often work quite well.

Most bikes come in the range of materials shown in the preceding list, but it's with road bikes that the greatest importance is placed on getting the right substance for your frame.

One of the easiest ways to make the bike you buy go faster is to get new wheels. All road bike wheels are fast, but a significant difference exists between entry-level wheels and the ones at the top of the range, with the better ones having far less rolling resistance. You can pay well over £1,000 for good wheels, but this upgrade probably provides the most readily felt difference in performance.

Upgrading your bike's tyres also makes a huge difference to the speed and feel of the bike. Many racers have fast tyres for training, but keep a spare pair of wheels with extra-fast tyres on them just for race day.

Most bike manufacturers these days offer what they call women's specific design (WSD) bikes – bikes that are designed specifically for women. These tend to have smaller frames (and even differently proportioned frames, with appropriately altered geometry), different shaped saddles, short-reach brake levers, narrower handlebars, shorter cranks and a wider gear range.

Getting to work – fast!

If you've decided to take the plunge and cycle to work, a road bike can be an excellent choice. Maybe you've seen bike lanes painted along your route and think enough of them have been created now to give it a go. Road bikes certainly are the fastest bikes and they're built for tarmac.

Once your legs have developed some strength, you can, if you want, beat everyone off at the lights. You can enjoy a healthy commute that isn't that much slower than a car, and may even be quicker. In built-up areas with lots of traffic lights and any roads where congestion hits, you'll leave motor traffic standing.

Road bikes aren't ever built to hold panniers or racks of any kind (see Chapter 3 for more on these) and if your route to work has lots of pot-holes the wheels might not cope too well. Road bikes are also definitely not built for riding off-road. Even the shortest distance on grass or gravel will cause big problems and is not good for the bikes. They're just not very tough that way. You need to stick to the (smooth) tarmac and, if you need to carry stuff with you, you need a backpack.

You won't want to commute on a road bike unless you've got somewhere secure to keep it; your own workspace or office is best. Not only will you want to keep the weather off it, you'll want to keep it safe from theft. Covered communal bike racks can be good, but only if you've got a really strong lock.

Paying for a road bike

Road bikes start at less than £500 and, although they're not going to turn heads, bikes at around this price always look good and can come equipped with carbon forks and gears that won't disappoint a beginner cyclist. Stretch to £1,000 and you can get a bike with a better gearing system and an aluminium frame with carbon stays as well as forks, meaning the bike is more comfortable and the gears switch easily and smoothly at high speed and on climbs.

When you reach £1,500 to £2,000, you can join the carbon club – with a full carbon-fibre frame – or stick with an aluminium frame (with carbon forks, seat post and stays) and add a very smooth and highly presentable gearing system. For not much more than £2,000, some companies produce models that have both a full carbon-fibre frame and a fancy groupset.

Hopping up to a gearing system from the top of the range offered by the manufacturer, or going for a titanium frame creates a big jump in price, into the many thousands of pounds. As you head towards £5,000, in addition to a titanium frame or an even better quality carbon-fibre frame, and the best gearing system, you can include top-of-the-range wheels, tyres, carbon bars and a razor-sharp saddle – and expect to be on a first-name basis with the bike shop owner.

You won't see too many titanium-framed bikes in the shops, as they are usually tailor-made to your needs and measurements. If you're really interested in getting one, ask at any bike shop, because they're probably able to get you one. A bicycle with a made-to-measure titanium frame costs between £3,000 and £8,000, depending on the gearing system and other components you choose, and it may take several months before you receive the bike.

Road bikes don't usually come with pedals, because most riders prefer to use the *clipless system* (cycling shoes with cleats in the soles that attach to the pedals). Because all the different makes of pedals are incompatible, the pedals aren't part of the package, so you have to buy the pedals separately and, if you're a first time buyer, you'll need to buy the shoes as well. The cost of buying both pedals and shoes starts at about £75 and can then rise quite considerably.

Going on tour

Wanting to race isn't just about buying the right road bike. Racing is a lifestyle decision that means spending many hours on your bicycle, including all the painful bits that make up your training. It also means planning your diet, keeping toxins out of your system and making sure you get plenty of sleep at the right times. For more on touring and racing, see Chapters 12 and 13; check out Chapter 16 for tips on nutrition.

Climbing Onto a Mountain Bike

Mountain bikes (MTBs) had a huge impact on the cycling scene when they hit the market with a big thump in the 1980s. They were strong bikes with a good range of gears and fat, grippy tyres. In the 1990s front suspension became standard, making trail-riding considerably more comfortable (see Figure 2-2). This comfort factor helped MTBs sweep the market, and they became the biggest-selling bikes in the country. Over the last decade, *dual* – front and rear – suspension and disc brakes have become common – and they have proven so popular for tough riding that these items are now essential.

MTBs were originally just built for the (rather vague) purpose of general off-road riding. Because of the rapid and very effective development of MTBs, a number of distinct types of riding now exist. Networks of *singletrack* (narrow, unpredictable and often steep paths built to wind through woods and hills, solely for the use of MTBs) have been crafted in locations handy to most population centres in the UK. Riding these tracks, or along the UK's thousands of miles of bridleways, is an exhilarating way to spend time away from buildings, cars and the stresses of modern life. And not just because you're getting some fresh air: these trails involve fast and furious action, merciless climbs and high-speed, jagged descents.

Every aspect of the design of a top-end MTB is tailored to a specific kind of difficult country, but the lower-priced bikes you see at supermarkets, department stores and in bike shops still have features that make them versatile and strong. These lower-end bikes are made for all-round riding that includes the occasional foray into field and forest. MTBs aren't specifically designed for riding on roads, but that doesn't mean you can't – and many people do.

Figure 2-2:
Mountain
bike with
front
suspension.

Getting to work

The fat, knobbly tyres of a MTB are built for traction on loose, broken trails. This makes their grip on a road surface more than you need for commuting. Their bulky, strong frames are also heavy and these factors will slow you down and make keeping up a good pace harder work. But that shouldn't stop you choosing a MTB to ride to work on.

MTBs are comfortable, easy to ride at a gentle pace and can roll off a foot-path onto unsurfaced terrain and deal with potholes without the trauma any other bike might bring. These bikes are tough enough to be ridden hard and if that's how you want to travel you'll build up great strength in your legs.

We've been among the cut and thrust of commuter cycling and seen men and women on MTBs take charge of the cycleways, passing bikes that should have been going twice their speed. Whenever we see a rusty, old front-suspension MTB leaving a coffee-set carbon racer standing, we always celebrate the heroic character of the triumphant MTB sprinter. If you're caging that kind of attitude, an MTB is a great way to let it out.

Front or rear suspension works by absorbing both small bumps when riding over uneven ground and large shocks when landing jumps. Some people worry about wasting energy pumping the bike up and down as they pedal if they've got any kind of suspension, but plenty of MTBs have a lock-out switch on the handlebars or the forks that only allows the suspension to kick in if you hit an obstacle. More advanced suspensions have what the manufacturers call a 'brain', which can tell the difference between pumping and collision and only let the system operate for knocks.

If you choose one of these bikes to get to work, you'll have a bike that's good for almost any other kind of riding in your free time.

Riding the trails

About 90 per cent of people who go mountain biking ride on trails in the countryside or in national parks. If you're just starting out with off-road cycling, look for tracks that are in good condition – with an even surface and not broken up or rocky – and you can cycle for hours without the technical knowledge you need for switchbacks or the sheer nerve required for rock gardens and drops. For off-road cycling on an even, unbroken surface, a *hard-tail* (a MTB with front suspension only) will do, but a *full* (a MTB with suspension at both ends) will always be better.

Plenty of trails have good long climbs, always followed by fast, freewheeling descents. Riding these trails is a great way to get super fit and see long tracts of countryside. Getting right out into wilderness on a bike brings on an exhilarating feeling of personal freedom and, because you pedalled there, an empowering sense of control.

For this kind of cycling, you need a bike that's light, strong and has a full complement of gears. Ensuring you have three chainwheels, which gives you a greater range of gears to choose from, helps a lot when it comes to slow, uphill struggles. A MTB from the lower end of the market – below the £500 price point – gives you everything you need when just starting out, or you can buy an expensive one with a few extra comforts to enjoy if you wish.

When choosing a MTB for trail-riding, the most important thing is that the bike feels right and gives you confidence. This self-assurance in the saddle helps you stay on course as you approach a difficult summit and enables you to let go as you roll down the other side. The confidence the bike gives you helps get you stronger and learning the tricks of the trail.

Spilling blood on the tracks

If you've graduated from country paths and bridleways and want to move on to the extra-tough stuff, you can take on more difficult tracks, or even start riding in competition.

To find out about more difficult mountain biking trails, check with your nearest MTB facility: you're likely to discover many miles of singletracks with obstacles, jumps and drops, steep banks on tight bends and wooden bridges that will keep you lost in the countryside for hours. You need a strong bike with dual suspension for this kind of riding. You also need nerves of steel, and to have built up certain skills in order to master the sharp bends on steep slopes at high speed – whether you're going up or down. And for most hardcore MTB riding you need very strong legs.

One relatively new MTB style is called *freeride*. It involves just heading out into the hardest and wildest country you can find. Freeriding isn't a competitive style, but freeriders may well be the fittest and strongest mountain bikers. Rather than trying to avoid the most challenging of obstacles, freeriders head straight for them, hoping to tackle and conquer them. Freeriders have to be nimble and may know all sorts of tricks, but they take on the toughest singletracks and do a great deal of climbing and fast downhills.

Downhill racing is the most notorious of MTB styles. Downhillers don't ride their bikes uphill – the hills they race down are usually too steep. They either push their bikes up or are driven. Because they don't have to do the climbs, downhill bikes don't need the same range of gears and so will usually just have one chainwheel. They go incredibly fast, often averaging over 40 miles

(64 kilometres) per hour over a whole course. These riders have plenty of skill and zero fear. They make huge jumps and drops, making split-second decisions about which line to take, with no time for hesitation. For these men and women, it's always, 'Who dares, wins.'

Many ordinary cyclists shake their heads in awe at the dangers of downhill racing and the damage the racers can endure. But downhill riders are quick (actually, they're very quick indeed) to point out that road bike riders may well have a greater accident rate as they take on the challenge of riding at very high speeds on a hard surface in motorised traffic. In fact, although injuries can be horrific in either sport, they are rare in both.

If you think downhill MTB racing is what you want to do, go along to an event and check it out at close quarters before you buy a bike.

Paying for the pleasure

You can get a reasonably good quality MTB, with hydraulic brakes as standard, for less than £750, though full-suspension bikes start at around £1,250. Spend a few hundred more, and you get smoother gears. Climb up to the £1,500 level, and you start to get stronger, more lightweight aluminium frames and bikes that can handle rough trails more comfortably.

Many MTBs come in the £2,000 to £8,000 range. Most of these bikes have sophisticated suspension systems built for cross-country or downhill mountain biking and racing. They may have carbon-fibre or superior aluminium frames and carbon wheel rims, and they all have excellent gearing and braking systems. The frames become more specialised, so you can get one designed for the specific type of terrain you'll be tearing through or down.

If you're looking for a MTB for a specific purpose and terrain, you can find a bigger range and the perfect advice at a specialist mountain biking shop.

Checking Out the Bikes in the Middle: Commuter, Urban and Hybrid

Defining bicycles that aren't road bikes or mountain bikes can sometimes be a little difficult. You won't find any rules that lay down how to pinpoint exactly a hybrid, an urban bike, a commuter or a street bike, although there are always features to look out for. Even a flat-bar road bike, which ought to be a simple thing to recognise – just imagine a road bike, then put flat handlebars on it – isn't always so easy.

Over time, the meaning of bike titles such as hybrid might change slightly, and the history in the definitions of these bicycles is far from consistent. What people are often after is just an old-fashioned bicycle – one that people used to ride with pride and that used to be called simply a 'bicycle' – but we dare you to walk into a bike shop and say, 'I know exactly what I want. I want a bicycle.' Go on, give it a go.

Historical knowledge only serves to frustrate when faced with all the choices in a modern bike shop. You might now call that once ubiquitous kind of bike a utility bike – they sell many millions of them in China and the Netherlands. These bikes are making something of a comeback, and if you go into a bike shop and ask for a Dutch bike they'll know exactly what you're talking about.

A trend at the time of writing is to make many modern bikes, such as commuters and hybrids, look more like traditional utility bikes. Manufacturers add full chain-guards, mudguards, leather-look saddles and sometimes wicker baskets to heighten the effect. However, you won't find the heavy steel frames, backward-curving handlebars and rod-lever brakes that are still common all over India and China unless you track down a fashionable, stylised retro roadster from a specialist shop.

You can also occasionally find old-style cruiser bikes. Bright colours and curved tubes are what single them out and although these bikes are mostly produced for and marketed at children (who love them), some great adult models are available.

The names used, however, are not the most important thing. That which we call an urban bike, by any other name would ride as sweet. If you have an idea what you need a bike for, you should be able to spot certain components and design factors to help you on your way. Then, when you are told, 'Yes, that's a commuter', you can take it home secure in the warm feeling that you now own the hybrid bike you always wanted.

Mixing with a hybrid

Hybrid bikes came along when MTBs started getting more specialised and better developed for off-road conditions. MTBs started getting lower bars, tighter angles and sharper saddles and many people began demanding something more relaxed.

The hybrid bike typically has an upright riding position, possibly more so than any other modern bike style. This position is achieved by manufacturers raising the handlebars and bringing the saddle closer to the front. A lot of the comfort factor also lies in the saddle. These are often wide and soft to cushion your behind, and are frequently augmented by *seat suspension,* which is a small spring system in the seatpost just below where you sit (see Figure 2-3).

Add mudguards and a wicker basket on the handlebars and you've got a variety of hybrid commonly called a Dutch bike. Hybrid bikes usually have wide tyres, though not as fat at those on a MTB and without such a bumpy tread. Another common feature is a stem head that you can easily adjust to alter the height of the handlebars.

Hybrid bikes usually come with at least 18 gears, you can load them up with baskets or racks and panniers (see Chapter 3 for more on these), and their wider wheels mean that you can take them over grass or gravel tracks. These features make hybrid bikes perfect for commuting, daytrips on rail trails or riding down to your local shops. Hybrids aren't the fastest bikes on the road, but there's no reason to think that you can't ride a hybrid for a long distance. On one of these bikes, you should be able to stay comfortable and keep pedalling all day.

Hybrids are a melting pot, and are a diverse breed. They fall somewhere in the middle of the bike family, and can quickly morph into other types of bike by making a few nifty alterations. By sticking some mudguards on a hybrid and giving it smoother tyres and a rack, it becomes a *commuter*. Give it tyres with white sidewalls and a snazzy paint job and it becomes an *urban bike*. Add a wicker basket and an upright riding position, and you've got a Dutch bike. Definitions can become confusing and unhelpful, especially when different bike manufacturers and bike shops call the same style of bike by different names. Just remember that the bike's features, design and your needs are more important than any label it has.

You can get a reasonably good-quality hybrid for £350. Quite a range of possibilities is available for under £600, but more variation probably exists in what are called hybrids than any other type of bicycle, so be sure that what you're being shown has got all the features you're after.

Figure 2-3:
A comfort bike with seatpost suspension.

Many people just aren't happy on a bike unless they can put both feet on the ground while sitting in the saddle. This position is definitely possible with a hybrid bike, so if you're trying out this kind of bike and you feel this way, get the salesperson to lower the seat so that you're sure that's what you're getting.

Looking cool on a retro bike

Whether it's a lugged steel racing bike from before the age of aluminium, a laid-back curvy cruiser or a utility bike with some retro stylings, these bikes are turning heads so that they spin. Modern bikes look great – we think – but these retro bikes are all stunners.

Setting the pace with a retro racer

Just a few years ago at big events all eyes would be on those rare, expensive beauties, the carbon-framed racers. Everybody wanted one – and then everybody got one. Now these types of racers are everywhere and if you take one along to a mass gathering of cyclists, nobody turns a hair. But if you pedal in on something like a steel-framed Hetchins or Rotrax, the surreptitious glances simply won't stop.

Old steel-framed bikes are heavier than modern road bikes, but they are a pleasure to ride: smooth and solid on the road. They were built back in the post-war bicycle boom and became immensely popular in the 1980s. These bikes evolved to have a huge ten gears – two chainwheels at the front and five cogwheels at the back – and gave everyone a new feeling of speed on the road. Compared to today's bikes, however, their weight and limited range of gears does make them harder work on hills.

Steel-framed road bikes started dropping out of the scene later in the 1980s when aluminium began to creep into frames and with the advent of the MTB. Many brands of bikes with steel frames were available at the time, but so many of these old beauties were sold they're still filtering out of garages and into bins.

A friend of Gavin's has a Repco Traveller – a 1980s bike made in Australia. He got it when somebody turfed it out for a council clean-up. That bike still functions beautifully and the curved chrome on the handlebars has barely a blemish. It's a unique aqua colour, not far from the celeste of a Bianchi (the sky-blue hue specially created for the famous Italian road bike company). Gavin suspects his friend might struggle a bit on hills with his Repco Traveller, but he won't admit it. He loves that bike. So does Gavin.

If you come across any old steel-framed road bike in a neighbour's garage or maybe at your local tip but it doesn't work perfectly, working on one of these gems is a fabulous hobby with a highly rewarding end product. Although it's not a cheap pastime, refitting a classic road bike with the best gear you can afford (and maybe getting a respray) is an immensely satisfying way to end up with a fast, strong, very stylish bike that will last a lifetime.

Check online if you want to buy a classic steel road bike that's already been rebuilt. Although you'll miss out on the fun of doing it yourself, some very classy old mounts are available.

Cruising with style

Cruisers are a style of bike that was very popular from the 1930s through to the 1950s, particularly in America. The frames had big downward curves from handlebars to bottom bracket, or sometimes a downward curve on the down tube and an upward bend on the top tube, making the frame form the shape of an eye bisected by the seat tube, instead of the usual triangles.

Original cruiser-style bikes are as rare as hens' teeth and very valuable, but the newer models are just as eccentric in design and as bright and bold in colour. Check out Figure 2-4 for an example of the audacious cruiser design.

Cruisers are quite heavy and generally have either no gears at all or a three-gear internal hub system. They usually just have one lever – for the front brake – and a back-pedal rear brake. Cruisers are great for short, easy riding, such as popping down to the shops, but aren't designed to work efficiently going up hills.

Figure 2-4:
Amazing
retro curves
of a cruiser.

Cruisers are a laid-back style statement and, just like the vintage bikes, some of the modern versions have the most amazing arches and curves built into the frames. But they aren't terribly ergonomically efficient, so while cruisers make you stand out and are just as good as any other bike for taking to the park or cruising the footpaths on the way to school or to visit friends, doing anything more challenging is a big effort.

It may be that the only bicycle your child wants is something that looks great but which isn't all that practical. This puts you in a difficult position. Your child is more likely to get out on a bike on which they think they look cool, but might well tire of it as they become keener riders. However, if you buy a bike that's more sensible it might not fire their imagination and will remain in the shed, despite being a better bike to ride. Dilemmas like these are just one of the many joys of parenthood, and only you know what will work best for your child.

You can find a few adult retro cruisers and roadsters available here and there. These also all look like the bee's pyjamas, but if you're thinking of going any distance on one, ride up a hill or two when you're test-riding your possible future bike to see how well it pedals under pressure and ensure it meets all your needs without exhausting you in the process.

Cycling old-school style with traditional bikes

As a reaction to all the carbon, graphite and titanium bling that's available, a good few people have decided to invest in a traditional bike. These bikes haven't changed much in design from the 1950s, though the modern versions have modern components sitting alongside more traditional features such as sprung saddles, fully enclosed chains, hub gears and wicker baskets. These bikes have the old-fashioned sit-up-and-beg riding position, which means they're pretty slow and aren't good in headwinds but, then again, they're not designed for riding fast in the first place, and if you're someone who likes to see the world go buy as you ride (and in a certain old-world style) they can be a great choice.

As well as classic British designs, plenty of traditional bikes are available from manufacturers in the Netherlands and Scandinavia, and you can find a few bike shops around that deal in these machines alone. Some of these bikes can be quite expensive, but they'll last a lifetime (and will probably outlive you).

Training on a fitness bike

Some people have described *fitness bikes* (also known as *training bikes*) as 'hybrids on a diet'. They often have the same frames and components as racing bikes but swap the drop handlebars for straight ones. The idea of a fitness bike is to give you something close to the feel of an all-out racer, whilst sparing you the need to adopt the racing position.

With a fitness bike, you get a smart, modern-looking style of bike, although they can get expensive: top models have excellent gearing systems and carbon-fibre frames, and a price tag to match.

One major international bike company claims to sell more of their fitness bike range than any other kind of bike, and this type of bike can be very versatile – they're marketed as everything from commuters to park playthings. If you don't want to be caught up in the bunch or join the road bike rat-race, a quality fitness bike is a great alternative for a fast commute.

Travelling on a touring bike

Tourers can be a great compromise if you want a bike that can fulfil several roles. They're strong and have low gears, so are good for carrying kids or your weekly shop, and can cope with light off-roading and the bumpiest of urban roads on your commute.

Tourers are fitted with drop handlebars, so you can get into a tuck position and go fairly fast. And, of course, if you want to take off and cycle your way around the world, tourers are ideal for tackling the variety of conditions you'd encounter. They aren't particularly light as the frames tend to be made of steel (easy to weld, though, if you hit a problem in Outer Mongolia) and the components are chosen for their robustness rather than for shaving off a few extra ounces. But these are bikes that go on and on. If you have space or a budget for only one bike, a tourer could be the way to go.

Grabbing a city bike

City or *urban bikes* can be very similar to fitness bikes (see the earlier section), although these terms also include some much more conservative models. Some city bikes have taken a leaf from the courier book and, although they're not the fixed wheel that couriers prefer (see the section 'Cycling fast and strong with fixies' later in this chapter), they don't have any gears. This always makes for simpler, but more energetic, riding.

If you're just cycling around a flat area, having a bike with no gears isn't an issue, but if you're operating in a hilly neck of the woods with this sort of bike, you'll have hard-working legs.

City bikes also come as much more relaxed machines. Perhaps being influenced by the kind of bike built for urban bike-hire schemes all over the world, these models have an upright position and wide, comfortable saddles, rather like Dutch bikes. They may also come with racks, acknowledging that a great many people moving around city centres need to carry stuff.

Flat-bar road bikes are also sold as *urban commuters.* They are similar to road bikes – with fast, light frames, high-end gears and large, narrow wheels – but have straight handlebars to give you a slightly more upright sitting position. Their geometry is far more relaxed than a road bike and they're heavier, with the frames built to allow racks to be fitted.

Flat-bar road bikes can have superior gear systems for easy speed and this feature can tip them well over the £1,000 mark. They're marketed as being perfect for commuting, trips to the store and getting around town.

Specialising Your Ride

Bicycles have adapted and transformed in many ways over the years in response to the changing needs of cyclists. Although all bikes are still instantly recognisable as bikes, a few types have really broken out of the mould, evolving into something that stands apart:

- ✔ **BMX bikes:** These bikes aren't about transport – they're about jumps, stunts and attitude.
- ✔ **Fixies:** These bikes are for undoubted urban cool and a different experience of cycling.
- ✔ **Tandems:** These bikes are for people helping each other or just enjoying the shared experience.
- ✔ **Recumbents:** These bikes give the lowdown on another way of cycling.
- ✔ **Folding bikes:** Bikes that fold are for people who know where they're going and need to use different modes of transport to get there.
- ✔ **Electric bikes:** Powered bikes are for people who need a little help.

All of the preceding are bicycles, though, and all part of the family. The following sections cover these different and distinct breeds.

Jumping around with BMX banditry

BMX stands for bicycle moto-cross. BMX bikes are small, tough bikes designed for racing over short, off-road tracks with jumps and tight turns, and are also perfect for doing tricks.

With BMX bikes, size doesn't matter. Although small, these bikes, just like their riders, are hard as nails. BMX bikes have definitely moved on from being solely for children (see Figure 2-5), and BMX riding is also a very grown-up sport, achieving Olympic status for the first time in the 2008 Beijing Olympic Games.

Figure 2-5:
BMX bike.

All sorts of different styles of BMX riding exist, and you'll find differences in the bikes used for each style. Street riders use tough steel bikes, may have pegs protruding from both sides of each wheel axle and often no brakes. They practise stunts and are always looking out for steps, rails, ramps and walls to show off their *grinds* (sliding along on different combinations of pedals and pegs).

BMX riders also use skateboard parks and perform some of their most spectacular tricks on structures called *verts*. These structures are built like a half pipe, with vertical extensions on either side that usually go up about 3 metres (10 feet), although some can be up to 6 metres (20 feet) high. Riders do various spins and flips while they're up in the air. Those using verts always use smooth tyres and, most commonly, 20-inch (50.8-centimetre) tyres with 36 or even 48 spokes for extra strength.

BMX bikes can also be used for dirt-jumping and trail-riding. BMX bikes used in this way have knobbly tyres and stronger, chromoly frames. Trail riders ride over built-up mounds of earth and learn mid-air flips and turns just like vert riders. BMX racers ride over similarly built mounds, doing long jumps on tight circuits.

Flatlanders are a tribe apart from the rest. These are the ones who stay on the horizontal in car parks and malls, climbing all over their bikes, spinning and rolling like break-dancing cyclists.

Most BMX riders get ready-made bikes as kids and practise on them, then get more specialised bikes as they become more proficient. The tougher chromoly bikes for racing or tricks can get very pricey and, of course, the cool factor can add many pounds to a BMX bike.

A great deal of skill is involved in all kinds of BMX riding, and a great deal of time and effort put in to learn the skills. That kind of skill isn't something you pick up over a weekend, so if you feel like joining these guys be prepared to put in many hard hours of training.

Cycling fast and strong with fixies

A *fixie* (a bicycle with a fixed wheel) has only one gear and the rear cogwheel is screwed directly onto the rear hub. This means that whenever the bicycle is moving, the chain is moving and therefore the pedals are turning. Because of this, when you ride a fixie you can't freewheel: your legs must turn with the pedals while the bicycle is in motion. Also, in theory, it means you can ride a fixie backwards, although this isn't often done.

Track racing bikes are all fixed wheel. The racers you see hurtling around the oval of the velodrome don't have any gears to help them go faster and they can't stop pedalling while they're moving. Track racing is what, until recently, most fixed-wheel bike frames were made for. They are also used for the specialised sport of hill-climbs, where riders make a short, sharp sprint up very steep hills. Not for the faint-hearted.

A fixie frame is different from a normal road bike frame. The difference is at the *rear dropouts* (the slots that the rear axle slips into when fitting the rear wheel), which point down and forwards on a normal bike and straight back on a fixie frame. These frames are built this way because moving the wheel backwards is the only way to increase the tension of the chain on a fixie, which can't be done if the axle is pushed right into its bolting position on a downward facing dropout.

Fixies are now ridden by urban bicycle couriers around the world. These men and women ride bikes in traffic and under pressure all day, every day and are some of the strongest and fittest cyclists you could find. They work bikes very hard and if they have to ride bikes made of stuff like aluminium they often break them. The fixies these riders use have steel track frames modified with different wheels for street use and, because fixies only have one gear and often don't have brakes either (though this is illegal when used on public roads), they're very simple machines, meaning there's very little to go wrong with them.

Couriers and other fixie fans buy and sell frames and make up their bikes how they want them, including adding tough wheels so they can jump up kerbs, but most riders keep things pretty simple. People who love these bikes like to heighten their simple appearance by removing everything that isn't essential, giving them a stark, clean look.

Riding a fixie is very strange at first and takes some getting used to. It gives you a strong feeling of being connected to your bike and gives you far more control. You have to learn to slow the bike down with your legs and it's a great way to build up strong muscles.

Fixie riders form quite a scene and many websites are devoted to photos of cool bikes, stories of get-togethers and trading of frames and other components. A fixie movie subculture is growing, and you can watch and hear couriers talk of their experiences of urban riding around the world. Search online and you can even get hold of stickers that read, 'If it ain't fixed, it's broken'.

You can now buy ready-made fixies at bike shops. Because fixies have no gears, they're not expensive bikes: you can pick up a good-looking fixie for £400. If you're not totally committed to the idea of being 'fixed', you can buy a bike with a flip-flop hub. This system allows you to take off your back wheel and flip it around – on one side of the wheel is a fixed cogwheel, on the other a cogwheel that allows you to freewheel.

Pairing up for a tandem

It's easy to think the romantic connection you make with riding a *tandem* comes from the classic song, *Daisy Bell,* which contains the well-known line 'A bicycle built for two'. But we think it goes the other way around. The song was written acknowledging the intimate link that comes with two people riding one of these magnificent machines (see Figure 2-6).

Riding a tandem isn't just a shared workload, and isn't just twice the fun. There's something about riding a tandem that brings two people together with great feeling. The complementary pedalling, the dual (or duelling for) control and the learning of silent signals forge a sympathetic bond.

Figure 2-6:
A bicycle
built for two.

When tandem teams start out, both riders have a lot to learn. Starting up, changing gear, even turning a corner can go badly wrong if these actions are not coordinated correctly. Messages have to be sent back from the *captain,* the person at the front of the bike, to the *stoker,* the person in the rear. But soon these signals become non-verbal and, as team members progress, they become almost telepathic – although no signs of communication are perceivable, riders can freewheel, alter cadence and stand in unison.

Tandems are very efficient bikes and, when you've mastered the technique, they can go very fast. They're also, after initial differences have been ironed out, a great way for a couple with imbalanced cycling experience to enjoy riding together. Tandems also enable people who aren't able to ride on their own – for example, vision-impaired people – to share the fun of riding a bike.

Many of the major international bike manufacturers make tandems. Some smaller, local companies also make them in as many styles as you find with single seaters. Tandems start at under £600, but can cost several times that amount.

Laying back on a recumbent

Bents. That's what *recumbent bikes* are called by people in the know. Recumbent bikes come in a vast array of shapes and sizes. Typically long and low, many of them have bucket seats, although some are more like camp beds with wheels. This dynamic is one of the axioms of recumbent design: spreading your body's weight over the whole of your rear and often your back as well (see Figure 2-7). A big feature of all recumbents is comfort, even after a long ride.

Figure 2-7:
The recumbent bike – ergonomic satisfaction.

The position a recumbent puts your body in is still an efficient, ergonomic one for cycling – and is made more efficient by the lower wind resistance. If you've ever seen a recumbent out on the road, you know they can go very, very fast. These bikes have been pitted against standard fast bikes in the past and on flat or downhill courses they always win.

Ben has bought a recumbent bike for his kids to share. Despite having a big height and strength advantage over them, when the kids get going, Ben struggles to keep up on an ordinary bike. He therefore includes a few hills on family rides, as recumbents aren't so good on climbs.

Bents come in quite a few basic designs. Here's a list of some of the aspects of recumbent bikes that are available in different options:

- **Chains:** Most recumbents have long chains that reach back to the rear wheel. Some are front-wheel-drive (FWD) and have much smaller chains that only have to reach down to the front hub. One disadvantage of this FWD system is possible wheel spin if riding uphill on a loose surface.

- **Crank system:** You cycle most recumbents by using the traditional pedal system where the momentum comes from your legs and feet. However, recumbents that use a *hand-crank system* – where the momentum comes from your arms and hands – are available. Bikes with hand cranks are a great asset to people without use of their legs.

- **Steering:** Some recumbents have handlebars above the rider's lap. This system turns the fork in the same way as an ordinary bicycle and gives the rider somewhere to place a bike computer, bottle cage or any usual bar attachment. Other recumbents have a handlebar that runs under the seat and is connected to a pivoted rod that turns the front fork. These bars have grips that rise vertically and are grasped on either side of the rider's thighs. This system takes some getting used to, but is more relaxing for the rider's arms.

- **Wheelbases:** The wheelbases can be long or short:

  - *Long wheelbases:* These have the chainrings in between the front and rear wheels.

  - *Short wheelbases:* These have the chainrings, cranks and pedals above, and possibly slightly in front of, the front wheel. These bikes look like they're sporting some kind of ferocious weapon at the front. (The protruding drive mechanism is reminiscent of a chainsaw – though chainguards are available on some models.)

- **Wheels:** Choose between two wheels and three (one at the back and two at the front), with three-wheeled options being more stable.

People often build their own recumbents. Gavin once knew a man who had made four of them, all from bars and scraps of metal he brought home from the workshop where he spent his days. Gavin got on one once and, although he's spent time in some of the world's most dangerous cycling locations, he's rarely felt as unsafe.

Professionally built recumbents don't give you the feeling of being exposed or at risk. Three-wheeled ones don't topple over if you get your turning wrong and, although you've got to relearn your balance skills for a two-wheeled recumbent, this shouldn't take long – no more than half an hour to understand what you're supposed to be doing and another half an hour to become proficient.

A common fear about recumbents is that they can't be seen in traffic and so are dangerous. Bent aficionados claim it just doesn't work that way, saying that if a large refrigerator drove down the road in traffic it wouldn't be missed and recumbents with riders are about the same size. The problem with this logic, of course, is that refrigerators may be driving on our roads almost constantly, but if we can't see them we don't know. That recumbents are more often seen in groups and at events, and bent riders often attach flags to their bikes to make them more visible, is true, however.

Recumbent bikes start at around £1,000. A large range is available for between £1000 and £2,000, including some beautifully hand-crafted machines from specialist companies. Pay more than £2,000 and you start to get suspension, high-quality gearing systems, carbon-fibre parts and aero-dynamic fairings.

Folding up your two-wheeled friend

Folding bicycles (or *folders,* as they're also known) have many different looks, with hinges and latches at various places around the bike. Some bikes just fold up so you can lift them into the boot of a car. Some pack down into a much smaller size and come with carry bags so that you can take them on buses and trams. Another selling point for some folders is the speed with which you can fold them – you can fold some bikes in under 15 seconds.

Most commonly, folders are hinged somewhere in the middle. Making the bikes step-through, with no top bar, makes this arrangement easier. In keeping with their compact nature, the bikes are often fitted with small wheels and long, extendable seat posts and front stems. These factors give the bike its characteristic look (see Figure 2-8), but also make it easy to adjust for a range of different-sized riders.

Figure 2-8:
The typical look of a folding bike.

Cyclists living in small apartments often appreciate the smaller space one of these bikes takes up. Folk travelling the world on yachts also like the easy storage of folding bikes that can be a great asset when exploring new places. More commonly, mixed-mode commuters, such as people who ride then take trains, buses or ferries, take advantage of bikes that fold.

If you don't have somewhere secure – or somewhere out of everyone's way – to leave your bike at your workplace, have a look at the options available with folders. Many people pick these bikes so that they can store them under their desks at work.

Folding bikes are usually marketed as being not for fast or long-distance use, but some models contradict this. The small wheels and frame design certainly don't disallow efficient cycling. Gavin knows a man who owns a Brompton folder who gets very defensive about its speed capabilities – even going so far as to offer to take on any other bike and rider in a race. The Birdy and Brompton companies make folders specifically for travelling and also produce travel cases, panniers and racks for these folders.

Folding bikes start at less than £300 and you can find many for less than £700. Of course, more expensive ones are available, and you can pay up to £5,000 or more if you really want to.

Electrifying your pedals

Electric bikes help people who aren't so strong in the legs to get up hills and ride distances they might not otherwise manage. They all give you the option of pedalling, pedalling with the aid of the motor or just letting the motor do the work. In the UK, electric bikes (or Electrically Assisted Pedal Cycles as the Government likes to call them) are limited to 15 miles per hour, which means that as soon as you reach this speed, the motor stops helping. You can go faster than this on an electric bike, but you have to rely on pedal power alone.

Travelling on a folder

Take a leaf out of Mel Huey's book. Mel took off from his home in Oregon in December 2009 at the age of 68, shortly after he retired. He flew to South America with a Bike Friday folding bicycle packed in its travel case, leaving behind his much-loved daughter and grandson.

He started from Bogota in Colombia and traversed the Andes to Ecuador, then travelled down through Peru, back up into the mountains and on to Chile. From there, he crossed the Andes once more to finish in Argentina. He spent a little over six months on the road and covered 7,069 kilometres.

Huey's Bike Friday had dropped handlebars. Its travel case, where he stowed all his things while riding, had robust wheels at one end and attached to the back of his bike as a trailer. It was the perfect set-up for the adventure of a lifetime.

The batteries on an electric bike tend to take between four to six hours to fully charge and last for 15 to 30 miles (24 to 48 kilometres), depending on how much work you make the motor do.

Electric bikes are a fairly new development in the bicycle world, and legislation has only recently caught up with the market. UK law says that 200 watts is the maximum allowable rated motor output for a pedalling machine to still be classed as a bicycle – and, therefore, need no registration or licence. This figure rises to 250 watts for a tandem or tricycle. The law says that no one under 14 years of age can ride an electric bike. If your electric bike is too fast or too powerful, you're liable for Vehicle Excise Duty, will need insurance, a licence and an approved motorcycle helmet. At the time of writing, this legislation is under review, so keep an eye out for changes in the law.

You can buy electric motors to fit pretty much any kind of bike and can even get motors that disappear inside the seat tube and connect into the bottom bracket. Fitting an electric motor to an existing bike isn't simple, but you can do it at home with a bit of know-how.

Conversion kits cost between a few hundred pounds and several thousand. Ready-made electric bikes start at around £300 and go up from there. Seat-tube fitted electric motors cost about £2,000 fitted to your existing bike.

Chapter 3

Choosing the Right Gear

- -

In This Chapter

▶ Heading for a helmet

▶ Adding accessories to your bike

▶ Dressing for success

▶ Putting the right shoe on the right pedal

▶ Topping up with water

- -

*O*kay, so you've bought a bike, but your work doesn't quite end there. Lots of other things are available for you to buy, both for your bike and for you to wear when riding your bike. No matter whether you love to shop or you prefer to keep your spending to an absolute minimum, this chapter provides a run-down of the range of basic accompaniments to cycling. Some of them might be superfluous to your needs, some of them might be essential elements for the image you're already beginning to project and some of them are required by law.

If you're not used to cycling, a bike shop can be a bewildering place. All sorts of strangely shaped objects are lined up in neat packages on the walls. Gavin was once told by the family that they were short of Christmas presents for him so he trotted down to his local bike shop and bought some top-quality bar tape. The tape was wrapped and placed under the Christmas tree, and on Christmas Day, he acted suitably surprised and delighted when he unwrapped the tape. Weeks later his loved ones confessed that even after pooling their not inconsiderable mental resources they had failed to establish what the tape was for. (It's for wrapping around your handlebars to make them look smart and new.)

Reading this chapter should give you a much better idea of what's available so that you can figure out what you need. It won't take away all the mystery of your local bike shop, however. That will always be a place to spend time in, investigate and marvel.

Getting Ahead, Getting a Helmet

While you're not required by law to wear a helmet when riding a bike any-where in the British Isles, doing so is a sensible idea. All helmets sold in the UK and Ireland should comply with European Standard EN1078. Helmets designed for children under seven years old should meet European Standard EN1080, which is similar to the adult standard, but which also includes tests to ensure the straps keep the helmet properly on the head. In plain English, all this means that they've been subjected to and passed various impact tests that ensure that you'll be protecting yourself well by wearing a helmet.

Before buying a helmet, have a look inside the helmet to check it has a sticker that indicates the helmet has met European safety requirements. You should also find other mandatory information, such as the helmet's size, when it was made and instructions for safe use. Leave the stickers and other information inside the helmet – these are your proof that your helmet meets the legal requirements. For ordinary cycling, not a huge amount of difference exists in build or design of basic helmets. The majority of helmets sold in the British Isles consist of a moulded polystyrene dome built to fit over your head and covered with a thin layer of plastic. Straps hang down and lock together under your chin, and a tightening device is usually included at the back. As helmets get more specialised or expensive, however, you start to find variations – for example, some helmets have an internal frame inside the helmet, and in some the plastic outer shell is moulded on, rather than being glued on.

If you pick off all the outside plastic or modify your helmet in any other way, you may reduce its ability to protect you in the event of an accident.

Bicycle helmets are built to only carry you through one impact. If you're in an accident with your bike and hit your head (which is very unlikely), you should replace the helmet as it may have sustained damage. The polystyrene foam that forms the dome of the helmet is likely to be crushed at the point of impact, and can even shatter, creating cracks in the foam that you may not be able to see. Either way, the helmet will no longer continue to offer the same protection. If the plastic outer shell has become loose or detached, that can reduce the helmet's effectiveness, too. Also avoid buying a second-hand helmet, unless you can be very sure of its history and know it's never been hit.

As well as protecting you from impacts, cycle helmets also work to keep you cool. You can get mighty hot whilst riding out on the trails and roads, or even on short trips to the park or shops. Exercise increases your body tem-perature and you need to be able to conduct heat from out of the top of your head. To keep your head as cool as possible, ensure your helmet has suf-ficient ventilation gaps to allow plenty of air to pass through the helmet and over your head.

The mandatory helmet debate

Whether or not cycle helmets should be made mandatory is a vigorous and ongoing debate. On one side of the fence are those people who argue that helmets help to reduce fatalities and serious head injuries; on the other side are people who say the evidence for this is mixed, and that making helmets compulsory results in fewer people using bikes.

One example of the debate in action comes from the Northern Ireland Assembly, who, in 2011, voted in favour of introducing a law to make the wearing of cycle helmets compulsory, but dropped the idea in the face of widespread opposition and because of the weakness in the arguments supporting the move. And in another example, the British Medical Association is in favour of making helmets mandatory, whereas a paper in the *Journal of Medical Ethics* argued against doing so.

The issue over helmets has also proved tricky for cities with bike-sharing schemes. In places where helmets are mandatory (such as Melbourne, in Australia), take-up of the scheme has been much lower than cities where you can just jump on a bike and go (such as London). And despite extensive support for helmets in litigation-happy America, New York has resisted introducing legislation so that people can ride helmet-less when using its new Citi Bike service.

Many doctors say the overall health benefits of using a bike outweigh the minor increase in risk of not wearing a helmet – an argument which seems to be winning, at the moment at least. You can keep up to date with the debate at `www.cycle-helmets.com/england_helmets.html`.

Hitting the right hard hat

Bicycle helmets start at about £20 and from there rise considerably in price. Bike shops usually have some options that are just as cheap as options in supermarkets or department stores, but will have a much bigger selection to choose from.

Helmets don't necessarily get safer the more you spend on them. Recent tests in the United States showed that impact protection was almost identical between three helmets that cost under $20 and three helmets that cost over ten times as much. However, you will find better quality fittings on a more expensive helmet, with more options for altering how it fits.

Many helmets have a plastic visor, or peak, projecting from the front and giving shade to your face. If you ride leaning forward with your head down, these visors may cut out some of what you can see. You can usually remove them very easily.

Helmets for mountain biking, road bike riding and everyday riding are all very much the same in design. They all try to minimise weight and maximise protection and airflow. They all also try to appear as a stylish accessory although, it has to be admitted, some do a lot better on the style front than others. Some people are tempted by fancy brand names moulded discreetly (or not so discreetly) into the outer shell of the helmet, but you'll always pay more for that pleasure.

However, if you're going to be using your bike for more specific purposes, you need a helmet that fits in with this, such as the following:

- **BMX bike helmets:** Although BMX riders sometimes wear full-face helmets, a more military style helmet known as the half-shell is more common. Half-shell helmets have a thicker plastic coating and don't usually have a lot of ventilation. These helmets cover more of your head – and BMX aficionados have far more crashes. (These riders push their riding to the max, trying to go one better and, inevitably, they don't always pull it off.) BMX helmets often have very stylish graphics printed on the outer casing. These graphics can make the helmets very expensive, as can going with particular brand names.

- **Mountain bike helmets:** When tumbling down cliff faces and learning your jumps and drops in the wild, you may need to get a full-face mountain bike helmet. These helmets more closely resemble something you'd see on a racing driver, but are very stylish with a sharp, projecting chin and peaked visor. They're heavier than standard helmets and may not have the ventilation you'd normally be looking for, but do offer far more protection for when you're riding at greater risk. These helmets are expensive, especially lightweight ones made of carbon fibre. Specialist mountain bike shops stock protective neck braces that complement this headwear for even more top-end armour.

- **Time trial helmets:** These helmets are the ones worn by racers when they're riding against the clock, and that also make the riders look a little like Alien, with the long pointy bit coming out of the back of the head. The helmets are fully enclosed and in the shape of a teardrop, and are tested for aerodynamic perfection in wind tunnels by the likes of Bradley Wiggins. These helmets are expensive, but you won't really need one until you're racing with the pros. If you decide to wear one on your ride along the seafront, though, you'll definitely turn heads. (Someone might even call the council alien catcher if you're not careful.)

Fitting protection

The first thing to do when buying a helmet is to put it on your head. Helmets come in many different sizes and you want one that doesn't feel tight but that doesn't wobble from side to side either. All manufacturers use a different head shape to create their helmets, so try on a few and find the one that fits your head best and feels most comfortable.

Tightening devices are a great development in helmets, because they tighten the helmet around your head, rather than just keeping it pulled down, and also stop the helmet from sliding up and backwards. When buying a new helmet, make sure it has a tightening device at the back, just about at the top of your neck. The device will either be a circular dial, called a universal fit ring, or a couple of clips on a ridged strip. You can finely adjust both systems so that your helmet fits just right.

Some helmets come with removable foam pads on the inside that you can adjust to make the helmet fit more securely. However, these pads come off easily and can get lost, so don't think of them as being a secure way of fitting a helmet – they aren't. Buy a helmet that fits well with just a little tightening, and the same goes for children. Don't buy a helmet for a child to grow into – get one that fits now.

When you're happy that you've got a helmet that fits, you can work on the straps. Adjust the sliding buckles on either side so that they sit just below your ears, with one strap leading up in front and one behind each ear. Make sure they all lie flat against your head, with no twists. When you're sure they're all in order, clip the last buckle under your chin. You should be able to slip just one or two fingers between the strap and your chin.

If your helmet tends to slip upwards at the front when the straps are done up, try tightening the front two straps a little. Similarly, if your helmet starts to slip forwards, try shortening the back straps.

Before you set off, run through the following final checks:

- **Comfort:** You should feel comfortable in your helmet and ready for anything. It shouldn't press on any one part of your head and the straps shouldn't pinch anywhere. Think of it like any other kind of hat: look in the mirror and smile.

- **Fit:** The distance between your eyebrows and your helmet should ideally be one finger, and two at most. Any more and you need to readjust the side straps.

- **Straps:** To test the chin strap, tuck your fingers under it, open your mouth wide and shout 'Pinarello!' as loud as you can. You should feel tightness as the helmet is pulled down onto your head. (You can actually do this check without the shouting.)

Putting Bits on Your Bike

You may like to leave your bike exactly as it was on the day you bought it. Maybe doing so will remind you of that very special day. But if you're itching to add attachments, plenty of items are available to think about. Of course, if you plan on riding after dark, it doesn't take much to work out how important lights are. Having a pump with you when you ride is also a very good idea; you can easily attach a pump to your bike so you never have to think where you left it.

You can buy no end of other things to bolt, clamp, strap or clip to some part of your bicycle and in the following sections we give a run-down of all the more common options. (We cover systems of securing your bike, including chain and D-locks in Chapter 8, which deals with safety and security.)

Lighting up

If you take your bicycle out at night, you must have a decent set of lights. You need a white light in front and a red light behind, both of which must be fixed to your bike, as a legal minimum, and you can certainly have more than this. Attach front lights to your handlebars and rear lights to your seat post as high as possible.

One important function of both front and rear lights is to help other traffic see you at night, but front lights provide another function – they light up the road in front of you if you're riding in a poorly lit area.

When choosing lights, consider the following factors:

✔ Your visibility is important from every direction. Have a look at the lights from the side and check whether you can still see the lit component. If you can, this means the lamp will help light you up for a vehicle approaching you from the left or the right.

✔ A good rear light gives you the option of a continuous or a flashing light. Flashing lights stand out more and also use less battery power.

✔ If you're going to ride in well-lit urban areas, choose a front light that you can dim, as the point here is not to see better but to be seen.

Over the last few years, light emitting diodes (LEDs) have come along in leaps and bounds and now make up the brightest, most efficient (for battery-powered lights) and most common lights.

When LED lights start to lose battery power they often dim very quickly. Always carry spare batteries when you go out at night and, when choosing a light, pick one that you can open without a screwdriver, so that you don't have to carry one of these as well. And remember: you may well be changing batteries in the dark.

If you ride at night a lot and really want to improve how much you can see and be seen, consider the following improvements to take you above the legal minimum requirement:

✔ Many people find that for good front vision at night, two lights are best. One can be trained onto the road directly in front of you as you ride, alerting you to any obstacles or road surface problems, while you can point the other a little higher to give a good general view of what's up ahead.

✔ Head torches can also be a very effective help for improving how much you can see, because they enable you to light up areas of the road without turning your handlebars. However, if you're riding in a group, bear in mind they can be terribly annoying for other riders: every time you look at them, you shine a bright light into their eyes.

✔ If you're wearing a backpack, consider attaching lights to the pack, because the more light you give off, the safer you are. If you can find battery-powered fairy lights, they're ideal.

Whenever you use battery-powered lights, make sure you take them off your bike when you park it so that they don't get pinched.

As well as the more common battery-powered lights, a couple of other lighting options are available, as follows:

✔ **Dynamo lights:** Dynamos are a terribly clever arrangement for powering your lights from the turning of your wheel. A roller is put up against your tyre (or inside a hub in more expensive systems), which spins when the wheel turns and generates electricity to produce light. Dynamo lights provide a good light without slowing you down. They tend to dim when you stop rolling along, though some systems do stay on for a short time when you stop, so keeping you safe at traffic lights and junctions. However, you'll never have to buy or recharge batteries again. Installation is more complicated than with battery lights, but not too difficult.

✔ **Rechargeable battery systems:** These can provide much brighter lights and are often used by mountain bike riders when they tear along trails in the dark. However, these systems do have some disadvantages, including the following:

- The battery, which has to be fixed to your frame, is much heavier than a standard battery-powered light.

- Battery life is likely to be less than three hours.

- The light cuts out very quickly when the battery runs low.

Ringing bells

Knock, knock. Who's there? Isabelle. Isabelle who? Isabelle necessary on a bicycle? Arf!

This joke is one of the all-time classics beloved of Christmas cracker manufacturers. The answer used to be a simple 'yes' – a bell *was* necessary, at least at the point of sale of a new bike. But now, this particular law is being done away with. This scrapping is a triumph for common sense, as most road and mountain bike riders wouldn't dream of burdening their bars with all that extra weight. However, bells do play an important role in warning other road and trail users of your approach or presence, and they sound bright and cheerful as well.

The classic *trrring* sound of a bicycle bell is unique. Even the modern *ding* is unmistakable. And nothing brings a smile to the face like the *parp* of a traditional horn. These sounds are instantly recognisable. Hearing them is always a moment we relish. Although they are designed as a warning noise, the sounds lift the spirits and can make you feel expectant, joyful, even excited. To us, they're friendly sounds.

If you find yourself without a bell, most bike shops have a box of them somewhere near the counter. They only cost a few pounds and they clamp onto your handlebars without any fuss. Look a little further and you'll find bells in the shape of burgers, beetles, soccer balls, cups of coffee or teapots.

Pumping it up

You need a pump to make sure there's enough air in your tyres. You often need to pump up your tyres before you leave home and may need a pump when you're out and about, and you'll certainly need one if you have to fix a puncture.

Several different kinds of pump are available, as follows:

- **CO2 pumps:** These devices release the contents of a small metal CO2 cartridge – similar to the kind you use in soda fountains – into your tubes. Mountain bike racers often use these gadgets as they're a very quick way to get you back on the track after a flat. You use one whole cartridge every time you inflate, however, and they cost a great deal more than just pumping.

- **Hand pumps:** These devices may have a tube to connect them to the valve on your tyre's inner tube, or just an opening for the valve. Most hand pumps come with some means of attaching the pump to your bike – this could be plastic ties that hold your pump at either end, fixing it to your top, down or seat tube, or a more solid, plastic attachment that fits under your bottle cage.

You may find that the means of attachment provided with your pump are adequate, but often the fittings are flimsy or leave you with an unendurable rattle. In this case, you'll have to carry your pump in your jersey pocket, if you're wearing one, or your backpack.

- **Foot pumps:** These pumps are actually designed for cars, but can be used with Schrader valves.

- **Stand pumps:** Also known as floor pumps or tracks pumps, these look very much like the plunger device used in cartoons for exploding dynamite, and may come with a meter attached to show tyre pressure. Stand pumps are a very easy, quick and (because of the meter) accurate way of inflating your tyres. Half a dozen pumps and your tyres will be as solid as your cranks. They're too bulky to lug around, though, so you'll need to carry a hand pump.

Getting your pressure right

When it comes to pumping up your tyres, it pays to know a couple of things in advance, specifically the pressure requirement for your tyres and the type of valve that's used on your inner tubes.

You can find the range of pressure required for your tyres printed or moulded onto the tyre wall (the side of your tyre). The numbers are listed along with the letters psi, which relate to *pounds per square inch* (a fine old imperial measurement) or *bar* (the more modern metric scale). If you pump your tyres to the higher end of this range, your bike will roll more easily, but you'll have less cushioning against any bumps. You can pump up road bike tyres to 120 psi (or 8.3 bar), or around four times the pressure required for car tyres, while the pressure required for wider mountain bike tyres will be between around 35 psi (2.4 bar) for off-road use and 70 psi (4.8 bar) for on-road use.

Knowing your valve

Two kinds of valves used on bicycle inner tubes are commonly available in the UK: Presta (or French) and Schrader. Schrader is used on most bicycles and is identical to the valves you get on cars. This means you can pump up your tyres at the air pump in petrol stations – although these pumps often don't take pressure to above 60 psi. Presta valves are used on road bikes and more-expensive mountain bikes.

Carry on cycling

Almost everyone has to carry something on their bicycle at some point. The simplest thing to do is just pop on a backpack, but if you know you're going to transport things regularly, you'll find it more comfortable to have bags, baskets or packs attached to your bike. A number of different systems are available, each with a different purpose and all with a very different look.

If you travel to countries where bicycles feature much more in general transport, you'll see all manner of precarious means of getting stuff from A to B. In Hanoi, Gavin once saw a man delivering a fish tank, at nearly two metres (or around six and a half feet) long, by balancing it across the handlebars of his bike. In Nepal, Ben saw a window-cleaner riding along with a full-sized ladder strapped to the rear rack – sideways.

We don't recommend using your bike to transport over-sized items (and you may well find that doing so is illegal), but this section does provide a run-down on the more common ways of carrying things around on a bicycle.

Basketry

Baskets on bikes can be a fantastic style statement. If any bicycle accessory can definitely be said to be cute – and in a really positive way – it's a front or rear wicker basket. They seem to come with the promise of freshly baked bread and picnics with bottles of wine.

Front baskets attach to your handlebars. Rear baskets need to sit on racks fixed securely to your bike. Baskets don't just come in wicker: they're also available in wire, or even wire-coated in plastic to look like wicker. Search around and you'll also find basket-lining bags in amazing styles that you can lift out and carry as shoulder bags.

Racks and panniers

Rear racks generally fix firmly to your seatpost (or seat tube) as well as having bars reaching down and fixing onto your frame close to the rear hub. (Some racks built for specific packs fix only onto your seatpost, but these won't support as much weight.) These fixtures give a strong frame that has a flat top surface for loading and enough side coverage to attach bags and keep them off your wheels.

Some racks have a spring-loaded wire flap to keep your bag pressed down against the rack, but these are less standard nowadays. More common are *panniers:* a pair of bags that hang down, fixed in position on a frame, on either side of your back wheel. You can generally lift panniers off their rack quite easily and carry them by hand. On a long bicycle trip, panniers on a rack are the set-up you need.

Panniers come in different styles for different uses. You can get fully water-proof ones, ones designed to carry a laptop, and even panniers that will store a suit and then fold neatly onto the side of your bike.

Any looseness in the fastening arrangements between your rack and pan-niers can cause damage to your fixtures if you ride on bumpy surfaces. When buying a rack and a pair of panniers, which come separately, make sure they are the same brand or are compatible, because this means they will fit together more precisely.

If you're planning to travel with the essential kitchen sink, you can also get pannier systems for the front of your bike. Front panniers won't fit on all bikes – fitting them is tricky if you've got front suspension – and are usually a bit smaller than rear ones.

Road bikes aren't designed as beasts of burden and most don't have any of the little bolt-holes in the frame necessary to attach racks. You can use a seatpost mount to attach a rack and panniers to road bikes, but these kinds of racks can't carry much weight and, depending on the material the frame is made out of, may even damage your bike. If using a road bike, you may have to resign yourself to using a backpack or courier-style bag.

Saddle packs and handlebar bags

Saddle packs, or *tool bags,* are little pouches that dangle from under bicycle saddles. Most are just big enough to fit a spare inner tube, tyre levers, a couple of Allen keys and perhaps a puncture repair kit, although slightly bigger versions, which will also fit a bag of sweets or another inner tube (for those who set out feeling particularly unlucky), are available.

Handlebar bags attach (perhaps unsurprisingly) to your handlebars, so they sit where you can reach them while on your bike. They're usually hard-walled containers with lids and some will lock onto your bike. Handlebar bags are usually not as big as a front basket, but are very handy for carrying a map, camera, phone, sandwich or drink.

Electronics on your handlebars

Bike computers, or *cyclometers,* are little electronic gadgets that sit on your handlebars and record a lot – and sometimes an enormous amount – of infor-mation. Basic bike computers can display your current speed, distance trav-elled, average speed and trip time. More-advanced devices can also display information such as altitude, temperature and how far you've climbed, and store personal training information and allow data to be downloaded to your home computer.

Most bike computers have a magnet that's attached to a spoke on one of your bike's wheels and a sensor attached to a fork. The sensor transmits information either along a cable or wirelessly to the computer, which then calculates everything for you. Computers that measure *cadence* (the rate at which your feet are rotating the pedals and cranks) have an extra sensor on one of the cranks. Some bike computers are also heart rate monitors. If you buy one with this feature, you need to wear a special transmitting strap around your chest. (For the usefulness of heart rate monitoring, see Chapter 11.)

The face of the computer has several different readings showing at any one time, with your speed usually shown most clearly in the biggest characters. You can then scroll through further readings by pressing buttons either at the top or side of the bike computer.

More-advanced bike computers use satellite global positioning system (GPS) technology to calculate all your movements and speeds, and some even come with a mapping system. Because these bike computers use GPS, they don't need a magnet attached to a spoke and are much easier to set up. The added bonus of a mapping system can be very handy if you're riding in unfamiliar territory, and also means you can download a map of your ride when you get home. Bike computers with GPS are, however, much more expensive than ordinary bike computers – and they race through the batteries.

Adding the finishing touches: Bar ends, mudguards and mirrors

For some people, their bike is not complete without a few final items that really make the bike perfect. Such items include bar ends, mudguards and mirrors.

Bar ends

On a long ride, changing the position of your hands on the handlebars can prevent aches in your wrists and shoulders. *Bar ends,* which are almost like extra handles that you fix to the end of your handlebars, give you another option for hand positioning. They point forwards and up a little (and make your bike look like a charging bull).

Some people reckon bar ends make hill climbing easier, because they allow you to point your elbows outwards and lean your body even further into the climb. And some riders feel bar ends enable them to pull harder on the handlebars and heave themselves to the top of a hill. They definitely give your bike a strong, assertive look.

You fit bar ends onto your bike by sliding your grips (the bits you hold onto) towards the centre of your handlebars (see Chapter 4 for detailed instructions on how to move your handlebar grips). You then fit the bar ends onto the very end of your handlebars, making sure the angle of the bar ends gives you another comfortable cycling position.

When you cycle gripping your bar ends, your body puts a great deal of pressure on them, especially if you're leaning into your handlebars or cycling out of your saddle and up on your pedals. Make sure you fit the bar ends very tightly so they don't rotate as you cycle.

Mudguards

Mudguards used to be standard on any bike, but now you usually have to buy them if you think you might end up cycling in the rain but don't want water shooting up into your face from your front wheel and up your back from your rear wheel.

Full mudguards are fitted close to your tyres, curving around with the wheel. The front guard usually covers about a quarter of the front wheel's circumference, while the back guard can cover as much as half the wheel's circumference.

The traditional way of fitting full mudguards is to use a rod that runs from the highest point on either side of the guards down to the tip of the forks on the front wheel or the end of the chain stays on the back, with a central bolt fixing onto your frame either at the top of the forks or seat stays.

Many modern adaptations of the traditional full mudguard are now available, including lightweight, tough plastic guards that have quick-release fittings. You can even get an inflatable mudguard that rolls up and fits into your raincoat pocket.

Although road bike frames don't have any bolt holes for mudguards, you can get guards that clamp around stays, tubes or your seat post. (That is, of course, if you're not worried about the extra weight.)

Mirrors

Until you're quite practised, you might find that you wobble quite considerably every time you look over your shoulder to check what's behind you. In this situation, mirrors attached to your handlebars can be a very useful addition to your bike.

Depending on your handlebars' space availability, certain mirrors may only give you a reflection of yourself. You attach different mirrors in different ways – some plug into the end of your handlebars, meaning the extra sideways projection can give you the picture you need. Before you buy a mirror, position it on your handlebars to check it does provide a view of what's behind you.

Wearing Thin: Bicycle Clothing

Many cyclists embrace the activity with such fervour that they want to dress for the occasion. Riders want to know they've got the right outfit and bike shops always have plenty of cycling-specific clothing to choose from.

In the following sections, we cover clothing made specifically for cyclists. If you're thinking about the best items to pick from your current wardrobe, check out Chapter 4.

Going hand in glove with your new bicycle

Wearing gloves while riding a bicycle is a sure way of preventing or reducing injury. If you do fall over or off your bike, your first response is usually to put your hand out. But gloves aren't just your first defence: they're a very effective one. The simple protection given by cycling gloves prevents cuts, scratches, grazing and bruising, enabling you to get up with only your ego damaged.

If you're planning on medium to long rides, gloves also stop the aches and discomfort that come from gripping your handlebars for too long. Quite a lot of pressure is put on your hands when you ride, and having a little bit of cushioning in the right places makes a big difference.

The most common cycling glove is the half-finger, which looks like a glove that has had the ends of the fingers cut off. These gloves are designed to leave your fingertips free for nimble operations such as changing gears (and they're also quite good when you need to stop cycling to answer your phone). They have padding over the heel and side of your hand as well as the ridge of your palm – areas you might hit if you fall – and lightweight backs so that your hands don't get too hot.

Full-fingered cycling gloves, which offer more protection in rougher terrain or simply colder weather, are also available. These sorts of gloves often have fingertip grips, giving you a better grasp of your brake lever.

All gloves usually have a velcro strap for tightening around the wrist and a towelling strip on the back, useful for wiping sweat off your face or even for your nose when there's a chill in the air. (Don't worry – these gloves are eminently washable.)

Getting into bottom gear: The joys of Lycra

If you're going to ride a road bike, you'll have to get into skin-tight cycling shorts made from stretchy material such as Lycra. These padded shorts may show your shape to the world, but they're built to keep a very important region of your body comfortable while you ride.

All cycling shorts have an internal strip of foam or gel padding that covers your front, your rear and the important stretch in between. (The shape of the padding differs between shorts made for guys and for girls.) This padding is known as the *chamois,* although these days it's rarely made from the skin of the goat-like antelopes it gets its name from. The chamois acts as a cushion between the rhythmic rubbing of your body against your saddle as you pedal along. Road bikes in particular have rather hard and narrow saddles and this padding protects a part of your body that doesn't normally take much pressure at all. Cycling shorts are also made with few or very flat seams to help prevent chafing.

The skin-hugging tightness of these shorts is designed to prevent the material bunching (you wear the shorts next to your skin) and to minimise wind resistance. Baggier shorts may billow out or ride up your thighs as you pedal along into the wind, but material containing Lycra sticks to your skin like, well, skin, making your ride more aerodynamic.

Cycling shorts are usually black, but they also come in many other colours, and can be loud and lurid if you have team replica shorts covered in sponsors' logos. Longer styles that go to just above the knee or even to three-quarter length are available, while full-length versions are good for winter rides.

If you have either a cool start or finish to your rides, or often ride in cold weather, you may find you need something warmer than just shorts on your legs for that part of your journey. Options that are both warming and lightweight are available. Lightweight cycling tights can go over your shorts, or you could try *leg warmers* – tubes made out of material containing Lycra which leave no gap of exposed flesh and which fold up to next to nothing.

Cycling shorts and longs are also available in the *bib style,* which many road bike users prefer. These have straps that reach up and over each shoulder under your jersey (think of the suits wrestlers wear), meaning they won't budge, no matter how long you ride.

Cycle shorts that are less anatomically revealing and offer just a bit more room inside are available. These shorts, sometimes called *baggies,* are designed to not flare up in the wind, without being skin-tight. Some options have liners made out of material containing Lycra and padding.

Even if you're looking for cycling shorts that offer a little bit more room, you don't want to turn your cycling into sailing. Try on a few pairs to see which ones look best and make sure you're happy with the fit.

Targeting the yellow: Cycling jerseys

Cycling jerseys are either short- or long-sleeved and have either a zip down to the chest or a zip all the way. Long-sleeved options keep you warmer, while options with longer zips allow you to let air under your shirt when it's hot. (Arm warmers, which are really just tubes of material containing Lycra, are also available to combine with a short-sleeved jersey to give you some extra warmth when you need it.)

While cycling jerseys should be fitted, they should hug your figure without being too tight. When trying one on, lift your arms in front of you and up in the air to make sure it's still comfortable in different positions. If the jersey isn't comfortable in the shop, it certainly won't feel good when you're out on the road or trail.

Jerseys are made extra long at the back. This extra length keeps you covered up when you lean right forward, as you might on a road bike. Also included at the back of the jersey is a row of back pockets, which are usually big enough to hold your phone, some snacks and your wallet. (And sometimes more, if you want to stuff your pockets as full as a hamster's cheeks, although most cyclists think this isn't a terribly good look.)

Cycling jerseys are mostly made of synthetic polyester microfibre fabrics designed specifically to draw perspiration away from the skin and have it evaporate quickly. This process is called *wicking* and it's done so that your shirt doesn't stay wet when you sweat, which in most circumstances will leave you cold and uncomfortable.

Jerseys always used to be made of wool, which some people say is an even better wicker than modern synthetics. Wool jerseys (most often made from Merino wool), which are both cool when the weather is hot and warm when it's chilly, are seeing a revival in popularity and are increasingly easy to find. One great advantage of wool is that it has an amazing resistance to getting smelly, which cannot be said for its synthetic cousins. However, synthetics are certainly simple and quick to wash and dry.

Accessing your pockets while on the move

Reaching back to retrieve items from your jersey's back pockets is something you'll have to practise, preferably on your own and away from traffic. The first move is to put the hand that isn't reaching back onto the top of the handlebars, close to the centre. If you're connected centrally to the handlebars you're much more stable. Then reach back and get what you need.

Keep your eyes on the road and be prepared to give up and put both hands back on the bars if you need to react to anything in front of you. You might find yourself wobbling rather precariously at first, but get the hang of this manoeuvre and you'll be able to happily snack while you cycle.

The yellow jersey – the famous *maillot jaune* that's worn by the leader and eventual winner of the Tour de France – isn't the only brightly coloured top available to cyclists. Most bike shops have a large range of jerseys with plenty of eye-opening colours and designs. If you still want more options, look online and you'll find a huge variety of jerseys, including ones with the Superman crest, a pink skull and crossbones, your favourite beer, Santa's little helper or the bones of your skeleton. If you're fond of a particular professional cycling team, you can also go to the team's website and purchase exactly the same gear they wear. You can also go for something unique – getting your own design printed on a jersey is easily done, although the companies that do it often have a minimum order number.

Topping it off: Jackets and vests

Many cycle-specific jackets and vests are available and the version that's right for you will depend on your local climate and season, and what conditions you cycle in. However, the various options available usually fit in to at least one of the following three main functions:

- ✔ **Jackets that keep you dry:** Waterproof cycling jackets come in a variety of fabrics, including nylon and polyurethane. Some are just a shell that stops the rain soaking through to your other layers of clothing, while others are made out of thicker material to also provide some warmth. Some waterproof jackets have mesh vents under the arms that you can unzip to keep air flowing under your jacket.

- ✔ **Jackets that keep you warm:** High-wicking materials such as polyester microfibre fabrics and wool are hopeless in the wind – it whistles right through them. You need a barrier against wind, so windproof jackets are made out of fabrics such as polyester and a range of modern materials designed specifically for the job. Some windproof jackets also have mesh vents under the arms that you can unzip to allow some ventilation.

Some cycling jackets are padded for extra warmth, but many riders prefer to instead add layers underneath a waterproof or windproof jacket. Adding layers gives you the advantage of being able to remove your defences bit by bit. If you ride energetically, it's probably better to put up with being a little bit chilly when you start off, because your body generates a huge amount of heat when it exercises and, no doubt, you'll be warm as toast in no time.

✔ **Jackets and vests that keep you seen:** Safety vests similar to those worn by roadside workers are available for cyclists. These vests improve your chances of being seen enormously, making them great at night or even when it's raining and visibility is poor, and generally fold up small enough to put in your pocket. Another option is to choose a cycling jacket or vest in a bright colour and with strips of reflective material along the front, back and arms.

You can often find jackets that provide all three functions covered in the preceding list. Lightweight jackets are available that are waterproof, windproof and brightly coloured with reflective strips to help you be seen at night and in poor light.

Your local bike shop will have a range of different jackets and vests. If you still can't find one to your liking, check online where you'll find a massive array of choices and blends of waterproof, windproof, warm and bright.

We love the look of the tailored cycling jackets now available. Modern fabrics used by most manufacturers mean the jackets no longer have a 'plastic' look, and they don't make a rustling noise every time you move. And the streamlined designs mean you can find jackets that are more fitted to your body. To us, these jackets are fashion items that you can wear to almost any occasion.

Accessorising with glasses, head warmers, masks and more

Bike accessories are available that, although they may not be absolutely essential all of the time, can really complete your look. These include items such as glasses, helmet covers, head warmers, masks and reflective bands and strips.

Glasses

Although cycling glasses have undoubted advantages, opinion differs as to how essential they really are. Some cyclists would rather walk the plank than set out barefaced, and see glasses as their most important safety item. Other riders just note that they cope very well without them.

Good cycling glasses don't just act like sunglasses. Although they do have UV protection, they also shield your eyes from insects, branches, flying bits of grit and even magpies. Cycling glasses are also a different shape from ordinary glasses: they come in a wraparound style that means you can see things approaching you from the side without them being blocked by the frame. Good glasses come with several interchanges of lenses that you can use depending on conditions, as follows:

- ✔ Clear lenses for when it's overcast or dark
- ✔ Orange or brown lenses to relax your eyes
- ✔ Yellow lenses to add definition in poor light

If you need prescription lenses, these can be fitted to several makes of cycling glasses. Just ask your optometrist about the options available.

When wearing full-rim wraparound glasses, the lenses are prone to misting up in some situations. Picking a pair with ventilation holes helps to prevent this.

Helmet covers

Helmet covers fit over your helmet and provide shade for your neck and face. Made of a light mesh that covers your helmet, with fabric hanging down over the exposed bit of skin at the back of your neck, helmet covers usually have a peak coming out at the front to also give shade to your face, and are most useful in hot environments – although they do tend to heat up your head. You can buy versions that go under your helmet.

Head warmers

For riding in colder climates, you can get *head warmers* (woollen caps that fit under your helmet), *ear warmers* (woollen bands that go around your head, covering your ears) or, for extreme weather conditions, *balaclavas* (woollen hoods that cover the whole head, with holes for the eyes and mouth). *Buffs* are also useful to keep with you as you can use them for all these functions.

Face masks

Face masks that filter the air you breathe are an option for any cyclist battling city traffic congestion every day, and most city or sports masks are pretty similar. They all have replaceable charcoal filters that keep sub-micron particles, including emissions, pollens and other irritant dusts, from entering your respiratory system. Any mask that acts as a barrier to air intake has an effect on your breathing, but most masks are designed to still allow you to get the oxygen you need to ride hard.

Reflective accessories

Some final finishing touches available are reflective bands and strips which you can fit around your wrists and ankles or cut to fit and stick to where you think best. You can even buy indicator lights that strap to your wrists. These detect the raising of your arm and start flashing when you lift it to indicate that you're about to make a turn.

Putting Your Foot in It

If you're buying a bike for casual use, you probably won't want to buy expensive shoes that lock your feet to the pedals. Your bike will already have pedals and no doubt you just want to make sure what you do wear on your feet is practical.

On the other hand, if you're buying a road bike, it won't come with pedals. You'll have to decide which system of shoes and pedals you want, bearing in mind that most road bike riders use the cleat system that physically connects you to the pedal.

The following sections look at the various pedal and footwear options that are available to you.

Pedalling options

Standard pedals – also known as *platform pedals* – come in either plastic or metal. The plastic ones are cheaper and can break, but if you're just riding down to the shops or even commuting, you're unlikely to ever snap off a pedal. The big advantage of using standard pedals is that if you need to get your foot off and onto the ground in a hurry, nothing's stopping you.

The majority of road bikes (and many other bikes too) have clipless pedals (see Figure 3-1). These consist of not much more than the frame necessary to lock the pedal onto the cleat on the underside of a cycling shoe. This locked-on system is very efficient. Once clicked together, the shoe (and so foot) and pedal will always be in exactly the right spot. You're also able to lift as well as push the pedal, meaning you can pedal far more efficiently – and develop your calf muscles.

The disadvantage of clipless pedals comes when you forget, or are unable, to unlock a foot before you come to a standstill, giving you only one option – to fall over.

Figure 3-1:
The clipless
pedal.

Every cyclist we know who has changed over to clipless pedals has subsequently fallen over on their bike at least once, and often more than once. You can easily forget that you need to unlock your feet when you're reacting to something in front of you and stopping quickly, or when you're just not used to the new system. Unfastening your feet does, however, become second nature after a while. We're not still falling off our bikes. Honest.

Clipless pedals are common on mountain bikes, but some MTB riders prefer a standard pedal, simply because the terrain they tackle is so unpredictable they may often need to *dab* (take a foot off the pedal and touch the ground). Special kinds of pedals are available, however, with the most popular type known as *low profile* pedals. These are extra thin, with a wide platform featuring *pins* – little spikes that help keep your foot in place.

A final set-up is available that is almost halfway between a standard pedal and the clipless system: pedals with *toe clips* or *toe cages*. These are sometimes called *stirrups* and are made up of a (usually) plastic, cup-shaped frame bolted to the front of the pedal and a strap that weaves through the pedal and round the outside of the plastic. This arrangement forms a kind of half-shoe that your foot slides into as it lands on the pedal. *Half-clips* are available which do away with the strap and enable you to take your foot out more quickly and easily than with full toe clips. Half-clips are a good way of easing yourself into using caged pedals.

Although now less common than clipless pedals, these toe clips also enable you to pull on the upstroke while still allowing you to quickly release your feet. As with clipless pedals, when learning to use toe clips you may occasionally forget they're there and fall over.

These shoes were made for cycling

If you don't attach specialist pedals to your bike, wear shoes that are comfortable and practical when cycling. Pedalling a bicycle is harder work on your foot apparel than walking and you may also find unwanted grease or other marks appearing. This means you should probably avoid cycling in your best pair of shoes, unless you're happy for them to wear out before their time.

Flat-soled shoes will put your foot on the pedal at the correct angle. A stiff sole will give you more pedalling efficiency, as less of your energy will be spent on compressing the sponginess between your foot and the pedal. And shoes with some grip underneath will help a lot in keeping your foot in the right position and not sliding off the pedal.

Using the toe clip system on your bike has the advantage of pedalling efficiency while still letting you wear pretty much what you want on your feet. While you don't have to buy any special shoes, the same criteria as outlined in the preceding paragraphs still apply.

If you buy clipless pedals, you'll also have to buy special shoes. Shoes made for use with road bikes are designed for lightness and efficiency. Some of them even have light but strong carbon-fibre soles for maximum energy transference between your muscles and the pedals. Unfortunately, though, you can't generally walk on them, or at least not very far. The metal cleats fix onto the flat sole and when you try to walk your toes will point skyward and you'll make an awful clacking noise.

Most mountain bike shoes are made with the assumption that MTB riders may well have to travel using their feet as well as their wheels at some point. The cleats are fixed into a recess in the sole and you can walk with ease. Some of them are very stylish and you could wear them almost anywhere.

You might think that you could wear your mountain bike shoes on a road bike and that no one would ever know. To most people that's correct, but other road bike riders will know straightaway and you'll have to work hard to be forgiven.

Quenching That Thirst: Cool Clear Water

Taking in fluid when you're riding is very important. Your body loses a large amount of water (and some minerals) when you perspire and if you have an efficient high-wicking shirt you may not even be aware that you've been losing it.

You don't have to lose much fluid before you become dehydrated, and dehydration will make you weak, nauseous and quite ill. For short rides, becoming dehydrated probably isn't something to worry about too much, but for anything longer, especially a cross-country route or a long ride on empty roads, carrying sufficient water is essential.

Work out how much water you need for a ride and make sure you're carrying enough. Try weighing yourself on a warm day, riding for an hour and then weighing yourself again. Most likely you'll have lost at least a kilogram in fluid through your skin. Most people can't absorb more than one to one and a half litres (or roughly two to three pints) of fluid an hour, however, so this is a good figure to use, especially in hot or humid locations. If you think you'll need more than you can fit on your bike or in your hydration pack, consider putting larger bottles in a backpack or even in panniers.

Caging your bidons

Bidon is the French word for water bottle and it's the term cyclists use – probably from watching the Tour de France – for the squeezy plastic bottles they fix to their bikes. To carry a bidon you need to fit a small frame, called a *cage,* to your down tube or seat tube (many riders have them on both). You can then learn to reach down, pull out the bottle, take a drink and then replace it, all without losing control of your bike.

As with other manoeuvres, you should practise using your bidon while cycling alone and away from traffic before trying it out in the middle of a pack.

To fit a cage for your bidon, just remove the two screws you find on the upper side of your down tube or the forward side of your seat tube, put the cage in place and replace the screws.

You can also get double cages that attach to the little rails on the underside of your saddle. To grab bidons in these cages, you just have to reach back instead of reaching down.

If you fix bottle cages in all the places covered in this section, you'll be able to carry close to three litres of water attached to your bike.

Wearing water: Hydration systems

The *hydration pack* is a marvellous invention that allows you to drink without reaching for a bottle. You carry hydration packs like backpacks and they have a tube that runs from their reservoir to close by your mouth. All you have to do is grip lightly with your teeth to open the valve and you have access to all that water.

Hydration packs carry between one and a half litres and three litres (that's between around three and six pints) of fluid (making them good for longer rides) and the better ones are well insulated. This means your water – or whatever you fill the pack with – stays cold for quite some time. If you're riding in a cold climate, you can fill the pack with hot water and the insulation keeps it warm for ages.

These days all hydration packs have some kind of mesh that sits between the body of the pack and your back, which allows some ventilation through to ease the perspiration process.

While you're not likely to see them in bike shops, online you'll find cycling jerseys with built-in pouches that can store two litres of water and also have a tube you can place in your mouth. They have insulation and are made of high-wicking material to keep you cool.

Chapter 4

Making Sure Your Bike Feels Good

*B*efore you ride your new dream machine away from the bike shop, you need to make sure all its adjustable parts are in the right spots for you. Knowing about adjustments that make your riding comfortable and how you want the bike set up is also handy so staff at the bike shop can make changes accordingly.

For anyone embarking on a future with a road bike, getting this kind of bike fitted exactly is very important: your body position and resulting limb movements are critical for the efficient transfer of energy. If your bike's not set up right, you're going to end up pretty sore. The first sections of this chapter deal with adjusting bikes that are going to be ridden fast or long distances.

Even if you're planning to take it a bit slower on your bike and prefer a bike that allows you to ride in a more upright position, setting it up so that you can pedal easily and not end up with sore knees, wrists or a pain in the back is still important. With that in mind, this chapter also provides tips on getting your commuter or weekender bike right from the moment you roll away from the shop, as well as giving you some ideas about adding comfort and style.

If your riding falls somewhere in between fast and casual, the whole chapter is a worthwhile read.

Getting the Perfect Road Bike Pose

Whether you want to be sure you're set up for fast racing or just a brisk ride into work, when you've chosen your road bike get the staff at the bike shop to make adjustments to make sure you're sitting right on your bike.

Arranging your bike fit at the shop

You may be spending a reasonable sum of money on your road bike, so make sure somebody at your bike shop takes the time to do a bike fit for you. The first thing a fit establishes is that you've got the right size of bike frame. From there, adjustments can be made to the height of the saddle, the forward or backward positioning of the saddle and even the height or the angle of the *stem* (the bar that reaches forward from the frame and holds the handlebars).

To ensure your bike fit for your new road bike is correct, your bike shop might use a complicated system that involves many measurements and calculations. They might need to track down your sternal notch or learn the length of your femur and then do calculations using difficult formulae. Or they might just be very adept at sitting you on the bike and working with lines of sight, plumb lines and elbow-to-fingertip comparisons to get the fit right.

If they're using hands-on techniques, some things staff at your bike shop may be looking at are the following:

- **How extended your leg is when your pedal is farthest from your saddle:** Your leg should be almost fully extended at this point, but your knee should not 'lock'.

- **Where your knee-bone is in relation to your foot on the pedal:** Your knee-bone should be directly above the ball of your foot or the pedal axle when the crank is horizontal and pointing forwards.

- **How far forward your head is towards your handlebars:** With your hands on the lower part of the handlebars and looking straight ahead, a vertical line from the tip of your nose should hit the point where the stem meets the handlebars, or be just one or two centimetres behind that point.

- **Where your head is in relation to your front axle when you lean forward on your road bike:** With your hands on the lower part of the handlebars and looking straight ahead, your view of the front hub should be obstructed by the handlebars.

Make sure your bike shop provides a full bike-fit at the same time as you buy the bike. If the bike's not quite right and you have to bring it in for a fit some time later, the bike shop could charge you for the service.

You can do a bike-fit yourself and helpful tips are available online on bicycle websites and forums. However, you need someone else to help you with measurements, and having someone look at you on the bike to make sure your riding position looks right is always a sound idea. The people at the bike shop are going to be far more thorough and accurate, and should provide this service for free at the time of purchase.

Adjusting your road bike saddle

Even after you've had a bike fit (refer to the preceding section), you might find the position of the saddle on your road bike is causing you trouble. You might suffer from numbness in your groin, which is very worrying, or regular soreness when you ride.

If your saddle is causing you discomfort, the first thing to try is a slight adjustment of the angle of your saddle. It may just be that the nose needs to be angled down slightly. Take it too far and you'll find yourself slipping towards the pedals, so just move it a very small amount and see if that makes any improvement. If your cycling is giving you sore knees, it could be that the height of your saddle is wrong. Again, make small changes in the height and go for a test ride after the adjustment to see if you can notice any difference.

If changing the angle or height of the saddle didn't make your ride any more comfortable, it may mean your saddle is actually in the wrong spot. Take your bike back to the bike shop so staff can move it backwards or forwards to correct it, or see Chapter 18 for specific tips on how to adjust your saddle yourself.

If adjusting your saddle angle and position doesn't help, you may need to look at some of the alternative types of saddle mentioned in the following section.

Finding the right saddle for your road bike

If you wheel a road bike into a crowded room, you can tell those who don't ride one by the glances of fear and apprehension directed at the saddle. It looks so sharp – how could you possibly sit on that?

However, on any bike that you're riding fast or for a long period of time, you're likely to be in a leaning-forward position (see Figure 4-1). This means that more of your weight is being put on your handlebars and pedals, so you don't need a wide cushion for your rear. You do put weight on your saddle, but only through the lower back tips of your pelvic bones. So, ideally, you should be able to pedal for many kilometres or miles on a road bike saddle without getting sore.

We are all made a little differently, though. If you find cycling with your existing saddle is a painful experience, you may need to experiment until you find a saddle that's right for you.

Figure 4-1: When a cyclist is leaning forward to ride, more weight is on the handlebars and pedals.

The nose of the saddle often creates the most problems. Road bike users tend to pedal fast with less resistance (it's more efficient and less tiring that way). This means your thighs move up and down beside the front end of the saddle at a great rate. Saddles for road bikes are made thin at the front for this reason: to give your thighs a clear passage. However, riders can still experience pinched nerves and sore flesh around this area. Saddles that taper more slowly to the nose point or allow greater clearance for your thighs are available to help with these problems.

If your saddle is just generally uncomfortable or causes numbness, several variations on the standard saddle are available. Some saddles have strategically placed grooves or holes to get you sitting more comfortably, and some have gel inserts where your sitting bones sit on the saddle, providing more give than the normal hard saddle. Or you may need a saddle specifically designed for your gender. 'Standard' saddles are usually designed to suit male anatomy, but you can also find saddles made specifically for women.

Fiddling with your bars

Another common cause of cycling aches and numbness is handlebars positioned at not quite the right angle. If you're getting numb hands or sore wrists from cycling on your road bike, it may be that you need to tilt your handlebars further forwards to give you better extension, or backwards to bring them closer to you.

You can swivel the handlebars by using an Allen key to loosen the bolts that clamp them into position. Start by moving the bars just a small amount – it may only take a tiny adjustment to solve the problem and you can always alter the bars more later. When you're happy with the angle of the bars, retighten the bolts, making sure they're tight enough so the handlebars don't rotate as you cycle.

If you don't have an Allen key in the right size for the bolts on your bike or aren't sure about how far you should be adjusting your bars, pop down to your bike shop and they'll fix it up in no time.

When you have your handlebars at the correct angle, another cause of soreness or numbness could simply be your cycling position. Make sure your wrists aren't bent and you're not putting too much pressure on the joint of your thumb.

Comforting Tips for the Easy Rider

If you're riding for comfort rather than speed, you may be approaching cycling a little less athletically. You may prefer to sit on the bike in a more upright position, for example, meaning more weight is on your saddle and less on your handlebars. It's still just as important to get the bike set up just right for you. While the handlebars and saddle are key elements, you can make other little changes or additions that will make your bike speak to you and draw you towards taking a ride every time you see it.

Sitting up and seeing the world

For many people, sitting upright on a bike is the only way to ride. Your weight is placed fairly and squarely on your rear, not shifted forwards onto your arms and feet (see Figure 4-2). In this position, you get to see and learn about the world you pass through – more so than by any other means of travel, except walking. And you can easily exchange a few words with the people you pass, without having to crane your neck and screw up your face at them.

You might be riding through rice paddies in Asia, orchards in Switzerland or just to your local shops – on an upright bike you won't miss a thing. Your head is already lifted, all set to greet anyone who wants to pass the time of day. Whenever we travel to a city where cycling is deeply embedded in everyone's way of thinking – such as Amsterdam – we see hardly any other kind of bicycle.

Figure 4-2:
An upright sitting position, where feet can reach the ground and all weight is on the saddle.

Your sitting position on a bicycle is partly dependent on the kind of bike you get. You won't ever be able to sit up straight on a road bike, for example. If you do want to sit up and watch the world go by, you'll need a bike with the saddle a lot lower than the handlebars. You also need to be able to reach the bars without leaning too far forward or hunching over too much – this prevents you getting a sore back as you ride.

Maybe you like to be able to put both feet on the ground while still sitting on the saddle. Feeling this way is not unreasonable – perhaps you've had a bike accident in the past and you only feel safe when you're able to get your feet on terra firma. Most bike shops have bikes that allow this, such as some hybrids or small-wheeled bikes, such as folders. If the bike you like doesn't quite match up, just ask the bike shop staff if it's possible to adjust it.

If you've already got the bike and want to change the height of your seat, see Chapter 18 for some simple instructions on altering the position of your saddle.

Gearing down: Casual clothes for bikes

If you're not going to wear clothing made especially for cycling – and no big reason exists why you should – give some thought to what you will wear. Your first concern should be safety, then comfort – without forgetting style, of course.

Avoiding getting caught in the works

Most bicycles these days don't come with a chain guard – although guards are more common on certain kinds of bikes such as retro-style bikes. Dutch bikes often not only come with a chain guard but a *dress guard* too, which stops a flapping dress getting caught in the back wheel. If your bike doesn't come with a chain guard, you're unlikely to be able to get one that fits so you'll have to be very careful about clothing that hangs around the lower half of particularly your right, but also your left, leg. Skirts or trousers that flap loosely anywhere near your chain are going to end up getting caught, not only stopping your bike but also ruining your clothes. Instantly.

The problem of protecting trouser legs or other hanging fabrics is really a matter of style. You can buy trouser clips to clamp down on your flapping trouser legs and keep them out of harm's way – and some even have reflective material on them to help you be seen more at night. Or you can tuck your trouser legs into your socks or simply roll them up. Or you can just wear shorts or a shorter, less flappy skirt. Shoelaces can also get caught, so don't forget to tuck laces away inside your shoes.

Avoid clothes that can interfere with any moving part of your bicycle. Take great care with any item of clothing that hangs down from your back, such as a long coat or the sleeves of a shirt that has been taken off and tied around your waist. These flapping peripheries of clothing can lodge in your rear brakes or anywhere around your rear wheel and bring your bike to a shuddering halt. They can also flap in front of your rear lights, meaning you'll have less chance of being seen at night or in poor light. Although less likely, also check you're not wearing or carrying anything that will interfere with your front wheel, because if this does happen, you and the bike are likely to take a tumble.

Cycling is not inherently dangerous; however, you might end up falling off your bike at some stage, particularly when you're just starting out or getting back into cycling after a long break. If you're feeling a bit nervous, wear long sleeves and clothing that covers your knees. Even quite thin fabric can prevent some painful and unsightly grazes. Gloves are a good idea, too.

Comforting costumes

As well as safety (refer to the preceding section), comfort is an important factor when dressing to ride a bike. While you are free to wear almost whatever you like on your bike, you need to be able to move freely and stay at a reasonable temperature.

Consider the following when choosing a cycling outfit that helps you stay comfortable for the length of your ride:

✔ **On warm or hot days:** Select loose clothing made out of natural fibres such as cotton, because these fabrics help keep your body cool and make you perspire less. Also remember that you're out in the elements, so choose clothing that provides protection from the sun.

✔ **On cool days:** Select layers of clothing that you can remove as you warm up and pack away without taking up too much space in your bag or pannier. Consider using scarves and gloves to keep you warm initially, rather than a bulky jacket.

✔ **On windy days:** If you wear skirts, select styles that still give you room to move without flapping around too much. Looser skirts blow up in the wind – you can either take this as an opportunity to create a scene worthy of Marilyn Monroe or you'll have to free one hand from the handlebars to correct your wayward attire. Another option to help preserve some of your dignity is to wear tights or leggings under skirts.

Cycling is exercise, so even after a short ride you may find your clothes are a little damp. It may be necessary to wash and change if you've got an important date or appointment.

Cycling chic

Apart from a few practical considerations you really do have the freedom to wear just about anything you like on a bicycle. Whether you like to blend into the flow of a busy city or stand out in any crowd, you can carry on with your usual approach to fashion – your bicycle will only help you with your chosen course. If you dress to impress, you can continue to do so as you pedal down the street. We've seen people riding bicycles while dressed as fairies, gorillas and even, dare we say it, naked.

For us, the natural sense of freedom you enjoy when you ride a bike is a perfect step towards further self-expression through the outfit you choose to wear while you cycle. Riding a bicycle enhances positive human feelings and is an excellent medium for telling the world all about you. So let your outfit be part of the conversation.

Saddles and seat pads for upright cycling

For slower, more upright riding, you need a cushioned saddle to rest your rear. But many different shapes and styles are available. If you've just got your bike, you're new to riding and you're not sure your saddle is quite right, stick with it for a while. It may be that your body just isn't used to such a seat, but that you'll settle into it.

The Tweed Run

If retro is your thing, why stop at simply riding a retro bike? The Tweed Run is for people who like all things traditional, so as well as being encouraged to sit astride a classic vintage machine, the wearing of tweed is expected. And not just any old tweed, either. The real aficionados go for tweed plus fours – traditional British cycling attire.

The Tweed Run began in 2009 and was developed out of the Tweed Cycling Club as a reaction against the Lycra and fluorescent garb that has come to dominate cycling today. It was an effort to rekindle an altogether more wholesome aesthetic, so wool, steel lugwork, canvas saddlebags and dynamos are in; anything carbon or acrylic is definitely out. Phrases such as, 'style not speed, elegance not exertion', give you the general idea.

The first Tweed Run took place in London, but the movement has spread around the world to cater for the previously unmet need of thousands of cyclists to wear tweed. Greece, Mexico, Russia, Japan and Latvia are just some of the many countries that have hosted Tweed Runs. So if you see a group of woollen-clad riders serenely gliding past you in some far-flung capital city, don't be surprised. And if you secretly harbour ambitions to wear tweed plus fours in public but haven't yet plucked up the courage, you now have your chance – and you'll be amongst friends.

You can find out more about The Tweed Run on their website (www.tweedrun.com).

If your saddle isn't comfortable after you've settled into your bike, it may be that the angle, height or position of the saddle needs a little adjusting. You can apply the same process as for adjusting a road bike saddle here, so refer to the section 'Adjusting your road bike saddle' earlier in this chapter for more, or see Chapter 18 for specific instructions on how to adjust your saddle.

Another easy way to adjust your existing saddle is to make it softer and bigger using a gel seat pad. These pads fit on top of your saddle and are tied in place underneath with drawstrings. Gel seat pads feel almost like flowing, formless things – even like living organisms as they alter their shape in your hands – but they provide an even layer of extra cushioning over your saddle once installed.

If you decide you need a different saddle from your existing one, check out the saddles on the bikes of any friends or colleagues who ride. Find out if you can have a go on their bikes and see how their saddles feel. Always give the saddle a fair go – take the bike around the block, rather than just taking a few short pedals – and move around on it. Nobody is going to stay comfortable sticking to just one position on a seat for a whole ride.

If all else fails, and particularly if it's the nose of the saddle that causes you trouble, you can try a more unusual bicycle saddle. A number of specialist saddles are made without any protruding front. These saddles are usually well cushioned with either one oblong or oval piece or, quite commonly, two adjacent soft pads, one for each of your sitting bones. Some of these dual seats actually pivot, moving each side up and down with your body's efforts.

Gavin once tried out one of the more unusual – and scary-looking – specialist saddles for a review for a magazine. When he eventually met with the editor, she noted his condition of nervousness and shock and they agreed never to mention the saddle again.

You won't find any of these special saddles at your local bike shop, (bike shop owners generally find them just as scary as Gavin does) but if you're interested in tracking one down, you can track them down easily on the Internet: just search for unusual bicycle saddles. They could be just right for you.

Ben is a big fan of leather saddles and is frequently ribbed by cycling friends for being old school (he's a fan of merino wool too – read more about clothing fabrics in Chapter 3). However, nothing is quite as comfy as a properly broken-in leather saddle, though it might not look quite as flash as the modern high-tech alternatives perched atop a carbon race frame. It may take a few hundred (relatively uncomfortable) miles before a leather saddle is moulded to the shape of your particular behind, but when that's done it's like greeting an old friend whenever you go for a ride.

The perfect bicycle saddle for you might be an elusive thing, but it does exist. Don't think cycling is out because you haven't had any luck finding a seat that's comfortable from start to finish. Persevere – the right platform for your posterior is out there somewhere and finding it is worthwhile.

Handlebar grips

An easy, quick way to brighten up your bike is to shop around for some new handlebar grips. Your grips are right in front of you, so you see them all the time, and because grips can be made of a range of materials, you can give your bike a very different feel for a small amount of work and expense.

The most important thing about handlebar grips is that you can do just that: grip them. Many are made of rubber, just like your tyres, which holds your hand like a sweetheart. They can also be made out of metal, plastic, leather, cork – and even bamboo. Grips are often ribbed or contoured to help with hanging on tight and some are designed ergonomically to help cushion your palm.

Decorating your bicycle

You can personalise your bike in various different ways. Here's just a quick look at a few of them:

✔ **Handlebar attachments:** These attachments range from the fun but slightly daft (rubber chickens and witches hats for kids' bikes, for example) to the noisy but practical (such as cow bells that warn pedestrians not to step off the pavement into your path).

✔ **Painting your bike:** Most DIY bike paint jobs don't look great. If you're not after a smart look, fine – go ahead and paint. If you want it to look like a proper job but you don't have any specialist paint tools, here's the best way to have a go using aerosol spray paints.

Scrape and sand off as much old paint as possible, finishing with a fine sand. Using a space where you have lots of light and ventilation, spray two coats of primer. Spray again with at least two coats of your chosen colour. Spray from about 30 centimetres (that's 1 foot) away and leave the right amount of time between coats.

✔ **Spoke inserts:** You can fix things to your spokes using wire ties or just weave the item between several spokes. Laminated items work best, but pieces of card with any kind of picture or words on them are a great way of defining you and your bicycle. Additional reflectors can look good and help you be seen.

✔ **Stickers and decals:** The fastest way to transform your bike. Bike shops often have stickers to give away and you can buy decals online. You can also use fancy tape on your frame to deliver any message or image, as long as it fits on your tube. Tape can also hide any decals showing how expensive the bike is (to stop it getting pinched), or can cover any damage and add colour and flair.

✔ **Tassels:** Available from many bike shops, *tassels* (coloured strands that dangle from plugs in the end of handlebars) are easy to install. Ribbons, flags and flowers are good alternatives. Just be sure anything hanging won't get caught in any moving parts.

✔ **Valve caps:** Valve caps screw onto your inner tube valves. Just unscrew the little black caps and replace them with the decorative valve caps. Plenty of designs are available.

But the greatest variety comes with the look. Many stylish black handlebar grips are available, but you can find them in any colour you like. You can choose a brilliant primary intensity or pick a bright, go-faster pattern, such as flames or love hearts.

Changing handlebar grips

The actual handles of your handlebars are fixed very securely to the metal tube of the bar. That's very important – you need them to be perfectly immobile as you cycle along, not swivelling around.

Some grips slip onto the end of your bars smoothly and easily, and then get screwed tightly into position. But most grips are made of such material and of exactly the right size that they hug snugly to the metal and simply do not move. And this makes them very difficult to get on and off.

We've heard of a number of household products that perform just as well, but hairspray works with great success. Not on hair, but on the inside of the grips. To remove old grips, find a thin metal rod or skewer (a bicycle spoke works very well) and slip it under the grip, as far as you can get it, being careful not to scratch the handlebar. Either end of the grip will do, but some grips are closed at one end, which means you'll have to choose the one closest to the centre of the handlebars.

Lift the rod, skewer or spoke slightly to create a gap and shoot in some hairspray. Although you will still need some force, the grip will start to respond to your efforts to remove it.

To mount new grips, give the handlebar a light coating of hairspray (not too much or it will take an age to dry) and slip the tight-fitting rubber down the metal of the bar.

Chapter 5

Finding the Time to Ride

· ·

In This Chapter

▶ Beginning your cycling commute

▶ Plotting out time to ride

▶ Dropping the excuses

▶ Scoring goals and rewarding yourself

· ·

For most people, the biggest hurdle to exercising is finding the time in a full weekly schedule. You probably already have other things you'd love to be doing, but just don't have the time for. Finding a spare few hours to ride your new bicycle each week can be a daunting thought. Riding to work can also seem to have some difficult aspects.

If you're in the situation of having no spare time, you can do a number of things to shift priorities around, with some changes being more mental than physical. Riding a bike is a worthwhile thing to do: it makes you healthy, it makes you happy and it's good for your environment and increasing your community spirit. So, shuffling things around in your life and thinking clearly about your priorities to allow some time for riding your bike is well worth the effort, though doing so may mean making different arrangements with some of the people in your life.

In this chapter, we cover some very practical changes you can make to help you get out on your bike, and also provide some tips and ideas that should make a big difference in achieving your goals.

You can find the time to ride. And if you want to do it, you will do it.

Starting to Commute: It's Easy

A great way to find the time to ride is to incorporate cycling into your daily journey time by cycling to work.

The most common reason people give for not riding to work is not having a bike. Well, if you've got one now, one obstacle is gone. (If you don't yet have a bike, check out Chapter 2 for tips on finding the right bike for you.) You may feel another obstacle is that you have to carry things that simply won't fit on a bike or the total distance between your home and your workplace is just too far or parts of the journey are too busy for you to feel safe. However, you can overcome these apparent barriers. What seems like a great distance now may become something you can handle before you know it, and you can avoid main roads that don't feel very friendly by finding another route.

Riding to work is one of the smartest decisions you can ever make. Making the switch from using a car or public transport provides numerous benefits, including the following:

✓ Your problems caused by scarce parking or public transport delays vanish.

✓ You help yourself and your environment to become healthier.

✓ You save all the cash you were forking out on petrol or public transport costs.

✓ You start your working day feeling fantastic.

✓ Your fitness improves, without having to find the time (or money) to go to the gym.

In the following sections, we look at issues around cycling to work and show that some reasons people give for not doing so aren't really reasons at all. We also provide some good tips to help you get started and iron out problems along the way.

The time factor

In 2007, the BBC television programme *Top Gear* conducted a race across London. In rush-hour traffic, different modes of transport were compared. One person was in a car, another was in a speedboat, one was on public transport and another was on a bicycle, all racing from west to east across the great city. Who won? The person on the bicycle. Hands down.

Joining the commuter racing championships

A factor that might spur you on when riding to work is the phenomenon known as the *Cat 6 Commuter Championships*. The term comes from American *criterium* racing (a race of a number of circuits, usually three to five kilometres (two to three miles) each or over a given time on closed-off urban or suburban streets). The racing categories go from Pro-élite, to Cat 1 to Cat 5. Cat 6 is the race you are in when you take to the cycleways on a work-day morning.

Cyclists can be very competitive, even during commuting. You may be pedalling along very

happily, thinking you're making good time, but then another cyclist shoots past you like their saddle's on fire. Likewise, if you spot a rider up ahead, you may not be able to resist picking up your speed.

Naturally, many bicycle commuters don't indulge in this behaviour, considering it to be unnecessary, even immature, to need to prove you can beat a stranger – especially one who may not even know you're racing them.

What most people who live and work in any of the UK's urban centres find out is that commuting by bike is quicker. The big arterial roads allow motor traffic to speed in to the outskirts of the city's centre, but then everyone slows to a snail's pace for the last part of their journey, bogged down in traffic congestion. Everyone, that is, except the smart ones on bicycles. Not everyone works in a city centre, but average speeds for bicycles on other kinds of journeys often aren't that much slower than cars either.

Gavin works part-time at an educational institution ten miles from his home. No significant traffic congestion ever occurs along the route (all main roads), although there are plenty of traffic lights. On his bicycle, the journey takes Gavin 38 minutes – sometimes 38.5. He chains his bike outside the front door of his building and walks straight in. One time he took the family car and it took 30 minutes, and then he still had to find somewhere to park and walk to the right building. When motorists speed past on open stretches of road, they're certainly going faster, but, overall, they may not be saving any time.

Ben worked in central London for 15 years, commuting by bike the eight miles from home. Despite being close to good public transport connections at both ends, taking the bus and train took at least twice as long, and often much longer, than did commuting by bike. That works out as saving around an hour a day – or an entire nine days – over the course of a year. Despite the UK's reputation for bad weather, the average number of times that Ben got caught in really heavy rain showers was just twice a year. So while it might rain a fair amount, you can generally find a dryish window in which to commute.

Breaking it up

If you'd love to ride to work but feel that pedalling the total distance every day just seems like too much of a hard slog, you may be right. But you don't have to tackle it all at once. You can start commuting slowly, and perhaps eventually build up to riding your full journey every day.

Consider the following when planning your commute:

- ✔ **You can start small:** If you're currently driving somewhere from which you then take public transport to work, try riding your bike to this spot instead. Most train stations have bike racks where you can safely lock up your bike. As you get more comfortable with this, you can try heading for the next station down the line to give you that extra time on the bike.

- ✔ **You don't have to cycle every day:** Start by cycling every other day and you'll still have clocked up a great workout by the end of the week. Even cycling once a week makes a big difference. Don't punish yourself for not cycling every day – just do what you can.

- ✔ **You don't have to cycle the whole way:** Perhaps the distance between your home and work is genuinely too far for you to cycle – even if your legs were strong enough, cycling the whole way would simply take too long. So, you can just ride part of the way. Have a look at a map and find a spot that, for you, is a good distance from your destination and where you can park or, even better, get public transport to. As soon as you get to this spot, saddle up and avoid the congestion with healthy travel the rest of the way. (See Chapter 12 for tips on transporting your bike.)

Talking to your workplace about facilities for cyclists

Being able to cycle to work doesn't just rely on roads and your legs. When you get there you need to be able to lock up your bike and then shower or freshen up. If you don't have the proper facilities at your destination, commuting by bike can be difficult.

Talking to your workplace generally means talking to your boss, who is likely to perceive any mention of providing extra facilities as an unnecessary demand for more spending. So start off by outlining the benefits your company or department would see if more people rode to work.

ANECDOTE

Finding a better route to work

Local governments are painting bike lanes all over the UK these days. You may have seen these special lanes roll out along your way to work and have felt inspired to get on your bike. These developments are certainly very positive, but a main road isn't necessarily the best road for a bicycle.

When you drive to work, the quickest way is usually to take the road with the most lanes, but on a bike it may not be. You travel at the same speed on a smaller road. Check out a map – an alternative, smaller, quieter road may exist, where you feel safer and happier, or you might be able to find an alternative route to avoid a big hill or a menacing roundabout.

At one stage, Ben was commuting a total of 20 miles (that's 32 kilometres) every day from south-east to north-west London. The roads were a bit stressful here and there, but he worked out a route that avoided any major roads and included a few big parks, and which added just 15 minutes to the journey. It meant the ride to work became a real pleasure, and he still beat his next-door neighbour, who made a similar journey by public transport, by at least half an hour.

In the UK, central and local government are both pushing to get more people cycling, whether it's to work, to school or to other local destinations. Local councils produce maps detailing designated cycle routes for riding in urban areas (and how you can best link up with public transport), as well as for cross-country routes which are quiet and go through fantastic scenery. Give them a call and ask, or check online. Sustrans, a charity that encourages people to get out of their cars, has all sorts of resources and useful information on its website (www.sustrans.org.uk).

Yet another valuable resource for finding possible bike routes is a website called Bikely. Tools available on the website allow you to map out a bicycle journey and post it for all the world to see. Cyclists use the site to show other cyclists the best way to get from A to B on a bicycle. So many routes have now been loaded onto the site (millions of them), we can almost guarantee that your trip to work is on there somewhere. Check it out at www.bikely.com.

Focusing on the benefits

When approaching your boss about improving the cycling facilities at your workplace, you can highlight the following benefits:

✔ A healthy workforce is a much more productive one. Statistics show that people who ride bikes to work take far fewer sick days. One of the reasons why expenditure on cycling infrastructure – bike paths and other facilities – is such a sound investment is because governments save so much money on health care. The same is true for businesses that employ cycling commuters: riding a bike is such a great way to stay healthy that far less money gets spent paying people to stay home in bed.

✔ Not only are cycle commuters healthier, they're also happier. Being happier – arriving at work every day feeling great – makes them more productive. They focus better and are more willing and able to get on with things.

✔ You can park ten bicycles in the space it takes for one car. Having the space for car parking is expensive, so cycling is a very quick way to save money. If your company pays for other car-related costs, all these are saved too.

✔ People in the UK are far more environmentally aware these days. To be seen encouraging green initiatives sheds a very positive light on your company, which can have a direct effect on how much business you do. It also attracts a much better class of candidate for any job opportunities. You'll get the really smart ones coming along – the cyclists.

Ensuring parking options are available

Bicycles don't take up much room, but they do need somewhere secure to be left. Bike cages are a good option. They are easy and cheap to build, can go in any covered parking area and every workplace cyclist can be given a key or the code for a combination lock. Having some kind of bike rack system inside a cage is necessary so that bikes can be stored efficiently and securely (and you can also then lock your bike to the rack for added security), and because bike cages are left largely undisturbed for most of the day, it's handy if they can be placed within sight of a security video camera.

Outdoor (uncovered) parking of bicycles in any facility is a very poor option. Cars can be left unharmed in the rain, but bicycles can't. If your bike's been rained on all day your chain will grind rustily all the way home, and you'll have a wet saddle.

Providing showers

If your workplace already has showers, or plans to add them during a building refurbishment in the near future, fantastic. However, if a workplace doesn't have any showers, would-be bicycle commuters can certainly be put off. Starting your working day feeling great is all very well, but being smelly rather spoils it. Unfortunately, putting in plumbing in a big building can be difficult and expensive, becoming a real stumbling block. However, a number of solutions are possible, including the following:

✔ Choose appropriate cycling clothing so you don't arrive at work any hotter and sweatier than you have to (which may mean starting your ride a little cold and warming up as you go). You can then change into your work clothes and perhaps splash some water over your face and arms. You could also ask for a lock to be put on the entrance to the bathroom to keep the washbasin area private.

✔ Check whether a gym is close to your workplace and, if so, ask staff there if you (and other workmates) can have use of the showers in the morning. If they agree to allow this for a small charge, ask your employer to pay. Your employer will find this is cheaper than plumbing.

✔ Join the *slow bicycle movement*, the main tenet of which is, if you're starting to sweat, you're cycling too fast. It may mean you need to leave home a little earlier, but taking your time on your ride means you can enjoy the scenery and company and still arrive feeling fresh.

After you shower, you need somewhere to put your towel and cycling clothes. Your desk may not be the most appropriate place. If you're getting showers built in, ask your employer if they can also include lockers.

Making Time: Planning Your Week

Where do you start to find time in your week to ride? Actually, *when* do you start is the most important question.

If you've bought a bike for a specific purpose – perhaps for riding to the library or taking your eggs to the local market (and, if so, please be careful) – you don't have to give much thought to when you can ride. Just go right ahead and start. Otherwise, it may be a little more difficult to get into the swing of it.

If you'd like to increase the amount of time you spend each week cycling but are struggling to do so, try one of the following techniques:

✔ **Announce your plans before anyone else does:** It may be that your family and friends are going to organise a day together at the beach, in town or meeting up with more friends. If you've already said you're going out on your bike, they're likely to make their plans (which include you) around your ride, afterwards or on a different day. If you haven't said anything, most likely it's goodbye bike ride or goodbye friends.

✔ **Write down your plan and tell someone about it:** If you intend to ride your bike for an hour on Monday, Wednesday and Friday, research shows that you are 50 per cent more likely to do so if you've written down those intentions. If you then tell somebody else that you're going to go on those rides, you're even more likely to get them done. And if you ask that person to follow up with you to see how those bike rides went, you're about 75 per cent more likely to tick off all the dates you made with your bicycle.

✔ **Create a schedule of your planned rides and goals:** You can mark up your planned rides on a calendar, or even just draw up a table for the week or fortnight ahead, mark down your rides and stick it up on the fridge. You can also include goals in your schedule. Perhaps your local cycling group is organising a big ride in a few months' time. Sign up for the ride, mark down the date it's being held on your schedule and then add in some smaller goals in the lead-up to the ride. Small goals could include riding for an hour instead of 40 minutes, getting to the top of a particular hill or riding to work four days a week instead of three. Setting smaller goals helps you reach the bigger one.

✔ **Reassess your priorities:** If no space seems to exist in your weekly schedule – blocking out time in your week to ride is too hard – try taking a step back from all the things you do. Is it all really necessary? Or enjoyable? Maybe you could stop doing something else so that you can ride your bike instead. Riding your bike is, after all, something you're not only going to enjoy thoroughly, but also an activity that's going to have a directly positive effect on your health, how long you live and the way you look.

We've known people who wanted to cut back from five days a week at work to four, and were in a position to ask their respective employers if that was possible. Cutting back on spending (and they were able to quite easily identify spending that wasn't essential) meant that they were able to create a significant amount of extra time in their weekly routine. That's a great way to make more time for riding a bike, which, when you've got one, only represents a minimal cost.

Your individual circumstances dictate the ease or possibility of taking up any of the ideas we've included in the preceding list. But even if you can't consider giving things up, getting a bike is a very positive event in your life and it's essential to follow through and make the time to ride it.

Planning ahead doesn't always work. Things crop up or other people make plans for you, meaning when you get to the time you'd set aside for riding your bike, it can seem unreasonable or impractical to actually do it. However, we're complicated creatures. Sometimes circumstances really do stop us, but sometimes we can show strength and carry on as planned. Where do we get that strength? We have to find it ourselves. It could be that a simple self-reminder is enough – for example, you enjoy riding your bicycle and you always feel great afterwards.

Stopping the Excuses for Not Being Able to Ride

Your mind and body can play tricks on you. If you're cycling up a long difficult hill, starting to think lots of 'give up' thoughts is quite natural. You don't have to go all the way to the top. You made no promises. You're the only one who'll know if you stop. If you give up now, you'll probably do better next time. Who's the boss of this cycling thing anyway?

This system of deception is complicated. Your body is sending sneaky and seductive messages of fatigue to quiet corners of your mind. Your brain is then conjuring up excuses and false reasoning to get you off your bike.

Unless you're injured or in real pain, or the situation you're cycling in has become dangerous, don't listen to those voices. If you've said to yourself that you will cycle up that hill, the best outcome for you is to do it. I know that doing so is hard, but you should at least be aware of how contrived your own reactions can be and what's really stopping you from getting or staying on your bicycle.

Sometimes it can be hard to muster up the enthusiasm to even get on your bike and excuses again come easily – 'It's raining,' or, 'It'll be quicker if I drive.' Or perhaps you've been held up and now don't have enough time for the full ride you'd planned or would be riding part of the way in the dark, so riding at all seems pointless.

You can just as easily find reasons to ride instead of excuses not to. For example:

- ✔ Even if rain is falling, chances are on a fine day you'd be damp from perspiration when you get where you're going anyway, so who cares if you get a little wet from the rain? Just like a pool that feels too cold when you dip in your toe, cycling in the rain is often fine once you're in – the rain is refreshing and that is the message you should listen to.

- ✔ Riding your bike is often quicker, especially if you're only going short distances, such as to the supermarket. (You'll also save money, as the amount of stuff you can buy is limited to the room you have in your backpack, basket or pannier.)

- ✔ A shorter ride still provides many benefits and is a great way to de-stress after a busy day. And just get some lights if you'll be cycling home in the dark. Simple.

There certainly are conditions you shouldn't continue to ride in. If you've been injured or are experiencing severe pain in your back, neck or knees, or numbness, you should stop and either rest or seek medical advice. If the conditions have become dangerous, due to changes in the weather or surface of the road or trail, you should also stop and either wait for conditions to improve or seek an alternative route.

Gavin was once at extreme altitude in a remote part of South America – higher than Everest base camp – where the temperature was minus 20 degrees Celsius (that's minus 4 degrees Fahrenheit) and a howling wind was blowing fine sand into every crevice. The track ahead was soft sand and volcanic ash at a gradient of 16 per cent. One of the team had become ill. It wasn't nice at all and he made the decision to get off his bike.

While exceptions do exist, deciding against a bicycle ride, particularly if you're choosing to drive instead, is rarely the right thing to do. In most cases, if you stick with your bike, you'll always feel better for it.

Motivating Yourself and Achieving

Riding a bike as a regular thing is a progression. The more you do it, the better you get at it and the more you get out of it. The more you ride a bike, the less you use other forms of transport and, quite likely, the less you'll want to.

As with any physical activity, your body adapts and gets stronger as your muscles build and learn the regular movements of cycling. You get gradually fitter, feel much better generally because of your fitness, and start to see how much better you're doing. As you become more skilful and strong, you feel a change in your life too. You're healthier and, because you spend more of your time with those magic endorphins released through exercise buzzing round your system, you're happier too. Although feeling fitter and healthier are rewards in themselves, you should also acknowledge when you've done well and reward yourself.

The following sections offer some tips to keep you motivated in your cycling and ways to recognise when you've met certain targets.

Watching benchmarks fly by

One of the really fabulous things about riding a bicycle (and many exist) is how easily you discover that the more you ride, the better you get at it. This is true throughout the range of cycling ability. Learner riders can just as easily see their progression as top professional cyclists can.

Ride your bicycle regularly and you'll soon be able to ride it further and further. If 20 minutes is all you can comfortably ride now, keep doing your 20 minutes several times a week and in a month or so you'll realise that you're not tired or out of breath after your ride. You'll see that you're very capable of riding for half an hour or pushing to go further in the 20 minutes you have available.

While hills can be a struggle, you can motivate yourself into cycling all the way up by turning conquering one into a goal. If you've got a sticky one that you can't avoid by choosing another route, don't punish yourself too much – ride until you need to stop and then stop. Note where you get to, and then keep at it. Each time you need to cycle up the same hill, again note how far you get – soon you'll notice that you're getting further and further up before you need to dismount. And one day you'll get to the top.

After a while you lose that sense of dread you feel when approaching a hill on a bicycle. Some people even start to enjoy them.

Using goats for motivation

Goats are lovely animals, masters of the mountain environment and a source of excellent cheese, but as far as motivation is concerned, they are practically useless.

Goals are what you need, not goats.

If you really want to get faster and stronger at cycling, you need to practise. Practice as much as you can. But your progression will be faster and easier to see if you set yourself goals. Goals give your cycling a purpose, because you're aiming to achieve something specific by a certain date. The goal could be an event or just a ride you want to do at a certain time, but set your sights and you've got a goal.

A good way of reaching your goal is to set yourself a number of smaller steps along the way, leading you at a steady climb towards your stated ambition. Stage by stage, you can see how you're progressing towards your goal. These smaller targets could be increased average speed, a longer time in the saddle, a larger number of hills or a greater distance than ever before. Just don't be too ambitious – a succession of easy steps makes your passage smoother.

You may experience setbacks as you try to achieve your goals, and this is only natural. You might get sick and have to take a break. Life might just get too busy for a while. Don't let setbacks become a defeat – just readjust your schedule and start again at a realistic pace.

Refer to the section 'Making Time: Planning Your Week' earlier in this chapter for more information on setting goals and getting motivational help in achieving them.

Giving yourself a pat on the back

So you've just achieved one of your goals. Perhaps you've ridden 25 miles (40 kilometres) – 3 miles (5 kilometres) more than ever before. That's a very solid achievement. Or you may have ridden 250 miles (that's 400 kilometres) in 24 hours. Either way – well done! In either situation, you've worked hard and you've got a good result.

Just the knowledge that you've accomplished something is a reward in itself. But don't just feel proud – give yourself a reward. You've earned it.

If you've reached a small milestone, a token gift to yourself might be appropriate. If you've achieved a major goal, consider something more substantial. Bicycle-related items include new gloves, a more stylish water bottle or even a fancy jersey.

Of course, any gift will do. And if your achievement involved using a great deal of energy, you don't have to feel any guilt about going out for dinner and eating exactly what you like. Or perhaps treat yourself to a massage. If you're generous and selfless by nature and just can't bring yourself to splash out on yourself, why not treat your friends? A great idea would be to buy several copies of this book and present them to your closest pals.

A streak of success

Streak cycling is the term used to describe a decision to ride your bike every day for any long period of time. Sometimes riders have competitions with their friends to see who can go for the longest period of time, or sometimes cyclists set themselves a goal and work hard to achieve it individually.

Jim Langley is a famous bike enthusiast who has a huge website devoted to all things bicycle. He has plenty of easy-to-read pages on fixing bikes, riding techniques and some great stories. His page on 'Stupid Bike Tricks' is a must-read classic.

In 1990 Jim set himself a goal of streak cycling for ten years. His conditions were simple: he had to ride for at least an hour each day (although he often did more). All went well until 1993 when, out cycling in the mountains, he hit black ice and broke his pelvis. Three steel pins put his bones back together, but he was off the bike for six days and the streak was over. (Yes – only six days.)

But Jim didn't give up. He started again, at first riding on a trainer one-legged, with his healing leg propped up, but determined to get to the ten-year mark. When he reached it he just carried on going and at the time of writing he has just passed 18 years of streak cycling. Jim's proud of his streak, but says, 'I believe anyone who's a little stubborn and determined can do this. It's just a matter of making up your mind to do it and making it happen; that and a little luck.'

And although Jim loves to tell the story of his streak, he has also gathered stories of other remarkable streakers, so to speak. One is Scott Dickson of Iowa, in the USA, who has ridden every day for over 27 years. In that time he has cycled over 550,000 miles (or 885,000 kilometres), including 1,472 centuries (that means riding over 100 miles, or 161 kilometres, in one day).

Jim's advice on streak cycling is the following: 'If you're interested in becoming a streak cyclist, my advice is to go for it. Just take it one day at a time, stay determined and you'll probably find that the more days you chalk up, the more you'll want to keep the streak alive. Good luck!'

Jim Langley has one of the best bicycling websites on the Internet – check it out at www.jimlangley.net.

Part II

Freewheeling Away: The Fundamentals

In this part . . .

- ✔ Saddle up, grip your bars, pedal away – master the basics of riding a bike.

- ✔ Know the rules that cyclists have to abide by and understand the rules about bikes for other traffic.

- ✔ Stay alive: find out what steps to take to ensure that you're as safe as you possibly can be on your bike.

- ✔ Plan cycling routes that you're comfortable with and know what road conditions you are likely to face.

- ✔ Leave the tarmac far behind you and discover how to get to grips with off-road riding.

Chapter 6

Ticket to Ride: Your First Lesson

· ·

In This Chapter

▶ Saddling up

▶ Steering around

▶ Getting to grips with your bars

▶ Pedalling with power

▶ Using gears for gain

▶ Stopping short

· ·

Your riding experience becomes a lot more fun when you've learnt the basics and all the simple functions of riding a bike become automatic. This chapter provides some guidelines and tips for you if you're new to riding a bike. If starting off down the road on your bicycle isn't yet an entirely smooth process, read through for help with making your mounting more graceful and comfortable and your pedalling more confident.

We know some people find gears on a bicycle a bit scary and don't bother using them much, but this chapter shows how simple gears are to use, making those undulations in the road roll past with a lot less bother.

Taking a Great Running Leap into Your Saddle

In the 1948 movie *The Three Musketeers,* Gene Kelly plays the 17th-century French hero d'Artagnan. In one of the scenes showing his dashing ability, Kelly runs up a steep hill, jumps into the air and lands squarely in the saddle of his horse. It's breathtaking. And this is exactly how you should mount your bicycle.

No. Not really.

You can actually get on your bike with movements so comfortable and slow, you'll hardly notice you've just straddled an item of traffic. And if you do it the right way, pedalling off also becomes far less of an effort or gamble.

Starting (and stopping) on a bike is a key vulnerable area for topples and minor accidents. Until you get good at mounting your bike and pedalling off comfortably, you should make sure you're not taking any risks.

The easiest way to get on a bike

On a bike blog Gavin once read, someone claimed you could tell where people grew up by how they got on a bike. He put the person to the test and based on the way Gavin mounted his bike, the blogger's prediction was that he was raised in northern Tanzania (which isn't the case, but we're sure many highly proficient cyclists do come from northern Tanzania).

It may be true that cyclists tend to mount and set off differently in different parts of the world but, wherever you are, one general approach is easier and safer – the method that first gets you onto the bike and then gets you started.

If you've got a bike that lets you put your feet on the ground while you're sitting in the saddle, then go right ahead – simply sit yourself in the saddle and there you have it. If not, follow these steps:

1. **Get one leg over the top tube and straddle your bike so that both your feet are on the ground.** (If you've somehow ended up with a bike that has a top tube higher than the inside of your leg, this bike is too big for you and not safe. Please get another one.)

   If you have trouble swinging your leg over the top tube – perhaps you're just not used to stretching that way – don't worry. Just take half a step back and lean the bike towards you. This significantly lowers the top of the bicycle and you should now be able to get your leg over. Another option may be using a *step-through* bike, where the top tube is lower, particularly in relation to the saddle, and closer to the height of your pedals.

2. **Raise one of the pedals with your foot so it's pointing up at an angle towards the top of the front wheel, and place that foot on it (see Figure 6-1).**

3. **Push forward with the foot that's on the ground.**

4. **Push down with the foot that's on the pedal.**

5. **Lift your behind onto the saddle.**

6. **Lift your foot that was on the ground onto the other pedal and start cycling.**

Figure 6-1:
Stand over
your bike
with one
foot on
a raised
pedal.

These steps may sound complicated, but following them means you're at lower risk of anything going wrong, and it usually all follows pretty naturally when you try it. Starting off this way means that you centre your body weight all the way through and you don't have to attempt to swing limbs around while you're in motion.

If you're able to sit in the saddle with both feet on the ground, go through the same process outlined in the preceding steps – you just don't need to raise your behind into your saddle as it's already there.

The best place to get on a bike

It might sound obvious, but a busy main road is not a good place to practise getting on and off a bike and starting to pedal. You need a soft surface, just in case you take a tumble, but also a surface that's easy to cycle on. (Sand is great to fall on, but awfully difficult when it comes to pedalling.) You also need a flat surface so that bumps and hollows don't hamper your first pedal strokes. A rough surface takes more strength to get going on and could mean the whole sequence of starting is spoilt.

The best surface on which to learn to ride your bike is grass, but make sure it's not too long and the area is flat, firm and free of too many holes or hollows. This means the best place to first get on your bike is often your local park. As soon as you're feeling more confident about staying on your bike, you can move onto paths with harder surfaces. Practise getting on from the left, as this corresponds to the side the pavement will be on when you get more experienced and start heading out onto roads.

Don't just head to your local park for your first attempt to get on your bike without thinking. If you want to be alone, pick a time when fewer people are likely to be about – and so fewer witnesses to any falls you may have.

Getting started on a bike isn't always completely smooth, and you might take a small tumble or two along the way. Wear long trousers and a long-sleeved top to protect knees and elbows from grazes. Gloves are also a good idea to help look after your hands.

Steering Clear of Trouble

When you come to think about it, the physics of steering a bicycle is a complicated affair. A moving bike is in a constant state of imbalance, which you are continually correcting by both leaning and turning your handlebars. A great deal of learning to ride a bicycle involves your arm, shoulder and leg muscles creating unconscious patterns of coordination and correction.

This elaborate system of forces and counter-forces makes even a simple turn a difficult thing if you were to list all the small movements and changes of angle. Thank goodness steering becomes an unthinking skill.

Steering is enormously important. If you realise suddenly that you're going to collide with something – whether a small object on the road or a large mass, such as a car, moving up on you – steering is what will save you, so practise getting it right. Smooth accurate movements show that you're in control and help prevent you coming off your bike.

When practising steering, keep in mind the following:

✔ **Balance steering:** This comes about by making sure you're turning the handlebars with shoulder and body movements, rather than bending at the elbow. Elbow steering can be wobbly and erratic, giving you less control and not working in with the natural leaning of the body that manages balance.

- **Counter steering:** This is something most people do without realising. It's when you give the handlebars a small turn away from the direction you're about to change to, which shifts your position on the bike and enables you to enter your move leaning in the right direction for the turn. A conscious or exaggerated counter-steer can help you swing into a sharp turn by having you lean quicker and further.

- **The rock-dodge:** This is a steering trick that can clear you of a destabilising collision with any small obstacle that appears suddenly in your path. This simple quick right–left or left–right flick of the handlebars should clear your front wheel of the obstruction and leave you still powering along in the same direction.

Handling Your Handlebars

Gripping the handlebars may seem like the easiest part of learning to ride, but you can still benefit from knowing about the safest position to keep your hands in and knowing how to safely reach for items you may need while cycling. That's where this section comes in.

Keep your hands – both of them – on your handlebars as much as you can. At the times when you have to reach for things or signal to other traffic with your hands, you are more vulnerable because you don't have the same amount of corrective force on both sides of your non-stop balancing act. If you remove both hands, you're giving yourself even less control – and you're also breaking the law.

Getting hooked

If your hands are knocked from your handlebars – for example, if you hit a half-brick-sized rock (or half a brick) – and you're in any leaning-forward position, your hands will be thrown upwards and onwards and your body will then fall towards the road in front of you.

If your body is shooting forward, your handlebars are your last protection between you and the road. Making sure your hands are always hooked around your handlebars makes it less likely your hands (and so the rest of you) will be knocked forward. With straight bars this means riding with your thumbs hooked underneath the bars. Never ride with just your palms resting on the top of your handlebars, as in this position a jolt will send you flying.

Bike polo

Some cyclists learn to be very skilful at using one hand to control their bikes by playing hard-court bike polo. This game originated many years ago when British military types decided to use bikes instead of horses and dashed around fields in their uniforms. These days, hardcourt bike polo is a hip urban contest that has young riders meeting up in car parks and disused tennis courts.

To play bike polo you have to hold a polo mallet in one hand. These are usually made from ski poles and plastic piping and are used to score goals with a street hockey ball. Rules vary, but *dabbing* (touching a foot to the ground) is generally not allowed. Being able to *track-stand* (hold the bike immobile with both feet on the pedals) is a big help, and using an old bashed up bike is a good idea.

Although most forms of contact, particularly mallet to player, are not allowed, it can still be a high-impact game. Difficult at first, players develop skills quickly, especially being able to fully control the bike with one hand.

Not many people play this game, so bike polo fanatics frequently travel, sometimes very long distances, to hold championships.

If you want to have a go, new players are always welcome. Many cities in the UK have bike polo clubs (search online to find a club in your area), and there's even a European bike polo championship. The best thing to do is turn up, watch, meet people and have a go – if you dare. A mallet is always available to people who want to try their hand.

Also make sure your fingers can reach the brake levers. This is sometimes an issue with children on bikes that are a little too big for them. Some brake levers include screws that enable you to adjust the reach for small hands. Few things are more terrifying than realising you can't stop, so if you don't want to put a child off riding for life, make sure they are able to use their brakes.

Reaching out and changing positions

As you start cycling for longer periods, being able to reach something while you're cycling means you (and any cycling companions) don't need to stop every time you need a sip of water or a snack. Being comfortable riding with your hands in a few positions on the handlebars is very handy.

If you're going to reach for something, perhaps a water bottle or an item in a jersey pocket, put one hand close to the middle of the handlebars before you do. This helps maintain central control of your bicycle. Take it slow and, if you don't feel comfortable, stop and put both hands back on the bars.

Moving your hands to different positions is a good way of relieving any build up of stress in your wrists, arms or shoulders. On *dropped* handlebars (as you'd find on a road bike) four different places to put your hands are available:

✔ On the lower curve

✔ Up on the brake hoods (where you can still operate your brakes and often gears)

✔ On the central, flat part of the bar

✔ On the curve just behind the brake hoods.

With straight bars, different hand positions are also possible if you add bar ends to the ends of your handlebars. (Refer to Chapter 3 for more on these and other accessories for your bike.)

If you're going to try anything new in the way you handle your bars, do so away from traffic and at a low speed.

Pedalling: Don't Stop Now

Your pedalling should come in a smooth stroke and should not tire you out. The pressure on the pedals should come from the ball of your foot, because this area of your foot is by far the most efficient spot for transferring energy from your legs to those pedals and cranks.

If you're using platform pedals, make sure the ball of your foot is doing the pushing, not your instep or toes. If you're using clipless pedals or the toe-clip system, your feet should already be landing in the right spot for proper pedalling. (Refer to Chapter 3 for more on the different pedal types and systems available.)

Pedalling is also much more effective (for you, not the bicycle) if you do it quickly with less resistance. A high *cadence* (the number of times the pedals go round per minute) means that you're using less energy for each muscle movement – each rotation of the pedals – and exercising more aerobically. Aerobic exercise gets your circulation going without overworking your big muscles – and it's what gets you fit.

If you're happy just trundling along at a natural pedal pace, that's fine. But if you want to ride faster or get further up hills, a higher cadence instantly improves your performance.

You might find yourself in certain situations where coasting is better than pedalling. You should stop pedalling if you're

- **Travelling fast and leaning into a tight corner:** On the side you're leaning into, raise the foot and pedal to the 12 o'clock position, then wait until you've straightened up before you start pedalling again.

- **Riding over an area of slime – or anything that's very slippery – on a path or road:** Continue to roll straight ahead, trying to stay as upright as possible until you reach a better surface, and then resume pedalling.

Easing Off the Pressure: Using Your Gears

Gears are a marvellous invention. They enable you to spin the pedals at more or less the same rate no matter how fast you're going or what kind of terrain you're crossing. Mountain bike gears go so low you could almost cycle up the side of your house. Road bike gears are so smooth you might at first think they're not there at all.

Gears are put on bikes to make them easier to ride. Some people approach them with caution, thinking they're a difficult thing – and the more gears a bike has, the harder they must be – but nothing could be more worth the effort than practising the use of and getting used to the gears on your bike.

What the gears are for

In short, the gears are there to help you. If you reach an upward slope and your legs start to slow down and work a lot harder, you can change *down* a gear or two – although you'll slow down, you shouldn't need to be using any more energy than you were on the flat. Then when you start to roll down the other side of your hill, you can change *up* through your gears if you want to pedal, but don't want your feet spinning round like a rat in a circular drainpipe.

Whatever cadence you're happy with, gears help you stay at that rate and, particularly, take the pressure off when the going gets tough.

Different systems

A number of different set-ups are available for changing gears.

Some bikes have *hub gears,* which is a mechanism that stays out of sight inside the hub of your rear wheel. This system has been around for more than 100 years and although it mostly used to provide just 3 gears, it can now give up to 14.

The advantages of hub gears include the following:

✔ The gears are much less vulnerable to water and grit thrown up by cycling.

✔ The gears require less maintenance.

✔ You can change gears even when the bike is not in motion.

One disadvantage of hub gears is that, if something does go wrong with the system, it will often be more expensive to repair and may even require replacement.

Most bikes, however, have a gear system that includes a dérailleur (a bar that pulls the chain off one sprocket and onto the next) at the rear and often at the front of the chain loop. When the chain moves onto a smaller sprocket wheel at the back, one revolution of the pedals will turn the rear wheel further, making it easier to cycle at a greater speed. When the chain moves onto a smaller chainwheel at the front, you get the opposite effect: one pedal turn spins the back wheel less, making it easier to pedal at a slower pace.

On most bikes, you change gears using one of two main systems, as follows:

✔ **Grip-shifts:** These involve turning your handlebar grip to change up or down a gear. Grip-shifts usually have a dial at the end of the grip to show you which gear you're in.

✔ **Gear levers:** These small levers are close to your brake levers, so that you can reach with your fingers or thumb to change gears. Some older road bikes have gear levers on the stem or down tube.

With any kind of lever system you have to reach to change gears. Modern road bikes have a fiendishly clever *integrated shifter* system that lets you push your brake lever sideways to change gears. The most modern advance involves an electronic signal being sent from the handlebars to the changing device.

Certain bikes, such as cruisers and single speeds, don't have any gears. These bikes are meant for particular uses – in the case of cruisers, that's little more than slow, cool rides to the beach, so they don't really need any gears.

Some people choose to train on bikes without gears, simply to make riding deliberately difficult for them when they want to build up strength in their legs. If that's what you're after, go for it, but most people are far better off with a few gears.

Using gears to best effect

One of the scary things about gears on a bicycle can be how many of them there are. Faced with the prospect of 24 gears or more, you may feel like you have far too many to deal with comfortably.

But the 24 gears aren't 'all in a row'. This number of gears means that you have eight different choices from each of the three front chainwheels. Think of them as three parallel lines of eight points, each starting a step ahead of the other, as shown in Figure 6-2. (**Note:** Figure 6-2 is a representation only. In reality, the sprockets would have fewer teeth as they get smaller, as would the chainwheels.)

Realistically, 24 gears laid out in this way only gives you a choice of about 12 gears, but 12 is still a pretty good number that helps you cycle happily in a big range of different conditions.

The best way to use the three sets of eight gears (or any number of different sets) is to pick the set that are most appropriate to the riding you're doing. If you're riding out on the flat with a good tailwind, then slip up to the top set (the biggest chainwheel at the front) and enjoy pedalling up to high speeds. If you're battling your way through a series of climbs, stick to the bottom set (the smallest chainwheel at the front) and you should have a good set of choices to carry you through.

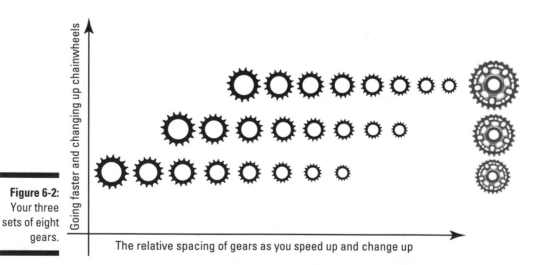

Figure 6-2:
Your three
sets of eight
gears.

Going faster and changing up chainwheels

The relative spacing of gears as you speed up and change up

Chains, chainwheels and sprockets wear faster if you use the extreme of each set of gears because doing so puts a bend in the chain and causes more of a strain on everything. So if you're using the big chainwheel (the one on the outside) avoid using the biggest sprockets at the back (which are on the inside). And, if you are using the small chainwheel (which is in the inside), it's best not to use the smallest sprockets.

Falling Off, Running Away or Just Plain Stopping

Brakes are an even better invention than gears: in fact, they're essential. Some people benefit by training on bikes without gears, but the same cannot be said for riding without brakes. At best you'll end up having to steer in directions to avoid potential hazards rather than going where you want to. You're more than likely to have some narrow escapes and at worst you'll have a collision. That's pretty much inescapable.

In the following sections you can read about the different systems of brakes on bicycles and some good tips on using them. We also provide some basic but important instructions on how to simply and safely stop and dismount from your bike.

Braking down

Three different kinds of bicycle brakes are common, as follows:

- **Back pedal (coaster) brakes:** These brakes slow down your back wheel as soon as you pedal backwards. These brakes are located in the hub of the back wheel. Some hub brakes are operated by levers on the handlebars.

- **Rim brakes:** The brake blocks clamp against the rims of your wheels and are operated by levers on your handlebars. Most bikes use this system.

- **Disc brakes:** The pads are squeezed against a flat metal disc near the hubs of your wheels, also by using levers on your handlebars.

All these systems work well, but disc brakes are the most effective. You commonly find these on mountain bikes and on an increasing number of hybrids.

You should test your brakes before you start riding your bike. Brake blocks can often need a little adjustment to sharpen up their effect. If you're new to a bike, you need to test the brakes to know how hard to pull the brake levers to slow down at a good pace.

Bicycles in the UK have their front brake lever on the right side. This is because the hand signal when you're turning right (and therefore turning across traffic coming from behind and in front of you) is more important than the one when you're turning left. The rear brake is less powerful but more controllable and therefore safer to use when you only have one hand on the bars. In countries where traffic moves on the right, front brakes are on the opposite side, which may take a little getting used to.

Always use both front and back brakes to slow down and stop. Using your front only can send the back of your bicycle – and you – up in the air. Because the front brake does about 75 per cent of the work of stopping a bike, if you use the back brake only, you may skid along for a while before coming to a stop.

Keep the following in mind when using brakes:

- Brakes with blocks on the wheel rims don't work as well in the wet. If you're riding in the rain and have to slow down quickly, brake, then quickly release the brake and brake again. (This tip has scientists puzzled but the wisdom of generations of cyclists insists that this helps your brakes to do their job.)

- If you're going fast downhill and round a corner, you're better off not braking, because it can cause your wheel to slip. But if you feel you're going too fast round a bend and that you're not in control of the bike, a gentle squeeze of the brake levers will slow you down just enough to regain control. Doing this is particularly important if you're riding in traffic, because you don't want to turn so wide that you end up on the wrong side of the road facing oncoming traffic.

Stopping good

Unfortunately, there always comes a time when you have to get off your bike. It's the end of the ride and you finally have to stop. It can be a difficult process emotionally to finish off such great fun, but the physical side shouldn't be too tricky.

To stop on your bike you need to slow right down, move your behind off your saddle and forwards, take one foot off a pedal and put it on the ground as you finally stop. This leaves you standing astride your bicycle. If you have a high top tube, you then need to swing one leg backwards and over your saddle to get fully off the bike. (If you have a step-through bike, you can just step your foot through.) If swinging your leg backwards and over is too much of a stretch, hop half a step away from the bike with one foot. This lowers the highest point of the bike as it leans over, making it easier to get your leg back over the saddle.

Getting off your bike in the direction away from the road, so putting your bike between you and the road, is a good idea. If you stop next to a footpath, dismounting this way puts you on it. If you're out in the country and suddenly you realise a truck, a dog or a great rolling boulder is coming at you, you're able to jump clear of danger without the bike blocking your way.

If you've got clipless pedals and shoes or the toe-clip system (refer to Chapter 3 for more on these), remind yourself you're attached to your pedals *before* you come to a standstill. Remembering once you've stopped will be too late and you'll fall over.

Chapter 7

Knowing the Rules

. . . .

In This Chapter

▶ Abiding by the law

▶ Understanding how you should be treated

▶ Staying alive

. . . .

*R*oad rules are there to try to keep road users safe. They generally also involve road-related areas, such as bike paths and footpaths, so they do concern you even if you're not actually on the road.

Bicycles are classed as vehicles and legitimate items of traffic. They have to follow the same rules and have the same responsibilities as other traffic, but some special rules – and the occasional exemption – also apply to bicycles. Your duty is to be acquainted with these rules. You're a safer cyclist when you know and follow them, so in this chapter, we cover most of the aspects you should be aware of.

While we deal with most of the important areas of the Highway Code relating to cycling, there isn't room for a complete guide here. You should look up the full details and make yourself familiar with them (see the 'Checking Out the Rules – in Detail' section at the end of this chapter).

Following the Rules for Bikes

Quite a lot of special rules have been put in place for bikes. They concern how you behave generally and how you act in specific circumstances and general aspects to do with your bike. Sometimes the rules overlap a little, but we've tried to split them here into the following three sections.

Getting up to speed on your required behaviour

Your rights and responsibilities when riding your bike include the following:

- ✔ The law requires you to ride with at least one hand on your handlebars. You're very welcome to cycle along waving two hands in the air, but only if you've got three of them.

- ✔ You must have both feet on the pedals, which means no waving your legs around in glee as you go down a hill.

- ✔ You're not legally required to take up any particular position on the road when cycling. However, cycle training endorsed by The Department for Transport refers to two riding positions: *the primary,* which is in the centre of the lane and *the secondary,* which is to the left of moving traffic but no closer than a ½ metre (that's 2 feet) to the edge of the road.

 The Highway Code says that cyclists should 'leave plenty of room when passing parked vehicles and watch out for doors being opened'. To do that, you need to be further than a ½ metre (2 feet) from the edge of the road, so a metre (1 yard) is a safer bet. (For more on avoiding car doors, see Chapter 9.) Staying further than that from the edge of the road also says to other traffic that you're traffic too – you're using a lane and they need to take all the usual care when overtaking you, rather than just squeeze past quickly, which is dangerous.

- ✔ Don't ride too close to the vehicle in front. Leaving enough space in which to stop safely is *your* responsibility – no matter how hard the vehicle in front hits their brakes.

- ✔ Holding onto a moving vehicle or trailer is illegal.

- ✔ Don't carry anything that affects your balance or gets tangled up with your wheels or chain – this rules out taking your pooch on a lead for a walk on you bike.

- ✔ While wearing a helmet and fluorescent clothing by day and reflective clothing at night is recommended by the Highway Code, doing so is not obligatory. But if you ride at night you must have lights and reflectors (see the 'Knowing the rules about your bike' section later in this chapter).

- ✔ You aren't allowed to carry more people than your bike was designed for, unless it has been properly adapted.

- ✔ Be considerate of other road users, particularly blind and partially-sighted pedestrians. Let them know you're there by ringing a bell if you have one.

- Overtake on the left only if the vehicle in front is turning right or if you're in queuing traffic and the lane to your right is moving more slowly than you are (note that these rules are the same rules for other vehicles – cyclists have no special dispensation in this case).

- Don't stop on the inside of a vehicle at the head of a traffic queue. This area is a blind spot for lorries and buses, but the driver of any vehicle can have trouble seeing you there. Particularly if the driver turns left, you're in a very vulnerable position. This is one of the most dangerous situations for a rider to put themselves in and is the cause of many serious accidents.

- Riding two abreast is allowed, but you should ride in single file on narrow or busy roads and when riding round bends.

- Don't ride two abreast when overtaking. When passing other traffic, you should always do so in single file.

Unfortunately, the special rules for cyclists are littered with phrases such as 'a safe distance'. Because the actual distance is not specified, it can mean vastly different things to different elements of traffic. To some motorists, if they got away with it, it was a safe distance.

Be aware of your rights and responsibilities on the road, but also stay alert at all times. Make sure your cycling is controlled and consistent, you give clear indication of your intentions in plenty of time and you make eye contact with other motorists as you approach a turn or roundabout. (See Chapter 9 for more on using the road with confidence.)

Knowing the rules about particular places and things

A number of laws apply specifically to cyclists in particular areas – including footpaths, bike paths and roundabouts – and situations, such as indicating to turn, merge or stop.

Checking out specific areas

Cycling on pavements is illegal. If you do it, you're liable to a fixed penalty notice of £30. (This law applies to children too, though the fixed penalty cannot be issued to people under the age of 16.) However, guidance issued by the Home Office when the penalty notice legislation was introduced said, 'The new provisions are not aimed at responsible cyclists who sometimes feel obliged to use the pavement out of fear of the traffic, and who show consideration to other road users when doing so.' This suggests that the police do have some discretion, but don't count on their interpretation of the guidance being the same as yours.

Alternatives to cycling on roads are to use cycle routes and cycle tracks. *Cycle routes* are located on roads (along with other bike-friendly facilities like advanced stop lines and cycle boxes). None of them are compulsory – so if you don't want to use them, you don't have to – but they can make cycling on main roads a lot safer for you. *Cycle tracks* are normally located away from roads, and sometimes alongside footpaths and pavements. Tracks are sometimes segregated and sometimes shared. Where tracks are segregated, you must use only the side intended for cyclists and take care at all times when passing pedestrians.

One piece of road design that can be a big problem for cyclists is roundabouts. Small ones are usually quite easy to get through, but large ones with fast-moving traffic can be a real menace.

While the Highway Code says roundabouts can be hazardous for cyclists and should be approached with care, no special provisions exist for cyclists. You are treated the same as any other vehicle. Drivers are told to watch out for cyclists who may be in the left-hand lane and are signalling that they intend to continue round the roundabout. They should allow cyclists to do this, but you shouldn't count on it.

Ninety per cent of the UK's roads are the responsibility of county councils; only the biggest ones are looked after by central government. Your local council is an elected body and is there to represent all voters. Roads are there for the benefit of all users – including cyclists. If you feel that particular roundabouts or junctions have been designed to put motor traffic flow as a higher priority than cyclist safety, put pressure on them to get it fixed.

We believe that as a cyclist, you keep yourself safer by being assertive, and that you should be given equal status and respect on the roads. We back away from very few road conditions. But when roundabouts get very large (which means they have been specifically designed for fast driving), they can become dangerous for cyclists, especially when laws treat bikes in exactly the same way as other vehicles. Being assertive does not mean the same thing as being unrealistic or reckless, however, so we do our best to avoid roundabouts that we feel unsafe using. And if no alternative route exists, we employ tactics to keep us out of harm's way. On a roundabout Gavin uses regularly, for example, instead of riding straight through he turns left, crosses at a pedestrian crossing, heads back to the roundabout and turns left again. If you're uncertain how motor traffic will behave, or are worried about your safety in any way, we suggest you do the same.

See Chapter 9 for more on planning a route you feel comfortable with, and some tips on dealing with more difficult traffic conditions, including roundabouts.

Indicating your intentions

Always indicate that you're about to make a turn. Do this by holding out your right arm to turn right and your left arm to turn left. In addition, if you're planning to slow down or stop, indicate this to other road users by holding out your right arm and moving it up and down below the horizontal. Always look first (normally over your right shoulder), before making any signal or manoeuvre and before setting off.

Knowing the rules about your bike

The rules relating specifically to parts of your bike include the following:

✔ You must ensure that your brakes are efficient. And you must have two brakes (one on either wheel), except if you're on a fixie (where you only need a front brake) or if it's a child's bike and the saddle is no higher than 635 millimetres (that's exactly 25 inches) from the ground. In this case, you only require one brake, on either the front or back wheel. These rules are very reasonable, because brakes are pretty essential if you want to stop and/or avoid a collision.

✔ You don't have to have a bell, but the Highway Code recommends that you do. Having a bell or horn is a good idea because it helps to warn people of your presence.

✔ Riding after dark without lights or reflectors is illegal. To ride legally, you need a white light at the front and a red one at the back. They can be solid or flashing. You're also required to have a red reflector on the rear of your bike and amber reflectors on the pedals (if the bike was manufactured after 1 October 1985).

✔ It sometimes happens that your light is still working, but the batteries are running low so the brightness of your beam is fading. You can't always see this from where you sit on your bicycle, so periodically turn on your bike lights and have a look from a greater distance. Ensuring your lights are working and bright isn't just about following rules – you need those lights for safety.

✔ If your lights have different settings, you can make your batteries last far longer by setting your lights to flashing mode, rather than being on all the time. But only set your lights to flashing mode where street lights keep the road surface well lit; otherwise, leave them on permanent beam.

You aren't restricted on what you're allowed to tow behind your bike, as long as there's no danger of anything getting stuck in your wheels or chain and your brakes are still able to stop you efficiently. However, do bear these considerations in mind:

✔ You can carry children of any age in a trailer and they aren't required to wear a helmet (though we recommend that they do). If the child is very young, make sure their neck muscles are strong enough to hold up their head. Be sure to follow the trailer manufacturer's weight limits, as you don't want to endanger your precious cargo.

✔ If using your trailer after dark, you must fit it with a rear-facing red light (just as you have on your bike) and a red triangular rear reflector. Most manufacturers appear unaware of this and supply the incorrect reflectors and nowhere to fix a light, so you may need to make an alteration or two.

Remembering the Rules about Bikes for Other Traffic

To pass your test to drive a motor vehicle you also have to know all the rules that apply to bikes and cyclists. But some of the rules about bikes are just for motorists. The Highway Code has plenty of advice about how other traffic should behave safely around bicycles and a few specific regulations.

The rules that relate specifically to motorists and bike lanes include the following:

✔ Cycle lanes are made for bikes and drivers aren't allowed to use them. In fact, driving or parking in a cycle lane marked by a solid white line during its hours of operation is an offence.

✔ Drivers should avoid driving or parking in cycle lanes marked by a broken white line, unless doing so is unavoidable.

✔ Drivers must not park in a cycle lane whilst waiting restrictions apply. Waiting restrictions are indicated by yellow road markings and yellow signs that display the times during which the restrictions apply.

Don't assume that drivers will actually stay out of cycle lanes just because the law says that they must. Stay alert to cars crossing into your path.

Remembering that Rules Are No Good If You're Dead

Unfortunately, although rules across the UK give cyclists certain rights, people who drive the bigger elements of traffic do sometimes act like the road is theirs and that they need pay no heed to the law. To show you what we mean, listen out for radio phone-ins about cycling. Invariably a (non-cycling) driver will call in to say that cyclists have no right to be using the roads because they don't pay road tax. Well, their argument has two massive flaws. Firstly, cyclists have every right to be on the road – exactly the same right as any driver; and, secondly, no such thing exists as 'road tax'. Vehicle Excise Duty, which varies according to the emissions of your vehicle, does exist, but because bikes produce no emissions, people using them don't pay anything. Check out `ipayroadtax.com` for more details.

As a cyclist, you'll experience this sort of attitude now and again. It could be that some motorists are unaware of the law or how they should drive around bicycles, or it could be that drivers sometimes just make the wrong call. Many drivers are well-intentioned, and some are cyclists too.

Although you can build up a romantic picture of a fair and just courtroom where your innocence and strength are lauded, if any actual conflict or contact occurs between you and a motor vehicle, you are much more likely to come off worse – and you could end up seriously injured or killed. This fact is especially true if you're a commuting male – you're in the higher-risk category. Four out of every five cycling casualties are male, and most accidents occur between eight and nine o'clock in the morning and three to six o'clock in the afternoon – commuting hours. Eighty per cent of cycling accidents happen during daylight hours, though those at night are more likely to be fatal.

Although being assertive when riding is important, as is feeling confident as a legitimate road user, the road is not a place for you to stick up for your rights. You must stay aware of how vulnerable you are and be at peace with backing off or just plain ducking for cover.

Checking Out the Rules – in Detail

We list here some website addresses where you can find out about the rules of the road in greater detail. Some of them help to interpret the rather complicated terminology used in legislation, and point out gaps and anomalies:

- ✔ **The Highway Code (www.gov.uk/rules-for-cyclists-59-to-82):** This website explains what is required of you as a bike rider.

- ✔ **The Cyclists Touring Club (www.ctc.org.uk/cyclists-library/ regulations):** The Regulations section of the website offers a good overview of the requirements for you and your bike.

- ✔ **UK Cycle Rules (www.ukcyclerules.com):** Written by a barrister, this website offers information and discussion about all sorts of topics to do with cycling and the law.

- ✔ **Bike Hub (www.bikehub.co.uk/featured-articles/cycling- and-the-law/):** You can find answers to some of the most commonly asked questions about legislation affecting cyclists on this website.

Chapter 8

Thinking Ahead for Safety

. . . .

In This Chapter

▶ Standing out with clothing and lights

▶ Ringing your bell and listening out

▶ Making sure you can stop short

▶ Firming up your tyres

▶ Locking in your security system

. . . .

*W*ith a few checks and a little thought and preparation, you can improve the safety and security of you and your bicycle. In this chapter, we cover some things you should do and some things you shouldn't do – and hopefully get you in the habit of taking care of yourself and your beloved bike.

Being Seen in All the Right Places

One of the major causes of accidents involving bicycles is motorists not seeing cyclists. When riding a bike, you need to use lights and other measures to help you stand out during the day and be clearly visible at night.

You need to make sure motorists can see you in all traffic situations. Consider the following:

- ✔ Car drivers rely heavily on a glance over their shoulders and at the rear-view mirror before changing direction or lane.

- ✔ Truck drivers have limited vision behind them and to either side.

- ✔ Bus drivers often expect to pull out from stops with little hesitation.

Your job is to ensure that drivers in all situations pick you out before they make their move.

Roads in many areas of the UK now have *bike boxes* painted on the surface of the road at lights and intersections. These allow cyclists to spread out across the front of waiting lines of traffic to help motorists clearly see you taking off when lights turn green. These boxes are a great help and an acknowledgement of the importance of bikes being seen, so don't hesitate to use them if they are available.

Some people fly flags on little poles from their bikes, which is a great idea, especially on bicycles that are closer to the ground. Gavin once drove past a recumbent in traffic and all he could see was a small orange flag passing by his windows. This caught his attention and was heaps better than nothing at all.

Anything you can attach safely to your bike to draw attention to yourself is a help. Give it some thought because being seen should become a major consideration whenever you're cycling.

Dressing to be noticed

Your bicycle might be a lovely and bright postbox red or clean and white as snow, but your bike isn't the major part of your bulk when you ride. The big part is you, and you're the thing that has to stand out.

Choosing to ride a bike is a statement in itself, so don't feel that you have to blend in or fade out when you hop on your two-wheeled friend. Be bold, show the world you're proud to be pedalling, dress in something that turns all eyes your way and have a safer journey because of it.

Bright is right

Imagine a cyclist dressed all in military camouflage gear, riding a green bike on a country road that runs through a forest. Then imagine some army tanks and armoured troop carriers, disguised for manoeuvres, heading down the same road in the opposite direction. It'd all be over in the spin of a wheel.

Of course, dressing in camouflage gear when you want to be seen is pretty daft, but just as crazy is wearing greys and drab colours in a city environment when you're weaving your way through traffic on a bike.

You need to wear bright clothes when riding a bike – and the brighter the better. Perhaps surprisingly, white has been shown to not stand out very well, but colours do, especially fluorescent ones (see the sidebar 'Finding your fluorescence'). And if you want to wear a full fluorescent suit, go ahead. Who cares what anyone else thinks? You might become known locally as the Orange Person, but at least you'll be a long-term feature, not just a flash in the pan.

Finding your fluorescence

Fluorescent pigments have special physical properties. They absorb light from the ultraviolet end of the spectrum and then re-emit that light in the visible spectrum. This extra light is why fluorescent colours – green, yellow, orange, pink – stand out so strongly.

Fluorescent colours are used by people who have to work near traffic or other dangerous machinery, and on emergency vehicles and signage, and are very useful indeed for cyclists. You can buy clothes, vests and tape in fluorescent colours. You don't have to know these pigments look the way they do because of electron de-excitation, but you will know that you'll stand out brightly in daylight (although fluorescence has no effect at night).

Whether you're slipping into your Lycra cycling outfit or popping on your comfy exercise clothes, be bright in every sense of the word.

Keeping clear of dangling gear

Whatever you wear or carry on a bike, you've got to be sure nothing's going to interfere with the bicycle's moving parts. Any dangling item won't just get spoilt if it gets chewed up in your chain or stuck in your brake pads; it will probably stop the bike and may knock you and the bike over.

Keep in mind the following when checking your clothes and baggage for any dangerous dangling bits:

- ✔ **Check all items of your outfit:** The bottom of trousers, or long dresses or skirts, is an obvious area to clear from danger, but any long pieces of fabric fly everywhere once you get going on a bike and could end up tangled in a wheel or chain. (Refer to Chapter 4 for more on this.)

- ✔ **Tuck away hanging straps on backpacks:** If you're sending children out on bikes, look them over for any straps or other dangling things they may not be aware of.

- ✔ **Avoid excess baggage:** Outsize bags loaded onto racks are unsafe as they can spill into the mechanisms of your bike. Anything hanging from your handlebars is doubly dangerous. You not only have to cope with a different balance set-up as soon as you start but, when you turn and the bag swings, your steering ideas will also move straight into chaos theory. Anything you carry should be contained and static.

Lighting up at night

We cover the rules for lights and reflectors on bikes in Chapter 7. Just fitting the lights required by law might be good enough, but if you want to increase your chances of being seen, more lights always help.

One of the weak points of many bike lights is that they don't send out light to either side. Traffic ahead and behind might be aware of you, but motor vehicles approaching from either side, perhaps entering your lane from a side street, may not see you straightaway.

Many bikes come fitted with reflectors in their spokes. These reflectors are side-facing and light up when headlights shine on them, so are better than nothing, but reflectors aren't as good as lights. Think about fixing some lights on your bike, your pack or yourself that shine light to either side.

You can get lights that clip on, strap on or even wind around things. Any kind of light is fine as long as it's fitted to your bike (rather than to your clothes or bags) and you have the minimum legal requirement of one red at the back and one white at the front. Check out what they've got at your local bike shop, but don't stop there – a hardware shop might have some good alternatives.

Lights attached to your helmet or backpack will be higher off the ground than those fixed to your bike and are great at helping you be seen. But the law requires you to have lights actually fixed to your bike if you're riding at night, so these other lights are not substitutes.

Having plenty of lights on you gives you more confidence when cycling at night. Knowing you're far more likely to be seen – and therefore safer – makes riding in the dark a pleasure rather than a worry. Imagine a great ocean liner ploughing through the waves at night with a thousand lights shining out into the darkness. Be that ocean liner.

Sounding Off

Sounds are all around us, and we interpret a great deal of the world through what we hear. Many sounds are warning sounds. As a cyclist, you should not only make warning noises, but also be able to hear them. When you can't see all around you, which is most of the time when you're riding a bike, you need your hearing to be receptive and alert.

Ringing your bell

Never be shy about giving a quick flick to that little noisemaker on your handlebars. If you think it might upset or alarm, then send that sound out with a smile and before you're right on top of someone – but always send it.

Plenty of people go through life (including areas in your path) without looking around to see what's coming towards them. You're a hefty mass on a bicycle and constitute quite a force, even when moving at a slow speed. So doing everything you can to alert anyone who might stumble into your path is important.

Many people are wary of using their bells in the very situations where they are most needed. You may feel that using a bell to warn a pedestrian stepping off a footpath into your path is easy enough, but that you need to be more cautious around, say, the elderly couple walking on a shared path because you don't want to frighten or upset them. However, using your bell in both of these circumstances is important, and everyone will end up feeling more comfortable if there's no risk of a crash or misunderstanding. Just make sure you slow down and ring your bell from enough distance away to give the person you're alerting sufficient time to react accordingly. (A distance of about 10 metres, or 30 feet, is usually enough.) If on a shared path, you can even clearly say 'Passing!' as you approach. And think positively about the noise of the bell: its ring is charming and the bringer of good news (a bicycle is always good news).

If you're not feeling self-conscious about your ringer at all, maybe you'd like to get a louder one. Bells aren't much use in noisy traffic, when many motorists can't hear them. But if you get yourself a horn, perhaps even an electrical one, you can turn up the decibels with ease. Just be careful that your horn is not so loud that people think you're being noisy or aggressive.

Some cyclists like to carry personal alarms, which you can wear on your wrist or strap to your handlebars. Set one of these off when someone strays into the bike lane and you'll grab everyone's attention. Of course, the loud noise will be closest to you, so you might end up being the most frazzled by it.

Unplugging your ears

Strapping your MP3 player to your arm and cycling off listening to the funkiest of grooves is a great pleasure but, sadly, one that we strongly recommend you deny yourself.

If you do ride along with earphones corking your ears, you won't hear a car coming up behind you. You won't hear other cyclists calling out politely 'Passing!' as they overtake and you won't hear the train chuffing down the tracks you're about to cross. (You also won't hear the loud voice warning you of unexpected quicksand or unexplained angry tigers just up ahead.)

Motor traffic is the biggest real danger you encounter on a bicycle and if you can't hear what's going on around you, you considerably lessen your awareness of what's approaching and how close anything is. You're vulnerable to start off with; block your ears and you become much more so.

If you want music while you ride, we recommend you show the world how happy you become when riding a bike. Throw your head back, puff out your chest and sing at the top of your voice. We do, and we love it.

Braking Up: Checking That You Can Stop

For safety's sake, checking your brakes is something you should get into the habit of doing every time you go out on your bike. The mystery is how brakes that worked fine when you got home have only a feeble grasp of your rims when you try them out the next day, but it does happen. Overnight they have somehow changed and are no longer safe.

The way to check your brakes is simple. You squeeze your brake levers tight and move your bicycle forwards. The wheels should lock tight and skid along the ground. This means that your brakes work, but your bike still might not stop as quickly as you'd like once you're riding it. When you're sitting on your bike, the extra weight forces your tyres onto the ground, giving them much more grip. But the extra weight also adds to your momentum, making your brakes work harder to stop you from rolling along.

Try leaning on your bike when you test the brakes, putting as much weight on the bike as you can. You may find when you push forwards the wheel slowly rotates. This means your brake isn't holding the rim tightly enough and you have to fix it before you hurry off down the road.

See Chapter 18 for some simple tips on how to adjust your brake blocks.

Squeezing In: Air in Your Tyres Is Like Wind in Your Sails

The other check you should make an everyday habit is a quick squeeze of your tyres. Just as with your wayward brake blocks (see the preceding section), your tyres can change overnight. This change is far less inexplicable, however, as tyres contain compressed air that will without fail find the smallest opening (if one is available) and slowly but surely escape.

Riding your bike with a flat tyre can damage your wheel and ruin your tyre. If you get a flat and can't fix it, walking home or securing the bike somewhere, getting a lift and returning with what you need to sort it out is a better move. Never leave home with a flat tyre.

To check your tyre pressure (if you don't have a meter on your pump) put your fingers under the rim at the top of the wheel and your thumbs on the top of the tyre. Squeeze your thumbs down. You can check by squeezing from the sides if you like, but make sure you do the same thing every time as these two different squeezes don't feel the same. You'll quickly get to know how your tyres should feel and your fingers become a very accurate gauge.

Tyre pressure

A tyre pressure guide for your particular tyre always appears on the tyre wall (the side of the tyre). The numbers you find there give a rough idea of what pressure you should use. The top number in the range is certainly going to be safe, so you can always go a little higher if you're not happy. Experiment and find what pressure is comfortable for you and the riding you do.

If you lower your tyre pressure, you have more cushioning and any bumps are absorbed more fully by your tyres. You might choose to do this on a very rough trail. Lowering your pressure also flattens out your tyre where it makes contact with the ground. This extra area of contact can be useful on a soft, pliable surface, such as sand.

But a softer tyre also has more rolling resistance, making it harder work to pedal. Low pressure on the tyre also allows it to pick up pieces of grit or broken glass, which may lead to punctures. Hitting a hard object, such as a rock or kerb, with under-inflated tyres can also cause punctures. Cornering can become dangerous with low tyre inflation as the rim can travel over and even off the tyre.

An over-inflated tyre, however, has less rolling resistance – making your bike faster – but the downside is that you feel every bump along the way, making riding uncomfortable on any roads that aren't smooth. And an over-inflated tyre can bounce on surface bumps, which can be dangerous if it happens while you are cornering.

If you find yourself pumping air into your tyres every time you ride your bike, you may have a slow puncture. Either search for and fix this leak or fit a new inner tube. See Chapter 17 for instructions on both these procedures.

Tethering Your Mount

If you use your bike to get somewhere – work, the shops, anywhere – you probably have to leave it on its own while you do what you have to do. Unfortunately, the UK isn't a place where people live in a climate of trust. If you don't secure your bike, chances are you'll lose it.

Most bicycle thefts are opportunistic – someone sees an unsecured bike and decides to take a ride home. So even cheaper, weaker locks reduce the chance of your bike getting pinched.

Some places are better than others when it comes to locking up your bike. But sometimes you don't have much choice, sometimes you have to be inventive and sometimes you have to be cheeky. If you've got problems leaving your bike at work, refer to Chapter 5 for suggestions about how to approach your employer for better facilities.

In the following sections, we cover a few of the more common options and things to beware of when securing your bicycle and then a couple of different locking systems.

You're leaving it where?

Although town-planning policies are often now demanding bike parking in new buildings and developments, finding a place to put your bike is still not always easy. Street facilities, such as loops and stands, may be available, but they're often full, driving cyclists to look for alternatives.

When looking for a place to lock your bike, consider the following:

 ✔ **If a rack only holds your front wheel, it's not secure:** A lot of bikes have quick-release front wheels and even wheel bolts can be removed quickly, enabling a thief to easily remove your front wheel and walk off with the rest of your bike. Also, if something falls against your bike it could bend your front wheel.

 ✔ **Sometimes you need to get creative:** In older shopping areas and malls, finding a spot to lock up your bike can be very difficult. Only a couple of spots may be available for bikes and they may well be difficult to find. Another spot, such as the railings of the trolley bays, may be your only option. Make sure your bike is out of the way of cars (so it doesn't accidentally get run over) and that people can still remove and return trolleys.

Watch out for places where parking a bike is banned. Security guards will take bolt cutters to your lock and your bike will be removed and impounded.

✔ **Lampposts and street signs are often a good choice:** If using a street sign, however, be careful of the shorter ones. Take a step back and have a look – would someone be able to lift your bike over the top? (Keep in mind that the thief could be taller than you.) Also, some smaller signs aren't fixed firmly into the ground. If you can wobble or lift a post at all, then someone else could steal your bike.

✔ **Leave small trees alone:** If you wrap your chain around a slender trunk, you could damage the plant. You might also find a thief comes along, cuts through the tree and then steals your bike, creating a double tragedy.

✔ **Avoid alleyways or places out of the way:** Your bicycle is less likely to go missing if you park it in an open public space with plenty of people around.

When you're locking up your bike at a stand that's already hosting several bicycles, be extra careful not to loop your chain through anyone else's bike. Locking your bike to another does make it extra secure, but also extra upsetting when the other rider comes along and wants their bike back.

The more of your bike you can chain up, the less likely you are to lose it. You may need more than one chain or lock, but securing the frame and both wheels is best. Always remove anything that comes off easily, such as your bike computer, lights or pump.

A good and obvious deterrent to bicycle theft is removing the pedals or seat. You can't ride a bike without pedals and riding without a seat is a winceworthy thought.

Teams of professional bike thieves operate in some urban areas. When such a team spies your bike, it might not stand a chance. But if someone's going to steal one bike and yours is locked up more securely than the next one, the next one is usually be the one that gets taken.

Professional bike thieves know their bikes. They might not want to sell yours in one piece but instead split it up into its component parts, which makes things more difficult to trace and can make them more money. Ben kept his and his family's bikes (a total of seven bikes) chained to the wall and behind a locked gate in the side passage of his house in London. He removed the wheels of the most expensive because with quick release hubs they would take seconds to steal and secondly because he thought it would make the bike less attractive to potential thieves. Still, one morning two had disappeared, including the one with no wheels and the next most expensive. The lesson here is – don't underestimate the tenacity and ingenuity of thieves. The inevitable conclusion is that if you want your bike to be really, really safe, you need to keep it inside your house.

Choosing your security system

Two main systems are commonly used to secure your bike: cables and chains, and D-locks. If you're locking up your bike in the same location every day, then you can be quite precise when you judge your needs. Otherwise you have to weigh up your decision considering the price of the locking system, its size and weight, how much of your bike you want to secure, how valuable it is and how vulnerable it's likely to be.

Everywhere in chains

Cables and chains are the most common means of securing a bike. They are usually longer than other locks, allowing you to secure more parts of your bike and giving you more options of where to leave your bike. Cheap ones tend to be quite thin and therefore easier to cut through. The thicker and tougher they get, the heavier they get – bear this in mind if you're planning on carrying one around. You can secure cables and chains with either a combination lock or a key lock.

You can wear a chain round your waist or across your body if you don't want to carry it in a bag.

You can buy lengths of chain at hardware stores, which enables you to ensure it's long enough to secure your frame and both wheels. Hardware stores have some very thick, heavy chains, but they won't have the protective plastic cover and so may be harsh on your frame.

Goal: D-locks

D-locks are the hard-framed devices with a U-shaped bar that locks into a straight piece, forming a D. You sometimes see them called U-locks.

D-locks are almost always stronger and harder to break than chains and cables. They require much bigger equipment and take longer to force open. Smaller ones can limit your choices for places to leave your bike, as the room inside the D-lock is cramped. Larger ones are heavier and more work to carry around, but definitely more secure. If you've got the biggest D-lock and a moderate-sized chest, you can wear your lock over your shoulder and chest like a bag, but many D-locks come with a bracket which fits to your frame and makes carrying them around very easy.

Security marking your bicycle

Police forces around the world tell of their frustrations when bicycle thefts are reported. Strangely enough, many cyclists often aren't even certain of the colour of their bikes, let alone able to give a detailed description of the bike. Consequently, when a stolen bike is recovered, nobody has any idea who it belongs to.

Keeping a record of your bike's brand, model, any distinguishing features – and its colour - is a good idea in case of a theft. Taking a picture is also a good idea – you can give it to the police if your bike's stolen (and you can carry it with you if you have to go away and can't take your bike with you).

An even better idea is to get your bike security marked or etched. Security marking or etching is usually done on the underside of the frame at the bottom bracket. A code number is registered with the police so if your bike is found, they can look up who you are and where you live, which makes returning your bike a cinch.

Police sometimes have officers security marking bikes at bike events, often setting up a special tent for this purpose and so officers can also answer any questions relating to bike security. You may even be able to just turn up at your local police station and have your bike marked – give them a call and ask.

If you're parking your bike in the same spot every day, you can just leave your lock there. If you've ever seen a lock left dangling on a rack, it's probably not because the bike was taken and the lock left behind, but more likely because the rider doesn't want (and doesn't need) to transport the lock every day. You have to leave the lock locked, of course.

Chapter 9

Planning Your Trip and Tips for Safe Riding

In This Chapter

▶ Mapping your journey

▶ Feeling positive about your place on the road

▶ Navigating through difficult intersections and roundabouts

▶ Handling hazards

*Y*ou've got a bike, you know where you want to go, but you're heading out onto roads and some barriers may still exist to your making that journey happily.

You need to give some thought to when to set off, and in which direction. If you're still asking yourself questions about how you feel about riding in traffic – What are you going to do when you reach a big junction and all the bike lanes disappear? Do you even know your options? And you've heard rumours about certain dangers cyclists face that no one else encounters. What are they and how do you deal with them? – it might be time to come up with some answers.

Don't be afraid. In this chapter, we set out all the planning you need to do to get successfully from one place to another. We provide tips on the best behaviour to practise on the road, and cover what your choices are at some of the more common junctions that give trouble to cyclists. And lastly we look at solutions to some of the perils that only cyclists have to tackle.

Devising a Route

Taking a different route on a bike is very often safer, easier and even quicker than in a car. The more you ride a bike on roads, the more you get used to thinking of alternatives. You automatically start to look at a road in terms of hills, traffic and big junctions and plan your route taking into account your personal preferences for all of these things. You do this as much for journeys as short as a trip to the supermarket as you would for a ride from London to Sydney. Bike trips, just like car trips, need to be thought through. You need to be aware of how long a ride is going to take you and whether or not you have any needs along the way.

You're protected from some environmental factors in a motor vehicle that you're exposed to on a bike, but a bicycle enables you to take in more of the scenery, and lets you stop more easily. The experience is different on a bicycle and, a lot of the time, a much better one.

Just how long is this going to take?

If you're replacing a car trip with a bike ride (almost always a good idea) you need to take a number of different things into account when working out how long it's going to take. Distance is obviously a major factor, but often not the biggest on shorter journeys.

If you're popping down to the shops and the trip is less than a ten-minute jaunt, your bicycle is likely to get you there quicker than your car. Even on longer trips in built-up areas, time spent pedalling is often the same or less than driving. If a couple of sets of lights pop up on the way and you get stuck in a jam, time on the road is likely to be the same, and then parking can add extra minutes onto the car journey.

You have to acknowledge that making your journey by bike is going to take you a bit longer – and plan your days accordingly – only on longer trips, where if you were using your car you could take advantage of big open roads such as motorways.

If you don't know how long a bike journey is going to take you, give yourself plenty of time. You may need to stop here and there to take in the scenery, buy a drink or just have a break. You should be able to average at least 10 miles, or 16 kilometres, per hour, including stops (that's 1 mile, or 1.6 kilometres, every six minutes), so a journey of 4 miles, that's 6.5 kilometres, will take less than 25 minutes.

Turning down time into up time

Deciding to take a journey by bicycle rather than a car almost always turns down time into up time. Minutes or hours that were wasted and useless become time spent achieving something positive and enjoying yourself.

Few drivers use their time at the wheel as part of an agenda to actually get something done. Occasionally drivers manage to learn a language, but otherwise listening to music or CDs (or someone reading *Lord of the Rings)* is just a way of distracting you while you're in that vacuum of down time. You can say you had fun when you get there, but it wasn't part of a programme.

When you ride a bike, though, every minute of pedalling is part of your schedule for fitness. All riding is exercise and takes you further towards such positive goals as improving your health, your shape and the strength of your legs, lungs and heart.

When someone asks you, 'Did it take you long to get here?' your 'Yes' can either be:

✔ 'Yes', as in 'I wasted 45 minutes stuck behind a wheel and then trying to find somewhere to park, with only loud music to calm me and ease my plight'.

or

✔ 'Yes', as in 'I enjoyed 45 minutes of great training, I found a new route that took me along a canal where I could smell the honeysuckle and look out for water birds, and I wished it had taken longer'.

Even a gentle bike ride on a warm day will have you at least glowing, if not actually perspiring. You may need a few minutes after you've got your breath back to freshen up and make yourself presentable.

Going from A to C via B for bicycle

In many places, big main roads have been built right next to original, smaller roads. These older roads become service roads or residential streets and can be perfect for bicycles. Cars would go much slower if they used these roads, but bikes go at just the same speed as they would on a main road and have to cope with less traffic.

Obviously, finding a quieter road basically parallel to or nearby a major one isn't always so easy, but doing so is often possible around shopping stretches and any arterial route into a city.

You often need to do a bit of research to find quieter routes. Online maps are a mine of information and a good place to start. Also check out your local library – your council might have funded a book of bike rides in your area and you can bet there'll be some hidden treasures in it. Websites such as Bikely (www.bikely.com), MapMyRide (www.mapmyride.com) or even MapMyRun (www.mapmyrun.com) enable people to plot routes for others to see and are well worth a look. But to know precisely what you're dealing with you have to get out on your bike and explore.

Don't be bashful: if a road appears to end in front of you or seems cut off to traffic, take a closer look. There may be a path or gap, even a tunnel, that enables you to get through to the next leg of your journey. Or there may be a 'No Motor Vehicles' sign, which allows you to continue through (and always makes you feel pretty special). Cyclists flow through streets like water, naturally finding the smallest of passageways and filtering through to their destinations. Just make sure the route you're on is legal for cyclists. (You can find details about the law in Chapter 7.)

Gavin was once part of a big bike count that had volunteers placed at strategic spots all around the city. Days later, he met with the man who organised the count and learnt that he was at a loss as to where a vast number of cyclists at one particular point were going. They had been counted heading towards one small area, but then they all just vanished. Gavin knew the spot and was able to tell him of a narrow paved path that curved around next to a building and emptied into a car park. He, along with all those other riders, used this short cut every day to avoid two sets of traffic lights.

Short cuts, quiet streets, off-road paths, green bridges (for walkers and bikes) – even gaps in fences – are all things you can use when working out your best line of cycling. Your route may end up complicated, even a little longer than it was before, but if you find these secret ways you might just discover the route you're happiest with and you're bound to see lots of other cyclists heading the same way. Get out there and explore.

When planning your bike ride, don't forget hills. That may mean avoiding them, it may mean including one because you know a great view awaits you at the top (or you know hills are good for you and you've already read Chapter 5 on motivation), or it may mean packing in as many as you can find on the map. However you feel about hills, do bear them in mind.

If you're travelling to the countryside, check with the National Parks Authority, National Trust or the local county council for tips and information about specific spots. For more detailed information about access, trail surfaces and local conditions, websites should provide contact information for local rangers who know the area better than anyone. And if you're just going on a roundabout amble on a sunny afternoon, why not pick out a shady midway spot or a grassy bank where you can lean your bike and have a nap, or a café where you can stop for a bite to eat?

ANECDOTE

Taking in the view from the top

The pace at which you travel on a bike lends itself superbly to taking in your surroundings. The UK has some beautiful scenery and in many urban areas we're spoilt with green corridors and splendid parks. You can't easily plan car trips around views, but if you're out on your bike you'd be mad not to.

If your legs can carry you up long, slow hills in the country, you're going to be perfectly placed for pulling over – and bikes can do this even where there isn't much room on the side of the road or path – and gazing out at the ever-unfolding rolling hills and valleys before you. Some urban river trails even have climbs that reveal spectacular views once you reach the top and – in our opinion – one of the great pleasures of life is to pedal hard to the top of a slope, then rest and take in an intricate panorama.

Some cyclists take this even further, and love to cycle up hills. To most folk, it doesn't make sense. Bicycles are best, surely, in flat places, because they're easier to pedal on the flat. Look at the Netherlands: flat as a Dutch pancake and bicycles everywhere. But some riders get the bug. They do some training on hills and all of a sudden they can't keep off them. These perverse pedallers are small in number, but scattered all over. If you live near a road that runs through mountains, go and check it out at the weekend. Just sit and wait – it won't be long before one of these hardy cyclists appears puffing round the bend, hell-bent on reaching the top of the highest peak.

And how do we know about these men and women of the hills? Well, we have to admit, we're among them.

Eyeballing useful spots along the way

If your journey by bicycle is going to be a long one, you may need some things along the way. You can only carry so much and you may not want to carry anything at all. If this is the case, you can plan your route via a series of accessible shops. It could be a farm shop, a service station or a fully-fledged shopping mall – any outlet will do for a drink or a snack if they've got what you want.

Consider the following when planning possible pit stops along your route:

✔ Refuelling is definitely one of the things you have to plan for when you head off on a bicycle, and either you carry food or you have to find it. Baked goods may not be your first choice for healthy eating in normal circumstances, but they're a great source of energy when you're riding a bike. If you find yourself on a long ride in the country on quiet roads through small towns, your tour could turn into a bakery trail. You could certainly do worse.

- ✔ Some people love to drink coffee after or during a bike ride. You can make a detour and take a break or simply take a roundabout route to your favourite café for an enjoyable trip on your bike.

- ✔ Regular intake of fluid is more important than food (or even coffee) and if you're not carrying enough for your whole ride, you have to stop and replenish your stocks. You must include this requirement in your planning, making sure you pass places where you know you can get water or drinks.

Service stations can be very handy along your way on your bicycle. Their main business is selling petrol, of course, which you don't need on this trip, but they do have some other very useful stuff. If you've got the option of riding by one, putting it on your route could be a good idea. (See the sidebar 'Fuelling up on more than petrol' for more on this.)

Of course, you may prefer to carry everything you need with you, either in a backpack, basket or pannier, and plan your pit stops around places that are nice to stop at, such as a spot with a picturesque view or a tranquil corner of a national park (see the preceding section for more).

Fuelling up on more than petrol

These days, service stations sell food and drink as well as petrol. Most of their customers are in the middle of a non-active pursuit – sitting down in a car – we've always been puzzled about why most of the foodstuffs they stock are high-sugar or high-fat snacks. Real high-energy stuff. To us, fresh fruit or even vegetables would be more appropriate. However, as a cyclist, you're turning up having exercised and with more working out to go, so you're fully entitled to make guilt-free purchases from any of their shelves.

Even if you don't want to have that kind of food and drink, service stations also offer some other advantages for cyclists. For example, you can always find a tap in the forecourt of a service station. If your bidon's barren, take the opportunity to fill up your bottle with cool, clear water.

Service stations also usually have toilets and telephones, if you're not carrying one or the battery on yours has just died. And another very useful feature of these places is the air pump. If, like some economies, you've had some trouble with inflation, take the opportunity to get some high pressure action.

Preparing to Get Out on the Road

The following sections are all about preparing you. If you're not feeling very confident about getting out on the road, these sections provide practical tips. We also offer tips to help any cyclist, even those with a bit more experience, setting out into traffic.

Your attitude makes a difference to what you encounter on roads. You can affect the way other traffic behaves, so your job is to help get everyone on the road acting as safely as possible. Doing so is very much in your interest.

Feeling confident

If you're worried about riding your bike among other traffic, try one or all of the following tips to build your confidence:

- ✔ Take your bike out on some quiet streets with few cars and no trucks. Just get used to being a part of the traffic yourself, because you are – even if you're, like Tigger, the only one.

- ✔ Ask a cyclist who is more experienced in traffic to come out with you and show you the ropes. Your friend can explain the best positions at junctions and in lanes, and you can start to notice how having confidence adds to riding safety. Bikes are allowed to ride two abreast, so go ahead: you will feel safer.

- ✔ Check whether your local or city council runs cycling confidence courses. Independent providers run them, too. These courses show you examples of situations you might be unsure about and help change the way you feel about riding in traffic. If your council doesn't run these courses, ask them to. These courses aren't expensive to organise and can be set up in conjunction with your local bicycle user group (BUG) or cycling club.

- ✔ Join your local BUG or cycling club. If the group doesn't already have some activity you can join in with to boost your confidence, you can suggest one or find other members you can team up with for some friendly rides.

You might notice that the more bikes are about, the safer it seems. This is true – as motorists get used to seeing more bicycles on roads, they learn to drive in a way that takes more vulnerable traffic into account. Each individual cyclist becomes safer when more people take to their bikes. So good for you for getting out there and making the roads safer for us all!

Being assertive: The lane is yours, too

One of the most important things to learn when riding a bike in traffic is to be assertive. Being assertive doesn't mean being angry, it means putting yourself in a position in the road where you're most likely to be seen and which encourages motor traffic to drive safely. Adopting this approach improves your safety considerably.

Beginner cyclists often try to ride as close to the left-hand side of the lane as they can in order to keep out of everyone's way. Their intentions are sound and they do believe they're safer this way, but this is not the case. When cyclists stay far in to the left, motorists take it as a sign that they can squeeze past in the same lane without leaving a reasonable distance between the bicycle and the motor vehicle. In this situation, the cyclist is virtually giving the motorist permission to do this, and most motorists will take advantage of the offer. The motorist will not feel they have transgressed and the cyclist will continue to feel that roads are a dangerous place for bikes – a lose–lose situation.

Keep one metre, that's three feet, between your bike and the side of the road or the line for parked cars. At this distance, you force motorists behind you to slow down and overtake only when doing so is safe, pulling out of the lane if necessary. You shouldn't feel that you're inconveniencing drivers, as the law requires them to do this – to drive safely – anyway.

Keeping a safe distance of one metre, or three feet, on your left side helps increase your safety in the following ways:

- ✔ **Your visibility is increased:** One of the biggest causes of accidents with bicycles is drivers not seeing bikes. Motor vehicles coming from behind, in front or from side streets are all able to see you more easily if you are farther out from the edge of the road or line of parked cars (see Figure 9-1).

- ✔ **You're farther away from the doors of parked cars:** *Car-dooring* is when the driver of a car (or sometimes passenger) opens the car door without looking and a cyclist goes straight into it. You can help avoid this problem by riding farther out to the right. (Also see the section 'Avoiding a car-dooring: The perils of parked or stopped cars' later in this chapter.)

Motorists and other cyclists are better able to take your presence into account (and react accordingly) if your cycling is consistent and predictable. Don't duck in around gaps in parked cars to get closer to the kerb and then back out again when more parked cars appear, but keep your cycling path consistent and as straight as is possible and safe.

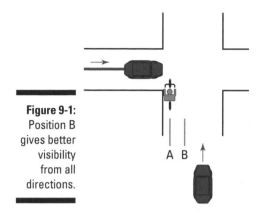

Figure 9-1:
Position B
gives better
visibility
from all
directions.

Knowing how to position yourself confidently on the road also helps increase your safety in specific situations, such as the following:

✔ **When traffic is congested or your path is blocked:** To remain safe, you may need to *take a lane,* where you move out from the left and effectively control that lane for any traffic behind. If you're travelling at the same speed as other traffic you won't slow anybody down and, as soon as space and other factors allow, you can move back over if you need to let other traffic past.

✔ **When you need to change lanes:** If you have to move across two lanes of traffic to turn right, do so boldly, taking lanes as you go. As long as motorists can see you, which is easier for them if you are centred in lanes, they will slow down and let you cross. If you hover on the broken white lines you appear not to be part of the traffic and give your consent for motorists to speed past you.

Never pull out from the left without looking over your shoulder to check what's behind. No matter where you are in the lane or road, someone could be about to pass you closely on the right.

You are traffic too and you have every right to use the road and position yourself for greatest safety.

Signalling clearly and making eye contact

Making bold moves is a great start (refer to the preceding section), but communicating with other road users is also essential. We explain the rules for what signals you are required to give in depth in Chapter 7, but signalling even when you're not obliged to – for safety's sake – is often a good idea.

Letting other people know what you're doing can only help prevent them driving your way. The more you make it very clear what you're up to, the safer you're going to be.

 Signals can be a good idea even when you're not changing lanes or directions. If the main part of a road turns to the right, but a side road leads off straight ahead, motor traffic may be used to taking this side road at high speed. Indicating right in this situation shows other traffic that you're staying in your lane on the main part of the road, and should have drivers slowing down to let you pass before they leave the main part of the road.

Another excellent idea is to always be polite on the roads. Politeness is all about concern for others, and if that's what you want back, that's what you have to give. For example, you may not be required to signal when you're about to turn left. However, if you're approaching an intersection where you're planning on turning left and a motorist is waiting to pull out from the turning, signalling so the driver doesn't wait in vain is always a good idea. This way, you lead motorists to think of you as a super cyclist, rather than a pernicious pedaller.

 Making eye contact with drivers when you're not sure what they're about to do is an invaluable tool. Just keep your eyes locked on them and when they make eye contact with you, that's the point at which you know you have been seen. If you don't make that connection, assuming that you haven't been seen and taking appropriate action is safer.

Dealing with Difficult Junctions

Approaching major junctions can certainly be very daunting for cyclists. On these parts of your journey you may be at your most vulnerable. Motorists are required to look in many directions (and so are you) and may not see what's right in front of them.

Some traffic authorities have worked hard to help bicycles at these points. For example, brightly coloured bicycle lanes that lead you all the way through a junction, making it clear to other traffic that they must give way, are a great help. When motorists know whose space is whose and bikes aren't forced to share or take lanes, different kinds of traffic can stay apart and stay friendly more easily.

In some places, steps to improve cyclist safety are even more advanced – off-road bikeways take cyclists through junctions in tunnels, or raised barriers separate bikes from other traffic at junctions. However, in some areas, more work still needs to be done to improve safety. The solution for some traffic authorities at difficult junctions has simply been to place signage that orders bicycles off the road. In almost all cases, it's unlikely that any legal requirement exists for cyclists to do so.

At an intersection Gavin used, a sign ordered cyclists onto a *shared path* (where pedestrians share the footpath with cyclists) in order to cross, which he suspected couldn't be a legal requirement. It took him nearly a year and much hard work to get an answer from his local authority, but finally his suspicions were confirmed: he did not have to follow the orders that sent him off-road.

You should feel proud to be a cyclist – you are doing great things for yourself, your community and your planet. So don't feel you ever have to get off the road. Approach all junctions with care, but with confidence. In taking up the safest position on the road you may have to assert yourself, but this is the best way to get where you're going without injury.

Avoiding them if you can

Although you're unlikely to come to any harm travelling through big junctions, you probably are more vulnerable at these points and you might just not want to cycle through them. That's fine.

Have a think, or check the street directory: is there another route with less traffic, fewer lanes and smaller junctions? Even if it involves a detour, this may be a better option.

Think your route through from start to finish. A detour quite early in your journey could put you some distance from the junction you're worried about and on a safer road, without adding significantly to your mileage. An easy left turn at a big junction on your route to work can be a problematic right turn on the way home. But do you have to take the same route each way? Think ahead and plan the minimum number of difficult moves.

If you're seriously worried about cycling through a big junction, you always have the option of tackling it as a pedestrian. If lights are available for pedestrians to make their way round the junction, you can walk your bike across when you get the green to go. If lights aren't available, crossing will be recommended at certain points. Just wait until the roads are clear, make your way to the road you want and set off once again on your bike.

Knowing what to do when the bike lane turns left, but you're not

We know of junctions where the bike lane veers with singular perversity to the left onto a slip road or side road. We wonder if the designers of those junctions just couldn't contemplate a bicycle going straight ahead and felt they should change cyclists' plans entirely, sending them off in a different direction. But if you do want to go straight ahead, then ahead you should go. The best way to get past this problem is to follow these steps:

1. **Pull out of the bike lane into the lane with other traffic, checking first that you are safe to do so.**

   You should do this before you reach the point where traffic turns to the left so that you have taken a clear position on the road before any motor traffic starts to turn.

2. **Carry on straight ahead, keeping a good distance away from the bike lane.**

3. **Move back towards the left when you're past the left turn, checking first that doing so is safe.**

If other traffic knows what you're doing – and which way you're going – far less chance exists of any conflict. By placing yourself out of the left-turning bicycle lane when you want to continue straight ahead, you're letting motor traffic know quite clearly where you're going. They'll slow down and let you carry on through before they make their left turn.

Carrying on when the bike lane disappears

Sometimes bike lanes just end. Maybe your traffic authority ran out of paint – you'll never know. We know that sometimes cyclists are just out to clock up distance, and happily change direction at the slightest whim, but most cyclists are actually going somewhere and if you want to carry on in the direction you're headed you have to keep going.

If the bike lane has just ended without warning or road markings, you're not being asked to give way: just carry on. If a broken line is marked for you to cross to join the main traffic lane, take these steps:

1. **Look behind you.**

   Make sure you know what other traffic is coming and how close it is.

2. **Signal that you're pulling out to the right and do so only when you have a gap in the other traffic.**

3. Position yourself appropriately.

If you're approaching a junction and you're turning right, take appropriate steps to get into the right lane and position for turning. If you're going straight ahead, locate the spot you're aiming for on the other side of the junction and travel in a dead straight line towards that spot. If no junction is coming up, just make sure you're positioned where you can be seen, and a safe distance from the kerb, parked cars or side of the road.

Turning right

If you're going to make your way across traffic to take up a position on the right for a right turn, position yourself assertively and clearly signal your intentions (refer to the section 'Preparing to Get Out on the Road' earlier in this chapter for more). If you need to stop before turning right because traffic is coming towards you, hold the lane so that no-one behind can squeeze past you on the left.

Triggering traffic lights

Most traffic lights don't just change as a matter of course. The lights for the major roads stay green for main road vehicles and only change to green on smaller side streets when something comes along on these minor roads. The lights are triggered to change by cables in the surface of the road that respond to metal disturbing an electromagnetic field.

The trouble is, these cables are always placed where cars can't miss them but bikes can. Not so long ago, many of them wouldn't respond to anything as small as a bike anyway, so cyclists could feasibly grow old waiting for lights to change. These cables work better for bikes now, but you've still got to look out for signs of the cables and make sure you set them off.

Look out for an oblong or rectangular shape in the surface of the road a couple of metres before the stop line (sometimes further back). The lines of the shape will be dark, smoother than the rest of the road surface and about two centimetres wide. This shape will have another line going off at an angle towards the traffic lights on your left (or right, if you're in a right turn lane). You've got to ride over this shape or line at some point or the lights won't know you're there and they won't change.

If other, larger traffic is coming, don't worry – just stay to the left and they'll set it off for you. If you have to trigger the lights, ride down one of the oblong's sides that run parallel to your front wheel. Riding along this part of the line puts more metal into the electromagnetic field and makes it more likely that you'll get the lights to change.

Just make sure that, if you're relying on larger traffic to trigger the lights, you don't end up positioned immediately to the left of a vehicle in a queue. This position is a dangerous one to be in as the vehicle may be turning left and the driver may not notice you. If you find yourself in such a position, you need to move. Get into the line of traffic, if possible, so that you're 'taking the lane', or move to the head of the queue. If neither of these options is open to you, get off your bike and onto the pavement until you can safely get back onto the road.

Some further tips for crossing traffic to turn right include the following:

- ✔ **If you're riding along a multi-lane road, you must cross over lane by lane, rather than in one uninterrupted movement across all lanes:** At each move, you must first make sure nothing is coming up behind you and then take the lane. Before moving into the next lane you must again make sure nothing is coming in that lane, signal, and then move over.

- ✔ **When you get into the right-turn lane you must take the lane again:** If a *bike box* (a space at the front of the waiting traffic reserved for bicycles, also known as an Advanced Stop Line) is present there, make your way up to it and position yourself in front of other waiting traffic.

- ✔ **Only make your way to the front of the right-turn lane if plenty of space is available in that lane to do so:** Never stray back into the right-hand forward-moving lane (to your left), which may have fast-moving vehicles coming through.

- ✔ **If no bike box is available, take a position behind the front vehicle in the centre of the lane:** If you start beside the front vehicle, its driver may not see you, and even the car behind may not know you're there. Instead, get into the middle of the lane as the traffic starts to move and take off after the front vehicle. Motor traffic doesn't usually start off into a turn any quicker than a bicycle, so taking the lane all through the junction is not going to hold anyone up.

When turning right with other traffic, you might think that the safest approach is to put yourself slightly behind and to one side of the leading vehicle, but you'd be wrong. You'd be in the car's blind spot. You're much safer where the driver can see you by glancing into the rear-view mirror. If you can see their mirror, then they can see you.

Finding your way across a couple of lanes may not be too hard. Although there may seem to be a never-ending stream of cars, motor traffic tends to travel in packs, meaning breaks do come and sometimes these are lengthy. But plan your moves before you get to the intersection. Pick out a spot to cross and if you haven't found a break in the traffic allowing you to move to the right by the time you reach that spot, you can always stop safely by the side of the road until a gap comes along or dismount and push your bike across.

When you've reached the exit of the junction, move back over to the left, but watch out for any immediate left turns. If you move left in your lane too soon, your positioning won't protect you from any motor vehicles turning left.

Tackling roundabouts

Small roundabouts don't take much effort to conquer, but larger, multi-lane ones can be more confusing and giant ones, designed to allow cars and trucks to whiz round at high speed, can be a bit tricky for bikes.

At all roundabouts, like all other traffic, you must give way to vehicles coming from the right as you enter the roundabout.

Conquering single-lane roundabouts

Most single-lane roundabouts are fairly straightforward, and even more so if they have bike lanes through them. However, bike lanes often disappear at roundabouts and, in this case, you should plan ahead.

Here are some tips for moving through single-lane roundabouts:

- ✔ **Look behind you to make sure the road is clear and move out into the lane in plenty of time:** Take the lane before you reach the roundabout to prevent any clash between you and a motor vehicle while you're actually on your way round.

- ✔ **When you're on the roundabout, do not leave enough space for a driver to overtake you:** You're both negotiating bends and your paths are far too likely to cross.

If you're carrying on straight ahead or turning right on a single-lane roundabout, watch any traffic that's approaching the roundabout in front of you. Try to make eye contact or slow down so that you can be sure they have seen you and are going to give way.

Overcoming multi-lane roundabouts

We cover the rules and regulations relating to cyclists and roundabouts in Chapter 7. However, some of these regulations are inconsistent (or even dangerous) and motorists may or may not be aware of them.

Here are some general tips for getting through large, multi-lane roundabouts – safely:

- ✔ Only enter a large roundabout if you can be sure you can reach a safe point.

- ✔ Always indicate if any traffic is approaching from behind, even if you're going straight ahead.

- ✔ Always occupy the lane you're travelling in.

- ✔ Be most wary of fast-moving vehicles crossing in front of or through your path to exit the roundabout from the right-hand lane.

- ✔ Always be sure that traffic entering the roundabout from your left is actually going to stop before you cycle in front of it.

Raised separators on roundabouts

Gavin was once asked to check out some raised separators that had been put in broken lines along the edge of a bike lane on the corners of a roundabout. The idea was to protect cyclists by discouraging drivers from straying into the bike lane as they entered or left the roundabout.

The engineers had been very careful in using a low-profile barrier so that cars would not be damaged if they bumped into it. His first thought when he saw the strips was that if he came into contact with one at a steep angle on his road bike, he would likely have a classic diversion crash, with his front wheel pushed out of line and no way for him to balance himself.

But, deciding to give the device the benefit of further study, he stood for about 20 minutes on this busy junction watching the effect of the raised strips on traffic. Over 90 per cent of motor vehicles continued to drive over them or round them, with a significant proportion going so far as to guide their left wheels into the bike lane between sections of the separator device and then out again round the bend through another gap. During the time he stood there every bus, taxi and council vehicle performed this latter manoeuvre.

Until councils and traffic authorities commit to a better form of separating bikes from other traffic at points like this, it may well be safer to stay among other traffic where you can be easily seen.

On larger multi-lane roundabouts a bike lane may continue through the roundabout, and this can be an asset. The bike lane may take you on a long, circular detour, far from other traffic, but that won't do you any harm. Showing other traffic that cyclists are well behaved, and that staying in a lane isn't such a big ask, is always good.

A bike lane on a two-lane roundabout can be the most dangerous place to be. If motor vehicles are turning left, the drivers will be studying closely any traffic coming from the right. If the drivers are used to cutting through the bike lane, they're likely to do so whether you're in it or not, because they won't be looking in your direction.

If you're not sure about your safety at a roundabout, move right out of the bike lane and into a lane of motor traffic. Take the lane before you get to the roundabout and travel round the roundabout in one of the motor traffic lanes where everyone can see you.

Don't feel weak if you decide to go through the roundabout using a series of left turns and pedestrian crossings. Your physical wellbeing should be your first concern. We've ridden in some genuinely dangerous places around the world without thinking of getting off our bikes, but we know of roundabouts that we won't enter from certain directions.

Dastardly Dangers

You face some particular – and sometimes peculiar – risks when you ride a bicycle. Some of the risks are because of where you're placed on the road as a cyclist. Some are just to do with not being protected by a roof. And some just seem part of a universal, elemental conspiracy against the common bicyclist. Consider them all with a smile and avoid them with intelligence and vigilance.

Steering clear of cars and trucks

The biggest danger to bicycles and their riders on roads is motor traffic – cars, buses and trucks. If it weren't for these motor vehicles, accidents would be rare events for cyclists. Occasionally, we see cyclists doing daft things, but more often we see motorists risking the safety of more vulnerable traffic, and we frequently have to take evasive action because drivers either don't look or don't know what to do when they see us.

Cyclists are quite right to perceive motor traffic as a danger. Data compiled by The Royal Society for the Prevention of Accidents (ROSPA) shows that of all serious cycle accidents reported to the police in 2011, 86% involved a collision with a vehicle. ROSPA also found:

✔ The most common contributory factor recorded by police in serious accidents between a motorist and a cyclist is 'failed to look properly', especially at junctions. 'Failed to look properly' is attributed to the driver in 57 per cent of serious accidents and to the cyclist in 43 per cent.

✔ The next-most common contributory factors attributed to motorists in serious accidents involving bicycles are a poor turn or manoeuvre (17 per cent) and being careless, reckless or in a hurry (also 17 per cent).

✔ For cyclists, the second-most common contributory factor in serious accidents involving vehicles is entering the road from the pavement, which was recorded in 20 per cent of cases.

✔ Two thirds of serious accidents involving cyclists happen at or near junctions. A particular problem is motorists who cut in front of cyclists when they are turning left and cyclists are not.

✔ While the most common vehicle involved in a collision with a cyclist is a car or taxi, heavy goods vehicles (HGVs) present a particular hazard, particularly in London where at least 20 per cent of cycling fatalities involve an HGV.

You can do your best to avoid the common causes of collisions by following these tips:

- ✔ **Dress in bright colours and use front and back lights at night or in poor light to avoid not being seen or being seen too late:** Refer to Chapter 8 for tips on how to become bright and be seen better on your bike.

- ✔ **Position yourself farther out into the lane when you pass a left turn to avoid being cut in front of by a motorist:** Doing so ensures that you are seen, and makes a dangerous cut-in far more difficult for a motorist.

- ✔ **Position yourself assertively to avoid motorists overtaking unsafely:** This reduces the likelihood of motorists thinking they can overtake by squeezing past in the same lane when doing so isn't safe. Over-taking unsafely is a very common cause of accidents, particularly in urban areas.

Car-dooring is another hazard which cyclists in towns and cities have to be alert to, and which we cover in the following section.

Avoiding a car-dooring: The perils of parked or stopped cars

Bike lanes that are just made up of white lines marking out a lane in the road, which are the most common type in towns and cities, are generally placed to the left of other traffic lanes – and right beside long lines of parked cars. Streets don't have to be too busy for the mixture of cars coming and going from roadside parking spots and cyclists enjoying their dedicated space to become a disaster.

When drivers or passengers of a car fail to look out for bikes and open a right-side door without a thought, sooner or later a cyclist is going to be almost on top of them – and then crashing into their open door. Similar perils present themselves when motor traffic is banked up but the bike lane is clear – meaning you can be cycling past just as a passenger on the left-hand side of the car decides to jump out.

To open your car door into traffic without looking is a clearly defined traffic offence with no doubt who's at fault. But that doesn't help the situation at all if you're a seriously injured cyclist. Car-dooring can even kill.

When riding alongside parked or stopped cars, constantly be on the lookout for passengers or drivers jumping out without looking, and travel at a safe speed unless you're at a safe distance from the cars. (See the sidebar 'Cycling intelligence' for more tips on avoiding being car-doored.)

Cycling intelligence

An enterprising German journalist who's moved to London has started a blog that aims to make riding in the capital safer. Olaf Storbeck shares all sorts of tips, advice and news. His blog lists cyclists' deaths and serious injuries and crucially, why they happened.

Here's what Olaf has to say about car doors:

✔ It's illegal to open doors into traffic:

- Paragraph 239 of the Highway Code says 'you must ensure you do not hit anyone when you open your door. Check for cyclists or other traffic.'

✔ To avoid doors, look:

- In wing mirrors and in car windows to see if you can spot someone moving.

✔ Also watch out for:

- Cars that have just parked.

- Cars' tail lights.

✔ Riding in the door zone:

- Ride on the outer side of the cycle lane, away from car doors.

- Be prepared to ride outside the cycle lane if you are still too close to car doors.

- If you can't avoid being in the door zone, slow down.

✔ General advice if a door opens in front of you:

- Hit your brakes and shout.

- Don't swing into traffic (this is how most fatalities occur).

✔ If you get hit:

- It is a traffic accident and details must be exchanged.

- Report uncooperative motorists to the police.

You can find loads of other information and links to lots of other useful sites on Olaf's blog at `cycling-intelligence.com`.

Testing the elements: Riding in hard rain, wind and snow

Being free to pass unenclosed through all kinds of beautiful country also means you eventually get exposed to harsher weather, some of which can be a challenge to ride in. Cyclists are a hardy bunch and very difficult to put off, and people ride bikes in all climates, under all conditions. Specialist items of clothing and bike parts are available that help with elemental difficulties, but the first big step is to pick up the gauntlet and say, 'Nothing is going to stop me riding my bike.'

Rain

If you ride in the rain, you're almost certainly going to get wet. Some people feel better about this than others.

A few years ago, Ben had an important final training ride planned before heading off to France to do the Etape du Tour (see Chapter 21) ride. As the day drew closer, it was clear from the weather forecast that there was going to be torrential rain, but he'd booked a day off work to do the 100 miles, or 160 kilometres, and couldn't postpone it. As predicted, it bucketed down all day long and widespread flooding occurred. Some roads were covered in six inches, that's 15 centimetres, of water and he got drenched, but it was a whole lot of fun, a real adventure. He didn't get cold (it was June) and traffic was minimal as few people had ventured out. And best of all, the experience turned out to be great training as the Etape, just five days later, was run in pouring rain, too.

In the UK, however, at certain times of year, the rain can be very cold and few things are more unpleasant than being both freezing and wet. To help you deal with such conditions, you can find cycle clothing that keeps out almost all water and you can also get extra protection for your head, hands and feet. (Refer to Chapter 3 for more details about cycle clothing.)

Make sure the cycling jacket you purchase to protect you from getting wet also provides adequate ventilation. Otherwise, unless you're taking it very easy, you can get awfully damp just from perspiration inside your cocoon.

Mudguards are also a big help in keeping you at least semi-dry, stopping jets of water flying over your legs, up your back and into the faces of cyclists behind. If your bike takes them, physically and stylistically, you can get big, thorough mudguards that keep practically everything off. These mudguards are also a great spot for extra stickers. Otherwise, you can get smaller ones that are easy to fit in a jiffy. Some people make mudguards out of plastic bottles, old bicycle seats and even pots and pans, but this may not be quite the look you're after.

Rain doesn't just get you wet: it throws up additional cycling hazards as well, such as the following:

- **Visibility on roads is lowered, and moving around becomes more difficult for all traffic:** Riders should slow down and be extra careful of motor vehicles in the wet. Seeing much at all can become especially difficult for cyclists in rain. Your glasses (if you wear them) don't have wipers and if you remove them or don't wear any, you might find drops getting into your eyes every time you raise your head. You need to slow down and even get off the road if you just can't see.

- **Stopping becomes more difficult:** Your brakes don't work as well when they're wet. You can give them a quick squeeze before you try to slow down. This gets rid of some excess water, but doesn't dry your brakes completely, so you still take longer to stop.

✔ **Potholes open up and quickly increase in size:** Potholes look like puddles when it's wet, so be careful what you're cycling through, even if you know the road well.

✔ **Roads become more slippery:** Any oil left on the surface can become lethal when it's raining, so avoid taking those downhill bends quite so fast or at such an angle.

✔ **Flash flooding can occur:** The water in flooded sections of roads may be deeper than it appears, so you should never attempt to ride through flooded sections if the water is fast-moving or you don't know how deep it is. Even if you get through safely, you may not be doing your bike any good if the water goes over its bottom bracket.

Your chain might start making awful grating and squeaking noises in the rain. These noises happen because all the lube, or lubrication, has been washed off and you've just got wet metal rubbing against wet metal. If you're riding through rain regularly, you can choose a heavier lube – some are better than others. Otherwise, just remember to keep relubing after rides.

Wind

For windy conditions you need a barrier. Woolly tops offer no protection, so refer to Chapter 3 for more tips on the best cycling jackets and vests to purchase for wind protection. Also think about protection for your legs. Cold winds can freeze your legs but, because your legs are moving a great deal while cycling, wearing anything but tights is going to hinder your movements. You can get woollen tights with windbreak fronts that keep you warmer for longer.

Wind is one of the toughest challenges to conquer on a bicycle, and battling against a headwind is one of the most dispiriting experiences you can have as a cyclist – cycle up a hill and you eventually get to the top, but winds just keep on going. If you're out for a fun or training ride and you know the wind is blowing strongly in a particular direction, plan it so that you get the tailwind on the way home and you'll have something to look forward to. If that can't be done, just take it easy: you won't get any medals for exhausting your legs.

Snow and ice

Cycling on snow and even ice is something some people can't get enough of, but it does throw up its own particular issues.

In very cold weather, you need to look after your fingers. When you're moving quickly through cold temperatures, it doesn't take much for your (essentially inactive) fingertips to become numb. Numb fingers stop you changing gears effectively, but more importantly could leave you unable to operate your brakes. Having use of your fingers is vital, so you might have to wear some pretty hefty plastic-coated gloves in severe cold, rain or snow.

If you step outside into the elements and are immediately cold all over, you're probably not wearing enough gear. Ride this way and you may never warm up. If, when you first step out, you feel lovely and warm, you've almost certainly got too much stuff on. As soon as you start riding you'll bake and sweat. If you feel just a little bit chilly when you greet a cold day, you'll probably warm up just fine after you've been pedalling for a while. (Refer to Chapter 3 for more tips on choosing cycling clothes for warmth.)

Follow these tips for safely riding on snow or ice:

- ✔ Wider wheels and tyres with studs and bumps are a must. You can find these easily and you can even get them for road bikes.

- ✔ On any kind of ice you need to slow down and stay as upright as possible. Only use the back brake and never brake while turning. With studded tyres you should be able to ride where you can't walk.

- ✔ Fresh snow makes for hard pedalling but offers no big dangers in itself. Watch out, and be prepared, for ruts and bumps under the snow. Falling over on a bike in fresh snow is much slower than falling elsewhere and the snow is quite soft to land on. Being the first to send your wheel crunching through a field of fresh snow on a bright cool morning is an exhilarating experience.

- ✔ Hard-packed snow is more difficult, especially if motor vehicles and other bikes have left ruts. Hopping in and out of these and bumping your way over unforgiving lumps of frozen mush is hard work. It may be easier to look for unbroken snow at the side of the road or track.

Weaving round walkers and dodging dogs

I've never felt anything but warm friendliness towards pedestrians, but I can tell they sometimes feel differently about me. How you react to pedestrians (and dogs) in your path depends in part on where you're cycling.

The law says that bikes must give way to walkers (and horses) on bridleways and byways and doing so is very important. A definite difference in perception often exists when cyclists pass pedestrians on a shared path: cyclists know full well that they are fully in control and no danger whatsoever to people on foot, but the latter often feel their lives are being endangered by speeding, reckless pedallers.

Cyclists are obliged to cater for these feelings no matter how unreasonable that may seem. Studies have shown that bicycle speeds on shared paths can be significantly lower than what complaining pedestrians have claimed, but, nonetheless, bikes should slow right down to pass folk on foot, especially if any small children are around.

ANECDOTE

Staring down swooping birds

Cyclists in parts of the UK have reported being attacked by birds. A few years back there was a particular buzzard in Devon which carried out a number of raids on peoples' heads at they rode unsuspectingly along, and in 2011 a man from the Isle of Wight needed three stitches in his lip after a seagull took a fancy to his moustache. However, bird attacks are very rare in the UK.

But they are very common in Australia, as Gavin discovered when he moved there. When he first rode the bikeways of Melbourne, he found himself mobbed by a crazed black and white crow which he later discovered was a magpie. He surmised that he was being punished, for no particular reason that he could fathom, in this almost biblically malicious manner.

Like good old Father Ted being mobbed by crows on the way to his car, it had a comic element, but he also felt a very real danger. He's seen *The Birds*. More than once.

When finally Gavin happened to be in a park one day and witnessed a young woman being set upon by one of these pied paratroopers, he felt a great feeling of joy. (Perhaps inappropriate as far as the young woman was concerned.) It wasn't only him. He now knew that they were evil birds generally.

Gavin's first persistent avian attacker lived along a quiet, picturesque stretch of Kororoit Creek in Melbourne. Knowing that he was going to cop it, one day he decided to take a detour along a residential street. As he made his craven way down the road, he noticed he was being followed. The malicious magpie was actually after him, swooping from power pole to power pole.

All set for a showdown, he dismounted in the street, took his pump off the down tube and stood ready. His eyes locked with the magpie's and they stood, him looking up, it gazing down. For a full minute they held this pugnacious pose, each intent on staring the other down.

Just then a car appeared at the end of the street and Gavin's eyes dropped instinctively. Within a fraction of a second there was a fury and a flurry of black and white feathers heading straight for his face. Ineptly waving his little silver bicycle pump, he hopped back on his bike and fled.

More than once he has returned home bleeding from the neck or ears after a magpie attack. On one occasion, two of them assaulted him on a road leading into some hills. He had no choice but to return through their territory, so he hit their stretch of road at over 35 miles (56 kilometres) per hour. How could they possibly swoop on him at that speed? But they did — no trouble at all.

Thankfully, bird attacks are rare in the UK, but if attacking birds do bother you, you have a number of options. You can dismount and walk. This doesn't always work, but they won't swoop on you as long as you're staring at them, so you can sometimes get away with a combination of the two.

You can also leave their territory alone until they stop swooping. Magpies attack in spring because they are defending their new chicks. Once you reach the fullness of summer, it should be safe to return to magpie-land. This plan isn't always practical but is often the best solution.

As well as slowing down around pedestrians on a shared path, also ring your bell or call out (something like 'bike passing' usually works fine) when you're coming up behind people. Follow that with a smile and you should reassure them that you were being helpful, not rude.

When cycling away from a shared path, people who walk straight out from the footpath into your path are a very serious danger. They can do so quite randomly and at full speed. If you're riding next to a busy footpath, watch out for anyone moving along quickly or erratically. Watch anyone stepping from the footpath in between parked cars.

Dogs are particularly difficult creatures to deal with when you're on a bike. They often have no traffic sense at all. We find it hard to understand how any sentient creature can't make the connection between large objects moving fast and injury, but most dogs just don't do it. Most of them are very capable of running straight under your front wheel, so beware. On a shared path, you must approach dogs with caution and slowly.

Small dogs that chase you in parks or on streets are a nuisance and can actually snap at you. A firm stare should get the owner acting responsibly and calling off the dog. Dismounting should also stop the dog's behaviour.

Other dogs are just mean, and telling whether the dog actually wants to attack you or is just chasing very aggressively is difficult.

If a dog starts to chase you very aggressively, you have a couple of options. Firstly, pedal like mad – sprint – and try to get away. The dog should have some idea of territory and not chase you forever. This solution is the simplest, and if it works, no harm is done. If you know that's not going to work, or you're just not up to it, stop and dismount, getting off on the side away from the dog, and use your bike as a shield. Then use a low voice to shout firmly at the dog, and back away. Don't crouch down. If anyone is around and you feel you need assistance, call for help.

Some cyclists carry an extra bottle filled with a mixture of water and chilli powder. If you pull out a bottle filled with this mixture and squeeze hard, you should definitely put off the dog. Just don't forget and drink from the wrong bottle!

Chapter 10

Toughening Up for Off-Road Riding

Mastering happy and successful rides on mountain bike singletracks involves a lot of learning and practice. Riders have to know how to react quickly to different obstacles and difficult surfaces. Mountain bike riders learn to ride fast along slender poles, over massive tree trunks, across ditches and through piles of rocks and rubble. They develop physical skills and knowledge of complicated environments.

That's all a big ask, but in this chapter we start with the basics, covering some of the beginner off-road skills that can either be a first step towards the rough stuff or a good grounding for anyone wanting to explore trails through forest or countryside.

A bike path doesn't have to be as smooth as silk to let you have a lot of fun on a bike, but not knowing where to aim your bike on a broken trail or how to hold yourself when shooting down a steep hill can send you flying. This chapter helps you to react confidently to different surfaces and inclines, making your ride in the country a satisfying and exciting pleasure.

Knowing What to Expect from Different Surfaces and Obstacles

When riding off-road trails, you need to keep your wits about you. The type of surface you're riding over can change quickly and hazards can suddenly appear.

Obstacles such as rocks, puddles, deep ruts and other bumps can knock you off your bike. You need to keep your eyes on the ground, looking as far ahead as you can to get yourself positioned on the trail to avoid big obstacles, but you also need to be looking at what is right in front of you. It doesn't take much to divert your front wheel so that you lose your balance and keel over. On a hard, slow climb, knocking your front wheel against a rock can simply stop you in your tracks.

No one can explain why, but a well-known cycling phenomenon is that if you look at the obstacle you're trying to avoid you're more likely to hit it. Look at the line you want your front wheel to take and that's the course you'll likely follow. You can attempt to disprove this if you like, but we assure you it will most often mean crashing into things.

The following sections outline the kinds of things you can expect to encounter when riding off-road trails.

Bumps and rocks

If your front wheel hits an obstacle at a low angle, the obstacle will push it from its course and you'll lose your balance – you just won't have any way of staying upright. Hitting a bump front-on will knock your front wheel up and to the side and you'll lose control of the bike. If it slows the bike quickly, you'll fly forward. Hitting a bump or rock with your back wheel will send your rear end up in the air, again throwing you forward.

If you can't avoid an obstacle and you think hitting it is going to make you lurch forward, raise your rear end off the saddle, so that your arms and legs are taking your weight. In this position, your arms and legs absorb a great deal of the shock. Move your body back and down so that any forward movement has less impact. Mountain bikers know this as the *attack position* (see Figure 10-1). Practise this position so that you don't have to learn under the pressure of a real jolt.

Figure 10-1:
Attack
position:
Take on the
bumps.

Gravel and loose surfaces

Gravel and loose surfaces are very common on trails. A bicycle has less traction on a loose surface and your wheels are vulnerable to sideways movement – a particular problem when you're turning. If you enter a bend on a gravel trail too fast, you may find you have to straighten your line of cycling to keep from falling sideways. This can mean riding straight off the path, which (needless to say) is best avoided. (See the section 'Staying on Your Bike on Rough and Loose Trails' later in this chapter for more on riding on loose surfaces.)

On gravel or loose surfaces, you should slow down, especially before entering bends. Don't use your brakes while turning and try to stay as upright as you can. On loose surfaces, you can easily skid and, if another bike or a walker appears in front of you, you can't stop or steer as quickly, so make sure your speed still gives you full control of your bike.

Ruts and grooves

Ruts and grooves can trap your wheels. Even on established bike paths, you sometimes find cracks and grooves have opened up. These can seize front wheels, especially narrow wheels like the ones you get on road bikes. If your front wheel gets stuck in a groove while you're moving forwards, you'll probably end up flying over the handlebars as the back of the bicycle goes up in the air. If you're in any doubt, steer well clear of any cracks in the path.

Larger ruts can seem like the best option on a rough trail, but they can end abruptly, with no chance to climb out, or steer you off course or off the trail. On a trail with a choice of highs and lows, the higher course is less likely to come to a dead end. Look ahead as much as you can to pick your route early.

Water

You don't know how deep a patch of water is just from looking at it. The water could just be a surface puddle or it could be a puddle surrounding a deeper hole. Cycling through puddles on trails is likely to at least get you wet, so you're best off avoiding them. If you do need to ride through water, slow down – when you're closer you should be able to get a better idea how deep it is and where. Give yourself time to stop.

Staying on Your Bike on Rough and Loose Trails

Riding off-road trails throws up a whole new set of considerations, but particularly so if the surface you're riding over is rough and loose. Your tyres have less traction and sliding or being knocked off your bike can happen quite easily. These kinds of surfaces are common on most off-road trails, so it pays to know how to deal with them.

Here are some tips for riding on rough and loose surfaces:

- **Keep your bike's momentum up:** Your bicycle is much more stable if you're travelling at a good speed – while you don't want to be going so fast that you're not in control of your bike, a bicycle wobbling along at a snail's pace is far more likely to get stopped or knocked over. If you're riding slowly because you're not sure of yourself, practise. Just keep your eyes glued to the trail and steer along the smoothest line you can see. If your line comes to a dead end, stop and shift to another part of the trail.

- **Avoid using your brakes when turning or going over bumps:** If you do find yourself going too fast and you don't feel in control, you must use your brakes; however, you should do so on flatter and straighter stretches, rather than just before you go over some bumps. Bikes take bumps far more happily while rolling, not braking.

✔ **If you're speeding downhill and can see bumps or ruts up ahead, lift your rear end from the saddle, move it backwards, and lower, or flatten your torso:** Using this position shifts your centre of gravity right back, so that any sudden jolts won't send you flying forwards. If you can't get very far back or very low, try lowering your saddle (see Chapter 18 for instructions).

Don't ever let your rear end get behind the saddle and lower yourself so that the back of the saddle is up against your abdomen. Any knock that throws you forward will cause much pain and possible injury. Lower your saddle to avoid this problem.

Avoiding Potholes

Potholes are formed when bitumen in the tarmac cracks and weakens. This often happens where the forces on the road surface are more complicated and include some sideways forces, such as before or on bends where vehicles brake and turn. When water flows over these cracks or weak points, it can get under the surface and erode the gravel platform underneath. If the water freezes, it causes even greater erosion. The bitumen then breaks into pieces and gets knocked away from its bed, creating a hole in the surface. If the hole then fills with water, more and more of the gravel under-layer gets forced out of the hole every time a tyre goes through it.

In this way, potholes can appear and become deep – and dangerous – very quickly. With the torrential rain the UK has experienced in recent years, alongside a couple of prolonged cold snaps and the fact that cash-strapped local authorities are cutting road maintenance budgets, potholes are everywhere.

Holes the same shape and size as potholes on tracks and trails aren't technically potholes, but they do present the same risks and you need to avoid them in the same way.

If you run into a pothole on a bike you could be in trouble. If you've got big, fat mountain bike tyres and a good suspension, you'll probably be okay, but for ordinary bikes, and especially road bikes, potholes can give you a powerful enough jolt to throw you. If your bike has small wheels this can be particularly severe. They can knock your front wheel out of your control or jerk your hands off your handlebars. And although road bike wheels can be very expensive, they're not very strong – a bump like this can put an irreparable dent in your rim.

You don't have to live in fear of potholes, but if you're riding on a road you know is prone to them, or a track you know can break up with water damage, always keep your eyes peeled.

Here are some tips for dealing with potholes:

✔ **Steer around, if you can:** Try to scan the path ahead and give yourself enough time to react. Sometimes, doing this just isn't possible but you do have a couple of options to increase your chances. Potholes are started by wheels, so try to stay out of the most used line worn on the road or track. Generally this means cycling just a little in from the left. Also be extra careful if it looks like any part of the road or trail has water flowing over it when it's wet. If you're too close to it when you see a pothole, you may not be able to avoid it.

✔ **Lift your front wheel over:** This move is known as a manual (where you lift the front wheel over a small obstacle). Just before you get to the offending bump or pothole, lean forward, then back and pull the handlebars up off the ground. It does take some force to pull this off, but you won't lose control of the bike: when the wheel lands you just carry on going. A big jolt to your back wheel could still do damage, but won't have the same effect of loss of control. Practise this manoeuvre somewhere like the park first, so you know how to do it before you're confronted with a pothole.

✔ **Jump both wheels over:** This move is known as a bunny hop (where you lift both wheels off the ground while riding) and is the best thing you can do if a pothole appears right in front of you. A bunny hop is more advanced, however, than a manual (see the section 'Going Bunny Hopping' later in this chapter for instructions).

If you're heading up a road or trail you're planning to come back down again, keep an eye on the surface on the other side of the road or trail and try to remember the location of any problems. If you're coming downhill in mottled shade and light, take off your sunglasses and keep your eyes glued to the road. You really may have to just slow down.

Balancing Your Centre of Gravity

All cycling is about steering and balance and the more you learn to move your bike with movements of your body, the smoother and more controlled your cycling becomes. Balance is particularly important for enjoying yourself on a bicycle, and is a key part of mountain biking. Having just some basic balancing skills lets you flow along trails and tracks like water down a pipe. Balance well and you won't be racing down a track with fear in your heart; you'll be bobbing and weaving and having the time of your life.

Use these exercises to improve your balance on your bike:

✔ **Ride in a straight line:** Riding in a straight line is perhaps the most basic exercise you can do, but is about balance rather than steering, and isn't as easy as it sounds. Find a quiet street and a line down the middle of the road, and give it a go. When you've got the hang of riding straight down that line, try standing on your pedals and moving your hips right back, then leaning right forward, then swinging your hips out to the left and right, all while still moving in a straight line. Getting good at these moves helps a lot when you get on a bumpy, up and down trail.

✔ **Cycle in a figure of eight:** This exercise is best done on grass, so go to the park and place two markers two to three metres (seven to ten feet) apart on the ground. Use rocks, bits of wood or items of clothing (as long as you didn't come in a bikini). Cycle slowly in a tight figure of eight around and between the markers.

Keep your eyes inside the circles. You may need to keep your fingers pressed lightly on the brakes. If you feel yourself falling inwards, press down on the pedals and speed up out of the fall. If you start feeling comfortable with this exercise, stand on the pedals and shift your weight around to different positions, keeping track of which positions make it easier and which don't help at all.

Anything that helps with your balance helps you ride your bike better – and you don't have to be on your bicycle to improve your skills. Just standing on one leg teaches your body about balance. Try it at work. Walking up a hill backwards is another helpful way of learning to bob from side to side when your legs are working, even if you do attract a few mystified sideways glances as you do it.

One instance when you need good balancing skills is on a steep climb. Short or long, if you're heading up a sharp incline you have to be in the right position or your bike just won't work, especially on loose surfaces. If a hill is very steep, you may find your front wheel lifting up in the air. If this happens, the line of your centre of gravity has gone slightly too far back and you'll start to topple backwards. Your reaction, of course, will be to lean forward, which will return your front wheel to the ground. But if you then put too much weight onto the handlebars when you're pedalling hard on a slope, your back wheel loses traction and starts to spin. With nothing driving you forward, you quickly come to a stop and it may be too much of a hill for you to start pedalling again.

If you find yourself on a short, steep stretch, stand on your pedals and find a mid-point that balances you against either your front wheel popping up or your back wheel losing traction. If you're going to ride up hills often, lower your seat to lower your centre and stabilise you.

Going Bunny Hopping

Gavin was once riding along a lane, heading towards some hills to do some climbs and singletracks with a MTB friend. As they pedalled on their way, he suddenly realised his friend was riding along the top of a big log lying alongside the path. He could imagine no means of getting a bicycle onto the log, certainly not while someone was riding it. As far as he could tell, a break in the great time-space continuum must have occurred. The progression of reality had been tampered with. There was a glitch in the matrix. But no: his friend had bunny hopped.

Bunny hopping is the extraordinary trick of lifting yourself and your bicycle skywards, right off the ground, and carrying on pedalling when you land as if nothing has happened. Performing a bunny hop can lift you over ruts, drains or even crevasses and it can raise you up onto footpaths, steps – and, yes, even logs. Bunny hopping isn't that difficult, but it does take time and practice to learn. And it looks really cool.

Here are some tips for mastering the art of bunny hopping:

- ✔ Practise bunny hopping on a flat surface and wear plenty of protective gear. Try first for small jumps – maybe put a twig out as your 'dangerous obstacle' and increase the size of your challenge as you go.

- ✔ Don't approach the jump too slowly or you won't have enough momentum to carry you over. As you approach the jump, get your cranks level so both feet are at the same height. Angle your back foot so that your toes point to the ground and keep your forward one flat. Keep your knees bent and put your top end over the handlebars.

- ✔ As you reach the obstacle, try to make all the next movements in one fluid succession:

    1. **Crouch down on the bike, flexing it towards the ground.**

    2. **Push your feet down, back and up.**

        If these movements are managed smoothly, you and the bike should surge upwards.

    3. **Land like a tiger.**

Your bunny hopping probably won't work at first, but keep at it and you'll get there. Before long you'll be hopping onto a double-decker bus, and then charging up the stairs to the top level. A glitch in the matrix? Just remember: you're 'The One'.

Riding rail trails

In the 1960s, 5,000 miles of Britain's railway lines were identified for closure. The *Beeching cuts* (named after the man who suggested them, Richard Beeching) destroyed many local rail services. But one man's loss is another man's gain, as they say, and these dismantled rail lines are just fantastic for bikes.

Rail trails often run through quiet, unspoilt countryside, linking rural towns and villages and giving us the kind of journey that hasn't been available since the age of steam. Some of them have hard-packed gravel surfaces and some of them are fully or partly sealed, so almost any bike can cope with them. Trains aren't great on hills, so these lines were never built with a difficult gradient.

For more information about these traffic-free routes, visit www.sustrans.org.uk. You can also find websites set up by enthusiasts extolling the delights (and secrets) of individual rail trails.

In Chapter 20, we provide details for what we believe are two of the best examples of rail trails in the UK.

Part III
Rolling beyond the Basics

Five Great Ways to Have Fun with Friends on a Bike

- **Bike dinners.** Get your friends to meet at a spot from where you can all ride to your favourite restaurant.

- **Full moon rides.** On the right day of the lunar cycle, take a train to a distant spot on a river trail or other bikeway, timing your arrival for nightfall. Ride by the lunar light, turning off your lamps if you feel bold. Take snacks and a bottle of wine for a moonlit picnic.

- **Rides to the seaside.** Just get together and head down to the beach for a paddle and an ice-cream.

- **Fancy dress rides.** Your options are limitless. You can arrange a ride in any kind of fancy dress – tog up as zookeepers, Zorro or zebras and parade together through a public space.

- **The World Naked Bike Ride.** This ride is an organised event that takes place in cities across the country and around the world. You don't have to be completely naked to take part, but how often do you get the chance to cycle down the streets of a major city completely starkers with a load of other similarly undressed people?

Pick up more tips on getting your kids outside and exercising - and enjoying it - at www.dummies.com/extras/cyclinguk.

In this part . . .

✔ Start training to improve your personal fitness and performance to take your cycling to the next level.

✔ Research your route, kit yourself out and prep your bike for heading out on a bike tour.

✔ Find out how to meet up with other cycling enthusiasts, discover the joys of going out riding with them and consider taking part in an organised cycling event.

✔ Get your kids up and running on two wheels and figure out how best to make cycling a part of their lives, too.

Chapter 11

Riding Faster, Tougher, and Longer: Training and Improving

*O*ver the last few decades, experts' knowledge of how an athlete's body works and improves has progressed in leaps and bounds. Where riders used to just practise a lot, a huge and booming science now exists, based on how muscles work and grow and how bodies become fitter and stronger.

With this knowledge, training techniques have been finely crafted. Cycling pros have their own dedicated personal trainers whose specialist knowledge takes them down esoteric paths of human biology. The expertise of top trainers remains secret until contracts are signed and substantial amounts of money changes hands. They all have their own individual take on the combining physical factors of training.

But certain fundamentals are easily understandable by all and training gets better results if you have some understanding of exactly why you do what you do.

In this chapter, we go through some of the terms and processes you may have heard mentioned in relation to pro cycling and disciplined training. Then we cover some basic techniques and tips for getting you out on your bike and riding faster, tougher and longer than ever before.

Exercising Lingo for the Cyclist in You

In the following sections, we explain some of the terms cyclists use to describe physical processes that go on inside them when they train. These aren't just words that are nice to know – having an understanding of them helps you to know what's going on with your body after certain events and when you feel a particular way. This understanding can influence the way you train and make your training more efficient.

Knowing when to slow down or when to step up the pace is partly about making you feel better, but mostly about getting faster and stronger, quicker.

Increasing your heart rate

Your *heart rate* is the number of times your heart beats per minute. Your heart is like a pump. It forces blood around your blood vessels to supply muscles and other tissues all over your body with nutrients and, what your body needs most when it's exercising, oxygen.

When your muscles are working, they need oxygen to convert the fuel your body has ingested as food and drink into energy. The more they work, the more oxygen they need, and the faster your heart needs to pump. Your body increases your heart rate automatically to supply extra oxygen to your muscles during exercise.

Your heart is a muscle and just like other muscles, the more it works, the stronger it gets. The more you exercise, the more blood your heart pumps with every beat – the reason why fit people have lower heart rates than less fit people when they're resting. Their hearts are still pumping more blood with each beat and so supply the required amount of oxygen with fewer beats. Also just like other muscles, your heart gets bigger if it works out a lot. In cyclists like Bradley Wiggins, you can imagine his heart taking up most of the inside of his chest. Mind you, he's got to have some pretty hefty lungs in there, too.

Working out your maximum heart rate

Your heart can only work so hard. When it beats really quickly it gets tired and it can't keep up a very fast rate for long. The fastest your heart can beat is called your maximum heart rate (known as *HRmax*), which is typically measured in beats per minute. HRmax differs from person to person, but is dependent on age, meaning your maximum heart rate slows down as you grow older.

The only way to accurately measure your HRmax is to get hooked up to an exercise stress machine with electrodes all over your body. This machine is a specialist piece of kit and requires a team of people to operate it and to make sure you remain safe, so is normally only available to élite athletes. It involves running uphill on a treadmill, steeper and steeper, faster and faster, until you've just about had it. The medically qualified people conducting this test notice certain changes appearing on your electrocardiogram and tell you to stop. You're then helped to a chair, gasping for air and with no strength left to support yourself.

A simple alternative to hooking yourself up to an exercise stress machine is to use a formula to calculate your approximate HRmax – and then just work everything out from there. The most common, and simplest, equation used is HRmax = 220 – your age. This formula has been, and is still, used a great deal, although folk of a scientific bent don't believe it's accurate enough. Many different, more accurate formulae have been invented, but the most accepted is HRmax = 205.8 – (0.685 × your age).

Determining your target heart rate

The reason for working out your HRmax (see the preceding section) is so that you can calculate something else: your *target heart rate range*. Your target range is when your heart is beating between 60 and 80 per cent of your HRmax, a level which should not overwork your heart and put it at risk, but at which you gain the maximum benefit from an aerobic workout. Generally, if you work out with your heart beating faster than this, your heart will not strengthen from the exercise, but will tire out – you won't be able to carry on for as long and you won't be doing as much good as if you'd kept your heart rate in the 60 to 80 per cent range.

To work out your target heart rate range, multiply your HRmax by 0.6 to get the lower figure, then 0.8 for the higher one.

If you're new to exercise, have a heart condition or any other medical history, you should go nowhere near the top end of your target heart rate until you've seen a doctor and been given the thumbs up.

Even after being given the all-clear from a doctor, if you're new to exercise stick to the lower end of your target heart rate range. If you're exercising to lose weight, sticking to the lower end is also wise – your body needs more oxygen to use stored fat as energy and you get more oxygen into your system at the lower end of this target range. At the higher end of the range you burn mostly carbohydrates. If you're intent on training to improve your strength and fitness, you should aim to exercise in the higher end of this range.

Monitoring your actual heart rate

You can monitor your heart rate as you're exercising in a couple of ways:

- ✔ **Wear a heart rate monitor:** This method is your simplest option. Kits come as a strap you wear around your chest and a monitor with a display face that you can either wear around your wrist or mount on your handlebars. Occasionally you see bike computers with a heart rate monitor function. Most monitors come with just the basic functions of displaying heart rate, including average and maximum for each session, and time and date. Or you can get top-of-the-range models that set personal training zones, display elevation profiles for your session, synchronise with your software, map your route, sound alarms if you slip out of your target rate and probably give you a foot massage at the end of your ride. These top-end monitors can be quite pricey.

- ✔ **Measure your heart rate manually:** To do this, you need both hands, so make sure you stop pedalling! Put the soft pads of your index and middle fingers on the inside of your opposite wrist, slightly to the thumb side. Feel for the beat: this is your *radial artery*. Count the number of beats in ten seconds and multiply by six. That is your *current heart rate*.

A rough guide to whether you're at the right level of exertion is to see how comfortable you find talking. If you're using plenty of energy, but can still talk quite easily, you're probably in the lower part of your target heart rate range. If you're working hard (but at a pace you can keep up for some time), but can only speak a few words before breathing becomes difficult, you're near the top end of your target range.

Measuring your VO_2

As well as your heart rate (see the preceding section), VO_2 and VO_2*max* are two more key measurements that help in understanding the physiology of exercise. VO_2 is the amount of oxygen you use per kilogram of bodyweight per minute. VO_2max is the maximum amount of oxygen your body can use when it's absolutely flat out – the most oxygen your body can physically take in. VO_2max is the figure most closely related to how fit you are.

About 20 per cent of air is oxygen and about 15 to 18 per cent of the oxygen you inhale with every breath is absorbed into your lungs. As air travels into your lungs it enters smaller and smaller branching and flowering clusters of tissue that provide an ever-enlarging surface area to absorb oxygen and expel carbon dioxide. These gases are finally exchanged in microscopic pockets called *alveoli*. Although sounding like a particularly nice garlic mayonnaise, these alveoli aren't spread on your food, but if they were spread out on the ground their combined surface area would cover about a third of a tennis court.

Oxygenated blood from the lungs goes straight to the heart, which fires it out into your arteries for transportation to the far-flung and diverse tissues of your body, including all your muscles. In the muscles, the oxygen is diffused into muscle cells and a chemical reaction occurs that finally produces energy. Your muscles need more of this energy to work harder and rely on a greater supply of oxygen during exercise. Fulfilling this need relies on your lungs and heart being able to absorb and pump more oxygen to your cells.

The following factors affect your rate of oxygen intake, and consequently your fitness:

✔ The effectiveness of your lungs to get oxygen in and carbon dioxide out

✔ The capability of your heart to pump the good stuff round your body

✔ The number and efficiency of the cells producing energy in your muscles

These factors are different in every person and are affected by age, gender, body mass and body composition, and genetics.

As with measuring your HRmax (refer to the section 'Working out your maximum heart rate' earlier in this chapter), to measure your VO_2max you have to see the medical scientists again and once more hop on the treadmill. Just like with the maximum heart rate, the boffins make you run faster and faster, on a steeper and steeper hill, until you're finally half carried away from the machine and dumped into a chair. This time, though, they catch all the air that you breathe out and work out how much oxygen is in it. As they already know how much oxygen is in the air all around you, from this figure they can tell you how much you're using.

Although your final VO_2max figure isn't much use on its own, if you get this test done at key points in your training programme, you'll be able to see solid proof that you're getting fitter.

If you can't get your VO_2max measured scientifically, you can use a number of methods to get a pretty accurate figure, either from your resting heart rate or heart rate after specific exercises. Do an online search for VO_2max calculators and you'll find various websites where you can feed in figures and obtain a number.

Many cyclists and athletes aim specifically to raise their VO_2max and use what's called *HIIT* (high intensity interval training) to do so. HIIT involves periods in training (usually for several minutes) where you exercise as hard as you can, alternating these with periods in your normal target heart rate range. This kind of training is said to produce the best results for increased fitness (see the section 'Training for Speed' later in this chapter for more).

Working out your lactate threshold

Lactate threshold, or *OBLA* (onset of blood lactate accumulation) has nothing at all to do with your capability to produce milk for babies.

Lactate is a substance made during energy conversion in your cells. It comes in a chain of substances, right after lactic acid. Lactate is not a waste product and is itself used as a preferred fuel source by the brain and heart. It either gets used where it's made, shifted elsewhere for use or deposited in the liver, which stores it for later consumption.

During exercise you produce more lactate. Up to a certain point, your production and removal of lactate both increase, but as exertion intensifies, production starts to dramatically outrun removal and blood lactate accumulation sets in. Roughly speaking, this point is your lactate threshold. Experts think that lactate is not the exact cause of muscle fatigue, but build-up of fatigue is directly connected to it.

So when you reach your lactate threshold, fatigue sets in: you're exercising at a level that you can't maintain. In theory, you should be able to exercise at a level just below your lactate threshold indefinitely, although other factors exist that will eventually slow you down.

Lactate threshold is often expressed as a percentage of VO_2max (see the preceding section). Ordinary individuals might reach their lactate threshold at 50 to 60 per cent of their VO_2max, whereas top athletes might get to 80 per cent of their VO_2max before crossing the threshold. Training can increase the amount of exertion you can endure in relation to your maximum physical capability.

The most accurate way to test for your lactate threshold is by taking blood samples at various stages of exercise. Naturally, for most people taking blood samples is neither practical nor desirable. It involves returning once more to those scientists and that treadmill, running faster and faster, steeper and steeper, then collapsing in the same old chair, but this time having the scientists analysing blood at certain points before you drop.

Luckily, more convenient ways of testing for your lactate threshold are available. You can buy portable blood-lactate analysers, which are hand-held machines that give you a lactate reading from a drop of blood in a matter of seconds. If you're using one of these to gauge your improvement through training, you need to set up exercise patterns that you can repeat more or less exactly to obtain comparable figures.

Other methods of calculating your lactate threshold that don't use blood samples are available. They involve studying your heart rate at barely sustainable levels of exercise over a fixed period of time, but they're not as accurate.

Lactate, or lactic acid, isn't the cause of delayed muscle soreness. This pain and stiffness typically comes on a day or so after strenuous exercise that you're not used to and can last for several days. Delayed muscle soreness is actually caused by micro-ruptures inside your muscle fibres. Blood-lactate levels peak about five minutes after the end of your strenuous exercise and you can expect levels to be back to normal within the hour.

Determining your recovery needs

You've been on the bike for a couple of hours and worked hard. You need to sit and relax for ten minutes, maybe have a bite to eat and there you are: recovered.

Not at all.

Recovery isn't just about feeling better after a ride, but is a vital and complex part of your training. If you ignore your recovery needs, you waste a great deal of your hard pedalling.

The process of training is simple:

- ✔ You physically challenge and overload your body's muscles.
- ✔ You go through a process of fatigue and recovery.
- ✔ The upward slope of recovery takes you to a higher performance level than you were at before.

So if you don't make sure you recover properly, you won't reach that higher level. Your body takes that step up during recovery, not training.

Apart from treating your body right after a ride, recovery also means not over-training. Training as hard as you can – riding your bike as much as you can – must surely mean you'll get fitter, faster, right? Again: no, not at all. If you don't allow your muscles to recover fully after regular, tough training, you gradually start weakening, not strengthening your physical skills. If you can feel yourself starting to fatigue earlier on training rides it might be time to reschedule, leaving longer gaps between rides and giving yourself more time to recover.

The first thing you need to do to recover after a ride is to replace your fuel stores. Replacing stores of *glycogen* (the stuff that carbohydrates are turned into for storage in the liver and muscles) is quickest in the first few hours after a ride. Your body is keen to refuel and it absorbs the glycogen much faster in this period. You don't have to restock in the first few hours, but you must do it within the first 24 hours or you won't get the benefits that come with full recovery from your training. (See Chapter 16 for more on fuel and refuelling.)

If you don't stockpile carbohydrates you simply won't have the energy in your muscles next time you hit the road. We also strongly recommend consuming some protein soon after you're off the bike.

As well as consuming carbohydrates and some protein, the other big factors in your recovery are rest and sleep. Take sleep seriously: your body does most of its recovery work whilst you're asleep, taking you up that next step of strength and fitness, so do your best to ensure you get plenty of undisturbed sleep. Many pro cyclists and athletes sleep during the day to help them recover enough from a morning training session to take on an afternoon one. As well as sleep, you also need to let your body rest. Don't go around refusing to ever sit down because you're the fit cyclist – sit whenever you can or even lean up against something instead of standing upright. Give your body all the breaks you can.

Some people swear by light massage after exercise. Gentle rubbing of muscles towards the heart helps to loosen any waste products after heavy use. Deeper massage can be taxing on your major muscles after training so you're better off leaving this until after you've recovered.

Training for Speed

If you think you can work out an effective training schedule for yourself, stick to it and address any weaknesses or problems that surface, good for you – go right ahead and watch your performance improve. But if you think you might need a hand – a professional hand – get a coach.

Qualified coaches put you on the right track with nutrition, recovery and a personalised training programme to suit your needs and your timetable. Coaches are automatically the best people to report back to and they always give the right feedback and encouragement. They spot problems you're not aware of and give good tips when you're not sure which way to turn. If you're worried about the cost, check out options in your area – they might not be as expensive as you think.

You can always find coaches through a cycling club. For information on cycling clubs all over the UK check out British Cycling's website (www. britishcycling.org.uk) and click on the 'Clubs' tab.

Training is an enormous field and depends very much on your individual aims. In the following sections we cover areas that can be strong components of any training.

Setting goals and programmes

Setting yourself a programme and goals is probably the most concrete step you can take towards improving your fitness and strength as a cyclist. But it isn't something you should throw yourself into as a beginner. Only start a programme if you're already riding regularly and are reasonably fit.

The perfect goal for a training programme is an event, such as a *sportive* (a timed ride over a set route normally between about 60 and 120 miles (100 to 200 kilometres) or a charity ride. An event has a date and a distance, so you can easily work towards it step by step. You can also look up previous results and get an idea of how fast you need to ride to be up with the best. You can set other kinds of goals, but to be effective they must be clearly defined and have a definite date. Saying to yourself, 'I'm going to become a stronger cyclist,' is not a clearly defined goal and will not work as something to train towards.

Examples of goals you could commit yourself to might include:

✔ **Doing a 50-mile (80-kilometre) ride every weekend for a month**

✔ **Riding at least 100 miles (160 kilometres) each week**

This distance sounds a lot, but if you add in commuting miles and trips to the shops, it can become very manageable.

✔ **Spending ten hours a week in the saddle**

Ten hours also sounds like a lot, but if you use your bike for regular journeys, you can quite easily achieve this target.

✔ **Reducing your average time on a ride**

If you ride a regular route, time yourself and commit to shaving off a few minutes or seconds each time you do it. Fitting a bicycle computer helps you to keep an eye on your average speed. This goal isn't about taking risks or cutting corners, but about gradually increasing and sustaining your pace over the length of a ride.

Follow these tips for creating effective programmes:

✔ **Write down your training programme:** Work out the steps you need to take, week by week, to reach the ability you need for the end goal. Adding 10 per cent increases in weekly mileage is a good rate – you might be able to do a bit more, but usually only to a maximum of 15 per cent increases. Apply these percentage increases to any long rides as well as to the weekly total.

✔ **Schedule one ride a week as close as you can manage to your end goal, both in distance and speed:** This weekly hard ride works as a guide to how you're improving.

✔ **Set yourself one long, slow recovery ride:** For this ride, cycle as long as your hard ride, but only at 50 to 60 per cent of your maximum capability.

✔ **Always make sure you take one day off per week, two if you can:** If you're not taking two days off, make one of your daily rides a short, very easy one. Schedule this easy one or the day off right after your hard ride day.

Following these tips leaves you with three days out of your weekly schedule. Make your rides on these days medium distance rides, but at about 80 per cent intensity. If you're going to use intervals (see the following section) as part of your training, do them in two of these rides, but make sure you leave at least 48 hours in between interval rides and between an interval ride and your hard ride. Remember: recovery is vital.

As you get very close to the day of your event or other major goal, you have to ease up. Some people recommend not doing any cycling in the three days prior to a big event. If you're going to cycle, make it only very easy, 'spinning' rides to keep your legs moving. In this last period, recovery is essential.

Some people get a great deal out of recording all their riding data. Analysing these figures tells them what's working and what isn't, what helps and what hinders. You can either write it all down or buy training diary software that won't just present your performance statistics, but at the click of a mouse also does all sorts of fancy calculations. This software makes it easy to share your data with your coach.

If you set goals that are too hard or a programme that is too rigid or difficult, you're most likely going to fail. Be flexible and realistic and you're much more likely to succeed.

Incorporating interval training

Interval training is a system in which, after warming up, you ride at an intense level for a set period of time, then recover by riding more easily for a while, then repeat the whole process several times.

Interval training is fast and furious – the kind of stuff that really pushes you to your limit. It has pro riders talking about the *Good Pain*. The key to interval training is intensity – this training requires you to work as hard as you physically can. One of the benefits of interval training is learning to deal with muscle pain, because that is what it puts you through. You're training until it hurts, over and over again, so that pain becomes a part of your routine, something you learn to ignore – the Good Pain.

Some disagreement exists among experts as to whether very short bursts (10 to 30 seconds) of absolute maximum effort are more effective than periods of a few minutes at 80 to 90 per cent of maximum ability, but it's certainly true that either approach brings big results in performance improvement.

You must already be reasonably fit and strong as a cyclist before you take on interval training. This regime is a tough one – 50 per cent of people who start interval training give it up – and it can injure you if you're not ready for it. If you're in doubt, ask a doctor or coach.

Interval training brings about several physical changes to your body. The biochemical processes of your muscles become more efficient and they start getting more oxygen out of each and every drop of blood. Your muscles grow more *capillaries* (the single-cell-thickness links between your smallest arteries and tiniest veins, where oxygen is transferred to muscle tissue for use in energy conversion). And your heart strengthens, pumping more oxygenated blood round your system.

For effective interval training, follow these tips:

- **Plan your high intensity minutes:** Aim for a total of 10 to 20 minutes of high-intensity work (or just 2 to 3 minutes if you're planning short intervals of absolute maximum effort). This time is just what you spend working flat out and doesn't include the breaks in between. When just starting out, begin with a total of just five minutes of high intensity riding on any one day. For high intensity training of 80 to 90 per cent of maximum, go for intervals of one minute to a top of five minutes. (You might need to work up to five minutes.)

- **Let yourself recover:** In between intervals, allow yourself to recover with easy pedalling so that your heart rate drops to 60 to 65 per cent of HRmax. If you're not wearing a monitor, this is roughly when your breathing returns to normal depth and rate. These recovery times should last about as long as the intervals themselves, unless you're doing the short maximum intervals, which take longer to recover from.

- **Train twice a week:** Interval training twice a week is plenty. Recovering fully from any interval-training session is most important, or you won't reap the benefits. A total interval-training time of 30 minutes per week is enough to improve your performance significantly. You can do intervals quite naturally on a succession of good hills or as sprints. If you do your intervals as sprints you won't just be training for greater strength, you'll also be getting good practice for racing.

You must always *warm up* (gradually increasing your level of effort and, with it, your heart rate) for at least 20 minutes before starting your intervals and *cool down* (gradually reducing your effort level and heart rate) for the same period before the end of your ride.

Mountain Bike Training

Mountain biking is a blast. The feeling you get when you battle your way to the top of a long, broken climb, or, even more, the rush of excitement as you start flying down a narrow track is better than anything you'll strap in for at any amusement park. But you can only enjoy these thrills if you're physically up for the challenge – and the more strength and expertise you build up, the more fun you're going to have.

The two major areas of preparation for a mountain bike rider are fitness and skills. For mountain bike (MTB) riding you need the same cycling strength as any other cyclist. You need to train and be fit with long hours in the saddle, but you also need technical skills. The environment is far more varied and complicated and you have to know exactly what to do in any situation to avoid ending up with boulders up your backside or your face in a puddle of mud.

Building fitness

Riding in the wild and on trails is an unforgiving pursuit – and short cuts home aren't always available. When you're way out in the countryside and hills, you're stuck there until the ride is done. Riding a mountain bike off-road is naturally more like tough training than riding out on *the black stuff* (MTB talk for bitumen). Repeated steep climbs on trails and singletracks are very much like interval training and experienced mountain bikers get to be very strong, fit cyclists.

Many MTB riders train out on roads, either on road bikes or mountain bikes fitted with *slicks* (smooth-surfaced tyres). Riding on roads makes training a more certain science. Duration and effort are easier to control and riders don't have to worry about trail skills. Riders can plan a clear, precise pro-gramme to execute without all the complications of the changing qualities of countryside trails. Longer, slower endurance training rides can be done without the problem of finding trails kind enough to ride easily for hours.

Road riding also helps with speed training for mountain bike riders. If you plan to do any MTB racing you need to be able to take off fast. Getting a good position at the beginning of a cross-country race is important when passing on narrow trails is difficult.

Practising sprint starts on roads is an easier way to improve your skills quickly, but riding unpredictable and arduous trails up and down hills is what's going to give you the toughest legs of any cyclist. To train off-road, you need to find a course that gives you as many different kinds of terrain as you can find.

When looking for a suitable off-road training course, keep the following in mind:

✔ If you use a relatively short loop with plenty of variation, you can set yourself a target number of circuits and vary this number according to how much time you have. Of course, this gives you the temptation to cut short your ride if you're not fully committed. A bigger circuit doesn't give you that option, but leaves you with no escape route should you have a fall or damage your bike.

✔ Including a steep climb in your training route provides a natural interval that usually has a downhill recovery straight afterwards. Practising steep climbs both in a standing position and seated, slipping down into your *granny gear* (the lowest gear on a mountain bike) for the latter position, is a good idea.

Regular resistance training for the muscles of your upper body helps with mountain biking. Your arms and shoulders do a big share of controlling your bike and strengthening them with some weight-training makes riding less stressful, puts off fatigue on longer rides and helps prevent injury should you take a tumble.

Increasing trail skills

You need to learn many skills if you want to be king or queen of the trails. We go over a few important points here, but for more guidance track down your local MTB club and find out when you can go riding with a group.

Balance is a key part of controlling a mountain bike. Good balance helps you in almost all situations, but especially in tight spots where you have to move slowly and stand on your pedals. Your balance is also a major factor in how well you steer your mountain bike. You should alter your balance to move your head and shoulders for steering, and never just swing your bars to change direction. Getting the hang of this kind of steering gives you far more control and assurance. (Refer to Chapter 10 for more on improving your balance while riding.)

The following list offers tips to help you improve your skills beyond the basics:

- ✔ **When you're making your way up a long steep trail, make decisions about the line you'll take early on:** Does the clearest way have a blockage of broken rocks halfway up? How easy is it going to be to cross over to take another line to the top? Have a plan.

- ✔ **Always think ahead for gear changes:** When you've hit the slope as you come out of a ditch, you're already far too late to start changing down. You need to be in that gear already. Anticipate what gear you're going to need and switch early to keep up your momentum with rapidly changing conditions.

- ✔ **Don't rely on your back brake on downhills:** Under certain conditions, heavy application of your front brake sends your rear up in the air, but if you're in the right position on the bike this won't happen and you definitely need the power of your front brake to keep control on a fast descent.

- ✔ **Use your brakes in an on and off pattern:** Using your brakes continuously heats them to the point where they may fail. Even disc brakes can overheat if you use them too much. Let the bike roll over big bumps or any ruts, just enough for you to remain in control.

- ✔ **Consider doing a reconnaissance on serious downhills:** Get off the bike and go and have a look. Work out the line you'll aim for and memorise the spot you need to hit to go over the edge – you won't see the surface of the slope as you approach and you need to know where to start.

- ✔ **Keep control when going over the edge on downhills:** Ride up to the edge in a standing position. Push the handlebars away from you and move your weight backwards as you roll over the top. Use your front brake to keep control.

Check out Chapter 10 for basic mountain biking skills, such as keeping your eyes on the trail – both right in front of your bike and further into the distance – and avoiding hazards and obstacles.

If you lose control of the bike on a downhill ride, you'll have to think and act quickly. Is there a clear exit at the bottom that you can risk hitting at high speed? If you have to get off to save yourself, go off the back, letting the bike roll ahead. Don't put out your hand or arm to break a fall. Aim to land on your shoulder and roll.

When you're flying round corners at speed, letting your back wheel slide as you lean is tempting – and fun. However, doing so not only gives you less control, it gives you far less power to accelerate out of the corner when you start to straighten up. Also, on blind corners, not hitting anything or anyone that might be on the path round the bend is your responsibility. Unless you can be absolutely sure no one else is on the track – such as on a course on a race day – you should approach a blind corner imagining a small child standing in the middle of the path just out of sight. Maybe you should slow down.

Endurance Training: The Long Steady Distance

Endurance training is for those people who want to race or ride long distances, spending many hours in the saddle. When you're trained and fit, this skill is a great one to have. To look at a map and know that you can cover long stretches of country on your bike is a powerful feeling. When you get to the stage where you can cycle hundreds of miles in a single day, you know you truly are fit and strong.

But, naturally, you have to train pretty hard before ten hours in the saddle isn't going to loom like a spell in the slammer. Training for endurance in a physical sense isn't that much harder – or that much different – than training for any other road racing, but you do need to acquire some other skills and consider other factors. You need to know a few mental tricks to keep you pedalling for long periods and one of the biggest problems you'll start to face when you hit the big miles is what fuel will sustain your efforts that your body will happily accept.

A training programme for endurance cycling should include all of the things we mention in the training sections earlier in this chapter. A rough schedule should be:

- ✔ Three days of medium to high intensity rides, possibly with intervals on two of them, but with intervals suitably spaced.
- ✔ At least one day off.
- ✔ One day with a long recovery – easy – ride.
- ✔ One day with a longer, tough ride.

Only this last day should be one that gets longer and longer.

On your long, tough ride, enjoy and cherish your *LSD* – your long steady distance. Keep your pace steady rather than slow: you still need to be exerting yourself, and your body won't improve if you just take it easy. You need to be setting yourself a route with a certain distance – say, 50 to 60 miles (80 to 95 kilometres) – then settling into a pace that taxes you, but doesn't exhaust you before you're halfway round. Increase your distance by ten per cent every week to build up your strength.

When starting out with endurance training, consider the following:

- ✔ The best route to map out is a big loop. If you can work it so no possible short cuts appear on the route, all the better. On a long ride, the most likely time you're going to want to give up is in the third quarter. If you know at that stage the quickest way home is to carry on and finish the ride, you're much more likely to ignore those voices whispering in your ear to throw in the towel.

✔ Carrying everything you need – food and drink – for a very long ride gets tricky. You might want to map in a shop or two along your route.

✔ Only take short breaks through the ride. You might feel like stopping for a long picnic at a scenic spot along your training route, but you're likely to feel better if you don't. Stopping for a few minutes when you need to causes no problems at all, but anything over ten minutes and your body starts wanting to recover. Your muscles think you've finished the ride. You'll certainly need to warm up again when you start and you may find that the rest of the day is less comfortable.

✔ When you first hit the 75-mile (120-kilometre) mark, assess how you and your bike are getting on. Is your saddle still comfortable? Are you having any problems with your ankles, knees, shoulders, wrists or back? If you're having a problem with the saddle, know that the perfect one is out there somewhere, but you can't go to the bike shop without know-ing where the problem is, so think your way round your nether anatomy and take note of the offending spot. Your seat may just need adjusting: take your bike and your list of ailments down to the bike shop and get the advice of the people there.

Do seek advice from bike shop staff if your saddle or any other part of your bike is causing you problems or pain. These problems won't get better the longer you ride; in fact, they will only get worse.

Many people recommend *cross-training* for endurance riders. Cross-training means incorporating some other form of exercise into your programme, and not focusing solely on riding your bike. Running and swimming are certainly both strenuous and strength-building, and swimming in particular exercises a huge number of muscles. *Resistance training* (using weights) builds up your core muscles, makes cycling less taxing on your upper body and helps to pro-tect you in a stack. Even just doing some different cycling can be a great idea. Getting out on the trails on your MTB or just plain old spin cycling can be a good variation and help you build your cycling strength.

Fuel for your ride is a big area for planning. You need stuff that's portable, goes down easily and provides consistent energy. Nothing's as individual as the likes and dislikes, cans and cannots, of endurance riders and their food-stuffs. When you start to ride longer distances, you'll probably find, as almost all ultra-distance cyclists do, that liquids are all your stomach is comfortable with. Whether you go with gels, energy drinks or hot cups of soup, you have to work out what's best for you.

If you're training for an event, make sure that whatever you end up thriving on is going to be available on the big day, because if you're forced to consume food or drinks you're not used to, you're going to be very uncomfortable. Avoid high-GI (quick energy, sugary) foods for your main source of fuel. Lollies can be a help for a burst of energy to get you up a steep hill, but they're a quick fix and soon leave you back with no juice.

Dehydrating when riding a bike for a long period can easily happen. Your sweat is wicked away into the wind and you may not realise just how much fluid you're losing, but you'll be losing precious water continuously, so you need to replace it just as constantly.

Lon Haldeman: Endurance pioneer

When Lon Haldeman won the first Race Across America (RAAM) – back in 1982 when it was called the Great American Bike Race – he shook the foundations of cycling achievement and brought bicycles into the media spotlight like never before. He rode the 3,000 miles (over 4,800 kilometres) in less than ten days and shocked the world.

Prior to that early achievement, ultra-distance cyclists had always ridden all day long, then spent most of the night sleeping and recovering. But Lon just kept on going. Endurance cyclists took him as their first and only role model and slaved away to try to copy his success.

Lon went on to win the Race Across America in different categories five times, including twice breaking the record on a tandem with his wife, Susan Notorangelo. He is now said to have crossed the continent on his bicycle over 50 times. Stories about his stubborn, two-wheeled persistence abound, with one of the best known involving the time he rode 50 miles (80 kilometres) with a flat tyre, mostly standing on the pedals so as not to collapse the wheel.

But Lon isn't just a hugely accomplished cyclist. Part of his devotion to ultra-distance cycling is a love of travelling, a love of seeing the world. For some time now he's been Race Director of RAAM. He's designed the route so that cyclists get to see spectacular scenery on their journey across the continent.

Many years ago, Lon first travelled to Peru. Having crossed the Andes from the Pacific side, he then spent months living with native Peruvians in the Amazon jungle. When he got back to America, he wrote passionately about his experience, and about how he felt other North Americans should try to have such an experience to increase their understanding of the world.

Lon and Susan started a bicycle tour company called PAC Tours. They go to all sorts of challenging places for different events and adventures. But every year Lon likes to return to Peru and cycle both the Andes and the Amazon. Aspiring riders pay to go along – for both the exhilarating ride and the chance to cycle with Lon Haldeman. But each and every one of the riders on the tour is taken to stores in Lima, the Peruvian capital, and asked to buy clothes for children before they start their trip. When they get to the jungle side of the mountains they all visit an orphanage, where they donate the clothes.

Lon has also gathered resources for and overseen the building of a school outside Iquitos, the isolated city far out in the Peruvian Amazon. And he collects bicycles and bike parts from all his cycling friends and clients to take down to Peru for the use of Peruvian racers.

Lon Haldeman is a man who likes to make a difference. He changed the way everyone thought about ultra-distance cycling by training and working so hard he lifted the sport to a whole new level. And he's made a fantastic change to the lives of many Peruvians living in less fortunate, less salubrious, conditions than their North American neighbours.

We tip our helmets to the man. Good on you, Lon.

Chapter 12

Touring and Exploring

· ·

In This Chapter

▶ Plotting your journey

▶ Readying your bike

▶ Loading up

· ·

Cycle touring could easily warrant a book in itself. Since we first packed up our bikes and flew overseas, not having any idea what kind of experience we were going to have, we've come to believe that journeying by bicycle is the most rewarding, educational, social and fun experience you could possibly have as a traveller. You don't have to go to remote and difficult parts of the world. Making your bicycle part of any trip gives you the same uplifting feeling and understanding of the country you pass through.

Researching your route covers everything from working closely with satellite maps showing distant foreign locations, to checking if there's a shop or café anywhere along the beach promenade you're cycling along one afternoon on holiday. In this chapter, we give you everything you need to get started, no matter where you plan to go. If you're going to put your bike in your car, on a train or on an aeroplane, we also provide tips to help you get it done smoothly.

Preparing your bike is simpler if you're taking it along on a holiday by the coast than if you're planning an Antarctic expedition, but wherever you're going you need to know your bike is ready for it. Having the right gear before you go might seem like a lot of work, but doing so makes your trip run far more smoothly – and finding the things you need is much easier in your home environment. Getting your bike serviced or fixed can be very tricky if you don't share any language with the bike mechanic, or if you're just too far from the nearest bike shop. We run through the equipment you're likely to need and how to prepare your bike for your big trip.

And what do you take with you? Advice changes like the weather, but we give you some good ideas to get you started on your packing.

Deciding Where – and How – to Go: The World Is Your Bike Path

You can go just about everywhere with your bicycle. Very few environments can't be conquered on two human-powered wheels. But having said that, turning up in the high Andes with your sights set on the heart of the Amazon, without having given the trip some forethought, isn't the best idea. If you don't have a very good idea of what you're going to encounter, you won't be fully prepared and the slightest problem could end your journey.

Although we would never recommend doing any travelling 'by the guidebook', having a certain level of knowledge about the place you're going is always an asset. Discovering things when you travel can be a brilliant experience, but having some idea of any obstacles, choices you'll have to make or things that appeal to you personally and that you don't want to miss is also very helpful.

You certainly can learn too much about a place. When Gavin first walked into Central Park in New York, past the horse carriages (you know the ones) and along to the footbridge where he'd seen so many people meet (in movies) it felt like he'd been there before. Many times. As he approached the bridge he felt it totally unnecessary to experience it, or even the park, in person: he knew it so well. He didn't need to be there, so he left. He went and found some much more interesting New York stuff that he'd never heard of before.

While you don't need to plan every detail of your trip, knowing something about where you're heading is essential and reading other people's accounts of similar journeys can be invaluable. Where to eat, where to sleep, where to take a short walk up a hill and get the best view in the world – you may not want to take other people's advice, but it can only help to listen to it.

Finding out that you'll come across a long and very dark tunnel somewhere in some foothills could have you packing those lights you were going to leave behind. Learning to your surprise that in the hot spot where you're headed it gets to nearly freezing temperatures at seven in the morning could mean laying your hands on those long-fingered gloves. Reading about notoriously angry lions along a certain stretch of your road might necessitate bringing along a top hat, a chair and a whip (let's just hope you don't ever actually run into any lions).

You may also need to plan your way through a number of complex situations. If you're getting on a plane, you need to be sure you'll have a bike box and know how to pack it. If your trip includes a bus, you need to know what you'll have to do to ensure your bike travels too? If you're off in the car, what is the best thing to do with your bicycle (other than ride it instead)?

Think it all through and your travelling will be less stressful, more successful and much more fun.

Finding the inspiration

Before you can start to plan a route, it helps to have some idea of the general area that you want to explore on your bike. Deciding this might be a no-brainer: perhaps you've hankered for years to ride from Land's End to John O'Groats, from Cape Town to Cairo, or to get to know the countryside of your own county better. If that sounds familiar, get stuck in and get planning.

Maybe, however, you just know that you like riding your bike and really fancy the idea of doing a spot of touring and exploring, but don't really know where you'd like to go. You need inspiration.

Inspiration can find you when you least expect it – perhaps on a television programme that's on in the background, in a postcard that lands on your mat one morning or in a conversation with a friend. You might just see or hear of somewhere that really grabs you. Our best advice here is to be curious; keep your eyes and ears open and be receptive to whatever comes your way. You could be struck by that elusive flash of inspiration when you're not actually looking for it.

If that doesn't happen, just do a little research. Follow your interests – watch films, chat in online forums, talk travel and read travelogues. Seek out destinations near or far that appeal to you.

We stand up for those ancient wanderers who wrote journals of their travels, then had them published in a solid hardback that perhaps lingered on a bookshelf for many decades before an eventual transfer to a charity shop. Accounts of adventures in distant places and faraway times don't give you much of a hint as to where to eat or drink, but they do give you a marvellous taste of the possibilities of a place, a version of your destination that's more like a dream.

Researching your route

Even 15 years ago, researching your route meant strolling down to your local library, seeing which guidebooks they had on the shelves and pulling out the atlas or road atlas. If you were lucky, you might find an intrepid cyclist had authored a regional digest about your preferred area and managed to get it published, or an ancient wanderer from the Victorian era had a journal of peregrinations put into print. If you were very lucky, you might have access to a specialist map shop. In short, you could get the basic facts and the rest was guesswork.

These days, life is easier – you can flick on your satellite mapping program, pick out a spot on the shores of the Sea of Okhotsk in far-eastern Russia and zoom in so far you can tell if the boy gazing up at the sky is smiling. And yes, he's smiling – because he's on a bicycle. Someone will have a blog describing the place you want to go, search engines automatically point you to sites that book accommodation and if you still don't get what you want there'll be a forum somewhere and you can just ask.

Now the Internet is here, you've got by far the best research tool ever known. And you have it right at home. But you also can't dismiss the tips and local knowledge you can gather from talking to someone in the know.

Consider checking out the following possible sources when planning your trip:

✔ Tourist bodies are always a good source of local knowledge. If you need to actually ask someone something, the people who work for these groups are always very helpful. Local councils that are concerned about the health and wellbeing of their constituents often have maps and other details of cycleways and good places to ride. National park authorities everywhere often have excellent information for cyclists.

✔ If you're planning a ride in the UK, you have no less than 13,000 miles, that's just over 20,000 kilometres, of the National Cycle Network to explore. You can get lots of information, maps and details from the Sustrans website (www.sustrans.org), which also has loads of links to cycling routes around the world – something to bear in mind if your UK ride is just a warm-up to something bigger.

✔ The Cyclists' Touring Club (www.ctc.org.uk) is a great source of inspiration and information for any rider planning a journey by bike. This club is the UK's national cycling charity and offers a wealth of expert advice and help for rides from just a few miles long to epic adventures.

✔ If you plan to head across the water for a cycle route, you can take advantage of the Europe-wide network of cycle routes, which is growing all the time. You can travel from the top of Scandinavia to the Mediterranean Sea on roads and tracks which are bicycle friendly. Often they are traffic-free or very lightly used by cars. A good place to start planning a European odyssey is the European Cyclists' Federation website (www.ecf.com) – just click on the link to Eurovelo. If you only want to cycle in France (and who could blame you – France is a fantastic place for biking) then try looking at the site for their Veloroutes and Greenways (www.af3v.org). CTC (see the preceding bullet) also offer information on touring in over 90 countries around the world and have lots of ideas and suggestions for your trip.

✔ Websites that enable riders to map their routes and share them are also a fantastic resource. Bikely (www.bikely.com) is probably the biggest, with over a million routes mapped out all over the world. If this website doesn't have your intended journey already, it's bound to have one very close by, wherever in the world you're looking. Bikely is easy to register with and use. Mark out a trip on the smallest roads in any quiet back-water and Bikely can give you an elevation profile, so you can even plan your days around climbs.

✔ Google Maps (maps.google.co.uk) can be useful and is very easy to use. The site can find anything for you almost instantly and give you a view at any scale. You can study your chosen area as a road map, a sat-ellite image or a combination of the two.

✔ Google Earth (earth.google.com) is the mother of them all. Check out your own home: is your bike leaning up against the fence? Click on the camera icon and swoop down to get a view up the driveway and a closer look. You can't do that for everywhere in the world, but you can follow any road or track, with a fairly good indication of altitude, any-where on the planet. Travellers pin their snaps on the satellite image and, although they do often put them in the wrong place, few areas exist where you can't get a fairly good idea of what the view is from the ground.

If you're planning on staying in very cheap accommodation, you may not find it on the Internet. You certainly won't be able to book it. Reading about it may be as close as you get, but just knowing that accommodation is there is a good first step. We love those accommodation sites that let people post their own reviews. When someone writes, 'The foyer was filthy. The bathroom was filthy. The sheets were filthy. Even the staff were filthy,' you know you're get-ting the lowdown.

Fitting racks to your car

Combining a trip with your car and bicycle (or bicycles) is an excellent idea. The car gets you over a long distance to a part of the country where you're free to just get away, let go and ride your bike. If you're not carrying a huge amount of stuff, it may be simplest to just put your bicycle in the back of the car. Quick-release wheels help in this situation, so does having an estate car. (Just watch where you put the oily chain and chainwheel.) If you've got pas-sengers or luggage, this often isn't feasible, so you have to look at some other system of carrying your bike.

You can choose from the following options for carrying your bike (or bikes) on your car:

- **Tow bar racks:** These are one of the most popular kind of bike racks for cars. They fit on to your tow bar and hold up to four bicycles out from the rear of your car. These racks are very sturdy, but can involve a bit of work every time you want to use them. Although they're designed to hold bikes steady, without swaying, tying your front wheels to your top bars is a good idea, so that they don't swing around. You have to pay to get a rear registration plate and a lights board to fix onto these racks.

- **Clip-on or strap-on racks:** These are good if you don't have a tow bar. They attach to the car by sets of clips or straps and stand out from the boot on rubber feet. The clip-on versions are more solid and have the advantage of allowing you to still open your boot when the racks are attached. These racks are a little less robust than tow bar racks, but often quicker to set up. Some racks lift bikes out of the way of your car's lights and registration plate. But, if not, you have to get extras.

- **Roof carriers:** These fit onto your roof rack and vary enormously in price. Some look positively space-age. You do have to lift your bike up onto the roof, so only get one if you're sure you can manage this. Roof carriers either take bikes with their front wheels on or off. Both types can have locks to secure your treasure. You can get as many as five bikes on your roof this way, but you have to buy fittings for each one.

  With the front wheel off, the forks bolt onto the roof carrier through the *drop-outs* (the slotted gaps at the bottom of the forks where your axle slips in and is fixed) and the rear wheel is strapped down. You can buy separate fittings to secure your front wheel onto the roof. With the front wheel on, both wheels are strapped and the frame is also supported and held by the down tube. With this system your bike(s) are secure from any rear collisions, but don't forget they're up there when you reach your garage.

You can also get racks to fit onto the rear of a caravan or motor home and special rails and stands that you can fix either inside your car or in the back of a van or pick-up. Plenty of drivers knock up their own systems of rails and straps to secure their bikes. These systems can be quite inventive and are usually very cheap.

Carrying bikes on public transport

The idea of mingling cycling with public transport is an excellent one. If distances are just too large to cover by bicycle alone, riding to a public transport connection, travelling in a far more environmentally friendly and efficient manner than a private motor vehicle, and then having the bonus of a bike at your destination is a great idea. Operators of public transport haven't always been hugely positive about carrying bikes – some still aren't – but changes are slowly coming about.

In the following sections, we cover different types of public transport separately. Rules do vary in different areas so check with the local service provider before you make any firm plans.

Although aeroplanes aren't really public transport, we cover them here too.

Trams

You can't take bikes on trams in the UK. Even though some of the models of tram now in use are similar to those in Europe which do allow bikes, for some reason bikes are not allowed in the UK. Folding bikes are allowed, but if your bike is loaded up with bags, taking them on and off, and having to fold your bike, might be more trouble than it's worth.

Buses

Buses, on the whole, won't take bikes either, though most allow folders (check if you need to bag it – some bus companies insist on it). The UK is a bit behind other countries such as the US, where a third of all urban buses have bike racks attached to the front. Although they've been successful, they slow the service down a little and, quite remarkably, cyclists sometimes forget their bike is clamped to the front of the bus.

As for coaches, some UK coach services take bikes as luggage but some don't, so it's important to check. You have to pack bikes flat, and coaches only have limited room, so if you're at the back of the queue you could find that your bike won't get on board. When rail companies replace train services that do take bikes with coaches (for example, when they're working on particular lines), they often refuse bikes on the replacement services, so be extra careful when making plans. (Websites for the rail networks post notices of upcoming works.) You sometimes find coach drivers put bikes on board if they've got room, even when they're not supposed to. To get this favour, you have to be nice to them.

In Europe, companies run double-decker coaches with massive bike trailers in tow. Catering solely for cyclists, they run all the way up and down France and cover much of Spain – you can just book whatever part of the route you want to travel. Greyhound in America allows you to take bikes if they're boxed up and the company also sells boxes. Greyhound charges extra for taking the bike, but the cost is a fraction of what you pay for flying with a bicycle in the United States.

In less-developed countries around the world, you usually find a more accommodating attitude towards carrying your bike, although you may be greeted at first with blank refusal and, of course, it may have to go on the roof. Often an extra payment (which may not be going to the bus company) is required, but the amounts are usually so low it's not worth being principled about.

Ben was cycling in the foothills of the Himalayas in Nepal and realised he was not going to get home before dark, so he waved down the first bus he saw. Within seconds, the bike was on the roof alongside some chickens, two rather bemused looking goats and a motorbike. The driver was used to carrying all sorts of cargo. A bicycle didn't faze him in the slightest.

Trains

The general rule for commuter or suburban trains is that you can take your bike with you, though some trains running on weekday peak times have restrictions. At these peak times, the ban is for trains heading towards the city in the morning and outward-bound trains in the late afternoon. Bike lockers are becoming more and more common at suburban stations, making it possible to ride at least part of your journey and leave your bike in relative safety.

Some suburban trains have no specific areas for bikes, so you have to stand yours as securely as possible in the area around the doors. Carrying a short bungee cord for such instances is a great tip – you can use it to secure your bike to a railing and not have to sit tensely waiting to leap up and stop it rolling between somebody's knees.

In the UK, bikes on trains are officially encouraged, but the nearly 30 rail companies all have their own rules. In general, a limited number of bikes are permitted on any train (often only two or three) and even this number is sometimes at the discretion of the guard. Some companies allow you to book a space for your bike, which may be a good idea during busy holiday periods, while for a few companies reservations are compulsory. Check your particular rail operator before you book a ticket.

Ben once had to get back home on pain of death. (His wife was going out that evening and he had to look after the kids.) As the train he had to catch drew into the station – a train which normally had plenty of space – he realised he hadn't done his homework. The train was full of hundreds of football fans heading to that evening's big match. The aisles and doorways were crammed and the bike racks were full. The guard gave him one of those pitying looks. Undeterred, and waiting until the guard's back was turned, he clambered on board. Conjuring up the spirit of Dunkirk, he found a few inches of room and, with a bit of jockeying, squeezed his bike into what at first appeared to be an unpromising gap. The guard protested, but when faced down by scores of fans, he sensibly withdrew.

Ben got lucky. Unfortunately, we've heard many stories of cyclists being less fortunate and getting refused space on trains, even when they've booked, and for no apparent rhyme or reason. This kind of unpredictable non-cooperation doesn't do any favours for the image of public transport and we can only hope things get better for bikes in the future.

Train operators

Here is a list of website addresses where you can find information about British and Irish train companies' policies towards bikes. The rules for travelling on trains with a bike vary wherever you go, so checking ahead every time makes good sense, particularly if your journey means using more than one train company.

✔ **For journeys in England and Scotland:** www.nationalrail.co.uk/passenger_services/cyclists/

✔ **For journeys in Wales:** www.arrivatrainswales.co.uk/bicycles/

✔ **For journeys in Northern Ireland:** www.translink.co.uk

✔ **For journeys in Ireland:** www.irishrail.ie/Bicycles/

We should make special mention of the train company Scotrail. It runs a cycle rescue service, so if you have an accident, a major mechanical failure or your bike is vandalised while you're in possession of a valid ticket, they will come and rescue you and help you continue your journey free of charge. You can check out their terms and conditions on their website www.scotrail.co.uk.

The Eurostar, which you can catch from the UK to mainland Europe, takes bikes if you box or bag them. You can then put them into the baggage car free of charge. If you don't want to dismantle your bike, you can make use of the limited spaces available on every train, but you have to pay £30 each way for the privilege.

Rules about bikes on trains vary everywhere you go in Europe. In France, only some of the high-speed TGVs take bikes. You have to check the time-table for the bike icon and book into the limited space for bikes. Regional trains and night trains all take bikes. If your bike is bagged or boxed you shouldn't have a problem on any train. In Spain, only the regional trains take bikes. You can travel all the way round Spain this way, but doing so takes a lot longer than using the intercity trains. In Germany, bikes are allowed on most intercity trains (not the high-speed ones), although you must book space. The German rail website (www.bahn.de) has information on trains all over Europe and a drop down menu on its homepage gives you the option of switching everything on the website into English.

In the US, Amtrak provide bike racks on some trains. Space varies between four bikes per train and three bikes per car and some trains don't take bikes at all, unless you box them up and send them as checked baggage. You must call the company when making a booking to check if you can take your bike on board.

Aeroplanes

On most long-haul flights bikes are just classed as part of your luggage and, as long as they're not individually too heavy, you shouldn't have a problem, though you do have to pack your bike into a box or bag (boxes are best as they protect your bike far better).

Budget airlines charge an extra fee for travelling with a bicycle, and you could incur extra fees if you bike goes over a particular weight limit, so check the conditions of your particular airline before you get to the airport.

A cheap way of preparing your bike for travel is to ask a bike shop for one of the big cardboard boxes that new bikes are delivered in. A bit of polystyrene, bubble wrap and heavy-duty tape can produce a robust container for your bike for next to nothing, and some cheap foam pipe lagging will fit perfectly around your frame tubes to give even more protection. Then, when you arrive at your destination, you can unpack your bike somewhere in the arrivals area and ride away from the airport. You may be able to store the box somewhere at the airport but, if not, find a bike shop that can supply a cardboard box for your return journey.

If you're flying overseas and travelling around, you need to make plans before you start as to how to pack your bike for the return journey. If you're flying in and out of the same place then most hostels or hotels will hang on to your bike box or bag for you while you go off on your travels. Sometimes they charge a small storage fee.

If you're returning home from a different city, give yourself time to get a new box. Depending on what kind of place you're staying in, your accommodation staff might be able to find one for you. Otherwise, you have to find a bike shop yourself.

Getting transport to or from an airport can be difficult with a bike in a box, especially if you don't speak the local lingo. Bike boxes don't fit in cabs and most taxis don't have roof racks, but it's rare to be unable to find a minibus or someone with a bit of imagination who will help shift you and the bike, though you may have a long wait and a more expensive trip. We've both certainly spent what seems like many hours dragging a bike box around the streets of foreign cities at night.

Unless your bike is very light, try to get a box or bag with wheels as boxes can be unwieldy things to carry. If your box is improvised and you're going to be walking a fair distance with it, pack a set of skateboard wheels to tape under one end. This saves it being worn to shreds as you drag it along (as well as stopping you from getting shoulder ache).

If your bike is expensive or on the delicate side (a full-carbon road bike with carbon wheels, for example) then investing in a proper padded bike case is well worth it. These cases can be expensive, but are very strong and are the only way to guarantee that your bike arrives undamaged. Many bike clubs and some shops rent these cases out for a fraction of the price of buying new. However, the downside is that these cases are heavy, they won't take as much of your other stuff (a cardboard bike box always has room for your sleeping bag, helmet, tent, jumpers and much more) and if you're not returning to your starting spot, you have no way of transporting the case.

If you're going to Australia with your bike – a long way, I know, but people do it – make sure you clean it really well before you pack it. In particular, ensure that your tyres are free from mud. Australian officials are very keen to keep out alien earth and always take a look. You save yourself a great deal of time if you're able to display clean black rubber through the top of your box.

Packing a bicycle in a bike box

As bike boxes are designed solely for carrying bikes, it ought to be an easy matter to pack your bicycle into it, but more than once we've witnessed groups of otherwise resourceful bicyclists utterly stumped as to how to fit a bike into a bike box. In this section, we provide instructions on how we pack a bicycle. We use the same method for any of our bikes, including the road bike. Just make sure you start with a suitably sized box – you're not going to get your full-size mountain bike into a box for a child's bike.

Bicycle cases should come with instructions. If you don't have any, check the manufacturer's website.

To disassemble or reassemble your bicycle you need the following:

- ✔ Pedal spanner
- ✔ Set of Allen keys
- ✔ Small adjustable spanner

To pack your bike up, you need the following:

- ✔ Half a dozen short pieces of cord (at least)
- ✔ Lots of bubble wrap
- ✔ Roll of five-centimetre (two-inch) width packing tape

Follow these steps to pack up your bicycle:

1. **Remove your pedals.**

   A pedal spanner works best, but if you don't have a pedal spanner, your small adjustable spanner works fine. Don't forget that your left-hand pedal unscrews in the opposite direction to normal (normal unscrewing is anti-clockwise). A good way to remember is if you stand behind your bike with the spanner pointing upwards, you pull the spanner towards you to unscrew both pedals. Don't leave this until the last moment if you haven't had your pedals off for a while – if the pedals are quite firmly fixed, you might need some help. And it's a chance to make sure your chosen spanner actually fits so you don't have any nasty surprises later on.

2. **Remove your seat.**

   Loosen the bolts that close the top of your seat tube around your seat-post. On some bikes you need a spanner, but more commonly an Allen key. When the bolts are loose, twist and pull the saddle until the seat-post is out.

   Before you move the saddle and seatpost, mark the seatpost with a marker where it emerges from the seat tube so you know the right height to replace it.

3. **Loosen the bolt(s) that clamp the stem to the steerer tube (above the top of the head tube) and twist your handlebars so that they are parallel to your frame.**

   Use a piece of cord to fix them in position.

4. **Remove the front wheel.**

   When the wheel's off, lift the bike into the box to make sure it fits. If your bike is still a bit long for the box, unfasten the handlebars completely and move them further towards the back of the bike, securing them once more.

   Leaving your back wheel on the bike takes less work and is less risky than taking it off. If you take off the back wheel, the bike's weight is resting on the jockey wheel of the rear gear mechanism. This wheel is sensitive and if it gets bent out of position your gears won't work properly. Of course, if you don't have that stuff on your bike, taking off your back wheel is no problem. If removing your back wheel is unavoidable, then turn the frame upside down so that the gears are uppermost and the bike is resting on the crossbar.

   If you have disc brakes and are removing a wheel, make sure you wedge something between the brake pads before you fly with the bike. If the pads aren't separated, they will close at low pressure in the hold of the plane and you won't be able to put your wheel back on. Fold some thin cardboard until it fits snugly or ask at your bike shop – they may have small plastic separators that they can give you.

5. **Deflate your tyres.**

   The airlines like you to deflate your tyres, so don't forget to pack a pump.

6. **Cushion your bike as much as you feel is necessary.**

   You definitely need to wrap (with bubble wrap or rags) the ends of your forks, the main triangle of your frame and both sides of the centres of both wheels. You may also want to wrap your handlebars and the top end of your seat tube. If your rear wheel has a quick-release mechanism, unscrew the plastic cap end and remove the skewer entirely. Screw it back together to carry it so that you don't lose the springs.

7. **Place your front wheel against the side of your frame where it sits as flat as possible and secure it.**

   Tie your front wheel up so that no metal is rubbing against your frame and so it won't move. Tie one of your cranks so they don't move either. If you've had to remove your rear wheel, do the same thing with it on the other side of the frame.

8. **Secure your seat and seatpost.**

   Either wrap your seat and seatpost first or just tie it up to the frame where it fits.

9. **Put your pedals, tools, quick-release skewer and any other bits you have lying around into a bag.**

10. **Pack the bottom of the box with other luggage.**

    Have a look at the bottom of your bike and work out where the gaps will be at the bottom of the box. Stow away your bag of pedals, helmet, sleeping bag or whatever you need to put in there.

11. **Lift your whole bike package into the box.**

    If anything is pushing against the side of the box you can put an extra layer of bubble wrap against the cardboard there.

12. **Stuff anything soft you've got in any space at the top.**

    If you've got two rolls of tape, put one inside the box; otherwise, pack your tape separately.

13. **Seal it all up and label it.**

    Use a huge amount of tape to secure the box. Write your name and flight number on the box with a marker, then pop the marker through one of the handle holes.

Most bikes, packed in a cardboard bike box with a few extra items stuffed in the gaps, shouldn't go over your check-in baggage allowance, but checking in early is always wise if you're flying with a bike. The airline staff won't be panicking about available space at that stage.

The check-in staff will ask you to take your bike to the Outsize Baggage drop-off spot, which can be some distance, where someone will take it from you. You have to find a similarly marked place at your destination to reclaim it.

When you reassemble the bike, do everything in reverse, making sure the seat and handlebars are both dead straight and nice and tight. Don't forget to replace the quick-release skewer. If you're keeping the box, shove all the bubble wrap, cord and tape inside. If not, dispose of it as neatly as possible. Some bike bags can roll up quite tight and you can carry them with you. These bags are bulky, but not at all heavy.

Specialist bike boxes can be worthwhile if your bike is worth thousands, but they aren't cheap. You can craft a perfectly effective and inexpensive home-made version with cardboard, tape and bubblewrap. Given a bit of time and ingenuity, they can be just as good at keeping your pride and joy safe and sound.

Arriving with a bicycle

Pedalling into a country village in Cambodia, Colombia, Calabria or Wales on a bicycle always ensures you a very warm welcome. People from small rural communities all over the world know about bikes, and if you ride into their domain they see you as the same, not different. You're not speeding through cocooned in a bubble of your own world, you're arriving as part of theirs. All you've got to do is smile and you've got friends.

Sophisticated city slickers can be less up to speed if they're more used to tugging a forelock for anyone with a fancy car, but keeping the right attitude wherever you travel almost always gets results.

What you require of accommodation when arriving with a bike depends very much on first impressions. If, for example, you notice gangs of indolent wastrels looking hungrily at your running gear as you pedal down a main street, you might well want to insist on having your bike in your bedroom. Ask nicely and this request isn't unreasonable. You can always offer to carry it there so that it doesn't touch the ground.

Most places to stay have a secure place where people leave luggage after checking out. If you can persuade hotel staff of the value of your bike, you should be able to leave your bike there. If you don't get a positive result, try staying somewhere else or just insist on the bike in the bedroom. Nothing is quite like opening your eyes in the morning and gazing up at your beloved handlebars.

We heard a story once about a man riding across Africa who used to chain his bike to a tree before entering a village on foot. One day he returned to find the bike gone. The awful thing was he had a great many banknotes rolled up inside the handlebars. Cyclists do get ripped off now and then – although we've read many stories about people travelling in remote parts of the world on bicycles and we're convinced this type of thing is a very rare event. If ever we're alone on an isolated road we split money and medication into three lots and carry some under out clothes, some in pockets and some hidden in panniers. So far, this trick has not been tested.

Communicating with the folks back home

Talking to the folks back home can be an uplifting part of travelling, and knowing that everything is okay is also enormously important for those you've left behind. Even 20 years ago, making international calls when travelling could mean booking phone time and using phrases like 'station to station'. Communication is now light years ahead of how it used to be and improving all the time.

A few years ago Gavin was bowled over – and delighted – when his companion in the high Andes picked up a payphone in a village square, popped about 50 pence in the slot, dialled straight through to a friend in Australia and had a good old chat. Doing this isn't yet as easy as that in every country, but things are always getting better.

What is almost universal now is online access. Internet cafés are everywhere and you can email, blog, Facebook or Twitter your way round the world with no problem at all. Staying in touch this way isn't quite the same as hearing the voice of your loved one, but is still a brilliant way of keeping in touch with as many people as you like. You can also recheck your upcoming travel arrangements, book accommodation for the following day's destination or just search for a picture of the strange-sounding animal you ate the previous night. (Let's hope it wasn't endangered.)

Many international airports have free web access now. You may only get 15 minutes at a time, but you can always take two turns. Internet cafés in less developed countries are always very cheap. Often these cafés are packed and the only problem you might have is finding an empty chair.

If your travels take you somewhere a bit more remote, consider taking a satellite phone. You can use satellite phones anywhere in the world, but they're expensive both to hire and to use. Bear in mind, though, that if you don't have an electricity supply for more than a few days, the phone will run out of juice. You can get very good solar chargers these days, but you'll have to rig up a clever system on your bike so you can ride and charge at the same time.

Staying in touch with people who care for you is important. You obviously know when you're having a great time, you've achieved what you set out to do and you're letting your hair down in a big way. But if you don't communicate this, all your devoted family and friends will think that you've been eaten by bears. Don't make any promises you can't keep, however. If you say you're going to call and you don't, you'll certainly disappoint and worry them, so be realistic about when and how often you'll be able to keep in touch.

Preparing Your Bike

New or old, get your bike checked out if you're planning on taking it away with you. Bikes need a certain amount of 'running in' and cables, gears and even brakes might need a little tweaking on a new bike. Older bikes could (almost) have a million and one things waiting to snap or burst, and if you're not trained in spotting these things you won't know.

Part of getting your bike ready for a trip is thinking through how you're going to use it. You may know the right kind of bags to carry (refer to Chapter 3 for a run-down on different panniers and racks), but by asking yourself what you're going to need and when, you gain a better understanding of where to put things so that you're not being constantly held up. Riding a bike is all about hassle-free travel and you should do your best to keep it that way.

Knowing that your bike is ready

Take your bike down to your local bike shop and tell them what you're planning. Be ready to tell them how many miles per day, how many days, what kind of roads and what kind of country. They'll tell you what kind of service you need. Bike services range from around £50 for a standard service, where staff check, adjust and lube gears, brakes and anything else they can spot check, to a gold-class, supreme service for upwards of £100. For this service, they'll be practically stripping down and rebuilding your bike to make sure everything's perfect. For that price we'd hope to get a foot massage and a glass of bubbly too, but we're sure a good explore around a bike shop would make us feel just as good.

Keep in mind the following when getting your bike serviced before a big trip:

✔ Think about how much gear you're going to be loading on the back and let staff at the bike shop know your plans. They may think you're going to put too much pressure on the chain and rear cassette and might suggest some new, tougher parts. Or they might have some ideas about spreading your load, depending on what kind of bike you have.

> ✔ Ask staff if they can suggest any particular tyre pressure for your trip, or if they have any other recommendations for things to watch out for or things to take.
>
> ✔ When you've had your service, take your bike out for a long ride. Whatever daily distances you've got in mind for your excursion, ride that many miles. Ask questions. How is your bicycle doing? Is it making any strange noises? Are the gears changing smoothly? And how are you feeling? Are you entirely comfortable on that saddle? If you've anything to report, get straight back down to the bike shop and let them know.

Prepping panniers

You're going to be living out of your panniers for a short while – maybe a long while – so put some thought into how you're going to use them. Some panniers have lots of little pockets, some are just single-cavity sacks, but you'll always have two – one on either side (unless you've got front ones too) – and they're not very big. The section 'Carrying Essentials' later in this chapter covers what you can put in panniers, but at this stage you can be fairly sure they're going to be full. And full means fairly heavy.

Try loading up your panniers with some books and clothes and have a good long ride with all your new, extra weight. Cycling with panniers is a bit different – harder work, and cycling uphill is more difficult. Even pushing the bike is much more of a chore. If you've got time, practise riding with full panniers more than once. The more training you get, the less of a shock to your system it is when you finally hit the road.

When you're shoving in the ballast, have a think about how much (or how little) room these bags have inside. Keep in mind that you're going to have to carry some water and food – possibly quite a lot – so you can't fill your panniers up entirely with other stuff.

When you're packing to get on the road, stay organised. Keep all your clothes together in one spot, all your food and drink in another. Have all your tools and spare parts in one bag at the bottom of one pannier, put your fist-aid kit and medicines together in another spot. Plastic bags are bad news for the environment, but very useful when packing panniers. They keep all related items together and also keep them dry, should you encounter a downpour. Having this extra protection for your stuff is worthwhile even if your panniers claim to be waterproof.

When packing your panniers try to balance the weight on either side of the bike. Proper balance helps you keep control when you go round corners.

Using handlebar bags and more

Panniers are a great way of carrying all your gear, but some stuff you need to get at more easily and some things you need to have on you all the time. Depending on how much stuff is involved, you've got a few options for these vital items, including the following:

✔ **Handlebar bags:** These are a favourite of many cyclists. They sit right in front of you, giving you easy access to your map, camera, bottle of water, sandwich or phone. They are often lockable and mean that you don't have to wear anything on your back. Being without a load on you is a definite advantage – not only do you not have the weight and constriction, but in a hot place any kind of backpack makes you sweat profusely. If you walk away from the bike, however, you may have to do some shuffling for the security of your valuables if you leave the handlebar bag in position. If you take it with you, most have removable straps so you can sling them over your shoulder.

✔ **Small backpacks or courier bags:** These work well for your few precious items, but getting things in and out takes more effort – you have to stop – and the delay in reaching your camera could lose you the shot. You sweat more with a backpack, but at least everything stays with you when you get off the bike without any moving or organising.

✔ **Clothes with lots of pockets:** These can be very useful, but whether this option works for you depends on how many items you want quick access to or safekeeping for; however, if your bidon cage is enough for your fluid supply, a pair of cargo pants and even a fishing vest should give you plenty of spots for essentials. If you're in a hot spot, putting vulnerable items, such as your passport, your phone or anything made of paper, in a plastic bag for protection against moisture, is a sensible idea.

We usually favour the pocket option for storing all our essentials and valuables, but a number of times this has brought wry comments at airport security checks when it has taken some considerable time to unload all our compartments into the plastic tray.

Carrying Essentials

When you decide to take a trip on your bicycle, you're leaving behind the world where you can say to yourself, 'I'm going to take this because, you never know, I might want to wear it.' You've got very limited space in your bags and you have to leave some of this free for the food and drink you buy as you go.

Even though you can only take the bare minimum of essentials, you still have to make choices, with your selections determined by the region you're headed for, the climate, the road conditions, where you intend to sleep and how long you're going for.

Before you make any decisions about what to take, check out these things about the place you're going to:

- ✔ **Climate and weather:** Is it going to be hot or cold, wet or dry?

- ✔ **Dangerous diseases:** Will you need protection? Visit a travel doctor.

- ✔ **Political unrest:** Are there any dangers from general civil disorder, terrorists or even bandits along your route? If so, perhaps you should go somewhere else.

- ✔ **Remoteness:** How far off the beaten track are you heading? This affects how much carrying space you need for your food and drink and also the number and type of spares and tools you need to take.

Have a good look at the size of your panniers and racks and start writing lists.

Compiling a small tool kit

The following lists the bike tools you might take on a bicycle expedition and notes how essential they may be:

- ✔ **Allen keys:** These small, cross-sectionally hexagonal, L-shaped, metal bars tighten almost all of the bolt fittings on your bicycle and come in different sizes. Make sure you've got one for every fitting on your bike or just take the full set. Essential.

- ✔ **Bicycle multi-tool:** These handy little combos have Allen keys, screwdrivers and often more, all in fold-away format. Saves taking Allen keys, screwdrivers and often more.

- ✔ **Cable ties:** These ties are amazing things – they have an almost unlimited number of uses and you never know when you'll need one. Pack a handful – you won't regret it.

- ✔ **Chain-breaker:** If you have to fix your chain, you won't do it without this lovely tool. Being able to fix your chain could make or break your trip. Chains rarely break, but it does happen. Only take one if you know how to use it.

- ✔ **Cord:** Some tough cord for tying packs to racks or just to hold your bike together can save your bacon. Essential.

- **Pedal spanner:** These spanners are so much easier than using an adjustable spanner and your pedals might be coming on and off like hazard lights while you're away. They do have some weight, but are very flat.

- **Pliers:** A small pair of pliers could come in really handy.

- **Pump:** Essential.

- **Puncture repair kit:** Splash out and buy the patches you don't need glue for, but just make sure you've got plenty. Essential.

- **Screwdrivers:** You have some fixtures, such as lights, that you need to screw on, so get yourself short Phillips- and flat-head screwdrivers. You'll probably need them.

- **Small adjustable spanner:** This 15-centimetre (6-inch) metal tool with the rotating adjuster isn't the toughest in the world, but it does a whole bunch of jobs. Essential.

- **Tyre levers:** Tyre levers are what you use to lever your tyre from its wheel and are small and usually made of plastic. Essential.

Keeping spares

You could take lots of replacement parts, but you also need to carry as little as possible. Take what you're comfortable with: I know some people worry about certain things going wrong more than others and you need peace of mind as well as the right spares. Some parts really are essential, so here's a quick list of spares to pack:

- **Batteries:** Pack spares for your lights, camera or hand-held fan.

- **Chain link connectors:** With a broken chain these get you going in an emergency.

- **Inner tubes:** Pack at least two spares.

- **Nuts:** If you've got any spare nuts and bolts lying around that fit your racks, chuck them in – you never know. The most common problem I've read about when bike touring in tough country – and one I've had, too – is rack fittings failing. A few nuts and bolts could save you a lot of grief.

- **Small bottle of lube:** Chains can keep on going for a long time, but when it rains they become bare and soon rust. Pack some spare lube to keep them running smoothly.

- **Spokes:** If a spoke breaks, even if you find a bike shop, they might not have the right spoke for your bike. Having a couple of spares could save a lot of bother and they don't take up any room.

- ✔ **Tyres:** If you're planning on a long trip on a road followed by a big ride along a rough trail, it makes sense to start with slicks and then fit some more knobbly tyres. If you do this, you must get tyres with a Kevlar bead, as they're the only ones you can fold. Tyres are bulky though – I always go for a compromise tyre.

- ✔ **Other items:** Some people like to take spare gear/brake cables and brake blocks – and I've even heard of someone crossing Australia with a spare roll of bar-tape. You decide what other spares are essential to you.

Packing clothes

Probably the most difficult list to write for yourself is the clothes you need to take. Most people take far too much stuff. We recently read the blog of a guy who seemed to be a very accomplished cycle tourer, but when we got to his list of clothes to pack we had to stop when we got to 'one tie'. A tie was the item that broke the camel's back as far as we were concerned. We had just hit the point where we couldn't carry everything he listed in our arms and we couldn't go any further.

When Gavin went to South America to spend three weeks in the Peruvian Amazon with his hardtail MTB, he took only one change of clothes. He did buy a T-shirt when he got there, but it was more of a souvenir than something he needed.

Consider the following when planning what clothes to pack:

- ✔ If you go to a cold place, you obviously need more clothes – the right layers to keep warm and waterproof things if you're going to face wet weather.

- ✔ If you have very few clothes with you, you need to wash things frequently or just put up with being a bit grubby longer than you normally would. Nobody expects you to turn up in the jungle fit for fine-dining.

- ✔ Divide the clothes you're planning to take into three piles. One pile is for things you might need, one for things you almost certainly need and one for things you can't do without. Take only the last pile. (This tip is good for everything you pack, not just your clothes.)

In order to cut down on your eventual 'pile for packing', try riding your bike in ordinary clothes rather than bike shorts and jerseys. Give it a go: you could find that the warnings about chafing are exaggerated. Cyclists rarely wear this stuff in the big cycling nations of the world and they seem to do just fine. You save a good amount of pannier space if you do without a specialist mode of dress for your cycling.

Carrying food and drink

One of the greatest joys of travelling for us is to sample foods we've never seen before and enjoy a wide variety of different meals. People of the world dream up some amazing concoctions and combinations – although consuming something the local people consider quite ordinary can sometimes be a challenge. But when it comes to packing your panniers with food and drink, you do have to get right down to basics.

Your needs as a cyclist are foods high in carbohydrate. These foods are your fuel, and if you don't get enough, you will weaken. You'll feel ill and tired and you won't be able to carry on. People eat carbohydrate everywhere, though: meals all round the world are based around rice, bread, pasta, potatoes or various other sources of complex carbohydrate. If you're eating out, you're unlikely to have any difficulty getting some of the right stuff.

If you're not planning on eating out that much, follow these tips for still ensuring you get enough carbohydrate in your diet:

- ✔ If you're camping and packing a stove, rice, lentils, rolled oats or noodles are all good carbohydrate choices. Two-minute noodles can give you more interesting flavours and we could carry on eating them indefinitely.

- ✔ For picnics and rest stops, biscuits are cheap and full of energy.

- ✔ Trail mix is easy to make from nuts, dried fruit, seeds and cereals. What you can get depends on where you are, but even a very simple mix will be tasty, nutritious and good fuel for your cycling.

- ✔ Fresh fruit is a great idea if you have access to it, but in a lot of places you should only eat what you can peel. (Consult your travel doctor for more precise instructions.)

Water is perhaps your most important consideration if you're crossing long distances and you're not sure what you'll find. Calculate what you'll need. A litre (just under half a pint) an hour is perfect, but you may not be able to carry or drink this amount. If you think you may not have enough, work out how much you have for each hour and ration yourself. If you're in a group, ration everybody and make sure water is shared correctly. Travelling companions do sometimes drink more than their share without thinking. You've got to keep an eye on them. A very close eye.

If you've been rationing your water and then come across an unexpected source, buy everything you can and guzzle down what won't fit in your panniers.

Taking toiletries and medical supplies

Without even thinking of medical matters, the first two items you should always carry on a bike tour are sunscreen and lip balm. Never, ever look at the sky in the morning and say to yourself, 'No, I don't think I'll need the sunscreen today.'

A small first-aid kit is something you should carry wherever you go, particularly if you're planning on a bicycle tour. You might think you already know enough about dressing wounds and what to do in a crisis, but we also strongly recommend doing an emergency first-aid course so that you really are ready for anything.

When you've got yourself up to speed, what dressings and tools to put in a first-aid kit is up to you. Here are some suggestions:

- **Alcohol wipes:** These are useful for cleaning your own hands quickly before dressing wounds.

- **Antiseptic:** Antiseptic is useful for cleaning wounds and can include tea-tree oil or iodine.

- **Bandages and sling:** A stretchy bandage is necessary for sprains.

- **Clear, waterproof surgical dressings:** You can leave these on for days. Pack a few 8 × 10–centimetre (3 x 4-inch) and 10 × 15-centimetre (4 x 6-inch) ones.

- **Diarrhoea medicine and rehydration salts:** That you'll have some sort of stomach upset is almost inevitable if you're travelling off the beaten track in a developing country. You can get diarrhoea packs which contain a variety of different medicines for different conditions. Carrying these with you turns something that could be very unpleasant into a mild inconvenience. Essential.

- **Latex gloves in sterile packs:** Make sure the gloves are the right size for you.

- **Non-stick dressings:** These dressings are great when you want a wound to dry out. You'll need surgical tape to fix them on and crêpe bandages for wrapping.

- **Plasters:** Sticking plasters are great for small cuts and blisters on your feet (or anywhere else).

- **Saline solution:** Basically, saline solution is salt water and is a natural, gentle antiseptic.

- **Sterile tweezers:** Tweezers are essential for picking grit from abrasions.

Also think about basic toiletries, such as soap, deodorant and sanitary items (if required), and medicines to carry, based on where you're going – although some medicines, such as paracetamol, are good to take anywhere. You can either see a travel doctor for advice specific to the part of the world you're headed for or look up the dangers in the region yourself and see your GP.

If you're travelling to anywhere outside the developed world, you may need to receive vaccinations for diseases such as hepatitis A and B, malaria, rabies, dengue, typhoid and tetanus. See a travel doctor or a travel vaccination centre for advice specific to the area you're travelling to. You could also take medicines, such as antibiotics, for use if you have a wound, get very sick or are travelling to high altitude. Any prescription medicine you do take should be in its original packaging, which will have your name on it, from the pharmacist.

If you have a medical condition, think about wearing a metal tag around your neck or wrist, engraved with your name and details. Consider having it translated into the language spoken at your destination. If you're on continuous medication, think about posting some of it before you go to a place where you can pick it up on your travels.

Fitting in a tent and survival gear

If you're buying a tent specifically to go bicycle touring, the first thing to consider is where you're going to put it. Bear in mind you'll probably also be packing a sleeping bag and one of those self-inflating bed-rolls. Will you have room in a pannier, or will they be tied to the rack between panniers? Size is the important factor as far as your bike is concerned.

Whether you're going to share the tent, how much you're going to use it, what the weather might be (and consequently how much protection you need the tent to provide) and what colour you prefer are all things for you to sort out personally.

If you're sharing camping gear, make sure the load is spread between bikes and you're not the one carrying it all.

Additional items that you might find handy to carry, and might be grouped into the category of 'survival gear', include the following:

- ✔ **A compass:** This is a particularly useful item if you're travelling with a map. You occasionally meet with a physical reality that doesn't correspond with what's on a map. One should never underestimate the imaginative powers and talents of cartographers, and you also need to bear in mind that people who draw maps these days very rarely visit the places they chart, most especially remote ones. It's often a question of filling in the gaps, and mistakes in map-making can travel through generations of their authors.

✔ **Personal locator beacons:** These send a signal to orbiting satellites, which is then passed on to the appropriate emergency rescue organisation. It's a worldwide system and when you set one off they run for a minimum of 24 hours, some of them for up to a week. The signal is personalised, and more modern devices have a GPS facility that sends out your exact location as part of the distress signal. These little machines are fantastic – but pretty expensive.

✔ **Space blankets:** These blankets are small and very light, and packing a couple could be a big help in an emergency. Not only good when someone is freezing, space blankets are also useful when someone is going into shock. They deflect heat (shiny side out) as well as retaining it, so can also help in harsh, bright sun – and because they're so shiny, you can use them to reflect light as a signal.

✔ **A whistle:** A whistle is also an effective signal, but only if you carry it on your person, not in your panniers. In the circumstances when you might need to use one, that you'll have access to your luggage is by no means certain.

Words of warning

You should and shouldn't say certain things to people when you're travelling around on a bicycle. And you should be very careful about answering – and asking – certain questions.

Obviously, don't even think about answering questions like, 'Where do you keep all your money?', but even give something like, 'Where are you camping tonight?' some thought. 'Where do you suggest?' is a good response, but it might be an idea to give a false indication of how far you intend to travel.

In my experience, meeting up with a person of evil intent is very rare when you travel on a bike, but it does occasionally happen, in any part of the world. The best thing to do is to say as little as possible and get away as fast as you can. If you find yourself with an unwanted companion as you make your way down a lonely road, try to lose them before they've learnt much about you and your plans. Stopping at a roadside café or service station and just staying put until your new friend has gone is one option. Alternatively, continuing to smile and tell the person as politely as you can that you don't want the pleasure of their company is better than putting up with it.

You can ask people 'How far is it?' as many times as you like, but be wary of the answers you get. Lots of people give hopeless answers when it comes to estimating distances, especially when they're quite small ones in places they've probably lived all their lives. Try it out: ask three people and see what different responses you get.

You often get similarly useless information if you ask about road conditions or hills. Most people have probably just never considered these things in the way that a cyclist does, and so will give you what they think is an informed reply, but which will most likely turn out to be nonsense.

Unfortunately, it seems to be a natural human response to try to be helpful and give someone an answer – even if you don't have any idea what the right answer is.

Chapter 13

Cycling with Other People

· ·

In This Chapter

▶ Bunching up with other cyclists

▶ Clubbing it

▶ Massing together at events

· ·

*R*iding a bicycle is fun. You may be the sort of person who enjoys solitary pursuits – and we wouldn't argue that spending hours riding through the country on your own isn't a great way to while away a day – but sooner or later you'll find yourself out with other people on bikes and you'll realise that's a lot of fun too.

Being with other riders who enjoy cycling just like you heightens your pleasure. You don't just feel the joy: you see it too. You share positive experiences and you learn from those around you. Whether you're just out for a casual half hour or you're meeting up with your training crew for a long, punishing session, your cycling has become social and you're part of the bicycling community.

People get together for all sorts of reasons to ride bikes. Sometimes to raise money for charity, or sometimes so people can meet to ride and talk about getting a better deal for cyclists. But for everyone, sharing the fun of riding adds a human element to enhance your cycling pleasure.

In this chapter, we cover all aspects of riding in groups, including riding for fun with family and friends, and riding in more organised groups.

Riding in Groups

In the following sections, we cover diverse clusters of cyclists who get together to do the same kind of riding. In each group, individuals may know each other, but even if they don't, they all want the same specific thing from being part of that group. Whether that thing is just local family exercise and fun, or a bunch of fast girls in matching jerseys, they know what kind of cycling they like and they know the advantages of doing it with other people.

All the instances covered here of people riding together show how participants benefit substantially from being with others. In fact, these groupings only exist because of these benefits. Members have organised their riding habits to get more out of cycling.

The following sections are really only examples of groups available for you to join or create. If you think you could do better with any kind of cycling, or could bring cycling into a social activity to improve it, then find some other riders and talk to them. Those riders are bound to agree and you only have to take some simple steps to get everyone together and having more fun.

Cycling with friends and family

Riding bikes with the family is always fun, as well as being a fantastic, healthy way to spend time together. Even if you've got tiny family members you can strap them on somehow (see Chapter 14 for the most appropriate way of doing this) and bring them along.

Even though family rides are a great activity, they often don't happen spontaneously and you may have to put your foot down to keep them going. We've certainly experienced middle-sized children complaining that they don't want to go out on bikes – and then, when they've been coerced into riding, having more fun than you've ever seen. It often can be a matter of, 'You think you don't want to, but you do really.'

Having a bike is an important part of being a child. It gives a young person a sense of freedom and achievement at the same time as having all the excitement of a go-kart or a roller coaster. But having a bike isn't just about enjoyment: when you give a child a bicycle, you give them a means of learning a healthy physical activity that they can take with them into adulthood as a positive part of life.

Enforcing the message that a bicycle isn't a toy is perhaps most important when children become young adults, when they start to distance themselves from childish things. Bikes are as much about good health, caring for your environment and being social as they are about efficient, responsible transport. And the best way to implement these ideas is by riding with young adult family members whenever you can.

Try following these tips to get (and keep) the whole family involved in cycling:

✔ Promise shorter distances than those you'd prefer or are used to in order to get the whole family out. And give some thought to other incentives along the way – a playground or a park are good carrots to dangle.

✔ Take things easy if you're trying to encourage beginners. If you get to be quite good at cycling and want your non-cycling partner to join in, remember how it was when you were a first-timer. Your loved one might have a great new bike, but even tiny hills are scary enough to put some people off riding at all. Keep it short and easy if you want to sell cycling to someone who isn't sure.

✔ Team up if you've got family friends who like to ride bikes. Doing this gives an extra incentive for any family member who's a little reluctant. If numbers permit, think about getting a rack at the back of your car so that you can drive the family and bikes to a new location (refer to Chapter 12 for different ways of carrying bikes on cars). This way you can get to the best spots on long trails, paths that lead to waterfalls or alongside rivers, or shared paths on long stretches of beach and seafront.

✔ Use regular rides as a great way to catch up with friends. You can exercise without the breathlessness of the gym, but with the privacy of a small group. Make it a Sunday morning thing and everyone will start looking forward to their regular session of gossip, news and exercise. Of course, because gathering for a ride is a healthy get-together, you can treat yourselves to sitting down at a café along the way and indulging in a coffee or more.

If you're in a larger bunch, or if your group has a newcomer, share your conversation as you ride. Pick a new partner to chat with and make sure the ride is a social one for everyone.

Catching the bike bus: Don't be late!

One ingenious way that cyclists get together is a bike bus. A *bike bus* is a commuting system where cyclists gather all along a particular route so that they can ride in a number that makes them safer. This arrangement is called a bus because it does have a particular, set route and even a timetable. When you know the bus is coming you just wait and join in when the bikes arrive.

Bike bus riders tend to all wear bright clothing for extra visibility and safety and they ride two abreast, also for extra safety. An experienced rider always leads the bus. Unlike regular buses, bike buses are free and, as with any bike commuting, riders get to work invigorated and ready for anything.

Different buses ride at different paces. Some go at a social speed, easy for chatting on the way to work. Some are known as *expresses* and riders are expected to pedal at up to 20 miles per hour for perhaps an hour. Speak to the organiser of the bike bus to find out if you'll be able to keep up.

If no bike bus runs on your commuter route, why not start one? Speak to bike commuters at work, try an online forum or even just stop cyclists you see (not the ones going very fast) and ask them if they're interested. We've stopped many cyclists to talk to them while we've been out riding over the years and we've never found a single one that wasn't helpful and friendly. Even two bikes riding together every day can be safer and give you more confidence on your morning (and afternoon) commute.

Tagging along with bunch riders: They're not bananas

Bunch riding, where cyclists ride in a tight pack, might look scary, but it makes a lot of sense if you want to ride far and fast. The reason for riding in this way is to lower wind resistance. Most sources say that riders in a bunch save up to 30 per cent of effort as they avoid battling against the air and wind in front of them, which means they can ride faster without getting puffed and keep it up for long periods.

Of course, the rider at the front of the group does face the wind and this makes work hard up front, but that's why bunch riders rotate. Riders only spend a short time at the front, and then move to the back of the group to wait their turn once more.

Getting up close and personal

Just how close you need to ride in a pack to save all this energy is quite difficult to say. Some people say riding behind someone at a distance of 50 centimetres (almost 20 inches) is enough to make a big drop in resistance, but if you check out a fast, experienced pack, you'll see they're much closer than that, sometimes never getting more than 10 centimetres (4 inches) apart.

Close bunch riding is absolutely not recommended if you're not used to cycling this way. The big danger of bunch riding is when your front wheel touches the rear wheel of the bike in front. If this happens, you hit the road and, even if you're not badly hurt, any bike behind will go straight into you and that rider could be seriously injured.

If you want to learn to ride this way you need some cyclists to tag onto. Tell them you want to learn and, as long as you can keep up, they won't mind you hanging on the back of the bunch just to practise proximity. As soon as you're comfortable with being up close to a leading wheel you can start to rotate and take turns at the front.

Keeping your front wheel slightly to one side, but never overlapping, the wheel in front is safer and allows you a better view of riders and the road in front. Staying squarely behind the cyclist in front gives you a very limited range of vision. And remember that if you take your eyes off the wheel in front you will be faced with an up-close posterior.

A few years ago a bike-clothing manufacturer produced some shorts that had a mesh section for ventilation towards the top of the bottom. This section was see-through, making these shorts very unpopular with riders used to cycling in a tight bunch.

Signalling intent

Riders in packs do have to steer away from obstacles and instances occur when they slow down, so you've got to be very alert in a bunch. Bunch riders use a number of signals and calls, and these signals get passed all the way back through the pack.

Hazards on the ground get shouted out (such as 'Glass!' or 'Pothole!') and the appropriate arm is pointed directly down on the side of the danger. If a walker or parked car has to be avoided the call goes down the line and a hand gets placed over the small of the back, palm facing to the rear, on the side of the obstruction. If the front riders are slowing or stopping they call out 'Slowing!' or 'Stopping!' If a car is coming from the opposite direction and the front riders think the bunch needs to know they call out 'Car up!' If a car is coming from the rear, those at the back call out 'Car back!' These calls and signals are just used when any of these situations is a hazard to the bunch.

One situation when a bunch is likely to slow and riders need to beware is when the pack hits a hill. Often a *rollback* occurs when cyclists step up onto their pedals and this unexpected slowing can cause upset to riders too close behind.

Rotating

You can use a few different ways of rotating in a bunch and riders need to agree the preferred method before they get on their bikes if they're not used to riding with each other. Four or more riders usually cycle two abreast, always doing so on a road with two or more lanes. Front riders do work a lot harder, so the other riders don't expect them to stay up front for long – maybe just a few miles – unless they're stronger cyclists and don't mind taking the lion's share of leading.

A common method of rotating is for the two front riders to move outwards (the left one to the left, the right one to the right) when the time comes to roll back, slow slightly as the bunch comes between them and then tuck back in at the rear.

Another method is for the rider on the right at the front to accelerate slightly and move in front of the rider to his left. The rider who had been behind him on the right moves forward (as does the whole right-hand line) and takes position as the right-hand leader. Using this method, riders have to be careful not to speed the whole bunch up at the changeover.

Riders have to learn not to *half wheel,* which is when one of the front riders lets her front wheel get a little bit in front of the one to the left or right. When the other rider moves forward to get even and the half wheeler tries to keep that very slight lead, the whole bunch can start to get faster and faster.

When riding in single file, front riders try to peel off to the side that the wind is coming from. If there isn't any wind, they'll usually travel to the back on the left-hand side of the bunch, as this is considered safer.

If a strong, angled cross-wind is apparent, riders move to the sheltered side of the rider in front, creating diagonal lines of cyclists. This technique isn't designed to emulate synchronised swimmers – it's all about wind resistance, and is called riding in an *echelon.*

By riding up close to another cyclist, you're placing a great deal of trust in that person. If you're not used to riding with an individual or group, be careful. If you don't know for certain how that rider in front is going to behave, keep your distance.

Having fun

We've mentioned already (a lot) that riding a bike is fun. It really is – the best of fun. But sometimes groups of cyclists get together and do things that are even more fun, including the following:

- ✔ Bike dinners are a simple idea. Get your friends to meet at a spot where you can all ride to your favourite restaurant.

- ✔ Full moon rides take a little bit of organising, but if you've got a few adventurous friends they can be a blast. On the right day of the cycle of the moon, take a train out to a distant spot on a river trail or other bike-way, timing your arrival for nightfall. Ride by the glorious lunar light, turning off your lamps if you feel bold. Take along some snacks and a bottle of wine for a moonlit picnic.

- ✔ Taking a ride to the seaside can be great fun. Just get down to the beach and have a paddle and an ice-cream.

- ✔ Riding your bike in fancy dress can also take a bit more planning but the options are virtually limitless. You can arrange a ride in any kind of fancy dress – tog up as zookeepers, Zorro or zebras and parade through a public space. (You can even go on special rides where everyone turns up in tweed. Refer to Chapter 4 for information about the Tweed Run.)

✔ Then there's the World Naked Bike Ride, which really is an organised event that takes place in cities across the country and around the world. You don't have to be completely naked to take part, but how often do you get the chance to cycle down the streets of a major city completely starkers with a load of other similarly undressed people?

Do an online search on Bike Fun and your location. If you're lucky, there'll already be a group of funsters organising exciting happenings. Otherwise, put your thinking cap on under your helmet, get some friends together – and go out and have some fun.

Joining an Organised Group

Whether you want to race against roadies, climb the ladder of mountain bike riders or just join in with a mixed bunch of local bicyclists, you can almost certainly find a group in your area and they'll be looking forward to seeing you.

You can join many specialist bicycle groups, but in the following section we just cover what local broad-membership groups, racing clubs and mountain bike clubs have to offer.

You probably already know if you're interested in signing up with either of the latter two, but the first of these could be the kind of group that you didn't even know existed and does the kind of riding – and other things – that has you hooked.

Catching BUGs: Your local bicycle users' group

BUGs, or *bicycle users' groups,* do a range of different things. Most commonly, BUGs are active within the scope of a local government authority and they organise regular rides and events, and advocate for better facilities for and treatment of cyclists, or both.

Workplace BUGs also exist, set up perhaps in a university, government department or large company, which have the same range of activities.

The great thing about BUGs is that they're local. If they put on a ride, it's going to be close by and all the people attending will live somewhere in the neighbourhood (or work in the same place). The advantage of this is that they pull together riders who have very similar interests and concerns, and when these cyclists get together and chat they soon have an agenda of local problems to fix.

And that's the other great thing about BUGs: they know exactly what needs to be done to improve the lot of local cyclists. They don't approach problems as part of a regional plan – they just know what they want sorted and how they want it done. They know about unused land and back streets when it comes to planning bikeways and they always know about spots that cyclists can't avoid that need fixing right now.

Too often authorities ignore major problems because they're too hard – or too expensive – and make a big show of putting in bike lanes where cyclists don't need any particular help (because plenty of room exists there anyway). BUGs can refocus attention on where real problems lie and force representatives and officials to acknowledge where work really needs to be done. BUGs don't normally have to get tough with anyone; they just have a much stronger voice because they represent quite a number of local people who ride bicycles.

As soon as you get riding around your neighbourhood, you'll probably develop some pretty strong feelings about the way some roads and junctions are laid out. You might feel strongly enough to start a campaign of writing to traffic authorities and politicians, and good for you – we wish you the very best of luck. But if you're lucky, you live in an area where a BUG is set up and you can go along to one of their meetings, or just join them on a ride, and chat with other people who may very well feel the same way as you do. If you then want to start approaching those people who make decisions about providing for cyclists, you can do it as part of your BUG where you have a much stronger voice.

If you find that nobody is listening you might try doing a bike count or organising a ride through a problem spot and contacting the local paper. If you're lucky enough to have accomplished cyclists living in your area and can persuade them to join in you'll have reporters along in no time.

But BUGs aren't just about changing the world. In our experience, the strongest BUGs, in all areas in which they're active, are those that have regular rides that get local cyclists out riding with each other. BUGs typically organise different rides to cater for different skill levels – they cater for fitter riders as well as beginners and families. You're bound to find that some of these rides suit your ability. Even if the rides sound too easy, if you go along, you'll be cycling with people who have a couple of things in common with you and strengthening a valuable asset within the local community.

If your BUG isn't doing something you'd like it to, we're pretty sure they welcome suggestions and input to fill the gap. BUGs are a vital part of getting better facilities for cyclists as well as an invaluable resource for many people who just don't want to go out and cycle alone. You may have to pay a small fee for joining a BUG, but often you can join for free. They deserve your support and if you've got one in your neck of the woods we strongly recommend you go along and check them out.

Racing road bikes

Bicycles hadn't been invented long before would-be winners were practising at high speed. In fact fewer racing clubs are active now than there were 80 or 100 years ago, but you can still easily find them. Cycling clubs dedicated to road and track racing are all over the UK, and some of them are huge.

To race in the UK you must be licensed by British Cycling – the organisation that regulates bike racing. You don't have to be Bradley Wiggins to race at a local club. You have to do your best, but not everybody is super-fast. If you're quite new to road bikes, just let your club know and they'll put you up against similar-strength cyclists. British Cycling issue different types of licence, which depend on your age and what level you want to compete at. You can organise this licence when you join a local club. You can also get day licences if you just want to give a race a go.

The various licences give you eligibility to enter certain races, accumulate points towards national or regional rankings and different levels of insurance cover for personal accident and public liability, both while racing and training, including training on your own. Check the British Cycling website (www.britishcycling.org.uk) for details of the insurance cover.

Some clubs have try-out membership fees. You pay a lower amount and get to compete in a few races – then, if you decide to join, they deduct this try-out fee from your full membership fee. This way, you get to learn if racing is really for you and what kind of people make up the membership of the club without being too out of pocket.

Cycling clubs usually hold events at least once a week and can tell you about training rides with other members that you'll be very welcome to join. These rides will be of varying length and speed, so there's bound to be something you can join in with.

As well as racing, you can train with cycling clubs, too. Club cyclists are likely to already have a programme worked out that may or may not have intervals (refer to Chapter 11 for more), but will contain some challenging elements. Any lone cyclist will probably slow down here and there without being aware of it, but when you're with a bunch you don't get that opportunity and your training is always more disciplined.

In addition to road racing events, an increasing number of cycling clubs hold track events, too. Track cycling is done on a sloping oval, and riders may do just a few laps or they may do hundreds. Riders here are in a more aerodynamically efficient position for track racing, with their saddles comparatively higher than their handlebars and also further forward.

The big difference with track racing is that the bikes have the *fixed wheel* system. This means that as well as having only one gear, the rider cannot freewheel – if the back wheel is turning, the pedals will always be turning too. Track racers have to pick a chainwheel they can push to get a fast start, but which also gives them a high cruising speed and enables them to give a kick in a sprint finish. When these bikes are ridden on the street they're known as *fixies* (refer to Chapter 2 for more on these types of street bike).

Track racing is hard work and highly competitive, but if you think you've got strong legs and like to win, why not see if you can borrow a bike to check it out and have a go. If you win a race you may get some cash to take home, but that's not the only bonus. Out of the ranks of local heroes do national champions emerge, so if you've got your eyes on the yellow jersey, track racing is the place to start.

Another staple of club competition is time trialling. In a *time trial,* riders set off at intervals over the same course and race against the clock, with the winner being the person to cover the distance in the shortest time. Slipstreaming is forbidden, so if you catch the rider in front, you can't just sit on his tail and get a tow. On long summer evenings and at weekends, it's not an uncommon sight on certain main roads around the country to see scores of riders with numbers on their backs spaced out every hundred metres or so in a tuck position. Distances start at just a few miles and go up from there.

A variation on the time trial theme are events where the winner is the person to ride the furthest in a given time, which can be as much as 24 hours. As well as club events there are national championships for time trials at all distances.

Mountain bike clubs

To compete in mountain bike (MTB) races you need to get a race licence from British Cycling. You can always just buy a day licence for a particular event, but a full licence doesn't cost that much more – only about three times the daily rate. Both licences include some insurance, so check with British Cycling for details (www.britishcycling.org.uk).

If you want to join a mountain bike club, first check whether the one you have in mind does the kind of riding you're interested in. Do they do social rides, competition or both? Many different kinds of competition events occur now, but most clubs are still focused on *DH* (downhill) or *XC* (cross country). Also check whether a local MTB facility is available and whether your club races there – or do they just get together to travel to other areas for competition?

Check the club has social activities as well as riding bikes. This latter point is very important for some MTB riders.

MTB competition styles

The styles available for competition mountain biking include the following:

- **Downhill (DH) racing** is the style that grabs all the attention and it certainly is fast and furious. DH can involve quite a considerable altitude drop, depending on the course. Courses run between one and three miles (that's one and a half and five kilometres) and races are always over in just a few minutes. Competitors get individual start times and are usually spaced 30 seconds apart. DH courses consist of rocky sections, fast narrow sections and some very steep drops. Top riders can average 40 miles (65 kilometres) per hour or more in these races. The person with the fastest time is the winner.

- **Olympic cross country (XCO)** is a mass- or individual-start race style usually on a three- to five-mile (five- to eight-kilometre) circuit. These circuits are very varied with some climbing, singletrack, forest trails. Along with DH, XCO is possibly the most common type of racing and riders with technical ability cover these courses in very fast times.

- **Short track cross country (XCC)** is typically done on an 800-metre (875-yard) circuit. These fast and exciting races are all over in just over a minute. Sometimes longer events – with multiple laps – are held on these courses.

- **4-Cross (4X)** is quite similar to BMX racing, but these MTB tracks get a little rougher. Logs and rock gardens join angled turns and rolling dirt piles. Four riders compete to do the built downhill course in the fastest time.

- **Cross country marathon (CXM)** is a mass-start race of anything over 40 miles and up to 65 miles (65 to 105 kilometres). These mixed-terrain races usually last over three hours.

- **Stage races** are a combination of different events on one day, or over several days. These races usually include downhill and cross country and although they have stage winners, the rider who is deemed the most versatile of MTB riders is the overall winner.

Be ready

Naturally, the more training and practice you get in the type of riding you're going to compete in, the better you do. Your legs get stronger, the rest of your body learns all the balance and movement needed for control of a mountain bike and your skills in tight spots improve. But you need still more to be ready at the starting line.

Courses are often open the day before events so you can go along and check them out. Some MTB venues allow camping, so you can go along, set yourself up, check out the trails and get to know other riders. Doing your first circuit of an MTB course during an event would be crazy, and you're certainly not allowed to practise downhill or cross country courses after other racing has started. Aim to ride or walk the course the day before or, if doing so isn't possible, do it at least on the morning of your race.

Learn what you're up against so that you know what's round a sharp bend or over a peak. Get familiar with the course so that you know in advance whether you're about to go over a cliff-face or into a *bomb-hole*. (A bomb-hole is a steep drop into a hole or trench with a tough climb back out again.) Taking a slow look at a downhill course enables you to map out a line to follow when you're flying down at 40 miles (65 kilometres) per hour.

Make sure you get to the start line at the right time. No one is going to come looking for you. Transport may be laid on for downhill riders to get to the start of their event (probably a lot higher than anything else around). If so, don't miss it.

MTB racing etiquette

Unsurprisingly, most MTB racing etiquette is to do with passing on narrow trails. Firstly, if you come off your bike and a rider is coming up behind, you must get out of her way, preferably off the trail. If you're racing and happen to be walking, you must let anyone racing – and riding – get past. Get yourself and your bike onto the least rideable part of the path.

If you're leading a race, or at least leading the rider coming up behind you, you don't have to let him get past. Finding a place to overtake is up to him. If a rider comes up behind you and is lapping you, then she is leading – and you should let her get past. When overtaking on a narrow trail you should call out 'track left' or 'track right', indicating which side you're passing on.

Don't try to squeeze past another rider if the room isn't there to do so. If the rider is thrown off his bike or suffers any injury, you'll be held responsible. If you do come across an injured rider in a race, the rules state you're not obliged to stop and help them. You are, however, obliged to inform the next race official or marshal you see. But you'll earn more respect if you do stop and help an injured rider.

Don't just throw your gel or food wrappers on the ground. Shove them back in your pocket and take them home with you.

Participating in Big Organised Events

Big organised cycling events can get enormous. Finding accurate figures on which bicycle event is the biggest in the world is difficult, but the London to Brighton ride is certainly a contender for the biggest A-to-B ride. Started in 1976 with about 60 riders, now one day every June something like 30,000 cyclists pour down the 54 miles (87 kilometres) into the charming seaside town. The Skyride in London, one of many open events held in towns and cities across the country on short closed-road loops, had an even larger 80,000 people in 2010. It surely won't be long before even this huge number is topped.

Of course, actually seeing that many riders at any one time is impossible – all you experience is many, many cyclists all around you, whichever way you go. But knowing how many bikes are out and being so surrounded by them is always a powerful feeling and something that should be celebrated.

Private companies, individuals and charities organise events all over the UK. A quick search online tells you everything that's going on in your area. In the following sections we cover some of the best-known big rides across the country. Some of them have been around for a long time, some of them are new, but they all offer a very diverse set of possibilities for you to gang up with a lot of other riders and enjoy your riding together.

One-day events

Masses of day-long events both for on and off-road riding are held everywhere across the country. While most take place in the summer months, an increasing number are organised in the depths of winter, too. You could quite easily do one every weekend of the year if you wanted to.

Many of these rides are organised by charities with the aim of raising money, but the big bike retailers are getting in on the act to raise their profiles among their core customers. A number of organisations also exist which do nothing other than organise big rides.

You can participate in a number of different kinds of event, including:

✔ **Audax (also known as randonée or brevet):** Meaning 'daring' in Latin, Audax routes are run over set distances which start at a mere 200 kilometres (124 miles), then step up to 300 kilometres (186 miles), 400 kilometres (249 miles) and go up to an eye-watering 600 kilometres (373 miles). Routes known as *Permanents* run over even longer distances.

Audaxes aren't races – instead, the idea is to test yourself – but they do have a cut-off time which makes no allowances for breaks, meals, rest, sleep or mechanical breakdowns. These events, which typically attract around a hundred riders per event, are generally not supported as self-sufficiency is one of the highly-regarded qualities of Audax riders. So don't expect to find regular food and drink stops along the way, unless you've organised them yourself.

✔ **Cycling Festivals:** Growing numbers of these festivals are taking place across the country. They often combine all or some of the other events in this list. Typically held over a long weekend, cycling festivals include lots of things to see, do and buy, all connected with cycling, so you don't even need to get on a bike to enjoy yourself, though of course that helps.

✔ **Cyclosportives:** Often simply called *sportives*, cyclosportives are immensely popular, with several thousand road cyclists taking part in each. Usually run in beautiful countryside, they attract all standards of rider from the semi-professional to the gloriously amateur. Distances match abilities, so sportives have several routes to choose from, typically around 35, 65 and 100 miles (that's 56, 105 and 161 kilometres respectively) long. Some are more family friendly so have children's routes, too. Every rider is timed which all adds to the spirit of competition. Routes are well signposted so you shouldn't have to look at a map all. The entry fee normally includes food and drink stops as well as a few goodies such as a T-shirt or bidon.

✔ **MTB sportives:** Variously called sportives, enduros or marathons (and other things besides), MTB sportives are similar in format to road events, but take place on some of the best and most challenging trails the country has to offer. They vary in difficulty from tough to superhuman, and their very nature means that you have to travel to some of the more remote parts of the country to participate, which only adds to their appeal.

✔ **Skyrides:** Organised in partnership with British Cycling, Skyrides are aimed firmly at mass participation and inclusivity. Free to enter, and taking place all across the country in cities, towns and increasingly at local community level, the great attraction of Skyrides is that you can choose to cycle for as long or as short a time as you like, so the emphasis is on having fun rather than being all about performance. Skyrides are a great day out for the family and one of the best ways to have a go at riding in a big group.

The major individual one-day cycling events in the UK include the following:

✔ **The London-to-Brighton:** The granddaddy of them all. Run by the British Heart Foundation, the London-to-Brighton ride raises huge amounts of money for this important charity. Overnight and off-road versions of the event are now run, too, and the BHF organises other equally challenging rides all over the country. A new 100-mile (161-kilometre) challenge following much of the Olympic road race route is planned from 2013. Some of the route will be on closed roads and 20,000 places are available. More information is available online at www.bhf.org.uk.

✔ **The Etape Caledonia:** Possibly the most spectacular sportive in the country, this 81-mile (130-kilometre) closed road event in the Scottish Highlands attracts over 5,500 riders. Organised by the Marie Curie Cancer Care Charity, the Etape Caledonia is one of very few rides to take place over closed roads, which creates a completely different cycling experience. You have to commit to raising several hundred pounds in sponsorship money to take part, but that doesn't seem to dampen enthusiasm. Places are usually filled many months in advance. Check out the website at www.etapecaledonia.co.uk.

✔ **Freecycle:** Part of the two-day RideLondon festival intended to celebrate the massively increased interest in cycling after the London Olympics and Bradley Wiggins' Tour de France victory, Freecycle promises to be the biggest mass-participating cycling event in the world. Organisers expect up to 70,000 riders to join in the 8-mile (13-kilometre) loop around central London. Great for sightseeing and great for kids (as the roads will be closed and traffic free), this event takes over from a previous events called The RideLondon Freewheel and The Mayor of London's Sky Ride. You can find more details online at www.ride london.co.uk.

✔ **Fred Whitton Challenge:** First held in 1999 in memory of the secretary of the local Lake Road Club, this ride includes over 4,000 metres (just over 13,123 feet) of climbing and covers 100 miles (161 kilometres) in the Lake District. Rated as one of the best events in Europe, the Fred Whitton Challenge includes some vicious ascents including Kirkstone, Honister and Wrynose and the formidable Hardknott Pass. Entries open on New Year's Day for a place in the ballot, which decides who makes it to the start line in May. Check out the official website at www.fred whittonchallenge.org.uk.

✔ **Dartmoor Classic:** One of several challenging rides over the rugged moors of southwest England, this June ride is hugely popular so you need to book up by the preceding autumn to guarantee getting a place. You can ride one of two distances – one of over 100 miles (161 kilometres) and the other of around 65 miles (105 kilometres), both of which offer a lot of climbing and both of which take you through the very heart of Dartmoor. The ride is organised by the Mid-Devon Cycling Club, who know these roads intimately and choose the very best for this ride. You can enter at www.dartmoorclassic.co.uk.

Find a cycling group near you

Thanks to the increase in cycle commuting and the amazing success of British cycling on the world stage, interest in cycling in the UK has never been higher. Consequently, cycling groups of all descriptions have witnessed phenomenal growth in recent times. In response, British Cycling (the National Governing Body for cycle racing) has launched Social Cycling Groups – a social networking initiative. This free online service enables you to link up with like-minded riders and find groups and rides in your area. It has dates, distances, durations and maps, so you can choose the group and ride that best suits you and your fellow riders. And if the rides in your area aren't quite near enough or aren't what you're looking for, then the site shows you how to set up your own group. Check out the details at www.goskyride.com/social-cycling-groups.

✔ **The Great Manchester Cycle:** This event was first run in 2012, and enabled 7,000 riders to tackle three different distances on completely closed roads in and around the city centre, including on a stretch of Manchester's busiest motorway – the iconic Mancunian way. The ride promotes itself as the biggest timed event in the UK, where everyone has a chance to rate their performance. With 13-, 26- and 52-mile (that's 21-, 42- and 84-kilometre) routes available, the ride is aimed at novices, children and occasional riders, as well as those who want to push themselves a little harder than usual. Find out more at www.greatcycle.org.

✔ **The Exmoor Beast:** This 102-mile (164-kilometre) ride often takes place in wet and wild weather. If that wasn't enough, the route includes some horrible hills too, where no honour is lost in getting off and pushing. These two factors, plus some outstandingly beautiful scenery, make it one of the toughest and most popular sportives in the country. Definitely one to work up to rather than using it to launch your sportive career. You can check the detail at www.exmoorbeast.org.

✔ **The Dragon Ride:** Definitely one of the UK's classics, this ride is now ten years old and one of the longest sportives in the country, with the Grand Fondo (the longest route) coming in at over 200 kilometres (124 miles). Combine this length with over 3,000 metres (just under 9,842 feet) of climbing in the mountains of the Brecon Beacons and you can see why this ride has a fearsome reputation. The immense popularity of the Dragon Ride means entries used to sell out within hours, so riders are now selected by ballot. The website for entries is www.dragonride.co.uk.

✔ **Dunwich Dynamo:** One of the more unusual rides – and free with it – the Dunwich Dynamo starts at London Fields in Hackney and covers 120 miles (193 kilometres) to a lovely, lonely beach at Dunwich in Suffolk. What makes the Dunwich Dynamo different is that riders set off from 8 p.m. and ride through the night, with the first riders arriving at first light. By 9 a.m., the beach is covered in cyclists having a well-deserved snooze in the morning sun. The café on the beach opens up especially early to serve big breakfasts, and you can book a place for you and your bike on a coach for the journey home, though a hardy few prefer to ride. The Dunwich Dynamo is organised by Southwark Cyclists (www.south warkcyclists.org.uk).

✔ **Cycletta New Forest:** Sportives tend to be very male-dominated, which can be a bit intimidating for female riders. So women-only events are shooting up all over the place. Cycletta is just one organisation which puts on such rides (British Cycling is another with their 'Breeze' events), and with Olympic champion Victoria Pendleton lending her support you can see why they get a lot of publicity. Their New Forest ride involves dodging wandering ponies and donkeys, takes in some lovely roads, and runs over distances of 40 or 80 kilometres (25 to 50 miles), so is well within the reach of the majority of cyclists. Find out more online at www. cycletta.co.uk.

Multi-day rides

If you've tried out a few day rides and fancy something more challenging, or just fancy communing with your bike for more than a few hours at a time, a multi-day event could be just the thing for you. While not as common as sportives, you still have plenty to choose from in the UK, Europe and beyond.

Here are some great examples of multi-day rides:

✔ **Lands End to John o'Groats:** Possibly the most iconic of multi-day events anywhere in the world, this ride used to be something that only experienced and self-sufficient riders would attempt. But now numerous companies and charities organise supported rides so that all you have to think about is pedalling – they take care of the rest. The Action End2End supported ride, for example, raises money for medical research and covers 1,000 miles (1,609 kilometres) in ten days. Accommodation is in hotels, which makes the ride pretty luxurious for those used to carrying camping gear. You have to commit to raising £3,000, which covers your costs for the ten days. Definitely one to tell the grandchildren about. You can find more details at www.ukend2end.com.

✔ **The Ridgeway 200 Mountain Bike Enduro:** Following a roadway that dates back to 3,000 BC, this two-day event involves an astonishing 11,000 feet (or 3,353 metres) of off-road climbing and covers 100 kilometres (62 miles) each day. Starting at Wendover in Buckinghamshire, it follows the Ridgeway to Swindon in Wiltshire, then goes all the way back again. Attracting cyclo-cross riders as well as mountain bikers, overnight accommodation is in a school hall, so you're not short of opportunities to get to know your fellow fanatics intimately. This ride is organised by Extreme Energy, which has a number of other similar events, if this isn't enough for you. Check online at www.xnrg.co.uk for more info.

✔ **London-to-Paris:** A ride which gives you a taste of continental cycling and the joys that lie therein. This route is turning into a favourite for charity rides as it gains iconic status, and is a big achievement to complete, but it isn't as challenging as something like Lands End to John o'Groats. Typically taking around four days and covering 500 kilometres (310 miles), the best routes take in some lovely countryside as well as the grandest sights in two of Europe's greatest capitals. A number of charities and organisations do this route at different times of the year, so check them out at www.londonparisbikeride.co.uk.

Hundreds and sometimes thousands of cyclists taking over roads, making them safe by their sheer numbers as they pass through, enjoying their country as they've never seen it before and taking part in an adventure they'll never forget is a powerful thing. Each of these huge cycling expeditions is a rare and amazing phenomenon. Getting all those cyclists together, swapping stories of close shaves, eying up frames and maybe even falling in love is a brilliant step towards all of us leading healthier, happier lives.

Critical Mass

Critical Mass is a meeting of cyclists that occurs at the end of the working day on the last Friday of the month in hundreds of city centres around the world, and is a unique secular phenomenon: as the planet turns and that special time is reached in different time zones, riders gather in their respective locations and then cycle as a group through their city streets.

The idea is that when the number of cyclists reaches a certain amount, they become safe. They dominate the traffic as they are usually dominated. The gathering becomes a celebration of cycling and Critical Mass rides are typically lots of fun. Cyclists sometimes wear fancy costumes, such as gorilla outfits or Santa suits at Christmas, and often sound systems are cleverly fixed to racks. The air of the circus arrives as the streets come alive with colour and life.

Critical Mass was born in San Francisco in 1992. For the first ride along a main commercial street, 60-odd cyclists turned up. Within months, hundreds were turning up every month and the phenomenon spread slowly across North America and the world.

As with other street parades, such as the carnivals of Notting Hill in London, Venice, Rio and New Orleans, Sydney's Mardi Gras, or the recent worldwide craze of Zombie Walks, Critical Mass enthrals passers-by and brings smiles to the faces of city workers, tourists and even most motorists.

In some cities, authorities have not welcomed the ride and this has caused conflict. Occasional impatience flares up from those briefly delayed and even some conservative cyclists raise their eyebrows at riders so flagrantly having fun.

Critical Mass is a way for cyclists to meet other cyclists in an atmosphere of celebration, and an opportunity for bike riders to experience streets in the heart of their city that might otherwise always be fraught with risk and worry. And Critical Mass is also an effective way of showing the population how much you really can enjoy riding a bike.

If you're interested in finding out for yourself, just search the Internet for 'Critical Mass' and the name of your city. Bring along your bicycle, make friends, have fun.

Chapter 14

Riding with Babies, Toddlers and Children

In This Chapter
▶ Incorporating a new addition to your bike
▶ Picking the right bike and making it safe
▶ Teaching your child to ride

*F*or us – along with many other people – riding a bicycle was part of grow-ing up, and the memories of the freedom and movement provided by a bicycle are a hugely positive part of our pasts. The exploring and adventur-ing, getting to places with friends and having a quick, independent way of get-ting to school are all things we look back on with great warmth.

If you want your children to have similarly big and wonderful experiences, you need to make it happen for them. And with sedentary lifestyles leading to an increase in childhood obesity, encouraging your children to spend time being active and having outdoor fun is now more important than ever.

Coaxing your young ones away from computers, televisions and game con-soles may be tedious, but rewarding – when you do get them out and get colour in their cheeks they always enjoy it. Cycling isn't just a great way of getting exercise into your lives; cycling is also a fantastic family activity – something that you all can enjoy together that builds up the strength of your little clan and makes all family members feel good about each other.

In this chapter, we cover moving really small ones around with you on your bike. A couple of options are available for stowing them away, and you can choose whichever suits you best. We also look at bikes and equipment you need when your children are a little more independent, and provide some safety tips that we're sure you won't want to miss. Finally, we cover that most daunting of chores: teaching a child to ride a bicycle, which isn't actually as tough as you might think. We also include some stuff on how your school can help with teaching children about bikes.

Two's Company: Adding a Small Child to Your Bicycle

If you're used to getting about on a bicycle, whether as a means of travel or just for fun, and you've got a baby, taking the baby with you on your bike is the most natural – and reasonable – thing on earth. It certainly beats strapping your little darling into a car or just not going out.

No matter what means you choose of transporting your baby on your bicycle, don't take her with you on your bike until she has developed enough neck strength to not only hold her own head up firmly, but also her head with a helmet. This isn't a legal requirement, but is a wise move.

Authorities suggest that 12 months old is a reasonable age to expect a child to be able to hold up his head firmly, even with a helmet on it. Most children are quite well developed by this age, so 12 months is probably quite a safe figure. However, all children grow at different rates and if you think yours is an early developer you could consider the bike seats that are available for babies from six months old. If you're not sure, ask your doctor or a relevant health care professional.

You don't have to check your child's ability to hold up a helmet on your bike. Just sit the babe on the floor and see how she copes with a helmet on her head. Many adults find helmets very bothersome, so don't be surprised if you get a negative reaction from your tiny offspring. Getting your child to accept a helmet is your first hurdle, so stick at it – don't be beaten before you've even got on the bike.

The big choice for carrying a baby on a bike is between seats and trailers. We cover both options in the following sections.

When you've finally got yourself set up, with whatever system you choose, take things slowly. Your small child might take to being with you on the bike like a goat to a mountain bike trail, but if any little doubts are present, just ease your child gently into the pleasures of being pedalled about.

Choosing baby and child seats

You can mount baby and child seats either behind you on a bicycle – where you attach them to either your seat tube or a rack – or in front of you – where you attach them to your top tube or a bar connected between your head tube and seat tube. Front and back seats are different and not interchangeable.

Choosing the safe carrier option – trailer or seat?

Some people are quite adamant that one style of child carrier is safer than the other. To support their arguments, they invariably describe the worst-case scenario for the option they didn't take.

Trailers seem more vulnerable to some people because they drag along behind the bike, meaning they are low and they feel that speeding motorists could easily miss them. Other people argue that if a child in a seat is knocked off a bike, they fall in a wide arc from adult head height, and that a bike toppling over is a much more frequent event than a cyclist being hit by a car.

Trailer pullers insist that motorists always give them a huge berth – far more than they could expect as just a bike. And trailers come with flags to alert motorists of their presence even more. Seat carriers feel strongly that proximity to their children is an important factor in protection and security. No statistics are available to support either side.

You must weigh up the arguments yourself and go with whatever option you're most comfortable and confident with.

The features of front and back seats include the following:

- ✔ **Front carrier seats:** These seats carry a child weighing up to about 15 kilograms (2 stone, 5 pounds), which typically means a three- to three-and-a-half-year-old child is the maximum load they can take. The big advantage of the front-loader is having your child in front of you. You can see that he is okay and easily talk to the excited little angel, making each journey that you take together much more of a shared experience. The disadvantages are that if you come off the bike you're more likely to travel forwards – into your child – and having extra weight up front destabilises your bike and makes turning more difficult.

- ✔ **Rear-mounted carrier seats:** These seats are more robust and carry a child weighing up to 25 kilograms (4 stone), which means most five year olds are still safe. Even some older children won't break the weight barrier, but they do start to get too tall and just won't fit any more.

Sporting both a front and rear carrier seat simultaneously is feasible, but you'd have to take it pretty easy before you got confident with this arrangement. Two seats add a lot of extra weight, quite high up in your complicated scheme of things, and you might find it all a bit wobbly.

You can't wear a backpack when you've got a rear-mounted seat occupied – your pack would be in the child's face. Neither can you carry rear panniers, as your child's feet inhabit that space. You can still use front panniers, though, which can help balance the weight and add stability. Some rear seats, however, are designed so that you can strap a small amount of gear to the back.

You may find that small children don't realise how exciting riding around on a bicycle is and that they fall asleep while they're out and about. Some sources express concern about the child's head rolling about when the little one's having a snooze. We haven't been able to track down any injuries reported because of this, but if you're concerned, a well-placed small cushion, or better still one of those inflatable, horseshoe-shaped cushions you can buy for air travel (which are available in sizes for children) should help ease any worry. Some seats are shaped so that the head can rest back when the child dozes. A backward space is necessary for this as the child's head is bigger than usual, owing to the helmet.

You must work out a system for putting your child into a child seat, so that you can be sure the bike doesn't fall over while you're strapping the young person in. As children are eminently capable of independent movement, it may well be that a kickstand is not enough. Never walk away from a bicycle that has a child secured in a child seat.

Following these steps gives you a good approach to putting your child in a child seat on your bike:

1. **Make sure the bike is standing as solidly as possible.**

2. **Get yourself ready so that you can get going as soon as your child is fixed in the seat.**

3. **Lift the child into the seat and fasten everything up as securely as you can.**

4. **Move both your hands to the bicycle and keep hold of it.**

5. **Climb into position and start cycling.**

Going with child trailers

With their metal frames, wheels and greater number of component parts, bike trailers tend to be more expensive than child seats. Prices start at about £150 and carry on up from there. They attach, usually quite simply and firmly, to brackets fixed to the bicycle's back axle or the chainstays.

Riding a bike with a trailer is a lot more stable than having a child seat and while it's also more work as they're quite heavy, they also give you a bit of a push when you're going downhill. Trailers are bulky, too, but they often fold up to the same size as a folded-up pram and offer a number of big advantages over the child seat, including the following:

✔ Trailers can carry more than one small child. In addition to two seats, they usually have storage space behind and even underneath. Trailers are built to last, so when your children are all grown up and off racing in the Tour de France, you can still use the trailer to shift up to 50 kilograms (8 stone), which is probably more shopping than you should be doing at any one time.

✔ Trailers are enclosed, so offer more protection to your child, both from any immediate flying objects and from the elements. Many come with a detachable plastic cover that keeps off rain, and many also have UV protection. Trailers tend to have brightly coloured exteriors to give greater visibility. Strapped in inside a trailer, your child can wear a helmet for extra protection, too.

✔ A lot of trailers convert into strollers, so at your destination you can chain up your bike and continue to provide seated transport for your small child or children.

✔ If you buy an extra bracket, you can fit one on more than one bike. This means you can drop the trailer with the child somewhere and have someone else pick up junior. Or if you're all going out together, one adult can tow the child one way, while the other gets the treat on the way back.

✔ The trailer provides room for your child to carry a toy, blanket, drink or some food, and because the trailer has a floor and is enclosed, your child can fling the item away without losing it.

Some little children love trailers. They think they're being given pretty high-class limousine treatment and relax back into thoughts of mocktails and their parents in livery. Some children feel left out, like they're part of the load, not the action. Try to find a way of trying before you buy, perhaps through borrowing a friend's, because a trailer can be quite an investment.

Buying a second-hand trailer can be a great money saver. Sometimes children simply don't take to them, meaning that you can often pick one up in virtually new condition and have it running well for years.

Here are a few points to bear in mind before buying a trailer second-hand:

✔ Check out trailers in the bike shop so that you've got some idea of how they work and how they attach.

✔ Take your bike along so that you can be sure the brackets fit your frame, rack or axle.

✔ Take your child along and, if possible, take them for a test ride – so that you don't end up selling the trailer for the same reasons.

✔ Spin the wheels and be sure that they run freely with no sign of uneven rims or wobbling.

✔ Check the bracket is not damaged and can still be fixed tightly.

✔ Try the hitching mechanism and be confident that it won't let you down.

Ben's kids loved their trailer. Going to nursery was never so much fun. So when he suggested a ride around the New Forest they were thrilled by the idea. The day came and everything was going swimmingly. It was a glorious summer's afternoon and everyone was enjoying the wind in their hair. Whizzing along country lanes, down hills and around corners was great fun but, unfortunately, around one particular corner, a herd of cows had recently been loitering. The road was awash with the evidence, which was impossible to miss. A lack of mudguards on the bike he was riding was a miscalculation, and while he got a little splattered, the kids got a faceful, and what should have been an idyllic ride ended with a few tears instead.

Roads are frequently wet or muddy, so if the bike you're using to tow a trailer doesn't have a rear mudguard, fitting one makes sense. Also think about adding a mudflap to give extra protection from the very worst that tyres can pick up and throw at your little ones.

Progressing to bike extensions or tag-alongs

Unlike a trailer (see the preceding section), a tag-along enables your child to help with powering your pedalling system. Tag-alongs are like bicycles, but instead of a fork and front wheel they have a curved bar that fastens onto the seatpost of your bicycle. The child behind can pedal away, but you get to keep control of the steering and brakes.

Using a tag-along becomes almost like a tandem, but with a bend in the middle, and, while the rear rider on a tandem must pedal with the front rider (or lift their feet off the pedals), with a tag-along the child rider can freewheel whenever she wants. So your child gets to be stoker, but without the compulsion to stoke. This setup makes tag-alongs useful for riding longer distances with your child, even when she might be capable of riding her own bike.

Children should be sensible enough to ride a tag-along from the age of about five. The most important requirement is for the child to do as he is told, but as this requirement is by no means guaranteed at any age it can be a bit of a moot point. So, important factors become whether or not your child is likely to bolt in traffic and if you can persuade your child not to make violent steering movements – while the tag-along's handlebars are just for gripping, not steering, big tugs on the tag-alongs bars will have you rocking precariously from side to side.

Consider the following when choosing a tag-along for your child:

✔ Some tag-alongs have gears, but if this is your child's first experience of pedalling, choose an option without gears. The process of you teaching and your child learning how to use gears is best left until they're more fully in control of a bicycle and riding independently.

✔ Some tag-alongs fold up, which is very handy if you need to transport the attachment in the boot of your car. You can get a spare permanent fitting for the seatpost and put it on another bike so that you can leave the tag-along somewhere with one carer to be picked up by another.

✔ Some tag-alongs come with a mudguard. Mudguards are a good idea – if you get one that doesn't have a mudguard, you could find your little cherub splattered with the brown stuff after rain. You can always buy one and attach it to a tag-along you've already bought (depending on how you feel about your child).

✔ When you buy a tag-along, you're getting most of a bicycle, so you have some maintenance chores, including cleaning and lubing the chain and keeping an eye on the tyre.

The biggest concern most people have about bike extensions is visibility. Will your child be seen in traffic? As with any other smaller cyclist, your young one should wear bright clothing and have lights at night, but if you feel vulnerable, keeping out of traffic – possibly riding on footpaths – is the best option. Having another cyclist ride behind might help, although motorists have been known to try to duck in between the large cyclists in such a situation.

When they grew too large for a trailer, Ben's kids progressed to a tag-along. He'd managed to find a tandem version which, when attached, turned their ride into a triple-seater. The summer holidays were around the corner, and plans were made for a family camping trip. One adult was hitched up to the tag-along, the other towed the trailer with all the camping gear. This setup was luxury – it was even possible to get a cool-box on board. And although going up hills required a bit of effort, particularly when the kids decided they were going to have a breather, turning up at campsites was a joy. People were so intrigued by the travelling caravan that Ben and family rarely had to cook a meal or put up their own tent.

Considering Bikes and Safety Gear for Your Child

Buying a bike for your child means he is about to take a big leap forward in development and start a journey of discovery and freedom. However, your little loved one will be in charge of an item of traffic, a mechanism capable of propelling him forward at quite high speed, for the first time, with all the consequent reliance on your child making the right decisions and doing the right thing.

Put that way, giving your child a bike sounds like a recipe for complete disaster, but it needn't be. With the right training and encouragement, and also the right bike and safety equipment, your child should only experience the joys and fun of becoming a bicyclist.

In the following sections, we cover choosing that right bike and then check out some extra safety ideas. Considering the nature of your child and the places she'll ride, and deciding what's right for you and your child, is up to you.

Choosing a child's bike

You need to get over certain hurdles when buying a child's bike. Some aspects of the bike's quality aren't going to be easy for you to assess. They may not be that obvious to the person selling it to you either, depending on where you shop. And your child, if part of the purchasing process, might well have something to say that throws a good-sized bike spanner in the works.

Many bike manufacturers know you're not looking at a child's bike as an investment. Your child will grow and may only use the bike for a couple of years, so you're not likely to spend a fortune. Bikes don't get handed down so much these days, as children expect to get new stuff, and although you might be able to give away a good used children's bike, you may not be able to sell one very easily.

So, to make their bikes cost less, bike companies use cheaper materials and components. If the bike is working when you buy it, it's probably going to be okay. Children don't ride for long hours like some adults and the bike probably won't need to last them for many years, so getting a high-quality bike isn't crucial. But some very real considerations exist that make a difference to how much your child enjoys his new bike and how safe he's going to be.

Selecting the bike that's right for your child

Even though the bike you choose for your child might not be of the highest quality, you still need to make sure the bike size is right for your child and has all the required features.

One thing you can easily check is the weight of a child's bike – just lift up a couple of bikes. Children's bikes are made of relatively cheap alloys that aren't especially light, but if you can feel that one bike is significantly heavier than another, that heavy one is going to be more difficult for your child to handle. Accelerating, steering and stopping are all going to be harder.

Size, too, is definitely important when it comes to buying your child a bike, and it really is the main thing you need to get right. Here are some tips to help ensure you find the right-sized bike for your child:

✔ If you're getting the bike anywhere other than a proper bike shop, chances are you won't be able to really figure out if a potential bike is the right size. Shop staff in these places are often unable to alter the saddle height or anything else on the version of the bike they've got made up in the store. The same of course is true for any bike you buy online. In a bike shop, however, you get all the help you need to ensure the bike can be set up to fit.

✔ Children's bikes tend to be sized by their wheels rather than their frames. When children get to a certain size, they take a step up in wheel size and you take it from there with the frame. This is because you can't put big wheels in a small frame – they just won't fit. But if you go to the right shop you should still get a good range of choices in every wheel size. If you don't think there's enough choice, go somewhere else.

✔ Your child should be able to sit on the saddle and touch the balls of both feet on the ground, stand over the top bar with a five-centimetre (two-inch) clearance and reach the handlebars without straightening arms and leaning too far forward. If your child looks like he has been stretched out on a rack or packed into a cardboard box, the bike is definitely wrong.

✔ Don't ever think of buying a bike that your child can grow into – the bike has to fit now.

Naturally, if your child has joined you for the difficult operation of choosing a bicycle, you may have to contend with a strongly voiced opinion that colour is more important than a proper fit. This situation actually isn't uncommon (even among adults) and you just have to persevere and work around it.

Brakes are the next important thing to look at. Here are some tips to help you ensure the bike you pick has the right kind of brakes for your child and to check they're in good working order:

✔ Children's hands are small and not very strong. Bikes for very small children should have *coaster brakes* (or back pedal brakes, where you pedal backwards to brake) at the rear. Coaster brakes used to be the most common type of brake, but are now mostly just used on children's bikes because of the difficulty children can have with brake levers. Children are often far more comfortable with coaster brakes.

✔ Check that the brakes work. Do the same test you'd do on your own bike: squeeze each brake in turn, leaning your weight down on the bike and pushing forward. If each wheel locks, the brakes are fine. For a small child's bike, try squeezing each brake lever with just your little finger. The brakes should still work with that amount of pressure because you're applying about the strength of a little hand.

✔ If your budding little Victoria Pendleton is with you, have a look at how easily her fingers reach over the brake levers. If necessary, bringing the levers in towards the grips by tightening the little screw that sticks out of the lever housing should be possible.

✔ Also look at the rims when checking the brakes. You may have seen shops advertising bikes in junk mail, proudly claiming alloy rims. Far from being just a cool-sounding attribute that makes a cheap bike seem like a racing beauty, the alloy offers far greater traction to the brake block when the brakes are in use and, when wet, alloy rims have been shown to cut stopping distance by 80 per cent over chrome-covered steel rims. If possible, go for the alloy rims.

✔ The last feature of the bike itself to look out for is a chain guard. Children's bikes with no front dérailleur (and most of them don't have front dérailleurs) should all have a chain guard to stop clothes, shoelaces or even fingers getting hooked up in a fast-moving chain and chainwheel.

Checking the bike is safe and in good working order

When it comes to looking at whether the bike has been put together properly and is in good order, you need to check a number of things, including the following:

✔ **Start with the frame:** Stand behind or in front of the bike and look down the line of the frame. Does it seem twisted or are the wheels not aligned?

✔ **Try spinning the cranks and the wheels:** They should both turn freely without any movement if you try to wiggle them.

✔ **Check the seatpost and stem:** These components should also not move if you try to wiggle them.

✔ **Check the brake blocks:** When you squeeze the levers, the blocks should be fully in contact with the wheel rims and not touching the tyres at any point.

Remembering safety essentials and optional extras

The most important piece of cycling safety equipment is a helmet. Helmets don't do anything to prevent accidents, but are just there in case you have one. It makes a lot of sense that children who are new to cycling and who are bound to have a tumble or two as they get to grips with a new skill, should wear one.

Fitting a child's helmet is just the same as fitting an adult with a helmet (refer to Chapter 3 for how to fit a helmet). You may have to keep an eye on a child wearing a helmet for the first time (or even the thousandth time) to make sure that it stays in the right spot on his head.

Children are smart. If a child starts a campaign against wearing a helmet (arguing that helmets aren't cool, their friends don't wear them, statistics show that they don't do any good, they impinge on freedom of choice, and so on), you can easily find that a helmet has been misplaced or 'lost'. A good tip here is to keep a cheap spare one around the house, just in case.

The other piece of safety equipment worth considering is gloves. Falling off a bike and putting a hand out is far more common than any knocks to the head. Putting your hand to the ground with your weight behind it can cause bad grazing or worse – it can break your arm. Because of this, some people argue gloves are even more essential than a helmet.

Having a glove to cushion any fall or contact with the ground is an unobtrusive and important protective barrier. And cycling gloves can look really cool. You can find them available in some pretty small sizes, but if you can't get any that fit your child, cut off the fingers of some other suitably padded gloves.

When you have your child kitted out in the appropriate safety gear, follow these tips to ensure they cycle safely:

- ✔ **Teach your child to always keep one hand on the handlebars:** You must resist the temptation to show your children how clever you are when you do three laps of the park with your hands on top of your head. They'll take it all in and attempt to copy it.

- ✔ **Keep small children off roads entirely when riding:** Children don't develop enough traffic sense to cycle on roads until they're around nine or ten years old, so even on quiet streets you should give this some thought and don't just assume your children are going to be okay. Most bicycle accidents do happen on minor or residential roads. While children aren't legally allowed to ride on footpaths, those under ten years old can't be prosecuted and the authorities tend to show discretion for pre-teens if they ride sensibly and with consideration for pedestrians.

- ✔ **Never leave small children alone with bicycle helmets on their heads and never let older children play away from their bicycles while wearing helmets:** Bicycle helmets have been the cause of several deaths of children. The straps get hooked on things, the children can't escape and they're strangled.

Putting Kids on Bikes

Getting your child to ride a bike can be a worrying prospect. It could mean a great deal of work and it might involve some falls and tears, not only from the child. However, little ones don't usually take very long to learn to ride. They generally pick it up much quicker than learning to swim and the child is less fearful. Pick the right spot and the right attitude and you'll soon both be proud of your achievement.

Getting your child to ride to school is a really positive step for him, for the school and for the community. But don't dive into it without some proper thought. Here, we cover some ways of making it easier all round.

Give some thought, too, to how your children's school helps to get children active. Getting your school to structure some time for teaching kids the skills and benefits of riding a bike is a big help for your family and your community.

The more anyone rides a bike, the better they get at it. The following sections cover how to help your beloved offspring to get on a bike and stay on it.

Teaching children to ride

If your youngster has been talking about friends with bicycles, studying bikes in the park, hanging out at the bike shop and devouring the Tour de France, take these as subtle signs that she is ready to learn to ride a bicycle. This could all start happening as young as four years old, but is a great sign at any age.

If your child makes it clear that he doesn't want to ride a bike, putting off the process for a while is a good idea. He'll get to it eventually. Don't force it on him – you may just put him off.

Training wheels (or stabilisers) can be a sticky issue. If children have them on their bike, they often then think they're only ever going to manage balancing on a bike with these wheels fitted (because they then don't have to balance at all). With these contraptions fitted, the young cyclist doesn't learn anything much and has to start from scratch when the little wheels eventually come off, so if you can dissuade a child from training wheels you'll all be better off. Try a phrase like, 'If you don't dive in the deep end, you'll never get to the top of the mountain.' That should silence anyone with an active mind.

Picking the right spot and the right technique

The park is probably the best place to go for your child's first riding lesson, unless you just happen to have the perfect garden. Learning to ride is best done on a grassy surface (as long as it's reasonably firm) and on a very gentle slope. You need to start about 20 metres (66 feet) up the gentle slope and have 5 or more metres of flat to run onto at the bottom.

The traditional method of teaching a child to ride is probably not the best. All that running along beside the bicycle, hanging on to the saddle is very hit and miss. The learner has to take on board all the associated skills simultaneously and doing that is simply not very easy. Some children learn in a matter of minutes, but others have you hanging on to that saddle for hours. The running's good for you, but you do end up running at an angle that's very bad for your back. Do yourself a favour – a much easier way is available. The following method is good for learning to ride a bicycle at any age and often takes just an hour.

Follow these steps to get your child pedalling on the bike:

1. **Have your pupil get onto the bike while squeezing the brake lever to stop it moving.**

   Holding onto the bike to start off with, while your child gets onto the saddle, is fine.

   Make sure that the saddle is low enough for the rider to place both feet squarely on the ground. Taking off the pedals for the first stage can help, but is not essential. (If you do decide to take off the pedals, remember that the left pedal unscrews in a clockwise direction, contrary to normal.)

   When your fearless apprentice is seated on the bicycle, congratulate her. You've all done very well.

2. **With feet barely above the ground and brake released, your child should roll forwards, down the slope until coming to a stop on the flat.**

   This won't happen on the first attempt, as your child will need to steer and balance as he rolls forwards. Most likely, on the first few attempts, the bike will fall to one side or your child will just stop. If junior is ready, repeated attempts will bring success.

   Your child can use the brakes, but it shouldn't be necessary. If you're asked to run alongside, that's okay, but it should be seen as unnecessary pretty quickly. You might have to coax your student to keep the handlebars facing forward, but otherwise the occasional dab of the foot should keep the bike on course.

Repeating this process ten times can be enough, but carry on if you think more is required. As soon as you – and your young Padawan – are happy with this basic balance exercise, move on to the next step.

3. **Get your child to roll down the slope with both feet resting on the pedals.**

   Have your child start from the same position as in Step 2, but with one foot on a half-raised pedal. (If you took off the pedals, now's the time to put them back on again.) Your child should have gained enough balance skill to roll down the slope successfully and now he has to focus on just lifting that other foot and resting it on the empty pedal.

   Remember that doing this might seem like the simplest thing on earth to you, but that foot lift can actually be a really big deal to someone in the throes of learning.

   Once more, ten repeats of this exercise can be enough to build skill and confidence, but if it's not, persevere. When your child has mastered this process, you can both move onto the next step.

4. **Get your child to start turning the pedals gently while rolling along.**

   If speed picks up too quickly, remind them about the brakes and suggest not pedalling.

When your potential Laura Trott is happy and confident with gently pedalling down a slope, move on to the next stage. Now you need to find a flat area of grass – where junior gets the chance to pedal properly. Pedalling will start as a wobbly process. Gently remind your student to keep the handlebars steady, but by now you should have a novice rider who is on top of balance and can happily keep both feet on the pedals.

Here are some tips to ensure your child pedals away with confidence:

✔ Have your child start with a foot on one pedal pointing up at the handlebars, so that when the bike is pushed off this pedal can be thrust forward and the rider has time to lift the other foot onto the second pedal as it reaches its high point. This bit is tricky and might take some practice. Ask your child to keep looking forward as this helps to keep the bike steady and moving in one direction.

✔ Teach your child to use both brakes at the same time. This gives much more solid deceleration.

✔ Practise some turning – suggest slowing before entering a turn and explain about using just a little steering and a little leaning. Tell your child how racing cyclists always raise the pedal on the side of the turn when they start to lean.

Realising patience is a virtue

Give your student plenty of space and time. Say only encouraging, positive things. Keep at it as if you've got all the time in the world (you may not have, but please pretend). And be patient – not putting off your willing trainee at this stage is crucial. If you find yourself for any reason becoming impatient, call it a day. Breaking up the schedule is far better than risking spoiling any enthusiasm from your child.

Keep up your enthusiasm and encouragement and you'll soon have a new cyclist in the family – a time for beaming smiles, hugs and much celebration. Well done everybody.

Cycling to school

The number of children who cycle or walk to school is now a fraction of what it was 25 years ago. Somehow, parents have been spooked and now perceive cycling, roads and whole suburban neighbourhoods as being dangerous. Ironically, areas outside schools at pick-up and drop-off times are often far more dangerous, as a vast number of four-wheel-drive vehicles and other gas-guzzlers double park and children either jump in or pile out into the street.

At school drop-off and pick-up times, experts estimate that one in five motor vehicles on urban roads is conducting the family taxi service for children to and from school. This makes a big difference to the air that children breathe in their learning environment and creates a great big carbon boot-print, too.

Gavin remembers gazing in awe at the tangled mass of bikes in the shed at his old school. (Actually, he says the memories of what went on behind the bike-shed are more notable, but he won't go into that here.) Suffice to say the bike-shed was a significant piece of infrastructure of great importance to many school children.

Cycling to school provides the following benefits to your child:

- ✔ **Increased fitness and mental alertness:** Children need at least one hour of medium to heavy exercise every day to stay healthy. The health benefits adults get from commuting to work on a bicycle (refer to Chapter 5 for information) are the same for children: cycling to school is a great way of getting exercise without finding extra time and without starting a special new activity. And children start their school day alert and ready to learn.

- ✔ **Increased road skills:** Cycling on the same route every day – one that you've worked out for your schoolchild – will help your young cyclist to develop cycling skills in traffic. Although you'll be picking streets that have few cars and trucks, your child will learn to check for traffic and get more confident about cycling on roads.

✔ **Increased social interaction:** When people dive into cars in their own driveways and only emerge right at their destination, they have no contact with other people who live close by, often even with their immediate neighbours. Instead, riding right past people in your street, perhaps seeing the same faces a few times, will build up social skills and a sense of community in your child. In fact, it won't just foster a sense of community – it will build a stronger actual community, with local people interacting better and more frequently.

Try following these tips for incorporating cycling into your child's trip to school and back:

✔ **Swap the car for the bike:** Most schools operate a catchment area selection policy, so the majority of students live within a few miles of their school. Obviously, the practical matters of a traffic-safe route are individual to your actual address and the location of your child's school, but for most people riding or walking to school is not too far. If you usually drive your children a short distance to school, you certainly won't find it any slower to ride a bike. Riding with your young ones every day increases the amount of your daily exercise and you know they're going the right way safely.

✔ **Ride part of the way:** Some families who live greater distances from schools drop their children off at a spot far enough away from the school to give the children some exercise and the students walk or ride from there. If they know other families in the same boat, car trips and walks or rides can be pooled and merged.

✔ **Join a cycling scheme:** You can find schemes which set up a cycling school bus. Usually for primary school children, young cyclists are accompanied by adults (always one at the front and one at the back), who are qualified through a relevant training course, on a worked out, specified route. Children are picked up and dropped off at pre-arranged stops, usually their homes.

Some authorities advise that children nine and under are not sufficiently developed to respond properly in traffic situations. If you don't have suitable footpaths (or aren't happy for your children to be doing something which is officially illegal), you might want to leave it until they're a little bit older before you allow them to cycle on their own to school.

If you're going to let children cycle to school on their own, go with them initially to find the best route. Find the safest, probably quietest, roads and the best necessary crossing points, and make it clear that they must use this route every day. If the route you devise is the best way to get to school, you're quite likely to see other children riding along the same roads, which should mean any regular motorists in these streets are used to looking out for children on bikes.

Cycling in the classroom

Getting your children to ride to school is a great deal easier if you get the support of your school. Bike racks at the school are a great start, but the first big step is getting the backing of the top teachers. Often when the principal's first reaction is that cycling to school is dangerous the real problem is storage – the principal doesn't want bikes cluttering up a tidy school.

If the principal at your child's school doesn't actively support cycling to school, calling on the initiatives and literature of Sustrans' programmes and transport department policies should get a more positive attitude without too much pressure. School authorities don't like the awful motor vehicle congestion that builds up outside schools at start and finish times either, and should welcome any movements towards alleviating this problem.

If you're lucky, your child's school already has a bicycle education programme, such as Bikeability (check out the scheme online at `www.dft.gov.uk/bikeability`). Bikeability is described as 'cycling proficiency for the 21st century' and teaches children both the knowledge and practical skills they need to ride a bike safely and independently on roads and paths. The programme includes off-road and on-road components. Bikeability providers can offer training so you can become a cycle skill instructor, too.

Bikeability courses ensure that students know the rules and responsibilities for bicycles on roads and generally get taught in three stages, as follows:

- ✔ **Level 1:** Children learn to control and master their bikes. The training takes place in an environment away from cars or traffic – usually in a playground or closed car park.

- ✔ **Level 2:** Children at this level get out on the roads. Doing this gives them a real cycling experience so that they become able to deal with traffic on short journeys, such as cycling to school.

- ✔ **Level 3:** During Bikeability Level 3 training children learn the skills to tackle a wider variety of traffic conditions than on Level 2. They get taught to deal with all types of road conditions and more challenging traffic situations.

Getting your children taught by Bikeability is a big help. The people who teach it are professionals – they know all about bikes and quite a lot about children too. The course also underlines to children that it isn't just their parents who want them cycling to school, but also the school that sanctions the idea. And the courses aren't just useful – they're a lot of fun.

The Department for Transport organises Bikeability, which is available across 80 per cent of the UK. Some local authorities provide the course for free, while others charge a small fee.

If no official Bikeability facility operates in your area, you may find other organisations or a private business that offers the same service. (CTC, the national cycling charity, has lots of information about training courses on their website, at www.ctc.org.uk.) If your school needs some encouragement to get bike training, why not offer volunteer assistance or suggest a fundraising event to help pay for it. There's no doubt that qualified, professional teaching of schoolchildren about bikes is a fantastic safety measure for everybody's family.

Part IV

Maintaining Your Bike and Yourself

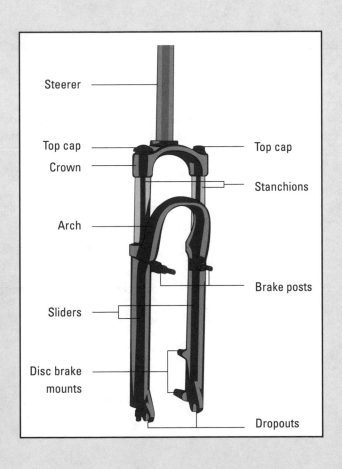

Run through a list of bike checks you need to make before you roll away at www.dummies.com/extras/cyclinguk.

In this part . . .

✔ Find out how to deal with those various aches and pains you come across as a cyclist and discover what you can do to your bike to keep bodily ailments at bay.

✔ Get up to speed with the essentials of energy intake and fluid consumption and establish a good diet for cycling.

✔ Figure out what maintenance tasks and repair chores you need to carry out in order to keep your bike running smoothly.

✔ Pick up some top tips for getting your bike to run more smoothly or more to your liking.

Chapter 15

Easing Ailments

· ·

· ·

A large number of places on the body can get sore after a bike ride. Little aches and pains here and there probably shouldn't cause any worry. Big pains and frequent pains in the same spot, however, are certainly worth some attention.

Some aches and ailments are due to how you ride the bike – how you move when you turn the pedals and position the rest of your body. Some fairly bad problems can be caused by some part of the bike being just slightly out of whack. And some persistent problems are caused by nasty little microbes that do their worst in hot, damp environments on tender flesh.

If you're not sure about fixing problems on your bike, your mates down at the bike shop (and they should be mates by now) can help you – they know all about this stuff. In this chapter, we cover some areas that might need adjusting on the bike, but we also offer some tips about getting yourself into the best position for riding so that your body can work efficiently and not feel like you're placing it under attack.

We also cover stretching and massage, and delve carefully into the trouble-some environment of your bike shorts. What is it that gives your groin grief and how can you keep your private parts secure?

Dealing with an Aching Neck and Back

The most likely cause of neck or back pain is posture, although it could be that your bike needs a little adjustment. Changing the way you position yourself on your bike may be enough to solve any problems, but stretching and strengthening exercises for your neck are also a good idea.

This section is focused primarily on riders of road bikes or other bikes that put riders in a forward-leaning position. If you ride your bike in an upright position and are experiencing neck or back pain, the neck exercises and stretches will also help you (see the sidebar 'Neck stretches and exercises'). Or it may be that you need to raise or lower your saddle or handlebars a tad. You could try doing this yourself (see Chapter 18 for instructions on altering your saddle) or pop down to the bike shop and talk to them about a bike fit, if you haven't already had one. You may also need some extra cushioning from knocks that are transmitting to the base of your spine. With all your weight bearing down vertically on your vertebrae (your spine bones) they have less of their own suspension and you might need to think about a more padded seat or suspension in your seatpost. Buying a seatpost with suspension is not expensive and fitting one is a quick job for the people at the bike shop.

If you're riding leaning right over the handlebars, a few things could be giving you neck and back pain. Here are some tips for alleviating the problem:

- **Position your helmet further back:** If your helmet sits too low on your forehead, you'll be straining to lift your head to see properly. Try positioning it slightly further back and see if you feel less strain when you're riding. If you've got one of those plastic peaks sticking out of the front of your helmet, take it off. The problem could even be just your glasses slipping down your nose, forcing you to raise your chin and flex your neck further.

- **Strengthen your neck:** If you're not used to being in this riding position your body might need some help to get used to bending your neck. Exercise helps to strengthen your neck muscles and stretches increase your range of comfortable movement. (See the sidebar 'Neck stretches and exercises' for some suggestions.)

- **Get a bike fit:** If you're training on a road bike and you haven't ever had a bike fit, get one done straightaway at your local bike shop if you're getting aches and pains. The people that do it will spot problems and make adjustments or recommendations. It could be that your bars are too low, saddle too high or effective top tube length too short or long, and the bike shop staff will know how to remedy these things.

✔ **Make sure your handlebars are positioned correctly:** If your handlebars are too low or you're too close to them, your back *overflexes* (bends too much) and this causes pain on a long ride. When you ride a road bike your back should be shaped like a bridge, strong and flexible. Your lower back has a vital role in controlling your bike, governing all your rear end balance and manoeuvring, so you need to look after it.

✔ **Don't overuse the lower part of your handlebars:** If you're not used to riding low with your hands on the *drops* (the lower part of the curve of road bike handlebars) then don't leap into doing it constantly. Leave your hands higher up on the bars for long periods and ease into the lower position. Your back and neck won't thank you for it, but they won't react so strongly for being overstressed.

✔ **Extend your thigh muscles:** If the muscles of your thighs are tight and not extending properly your pelvis can be forced into a position slightly too far back or too far forward, depending on which muscles are pulling on it. The pain that comes from this misalignment will be in your lower back. Stretching your thigh muscles helps get your pelvis back in the right spot when you ride.

✔ **Relax your upper body, especially your shoulders:** A less rigid body absorbs more shocks from a bumpy road.

✔ **Try different hand positions on the handlebars:** Don't just leave your hands in the same spot for the whole ride. Spending some time with your hands on the drops and some time holding onto the brake mounts gives your back and neck two quite different positions.

✔ **Try different positions in the saddle:** Try moving further back in the saddle for long climbs and forward for sprints.

✔ **Keep your cadence high:** If your *cadence* (the rate at which your legs go round) is too low, the strain you put on your leg muscles transfers to your back as you attempt to keep your body straight. Keep your pedals spinning around faster and all your little back muscles have a much easier time (and you tire out less quickly).

Neck stretches and exercises

These stretches and exercises help you stay comfortable and relaxed when you have to get right down and look right up. With your neck stronger and freer to move you are much less likely to suffer pain from putting yourself in an efficient riding position.

You can do these exercises anywhere. Just remember to keep breathing and breathe out on the stretch. Hold stretches for 20 to 30 seconds. Never 'bounce' a stretch and if it hurts, stop doing it.

(continued)

(continued)

Stretches help to increase your range of movement. If you regularly stretch your muscles, you'll be more comfortable every time you have to make a movement that uses those muscles close to their limit. Stretching can also help relieve muscle pain. Repeat each of these stretches five times:

✔ Stand with your feet about 30 centimetres (12 inches) apart to give you balance and keep your back straight up and down. Tuck in your chin and slowly move your head forward and down, trying to touch your chin to the top of your chest. Slowly move your head back as far as it will go. The forward movement is especially good if you have a pain in the neck and can feel great even if you haven't.

✔ Put your hands at your sides, keep your head facing forward (no turning) and bring your right ear down towards your right shoulder. Then do the same with the left. Be careful not to bring your shoulders up.

✔ Leave your hands at your sides and your shoulders down. Keeping your head level, rotate your head to the right as far as it will go. Then do the same to the left.

Exercises strengthen muscles, making them less likely to strain, fail or give you pain when you have to use them. These exercises are called isometric, which means that you use and strengthen the muscle without shortening and extending it: you use the muscle with power, but without movement.

Hold all these exercises for about five seconds and relax slowly. Repeat each one three times. Stand in the same position as the stretches – feet apart for balance and back straight:

✔ Tilt your head slightly forwards and put the palms of both hands on your forehead. Push against your palms with your head. Resist the movement with your hands.

✔ Put your right hand against the right side of your head. Push your head to the right, trying to get your ear to your shoulder. Resist the movement with your hand. Repeat on the left side.

✔ Put both hands, overlapping, over the back of your head. Push your head backwards and resist the movement with your hands.

✔ Put your right hand up against the very right end of your temple. Keeping your head level, try to turn your head to the right. Resist the movement with your hand. Repeat on the other side.

Tending to Joint Responsibility

Cycling hard can cause little problems to almost any part of a body, especially if that body isn't used to it. Aches and pains can crop up in the least expected places and for no apparent reason.

In the following sections, we cover human parts that move and bend: *joints*. Knees do a massive amount of bending and straightening when you cycle and the tiniest snag can cause them lots of trouble. Wrists and hands don't get to move around quite so much, but are still vital pieces of your equipment.

Shoulders might seem static, but they do a lot of work to control the movement of your bike and need plenty of strength. Concentrating on these areas, we provide tips on how to keep them moving freely without causing pain or other problems to themselves or any other part of the body.

Looking after all these bits is your job – call it a joint responsibility.

If you have some part of your body that causes you chronic pain, see your doctor or other health professional and ask for a treatment plan that's tailored to your specific needs.

Nurturing your knees

A pharmacist from whom Gavin was seeking help once asked him, 'How would you describe your knees?' Just as the word _knobbly_ was about to leave his mouth, he intercepted: 'No, I mean small, medium or large?' He'd obviously asked about knees before.

You don't have to feel great about the way your knees look to be proud of the job they do. When you're cycling, they work fantastically hard, bending back and forth nearly twice every second for sometimes hours on end. Cycling is, in theory, much better for your knees than activities such as running or even walking, because the continuous, repetitive impact isn't there. But knee pain among cyclists isn't uncommon and is usually caused by the way you're using or positioning your knee.

A couple of things about your bike, however, can make a difference to your knees, including the following:

- **Saddle height:** If your saddle isn't high enough, you won't get full leg extension. You can still pedal effectively, but after a while your muscles and joints start to get sore.

  You get a rough guide to correct saddle height when you sit on your bike and push the pedal as far away from the saddle as possible (at about five o'clock, if it were a clock face). This position should have your leg bent only slightly – just not quite straight. If you think you need to raise your saddle, do so in small (say five-millimetre) amounts and ride around to see how it feels. If you get a bike fit at your local bike shop, this setting will be done for you.

- **Saddle position:** An awful lot of people have one leg longer than the other. If the difference is only a couple of millimetres, it shouldn't be a problem. A difference of 3 or more millimetres (slightly more than $\frac{1}{100}$ of an inch), however, can cause knee problems and you may need to refit your saddle to get the right leg extension when you pedal. This repositioning should favour the longer leg. If your leg-length discrepancy is over 6 millimetres (just under ¼ of an inch), you may need to get a platform fitted under the cleat of the shorter leg.

✔ **Crank length:** How far your leg rises (and knee bends) at the top of the pedal rotation also influences how efficient your cycling is. If your cranks are too long, you can be fitted for the right leg extension, but find your knee bending too much as it rises. This can be a cause of knee pain and even injury. Talk to the people at the bike shop if you suspect that your bike's too cranky.

✔ **Cleat positioning:** Although your cleats are on your feet, not your knees, they can have a big effect on your mid-leg joints if they hold your foot in the wrong position. They can twist your leg in a way it really doesn't want to go and cause some nasty, painful problems.

Everyone's feet are different. Some people have pigeon toes, some have duck feet, and some even have willie-wagtail heels, which jump about all over the place. These different feet have different natural angles and cleats have to be fitted to take this into account. It doesn't matter at what angle your foot sits on the pedal, as long as your leg, as it carries on up from there, is straight and can move comfortably. Ill-fitted cleats force your knee to rapidly and repeatedly fit together in a way it isn't quite meant to, causing pain and possibly damage to the cartilage that makes up the joint and muscle that surrounds it.

Try repositioning your cleats by just a millimetre at a time and see if your legs feel like they're in a better position. If you don't know how to do this, get on down to the bike shop.

If you have your bike and accessories set up correctly and start to experience knee pain, you may need to change the way you cycle or train. These tips offer some ways in which you can do so:

✔ **Increase your cadence:** Possibly the most common cause of knee pain is working your legs too hard. When you're training or riding long distances keeping your pedals spinning at a high rate is important. This means changing gears until you can spin comfortably. If you habitually stay in too high a gear, your legs are working too hard. This overwork tires out your legs quicker, but also risks bringing pain and injury to your knees. The heavy work of pushing hard on pedals over a long period is just too stressful for knees, which aren't built for it.

One of the reasons you're cycling, rather than doing some other form of exercise such as running, is most likely so that you don't stuff up your knees. So don't stuff up your knees.

✔ **Strengthen the muscles around the knee:** Another cause of knee pain is lateral movement. Medically, lateral movement means side-to-side movement inside the joint. The bones of your leg meet at the knee in a mass of cartilage, which cushions them together. On the outside of this you have muscles that try to keep it all tightly in place. Sometimes the repeated movement of cycling can result in some sideways movement inside the joint, which disturbs and sometimes even frays the cartilage. This slight damage causes pain. Some people believe that *external sideways movement* (your knee not moving straight up and down, but swinging out or in as it does its bending and straightening) can also have the same internal effect on the joint.

If you do get this condition, which is known as *chondromalacia*, the solution is first to cut your cycling right down, or even take a break. Muscle strengthening is also recommended. This helps hold the joint in the right position as it moves. The usual suggestion for strengthening the muscle (your quadriceps are the muscles that need work) is to sit with your unsupported foot raised and pointing horizontally. Some people say to balance a pillow on your foot for extra effort.

✔ **Keep your knees warm:** This recommendation comes loud and clear from cyclists, but not anywhere from the medically inclined. If you cycle in cold conditions, many people believe that unless you cover up your Tweedle-Dees you're going to suffer knee strife.

Looking after your wrists and hands

Many people suffer from sore wrists from cycling and the most common cause is the positioning of hands on handlebars. Sometimes you can solve this with just some conscious effort, but sometimes you need to move the bars to a better position.

Your hands take a fair bit of weight and stress when you ride a bike, especially if you're in a forward-leaning position. If you ride with a sharply bent wrist, it will soon become painful for both the bones and the muscles.

Your hands need to be holding your handlebars in line with your forearms. Whether your palms are facing downwards on a straight, or nearly straight, bar, or facing inwards on bar ends or placed on the brake mounts of dropped bars, your wrists should not be bent. Your hands should be straight extensions of your arms.

Some people just aren't aware of the correct position for wrists when cycling. When they become aware, they find they can just as easily ride in the correct position, with unbent wrists, and no longer get the pain. Problem solved.

But for some riders the bike isn't set up to get a proper grasp of the bars and needs adjusting. Your handlebars might need lowering or rotating, or the solution might be in lowering or shifting back the saddle. If you can't figure out what's needed and fix it yourself, off you go to the bike shop.

Cycling gloves are possibly the most important cycling accessory, considering the protection they offer if you fall off your bike. They also do a great deal to soften the effect of vibrations that come up through your bicycle frame to your handlebars. Without gloves you increase the stress on your wrists and hands and this stress could be a source of some pain, especially on a road bike or any other bike without any kind of suspension. Not wearing gloves can also mean that you're forced to hang on more tightly if your hands get sweaty and slippery. This again increases stress and can bring on pain. (Refer to Chapter 3 for more on choosing the best cycling gloves for your needs.)

Another big area of concern to cyclists is numbness in the hands. This numbness can either be caused by poor wrist positioning affecting nerves or direct pressure to nerves that run into your hands through your wrists, as follows:

✔ Riding with your wrists bent right back can easily bring on numbness and exacerbate *carpal tunnel syndrome,* a condition of compression of the median nerve as it runs though the cluster of bones in the centre of the wrist (through the carpal tunnel). The median nerve gives feeling to the thumb side of your hand – the thumb, index finger, middle finger and part of the ring finger. When this nerve is put under pressure, you may get tingling or numbness in this part of your hand (which is most of it). If pressure is too great or prolonged, you may sustain damage to nerves or muscles in your hand. Changing gears and braking with numb fingers is also very difficult, so riding with your wrists bent back is really best avoided.

✔ A less-common, but also possible, effect of hand positioning is compression of the ulnar nerve, which gives feeling to the little finger and part of the ring finger. This nerve is actually the one you set off if you hit your funny bone. It runs into the hand much closer to the surface than the median nerve, through the heel of the hand. Even if your grip of your bars is perfectly good, putting pressure on this nerve and getting tingling and numbness in this part of your hand is still possible.

✔ If you think your wrist position is good, but are still getting numbness, you are putting pressure directly onto one of the nerves in your hand. You may just need to change your hand position slightly, but you do need to figure out how to fix it as nerve compression is not going to go away and can cause harm if it's prolonged.

If you've got flat handlebars, it may be that just a slight rotation will help any numbness in your hands. If your grips are shaped, try turning them to alter the points of pressure on your palms. If you get numbness when you have your hands up on the brake mounts on dropped bars, consider moving the mounts just slightly to change where your weight is being taken up.

Shoring up your shoulders

If you ride in an upright position, sore shoulders can mean that you're just not upright enough. Your forward tilt is forcing you to take some of your weight on your hands and this riding position is stressing your shoulders. If you think this tilt is the problem, you need to lower your seat (see Chapter 18 for instructions).

If you're riding a road bike or some other bike that has you leaning forward, the most likely cause of sore shoulders is posture. Pinning down the perfect posture for a cyclist is tricky. Some people have a big curve in their backs and sit on top of the saddle. Others have a much straighter back and have their pelvis tilted forward. You'll find all sorts of positions in between as well. The key thing is to find what you're most comfortable with.

The principles guiding posture are pretty much the same. Although the leg muscles are obviously doing a lot of the work, the top half is also strong and busy. Core muscles are keeping the back and pelvis stable, aligned and in control of all the balance work they have to do. Shoulders have to be forward and relaxed, but also able to take any shocks and keep control of much of the steering of the bicycle.

Given the differences in cyclists' stance, it has to be said that good posture is highly individual, and comes down to finding a position that's both comfortable and efficient. Avoiding having hunched or tense shoulders when you ride is certainly very important and, if you bear this in mind, hopefully, you'll end up in a position that's right for you.

Riding in one, fixed position for long stretches of time can bring on shoulder pain. Make sure you change hand positions to alter the pressure put on your top arm joints.

One thing you must not do is ride with your arms locked straight. This position stresses your shoulders, transmitting knocks from bumps in the road straight into your joints.

If you're riding with elbows slightly bent, as you should do, and you still get stressed from vibrations or experience sore shoulders, try some or all of the following options:

- ✔ **More bar tape:** Wrap more or thicker bar tape around where you grip your handlebars. Every little bit does help.

- ✔ **More shock-absorbent handlebars:** Consider getting new handlebars made out of material that absorbs more tremors. Carbon bars are a little expensive, but good for this.

> ✔ **Wider handlebars:** Another cause of sore shoulders is having handlebars that are too narrow. If you think that narrow handlebars might be the problem, pop down to the bike shop and see what they suggest there.

Unfortunately, on the very rare occasions when cyclists go flying off their bikes, two common injuries are dislocated shoulders and broken collar bones. Both injuries are painful, take weeks to heal and, worst of all, keep you off your bike for far too long. Obviously you can't insure completely against this happening to you, but resistance training for the shoulder muscles can help in these unfortunate circumstances.

Pumping some iron, specifically to build up the shoulders, has three distinct benefits for cyclists:

> ✔ The greater strength of the muscles helps prevent serious injury in the event of a fall. Your arm bone is less likely to come out of your shoulder socket and your clavicle is better cushioned for a snap.

> ✔ You make yourself less vulnerable to fatigue on long rides. Your legs get stronger the more you ride, but you use your shoulders a lot too and more strength lets you last longer.

> ✔ A lot of people think that working out makes you look attractive.

Shoulder pain can come from simply having one arm slightly longer than the other. If you know this is the case, you can loosen and turn your handlebars, pushing the long-arm side very slightly forward. Make sure you tighten your handlebars up again properly.

Stretching It Out

When you use a muscle it contracts, or shortens. When you stretch, you elongate the muscle, pulling it out in the opposite direction to when it's working. Humans, and a lot of animals, stretch naturally and without thinking. You do it when you wake up and yawn, for example.

Stretching increases the comfortable range of movement of a muscle, which means that, if you stretch all over, your whole body will be able to flex, bend and turn further and without pain. The benefit of this in exercise is simply that the routine, repeated muscle actions you do become less extreme within the range of movements you're capable of. You're much less likely to damage a muscle if you work more in the middle of its capabilities.

You can use stretches with great effect as part of warm-up routines, shortening the amount of time you actually exercise before you're ready to drop the hammer. And, just like massage, stretches help your muscles get rid of toxins and products of exertion after exercise, allowing oxygen and nutrients to flow into your fibres for recovery.

In this section we cover stretches for the muscles you use heavily when you ride a bike:

- Gastrocnemius and soleus (calf)
- Gluteus maximus (glutes, backside)
- Hamstrings (rear thighs)
- Psoas (hip flexor)
- Quadriceps (quads, front thighs)
- Tibialis anterior (shin)

Do all the following stretches first on one side, then the other. Stretch until you feel a stretch, not pain. Breathe out on the initial stretch – and keep breathing. Hold the stretch for 20 to 30 seconds.

Stretch each muscle group in the following ways:

- **To extend your shin:** Kneel down on the floor with your legs folded under your thighs. Use one hand to steady yourself and lift one knee with your other hand. Your knee may only rise ten centimetres off the ground, but this stretch is still very effective.

- **To lengthen your calf:** Stand with one foot one stride forward. Keep your rear heel flat on the ground and transfer your body weight forward. Do this with your rear leg straight, then with knee slightly bent to stretch both calf muscles.

- **To get your glutes:** Lie down on your back (you might want to put something soft under your head, for comfort). Bring one knee up towards your chest, clasp both hands over that knee and pull down until you feel the stretch in your rear.

- **To help your hamstrings:** Sit on the floor with one leg extended. Reach out towards your foot. Bring your body forward and your chest down towards your thigh. Rest your hands wherever you can reach comfortably – on your knee, shin or ankle or around your foot.

- **To elongate your hip flexors:** Stand with one foot one stride forward with your forward knee bent. Move your body forward then push your pelvis forward.

> ✔ **To pull on your quads:** Lift one foot up behind you and grab it with the opposite hand (you might need to steady yourself against a wall with the other hand). Pull your foot up and move your knee back as you keep your abs flat and move your hip forward.

Rubbing the Right Way: Massage Your Cares Away

Massage isn't just a way of helping your muscles recover; it feels great, too. Massage helps to remove toxins and other products of strenuous exercise, but it also relieves tension, ironing out painful knots and relaxing stressed and overworked muscles.

Top pro cyclists travel with their own personal massage therapists and enjoy the benefits of faster recovery, quicker warm-up and pleasurable relief. You often see massage tents at big events and you might decide to queue up and receive your own very special treatment.

If you're going to pay for a massage, find a therapist who understands the needs of cyclists. You can phone therapists and ask them if they cycle themselves, or go online and check cycling forums – people often add posts recommending good spots to get a rub. If you're lucky, you'll find that a therapist who's worked with a cycling team has set up a practice in your area.

Asking a friend to give you a knead can be wonderful, but bear in mind that massage therapists go through very lengthy training and only a qualified person is going to know how your muscles work and respond appropriately to any body problems you have.

While letting someone who's not a qualified therapist give you a full massage may not be the best idea, you know your own body and you can do a pretty good job of pummelling your quads and glutes yourself.

Follow these techniques for rubbing your pains away:

> ✔ If you're rubbing bare skin, use an oil. Some people use baby oil; however, baby oil is a mineral oil and you might find it too harsh. Vegetable oils you can use include safflower, apricot and almond. At a pinch, you can use olive oil (and you'll know that after your treatment you'll be perfect with some Mediterranean food).

✔ When massaging a muscle, start at the bottom and work in the direction the blood vessels take towards the heart. Using the pads of your fingers or thumbs (or both), make circular movements, feeling the fibres of the muscle.

✔ Use gentle pressure to stimulate the *lymphatic system*, which runs close to the surface of your skin and removes toxins and other products from your muscles. Use deeper massage to get to aches and pains. If you find a knot, linger on it, but don't cause yourself pain. For areas that need more force than your fingers can supply, use the knuckles of your fist and try to get weight behind them.

The longer you spend rubbing, the more good you'll do. Make sure you're lying down or in the most comfortable position you can find, relaxing as much of your body as possible. During massage, some people like to listen to the voices of whales calling to each other across the vast empty spaces of the ocean. Some people prefer AC/DC.

Enduring Saddle Sores with a Nasty Rash

A number of things can turn the area from your groin to your behind quite nasty when you ride a bicycle. Bike shorts are supposedly designed to help in this area, and bike shorts manufacturers are happy to tell you that the more you pay for your nether wear, the less likely you are to have problems. Manufacturers certainly make claims about diminished or non-existent seams that ought to cut friction in that constantly moving area of your body.

Although the material bike wear is made out of – which usually contains Lycra – is high-wicking and therefore removes moisture steadily from your skin, it is still a synthetic one that produces more sweat in the areas of contact. After a long ride on a hot day, there's no way you're going to get home with dry shorts.

The most common problem riders face is *chafing*. Chafing is when skin gets damaged through friction. As soon as your flesh gets a little inflamed, the problem gets much worse very quickly. Skin can break and become swollen and you can have a very painful problem before you know it. Typically, on a single ride, chafing can start and quickly get to a stage that takes days to heal enough for you to feel comfortable getting back on the bike. Don't try riding with untreated chafing. It will get a lot worse very quickly.

If you do get chafing, you can use a couple of moisturising ointments and creams to lessen discomfort and help with healing. Petroleum jelly, for example, is refined from a product known as rod wax that builds up at oil wells. People widely use this product as it quickens healing and works well with chafing. Shea butter is made from the ivory-coloured nuts of the African shea tree and is also a very effective healing moisturiser. Nappy rash cream is also widely recommended. If you use any of these creams on chafing, you should be able to still cycle. You can also apply these creams as a preventative measure, before any chafing appears. And the late, great bicycle guru Sheldon Brown had this terse recommendation: 'Many cyclists find relief by generous application of corn starch [cornflour] before longer rides.'

Saddles that are too wide or have too much gel in them can cause chafing if you're pedalling fast, especially on a road bike. Your thighs need to have free up-and-down movement without rubbing on the side of a saddle and your sitting bones need firm support, not a spongy mass.

Saddle sores are a stage further on from chafing. They can develop from chafing, although other causes are also possible. Saddle sores are painful, infected spots a bit like boils and need to be treated as such. They require antiseptics and possibly antibiotics.

The hot, damp environment inside your shorts can also bring on fungal eruptions that appear as a slightly inflamed and itchy rash. This problem is not unique to cycling and sportsmen in general tend to refer to it somewhat graphically as *jock-rot*. Jock-rot won't go away unless you treat it with an antifungal cream, which you can buy from a pharmacy.

Another problem is that heat and damp can simply block pores and bring on a condition similar to acne. Surgical wipes can help clear this up.

If you get any problems such as fungal infections or blocked pores, do some checks on your routines, such as the following:

- ✔ Make sure you get out of your bike shorts as soon as you finish your ride.
- ✔ Wash yourself – and your shorts – as soon as you can.
- ✔ Never re-wear bike shorts without washing them first.

Bacteria are everywhere. You can't see them and generally they do no harm, but in certain conditions – warmth and wetness are good – bacteria multiply at a phenomenal rate. When tonnes of them are present, they start to interfere with your bodily functions and cause unsightly or uncomfortable problems. And just because your bike clothing is no longer warm and wet, it doesn't mean the bacteria have gone – they're still in there. Washing gets rid of most bacteria, but if you think that's not enough special soaps and detergents are available that kill even more of them.

You can also get pain in your undercarriage from physical pressure and knocks, bumps and vibrations can cause a lot of pain in your saddle area. If you're new to cycling you may just need to get that part of your body used to taking weight and getting some knocks. Or it could be the saddle angle or just the seat itself that doesn't agree with you. Depending on what kind of bike you have and what kind of riding you do, more cushioning might help. To really soften the blows to your backside, you could get a seatpost with suspension.

If you think the saddle is the problem, take the bike down to the bike shop, show them your saddle and show them your sores. Go on – they're your friends, remember. Okay, just tell them what the problem is. They'll understand and be able to recommend possible replacement saddle options.

Chapter 16

Fuelling Your Cycling

· ·

In This Chapter

▶ Storing energy by increasing your intake of carbohydrates

▶ Eating the right stuff and the right amounts

▶ Watering well

▶ Cramming it in when cycling hard

· ·

*W*hat you eat and drink is what keeps you going when you ride a bicycle – your fuel. Without it, you sputter to a stop at the roadside and won't budge until your tanks are filled.

When you consume food and drink, your body breaks down carbohydrates into glycogen and stores that glycogen in your liver and muscles. You also have stores of fat around your body. In medium-intensity exercise, more than half the energy used comes from the fat. In higher intensity workouts, the carbohydrate becomes more and more important. The protein you consume also contains energy, but your body hardly ever uses this energy. Instead, it uses protein in other ways, including repairing muscle tissue after exercise.

If you're training hard, you need to pay special attention to what you eat and drink. Consuming nourishment can get very difficult when you exercise and different people work out very individual patterns of refuelling, depending on what they feel comfortable putting into their stomachs.

In this chapter, we cover some essentials of energy intake and fluid consumption and provide some tips for those cyclists already struggling to get down the calories they know they need to replace.

Carbing Up

If you're cycling in the hope of losing weight, you must stay in what's called *calorie deficit*, which means using more energy on a ride than you're refuelling with. Medium-strength exercise burns a lot of fat and will help you achieve your weight-loss goal. (Medium-strength exercise is where you work at around 50 per cent of your VO_2max – refer to Chapter 11 for more on VO_2max.) You can treat yourself with some tasty carbs after a ride, but keep fats low and don't overdo it.

It might seem illogical, but training hard is not going to knock off any kilos. If you want to strengthen and compete, you have to do it with your weight still on.

Carbing up is a phrase used to describe the process of eating more carbohydrates than normal for a few days prior to an event. Your liver and muscles store glycogen (made from carbohydrate) at a certain level, but can hold more. Cyclists and other athletes often choose to eat twice as much carbohydrate as they normally would with every meal for about three days before a big race or long event.

Although these athletes consume carbohydrates before and during the event, having larger stores to start with puts off the time when they begin to rely solely on the food they take in as they ride or run, and so delays the risk of running out of energy. (This running out of available calories is known as *hitting the wall* or *bonking*.)

Here is a list of common foods from which you get carbohydrate:

- Bread
- Cereal
- Noodles
- Pasta
- Potato (and some other root vegetables)
- Rice
- Other wheat products, such as pastry or couscous

All these foods are complex carbohydrates that take longer than sugary things to digest and from which you get a steady flow of energy. Many fruits have simple carbohydrates in them, and you can eat those fruits to boost energy, but too much fruit sends sugar levels rising too quickly (and also possibly opens the floodgates of your alimentary canal, leading to an upset stomach).

Chocolate and sweets are simple carbohydrates that also give you an energy boost, but this doesn't last long – meaning these foods are not a solution if you're nearing the end of your glycogen stores and have some way to go.

If you're consciously carbing up, you need to aim at doubling the amount of complex carbohydrate foods you take in with every meal. This means less of the protein element (sorry, less steak) and less greens (sorry, less salad), just so that you can fit in the carbohydrates. Having so much of your meal as carbohydrate can make your food quite boring, but you're only making the change for a few days.

One of the things athletes warn about most is to not do anything out of the ordinary with your system immediately before a big event. Eating foods you're not used to can be disastrous if it upsets your system and has you pedalling off down the road feeling uncomfortable. Carbing up, if you've not done it before, could have this effect, so think about it and perhaps take it easy, only adding a small amount of extra carbohydrates in the days before a big race.

Carbing up is only necessary when you have a serious ride coming up, when you're going to be burning calories in big quantities and where your body's normal reserves wouldn't be able to cope. For everyday riding, such as commuting or getting to school, you don't use much extra energy, so simply eating properly at your regular mealtimes provides you with all the calories you need.

Knowing How Much to Eat

Working out roughly how much energy you use to do a certain amount of work is perfectly possible. This work could be chopping down a tree or cycling 100 miles (just over 160 kilometres). Although some people's muscles work more efficiently than others, you can get some idea.

So, in theory, you should be able to calculate a programme of eating and drinking that supplies the necessary energy at just the right time, keeping you fuelled and content. But complicating factors do arise. You may not feel like a big meal before a long bicycle ride, or you may not find it very easy to eat anything at all while you're cycling. And when you're done, although you know you need to replenish your stocks pretty quickly, you may not want to put anything at all of substance inside your stomach.

Because you definitely need the energy – if you don't get it, you won't be able to finish the ride – you have to find a way around your discomforts and get the right foods and drinks inside you.

Stocking up before

Most athletes warn against doing anything out of your routine before an event. This holds the same whether your event really is a big day you've been training for or just a training day that's part of your programme.

Here are some tips for fuelling up before a big event:

- **Use your training days to get your body used to the routine you'd like to use on big event days:** Make the start of your training days a big refuelling moment. Get in the habit of taking in plenty of carbohydrate at the start of the day, so that when you reach the day of your goal you are used to a big feed. If you're exerting yourself, keep the fat content of your fuel-meal low. You won't be using the fat for energy, and fat has been shown to slow down the absorption of carbohydrate. And, of course, a healthy diet is low in fat anyway.

- **Know in advance what food options will be available on the day of the event:** Will you be eating at home at the start of the day of your event-goal? If not, do you know what will be available for you that morning? Try to find out – if the food available on the day is not what you're eating now, you either have to take your pre-ride meal with you or switch your diet now so that you're not eating new food on the day. Carb up if you can, but don't stuff yourself so that you start your ride with an awkward, swollen belly.

- **Drink plenty of fluid before a big ride:** Drink when you first get up, then before you eat and after you eat. If your bladder feels full, try to keep it that way. Your body is quite capable of withdrawing fluid from this waste sack if it needs it. Don't try this if it's uncomfortable, however (some people are better at holding on than others).

Keeping up your energy during

If you're out on a recreational ride, you might want to stop and relish the scenery when the time comes to snack. If you're enjoying a low- to medium-intensity ride, you'll be burning fat, so having some fat for energy in the food you use for fuel is fine. Foods such as choc chip cookies or even chips are okay, but don't overdo any foods that you know aren't good for you.

If, however, you're burning rubber with a pounding heart, you need carbohydrates, and you need them frequently. Your glycogen stores should last a couple of hours, but you want to put off their depletion for as long as possible. After they've gone, you've got to take in all the energy you're using. Complex carbohydrates (such as pasta and cereals) are best for a steady input of energy, but if you ride close to your lactate threshold (refer to Chapter 11 for more about this) you might be better off getting energy from quicker sources – simple carbohydrates such as sweets or fruit or a mixture of both.

Consider the following when planning what to eat and drink during an event:

- ✔ As a rough guide, on a hard ride you need to be taking in 200 to 300 calories (about 60 grams or 2 ounces of carbohydrate) per hour. This intake isn't too difficult to manage, but you have to try to snack every 20 to 30 minutes if you want to keep your food in small portions.

- ✔ Your body probably won't like being given food while you're riding a bike if it's not used to it. The food may sit in your stomach and feel uncomfortable. But eating on a long ride is vital, and you can train your system to accept solids during exercise. Stick at it: eating whilst riding is a skill you need to have.

- ✔ Energy bars, energy gels and sports drinks are very popular. They give a mixture of simple and complex carbohydrate without any fat. On the whole, the taste and texture of these energy products is much better than they were a few years back, but you can still come across some truly awful ones that we can only describe as grim. Be sure to test one out before buying a year's supply. The newest on the scene is the energy gel, which is easy to carry, easy to open while riding your bike and easy to ingest. You simply tear off the end of the sachet and suck out the gel – no chewing is involved. We haven't sampled them all, but we've yet to try one that tastes truly lovely and they're far from being the cheapest option. Having said that, carrying a few with you is worthwhile.

- ✔ Old favourites are bananas and dried fruit. Bananas have lots of energy and dried fruit (such as prunes, apricots and raisins) has far more energy than just about anything and has been described as indestructible.

Follow these tips when you want to snack:

- ✔ Slow down, if you can, and keep all of your focus on the road as you reach for your food and as you consume it.

- ✔ Keep mouthfuls conservative so that you can still breathe easily.

- ✔ Stop eating if you start a climb and only start again when you reach the top (because you're going to be breathing much harder on the way up).

- ✔ If you're in a pack, move to the back for the whole process of scoffing and swallowing.

Refuelling after

Whether you've had a long Sunday afternoon ride with the family or have just finished a double century (200 kilometres or 125 miles), you need to refuel as a very important part of recovery. Your body gives you a window in which glycogen can be restored to your liver and muscles at a super-fast rate. By four hours your reabsorption rate is back to normal, and at two hours it'll be halfway there, so to do the best job of packing that glycogen back in you have to get chomping straightaway.

You need a certain amount of protein after a ride. Protein does many different things in your body, but getting repairs underway to damaged muscle fibres is essential. Aim to consume about 20 to 25 grams (just under an ounce) of protein after a ride, which is about what you'd find in a chicken breast. Powdered protein products mixed in with other foods also work well.

The trouble with needing to refuel after a ride is, if you're like us, the last thing you want to do after a tough ride is sit down to a big plate of food, especially something like chicken cordon bleu. We just can't do it – we'd rather go to sleep and forget the whole thing – but we know we've got to get the carbs in somehow.

What you decide to refuel with is up to you. Food is a very individual matter and different cyclists are able to eat different things after cycling. Gavin goes for a banana smoothie made with milk, vanilla ice-cream and one or two bananas. A banana smoothie is cold, full of fluid and energy, tastes great – and 1½ pints (750 millilitres) of milk (full cream or low fat) contains almost exactly 25 grams, just under an ounce, of protein. Ben, on the other hand, craves something savoury following a big ride, particularly after having consumed various unappetising gels and bars throughout the day. Really tasty bread is good in something like a cheese, celery and mayo sandwich, followed up by a scotch egg. That tends to hit the spot.

Bodily Fluids: Keeping a Balance

No matter whether you're in a race or just going for a ride in the country with the family, maintaining your bodily fluid levels while cycling is enormously important. If you lose enough fluid to actually become dehydrated you become quite ill, and even after replacing lost water it takes hours before you're able to get back on a bicycle.

Becoming ill at the point of dehydration isn't the only effect of not keeping your fluids up while cycling. As your fluid levels slowly drop, your performance diminishes. Your blood volume level is affected and the fluid level of your muscle cells gets lower, affecting how well they can work.

Healthy bodies seem to be able to lose up to two litres, just over four pints, of fluid and bounce right back, but more than this can cause you big problems. Fluid replacement is something you should be thinking about before you even get on your bike.

Follow these tips for staying hydrated while cycling:

- A glass of water is pretty easy to drink any time, so before you start cycling, why not drink four? This puts you ahead, but you still need to start taking swigs from your plastic bottle fairly soon after you start.

- If you plan to drink 750 to 1,000 millilitres (approximately 1½ to 2 pints) of fluid per hour while you're cycling, you should stay on top. Most stomachs can't absorb more than a litre (just over two pints) an hour and you can continue your rehydration process after you've finished cycling. If your bidon capacity doesn't cover the amount you need, think about getting a hydration pack or just wearing a small backpack filled with bottles of water. (Refer to Chapter 3 for more on these options.)

- If you live or go cycling in a warm place, your chilled water bottle, placed strategically on your hot down tube, will be as warm as bath water in less than an hour. Freeze it beforehand and you'll have ice-cold trickles until it's all gone. If you're carrying two bidons, drink first from the one on your down tube where you can easily reach it. When this one's empty, switch them over and start on the new one in the same safe spot.

- On longer rides, continually drinking lots of water can become tedious or even physically difficult. If you find that sports drinks go down easier, use them to your advantage. They do contain some energy to help keep you going.

- Studies have shown that on rides of two hours or less no advantage exists in drinking sports drinks. On longer rides, or in places where conditions are very hot or humid, it may very well be a good idea to use these drinks because they contain sodium and potassium. Check the contents of your chosen drink, however, because some of them don't have very much sodium and it might be an idea to add extra salt or swallow salt tablets.

You can lose a great deal of fluid through perspiration without being aware of it when cycling. On warm days, for example, your high-wicking jersey spirits away your sweaty fluids and you won't even get a damp shirt. Try weighing yourself before going out for an hour on a bike without any fluids and then weighing yourself again when you get home. The measurable difference you see is all water lost through your pores. A kilogram of bodyweight lost is equivalent to a litre of water.

Some riders think that if drinking water is so important they should drink a huge amount to keep well and eliminate the risk of dehydration. Drinking lots of water is a good thing, but you can drink too much. Over-hydrating results in the condition of *hyponatraemia,* where the water level in the blood becomes raised compared to the sodium level. When the sodium level in the blood is lower than the sodium level in cells, water transfers into the cells by a process of osmosis. The cells get bigger. This increase in size is not a problem throughout most of the body, but is a big problem in the brain. The brain is constricted by the skull and if it starts to swell it begins to squeeze its way out of the base of the skull. Symptoms of hyponatraemia include general swelling, nausea and headache. Seizures, coma and death may follow.

At marathon events in the US, drinking stops have been moved further apart because some competitors have ended up taking in far too much fluid and dying. If you aim to consume about a litre of water per hour while cycling, you shouldn't put yourself at risk of over-hydrating.

Diet Hard: Food for Hardcore Cyclists

Hardcore cyclists ride hundreds of miles every week. Some of them can do that in a day. They burn up calories everywhere they cycle. Perhaps you've seen one standing in a supermarket, closely studying the nutrition box on a product label. He's not worrying about putting on weight – he's checking the item has enough calories. He might look up and give you an almost (not quite) smug smile and say, 'I can eat anything I want'. Because hardcore cyclists can. They can eat anything at all and are never going to put on any weight. Elite cyclists typically get through more than 6,000 calories per day. They need so much food that meals don't really cover their needs and so they tend to graze, just eating high-energy foods in small amounts almost constantly.

Of course, saying they can eat anything they want doesn't mean they binge. Very fit cyclists, like any other athletes, give themselves strict guidelines as to what they eat. Apart from a high intake of carbohydrates, pro cyclists also go for a diet that's low in fat and high in protein, vitamins and minerals. They also try to keep constantly well hydrated. You should do the same if you're training hard or hoping to regularly compete in cycling events.

When you're training or competing in events, and so hoping to keep at your peak performance level, keep your alcohol intake to a minimum and certainly don't consume it every day. If you do consume any alcohol, rehydration becomes supremely important. You also need to watch your intake of caffeine. A coffee here and there does no harm – in fact, it can give a boost to your energy levels halfway through a ride – but caffeine is a diuretic, which means it decreases your body's efficiency at hanging on to fluids.

Eating solid foods can get difficult after intense exercise, but eating is, of course, essential for recovery and refuelling. Gavin once spoke to a man who had recently completed the Simpson Desert Bike Challenge: five days across hundreds of loose sand dunes in scorching heat. He told me of the physical repulsion he felt at the end of the day when he cowered in his shade tent and was handed a plate of pasta. He couldn't have wanted anything less, but he had to eat it.

In hot places, cold items are a much more appealing prospect. In cold climates, hot things make you feel better. Some sweet foods that you can take more easily after intense, prolonged exercise are:

- Chocolate milk
- Flavoured, pre-made custard
- Hot chocolate
- Ice-cream
- Plain yoghurt with fresh or frozen berries
- Smoothies

And some good savoury foods are:

- Instant soup
- Risotto
- Quick oats
- Noodles
- Cous cous
- A triple-decker sandwich

If your glycogen stores have been emptied, as they will after several hours of heavy exercise, you need to take in 200 grams (just over 7 ounces) of carbohydrate within the first two hours of finishing your ride. However, as refilling your stores is done so much more effectively straight after you stop moving, you should try to get at least 50 grams, or 1¾ ounces, (and even more is better) inside you in the first 15 minutes.

Chapter 17

Troubleshooting: Can You Fix It? Yes, You Can!

*Y*ou need to frequently carry out a few maintenance and repair chores when you own and ride a bicycle. Keeping your bike clean, for example, is important for keeping it looking good and working well. Some things can go wrong or need fixing now and again and although you can always get them fixed at the shop, being able to fix them yourself is very handy (and much cheaper).

In fact, problems with your bike can arise while you're out on the road or trail and if you can't fix them there and then your ride is over. Some people learn these skills when they're young and they become second nature, but if that didn't happen for you, getting some of this know-how under your belt as quickly as possible is a very good idea. This chapter provides that know-how.

None of the techniques we describe in this chapter are perplexing or difficult, but it may take practice before you're a smooth operator when it comes to doing things like flipping over your bike and ripping out an inner tube. If you've got a bit of spare time, get your bike out and have a go at some of these jobs at home so that you're not performing them for the first time alone and surrounded by trees or traffic. If you've got friends who are good at these things, invite one of them over to show you the ropes. Promise cake, massage or beer, depending on your friend's tastes, and you'll be getting a fair swap.

Keeping Your Bike Clean

Many road bike riders give their bikes a thorough wash and blow dry immediately after a ride. They simply cannot be seen starting their next ride with little flecks of mud spattered over their down tubes or gritty streaks on their rims. Washing your bike every time you take it out may not be essential – it just depends how you feel about it – but giving it a good soap down every now and then will bring it back to life. You'll stand back when you've finished and feel proud of its sparkle.

Keeping your bike clean also lengthens its life, or at least the life of some of its parts. Getting any mud spots off chrome stops them erupting into rust. Mud can also eat into the paint on your frame, depending on its acidity. Getting mud into your brakes can scratch your rims or discs and getting muck into lubricated parts can cake them up, slow them down and wear them out.

Mountain bikes, or any other bikes used for riding on trails, are especially prone to getting filthy and you do need to clean them more often than road bikes. You might be tempted to think that a dirt-caked bike is a good look because it suggests you do hardly anything but tackle tough trails and live mostly in mud. In fact, mud slows you down, clogs up your *drivetrain* (chain and rings) and wears out moving parts.

Washing your bike shouldn't take you more than ten or fifteen minutes. Cleaning and relubing your chain at the same time (see the following section for details on this) adds on another five or ten minutes, but is really not a lengthy job.

Cleaning your bike isn't a huge job and you won't be crouching down or bending over for long. Make sure your bike is propped up securely before you start. Some people remove their wheels to wash their bikes, as this gives them better access to tucked-away parts of the frame. Taking off the wheels isn't essential, though, and you need a repair stand or some other means of holding the bike off the ground if you do. Some people turn their bikes upside down to clean them, but this allows water to get inside the steerer tube, which may cause damage if it lingers.

To clean your bike you need:

- Bucket of soapy water (use just a tiny bit of an eco-friendly washing-up liquid)
- Clean water
- Rags

✔ Small brush (an old washing up brush will do)

✔ Sponge

✔ Wax (optional)

Follow these tips to thoroughly clean your bike:

✔ **Start at the top and work your way down:** A sponge works well on the saddle and bar tape if you have it. Otherwise, use a rag on these areas as well as the frame and any bolted on bits. Don't forget to clean under your seat. Dirt can lurk here in alarming quantities. Remove any detachable accessories, such as your pump, and wash these separately. Get right into any hidden away corners by winding your rag and rubbing it in a small, circular motion.

✔ **Be thorough and clean your wheel rims, spokes and even the rubber of your tyres:** Having a shining clean bike with muddy or dusty tyres just doesn't quite make the grade. Don't forget to wipe under your bottom bracket because plenty of dirt gathers there. Leave your rear cassette and front chainrings until you're cleaning the chain.

✔ **Rinse your bike by trickling water over it:** When you've cleaned everything, get some clean water in a bucket or watering can and gently pour it over the top of the bike.

Never use a high-pressure hose to clean or rinse your bike. Bicycles have enclosed, lubricated parts that are not completely watertight – if you jet water into them, your bike will be in big trouble.

✔ **Dry your bike in the sun or wipe it dry with rags if you have plenty:** Some people, possibly surfers who like to wax their boards, enjoy waxing the frames of their bikes. Waxing bikes is a lovely show of dedication and affection, but isn't essential.

If you find any upsetting scratches on your paintwork and can't find a matching paint, nail polish works for small touch-ups. (Sit with your fingers raised until it's dry.)

Joining the Chain Gang

Your chain is probably the most important part of your bike to keep clean. It does tremendous work under huge pressure and if it starts to fill with grit or lose its lubrication it works far less efficiently and can break.

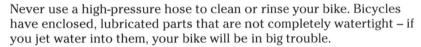

Even a clean chain needs some attention if you've been riding in the rain. The water eventually washes off your lube and leaves your mechanisms grinding and squawking as you pedal. You can't very successfully relube while your bike is still wet, but you must get to it before you take the bike out again.

When degreasing (cleaning) and relubing a chain, different people have different techniques, and even use varying materials. In the following sections, I describe how I perform these two different stages of restoring a bicycle's chain to smooth working order.

To degrease and relube your bike you need:

- Brush (an old toothbrush works well)
- Clean water
- Degreaser, aerosol or some other solution
- Lube (whichever kind you prefer – see the sidebar 'Bicycle lubes' for the most common types)
- Rags
- Soapy water

Degreasing

To degrease your chain and other lubricated moving parts, you need a solvent of some kind. You can use an aerosol degreaser, which is cheap and lasts for ages. Some people use diesel fuel diluted in water. Citrus degreasers cut through grease very effectively, but are acidic and you should take care to keep this stuff off your frame. Actually, none of these substances is particularly pleasant, so try to keep them off everything if you can.

Follow these steps to degrease your chain:

1. **Apply the degreaser.**

   Most of the dirt that gets into your chain comes flying off the front wheel or onto the outside of the chain loop from other directions. Because of this, be sure to send the degreaser the opposite way, applying from the inside of the loop, spraying downwards onto the lower run of your chain. Turn your crank backwards and make sure you get the whole length of your chain covered. Spray down onto the top of your rear cassette and down onto your chainwheels.

2. **Leave the degreaser for a moment to do its degreasing work.**

3. **Rinse all the gunk off.**

   Pour water over the cassette, chainrings and lower loop of the chain (turning the crank to give you access to the whole chain). If your chain is particularly dirty, you may need to repeat this whole process.

4. **Scrub the chain.**

   Get some soapy water (the same as you used to clean the bike) and a brush and give the chain a scrub, getting the bristles right into the gaps. Also scrub what you can get at on the cassette and chainwheels. Use a thin rag and a flossing motion to get between these cogged wheels.

5. **Dry the chain.**

   Use clean, dry rags to wipe your chain dry, running it between your fingers and giving it massaging movements to be as thorough as you can. Wipe in between the cogwheels on your cassette and also your chainwheels at the front.

Leave the bike for a while before relubing, just to let any inaccessible damp bits dry off.

Relubing

You don't generally need to put any lube on anything other than the chain. Here's how you do it:

1. **Hold a rag underneath the lower run of the chain.**

2. **Apply fresh lube drop by drop, link by link, turning your crank backwards with your third hand.**

   We know, you've only got two hands, so either you put the rag on the ground or you hold the bottle of lube in your teeth. Lube bottles aren't very big, so you could give this a go. Putting the rag on the ground is usually easier, though.

   You must make sure that lube doesn't drip onto the rims of your wheels. If it falls onto the strip where your brake blocks grip, your brakes won't work. You'll have to clean the wheels and you might have to replace the brake blocks before you have the power to stop once more.

3. **When you've applied lube to the entire chain, get another clean rag and wipe along the chain again, using the massaging movement to get the lube working its way into all the little joints and crevices.**

Bicycle lubes

In addition to the factory lube that's on your bike's chain when you buy your bike, three different kinds of lube are readily available that you can use on your bike chain. Each has advantages and disadvantages and some perform better than others in certain conditions.

Never use anything other than a purpose-made chain lubricant on your chain. Other oils won't do the same job, they may collect a colossal amount of debris and they may damage your chain.

Dry lubes are a recent invention. They combine a dry lubricant with a solvent that carries the lube into all the tiny spaces it needs to go. The solvent evaporates, leaving a dry coating on all the moving parts. Dry lubes don't pick up any dirt, but they have a low water resistance and will wash off if you have to ford a creek or cycle in the rain.

Factory lube is what is on your chain when you first get your bike. This lube varies in quality, but will have been very well applied. Leave it until you're sure it needs changing.

Wax lube goes on wet, but dries leaving a thick wax layer that won't carry any dirt. Old wax and any contaminants will come off with reapplication, so you hardly ever have to actually clean your chain. You do need to replace wax lubes quite frequently, and they wash off quite quickly in wet conditions.

Wet lubes are the traditional kind of oily lube. Although they do need traditional cleaning and pick up some dirt, they last better than any other in wet conditions and actually lubricate better than dry or wax.

Over time your chain lengthens, due to the wearing down of the rollers and rivets in the links. The mechanic at your bike shop can test for this just by measuring a section of your chain. If it has stretched, you need to replace it, and you might find the teeth of your sprockets have worn. They also need to be replaced before your chain starts jumping and slipping as you ride.

Fixing a Hole

Fixing a puncture is the first piece of bicycle maintenance any cyclist should learn. An unfortunate, and sometimes quite upsetting, fact of cycling is that punctures can happen at any time – and always happen when you're least expecting one.

Being prepared for a puncture is important. Always have with you what it takes to get yourself back on your bicycle and pedalling. Get one of those little saddlebags (the ones that hang underneath your seat) and fill it with the things that you need. Either fix a pump to your frame or make sure you always take one with you (I store mine next to my helmet).

Puncture repair equipment to put in your saddlebag includes the following:

- Adjustable spanner (take two if you don't have a quick release on your wheels)
- Allen keys (you don't need them to fix a puncture, but they're very small and are the most likely tools you'll need for anything else)
- Chalk, one small piece, any colour
- Puncture patches
- Rubber cement
- Sandpaper, one small square
- Spare inner tube (make sure it's the right size)
- Tyre levers (two of them)

Finding the puncture

You may find you have a puncture when you get your bike out for a new day of cycling, when you come back to your locked-up bike while you're out and about – or even while you're cycling.

If you suddenly feel a strong, rhythmic bumping as you roll along, have a look down – has either of your tyres become very quickly flat? If it has, get off your bike straightaway and get off the road. Riding with no air in your tube is dangerous, can very easily damage the tyre and even damage the wheel.

When you realise that you have a puncture, the first thing you need to do is find out where in the inner tube it is.

If you're riding in traffic, try to get yourself away from the noise – to where you can hear the hissing of a tiny little hole in your inner tube – and find a spot where you have space to work on your bike. Take your little saddle pouch off your bike and turn your bike upside down. (Don't forget to remove your bike computer if you've positioned it on a high point on your handlebars.)

Taking your wheel off to fix a puncture is extra work, but it makes the process easier. If you have to replace the inner tube, you have to take the wheel off the bike. (See 'Removing and Replacing a Wheel' later in this chapter.)

Follow these steps to finding a puncture:

1. **Remove one bead (the hard edge) of the tyre so that you can pull out the inner tube all the way around.**

See the section 'Changing a Tyre' later in this chapter for how to get one side of the tyre off the wheel.

2. **Take off the cap from the valve.**

   Also remove the small metal ring that screws down the valve if you have Presta valves.

3. **Move the loose tyre side back over the wheel at the valve point, lift the valve out of the hole in the wheel and remove the inner tube entirely.**

4. **Attach your pump to the valve and inflate the tyre so that it's bulging and tight.**

   This should take about 20 or 30 pumps.

   If you've taken off your wheel, you'll now be holding your inner tube independently in your hands. If your wheel is still on the bike, your tube will be hooked around the fork or stays and you'll have to work close up to the bike. Working this way is less convenient, but then you didn't want to take off the wheel.

5. **Put the tyre to your ear and, starting at the valve, move it around slowly, listening for the hiss of escaping air.**

   If you're lucky and you have a quiet environment, you may hear hissing quite easily and so find the hole quite quickly. If your tyre deflates before you've found the hole, pump it up and have another go.

6. **If you can't hear the leak, inflate the inner tube and put it in water.**

   Buckets are good, but even a puddle will do. Work the inner tube round so that all of it passes through the water until you find the hole. When you get to the hole, you'll see an unmistakable line of bubbles rising from the rupture.

7. **When you find the puncture, mark its position on the inner tube with your chalk.**

   If you had to submerge the inner tube, dry it before marking it with the chalk.

Patching options

When you've located the offending and troublesome puncture (see the preceding section), you need to patch it. Here's how:

1. **Make sure the area around the hole is clean and dry.**

2. **Use a little square of sandpaper to very lightly roughen the surface around the hole.**

3. **Apply a patch.**

   If you've got glueless patches, just slap one on, making sure it's firmly stuck down.

   We love glueless patches and don't mind paying the extra amount they cost. Some people say they don't work as well, but that hasn't been our experience at all.

   If you've got the old-fashioned type of patch, you have to reach for your little tube of rubber glue. Squeeze out plenty of the goo in an area just bigger than the patch you're going to use. Then you have to sit and count buses, wave at rowers or swat mosquitoes, depending on where you are, until the rubber cement is tacky. When it is tacky, place the patch over the hole and the glue and make sure you've firmly attached it all over. Then head back to the buses, rowers or mosquitoes for another ten minutes until the cement is dry.

4. **Using your nail or the dimpled section in you puncture repair box, if it has one, grate a little of the chalk around the patch.**

   Doing this dries up any excess cement and stops your tube sticking to the tyre when you put everything back together.

5. **Locate the cause of the puncture.**

   Around half the time the sharp item that caused the puncture is still in the tyre. Have a look at where the puncture is in relation to the valve and work out roughly where the tyre must have been breached. Look carefully at the outside of the tyre – often you can see the thick end of whatever the sharp object was from the outside.

   If you don't see anything on the outside of your tyre, start running your fingers around the inside of the tyre, feeling for the slightest imperfection. The sharp thing, whatever it was, may only be protruding a tiny amount now the tyre isn't under any pressure.

   Have a very good feel and look for the item that did the damage. Only proceed with getting back on the road if you're very sure nothing is still stuck in your tyre. Nothing is more disappointing and frustrating than cycling off after all the rigmarole of fixing a puncture, only to roll to a stop just down the road with another flat.

6. **Start reassembling your tyre and wheel by putting a little air into your tube.**

   Don't pump in so much air that the tube is tight, but pump in just enough to give the tube enough body to allow you to work it back into the tyre. Tubes that are too floppy at this stage get tangled and fall out.

Start by moving the tyre out of the way and re-inserting the valve through the hole in the wheel. Make sure the tube is not twisted as you work it right into the tyre all the way around.

7. **Put the tyre back on.**

Refer to the section 'Changing a Tyre' later in this chapter for instructions on how to put the tyre back on.

8. **Pump up the tyre.**

Before you pump up the tyre completely, have a look all the way round the rim on the side the tyre came off for any sign of inner tube caught under the bead. If you see anything, carefully use a lever to get the tube tucked in and out of sight. Then pump up the tyre.

If you can't find the puncture, don't have time or simply can't be bothered, use your spare inner tube. If you do this, make extra sure that you check to see whether the alien body that did the damage is still hiding in your tyre – or you may end up with two punctured tubes. We always just whip in the spare tube, promising that we'll fix the old one when we get home. We've each now got quite a collection of damaged tubes waiting for that special moment.

Removing and Replacing a Wheel

You may need to take off a wheel to fix a puncture, change a tyre, fit a bike into a car or pack a bike in a box. Taking off the front wheel is easier than the back and taking off either wheel is a lot simpler if you have a *quick release* – a lever on the hub which you operate by hand and which, when closed, clamps your wheel in place and, when opened, lets you remove it, all in a matter of seconds.

Quick releases make things much easier for you in certain common circumstances, but are also a bit of a security headache. When you lock up your bike, you have to make sure that your frame as well as any wheel that has a quick release is included in the locking system, which may mean carrying more than one chain. If you don't have quick releases and would like to be able to get your wheels off quicker (and the extra locking requirements don't bother you), pop down to the bike shop and ask them if they can fix quick releases to your bike. They will have to fit new hub axles, but most hubs are suitable for the conversion.

Removing the front wheel

Taking off your front wheel is a very easy job. If you've got a quick release, follow these simple steps:

1. **Pull the lever away from the bike to make the fitting looser.**

2. **Hold the lever steady and unscrew the little cap on the other side.**

   Give it about ten turns.

3. **Lift the wheel out.**

   If you've got the bike resting upside down, just lift the wheel out of the forks. If the bike is the right way up, lift the front by the handlebars and the wheel should simply slip out of its housing.

4. **Rest the bike down – gently – on the end of the forks.**

If you've got nuts on your front wheel, you need a spanner and to follow these steps:

1. **Loosen the nuts on either side of the hub.**

   You don't need to take the nuts right off – just give them a clearance of a couple of millimetres (about ⅒ inch) from the forks.

2. **Disengage the security hook, if present.**

   Some older bikes have this extra security gizmo, usually a little metal hook, one end of which tucks into a hole in the fork.

3. **Lift the wheel out.**

With either system of releasing your front wheel, you might find, after freeing the wheel from the forks, you still can't get it off. This could be because the brake blocks don't move back far enough to allow the wheel to pass through them – common with the fat tyres you find on mountain bikes. The most common kind of brakes are linear-pull brakes and to get the wheel off with this kind of brake you need to release the brake cable from the cable housing at the top of one of the brake arms. Squeeze the arms together tightly to get the cable free. On side-pull brakes, look for a small lever which opens up the gap between the brake blocks by a centimetre (⅜ inch) or so, which makes getting the wheel through easier.

If you take the brake cable from its housing, or open the lever, putting them back when you replace the wheel is vitally important. Otherwise, you ride away with no brake.

If you have disc brakes, you have to guide the wheel (front or back) into position getting the disc carefully into its slot and between the pads before the axle reaches the dropouts. Other kinds of brakes are uncommon on fat-tyred bikes, but if you have them you may have to loosen the brake blocks to release the wheel.

Removing the back wheel

As with a front wheel, a quick-release mechanism makes removing the back wheel a lot easier. To remove the back wheel, follow these steps:

1. **Turn the bike upside down.**

2. **Turn the pedals and change the gears so the chain is on the smallest sprocket at the back to make getting the wheel on and off easier.**

3. **Loosen the wheel.**

   Depending on whether you have quick release or nuts, follow the steps outlined for loosening your front wheel (see the preceding section).

4. **Remove the wheel.**

   Lift the wheel upwards and towards the middle of the bike. If you have a rear dérailleur you may have to push the pulley wheel back out of the way. As you lift the wheel, the cassette will catch on the lower (now upper) loop of the chain. Just lift the chain off and the wheel clear.

Similar to the front wheel, you may again find that the wheel only comes away if you release the brake cable from its housing or move the lever. Don't forget to put them back to how you found them when you've finished.

When you return the wheel, do everything in reverse:

1. **Move it into position, hooking the chain over the cassette.**

2. **Push the pulley wheel back so you can get the wheel down and the axle spindle into the dropouts.**

3. **Manoeuvre the wheel into the dropouts.**

   Check that the wheel is straight by seeing if the tyre is centred between the chainstays.

4. **Tighten it up.**

   Give the cranks a couple of turns to get the chain onto the right sprocket on the cassette. Replace the brake cable or lever to the original position, turn the bike back over and away you go.

Changing a Tyre

To change a tyre you first have to remove the wheel from your bicycle (refer to the preceding section). When you have the wheel off the bike, follow these steps to remove the tyre:

1. **Deflate the inner tube if it's not already flat.**

2. **Insert one tyre lever between the rim of the wheel and the tyre, pointing down towards the hub, with the little bent end towards the tyre.**

3. **Work the lever in so that you can feel you've caught the bead (the hard edge of the tyre).**

4. **Pull the lever right over the rim and down towards the hub.**

   The bead lifts out of the rim and off the arc of the wheel. Most plastic tyre levers have a slot that is there for you to hook the lever onto a spoke. If you've got one, do so: this frees up both hands.

5. **Put the second lever in between the rim and the tyre, two spokes down from the first one.**

6. **Lever the bead off the rim.**

   You now have a longer section of the bead clear of the wheel.

7. **Hold the second lever in its down position and move it away from the first one freeing more and more of the bead from the wheel.**

   This gets much easier very quickly and soon the whole of that side of the tyre will be off the wheel.

8. **Pull the other side free with your hands to get the tyre off completely.**

Before you start fitting a new tyre make sure you're putting it on the right way. Most tyres are directional and somewhere in the relief writing on the side is an arrow or words indicating which way the tyre should go when your bike is moving forwards. Your back wheel can only go on one way, because of its sprockets, and your front wheel may have a magnet on the side of your computer transmitter, so have a look and work it out.

Getting a new tyre on a wheel can be a little tricky at the start. The tyre has never been on a wheel or been under pressure from inflation before and is not used to being in that shape. The tyre will seem like a floppy, useless thing. Be patient.

Here's how you get a new tyre on the wheel:

1. **Work the first bead over the wheel.**

2. **Get your inner tube valve in place and your slightly inflated inner tube tucked into the tyre.**

3. **Start tucking the second bead over the edge of the rim and onto the wheel.**

   You should be able to get at least halfway around. Keep checking that the tyre bead is seated correctly as this makes things easier. Sometimes you can get the whole tyre on with just tough fingers, but you may need to use levers.

If you need to use levers, get one lever under one end of the stretch that's off the wheel. Hook it over the rim and lever up to get the tyre in place. Hold it there and get the other lever at the other end of the section off the wheel. (This is one of those occasions when you need to use all three hands.) Lever up. You may now be able to just push the remaining bead over the rim and onto the wheel. If not, close in on your levering until you have it all in place.

Check all round both sides for any part of the inner tube caught under the edge of the new tyre. If you find anything, lever the bead over the caught tube. Then get pumping.

Spotting a Problem

Things can go wrong with your bike that you're not able to fix, but if you spot a problem you can get help to sort it out before it gets much worse. If you can identify what's wrong, even though you don't have the skills to repair it you've done half the work by getting your bike into the right hands before it's too late.

In the following sections I cover the things to look out for generally and provide some tips if you think something's wrong.

Spoke too soon

Have a think about your wheels. The two of them carry all the weight of you and the bike, sometimes going quite fast. And they do it all on those thin sticks of metal, your spokes – which are the only things keeping everything from clunking to the floor.

If you were to hold a spoke in your hands and try to bend it, you would see that it's actually – individually – not very strong. Spokes show their strength on bikes only because they are so cleverly placed, and because so many are used.

So keep an eye on them. If you can see that a spoke might be more use opening an old-fashioned bottle of wine (one with a cork in it), get it fixed. Because a bent spoke is as good as a broken one, and if one's gone, that whole intricate pattern of spokes that provides the strength to keep up your bicycle is compromised. You may be still rolling along nicely now, but you could be headed for trouble.

Full (loose) stem ahead

You might notice a little looseness in your bars that isn't quite right. If you pick up and put down the front of the bike you might feel an extra little clunk. If you hold the front brake on and rock the bike back and forward and find there's some give, that's another indication that things aren't right. Stem heads commonly work themselves loose and when this happens, parts inside the headset could wear or even break – so checking that yours is fixed securely is well worth doing regularly.

Pick up the handlebars again. Do they flop to one side? They should – if they don't the stem could be fixed too tight. If the stem is too tight you won't be able to steer properly.

Riding around with a maladjusted stem isn't safe, so if you think yours has a problem, get on down to the bike shop.

Not true (your wheel, that is)

As you ride along, you should be able to look down on the top of your front wheel and see it spinning round in a nice straight line. If you suddenly spot part of it darting out of the line, your wheel is not true. That doesn't mean it is in any way false or not existing anymore; it means the wheel isn't a circle in a flat plane. Your wheel is out of whack.

You can also check your back wheel. Look down and check the wheel where you can see it spinning through the chainstays. Is it on the straight and narrow, or can you see that telltale flip to the side?

If you see a variation in the spinning front or back wheel, get it fixed. Your spokes should all be tightened to a certain tension and if one of them gets too loose or too tight your wheel goes out of 'true' alignment.

Your wheel doesn't have the same strength if it isn't properly aligned and when one spoke gets out of line, others may follow.

At the bike shop they have a piece of equipment called a *truing stand*. They can fix your wheel to the stand where *callipers* tell the mechanic very precisely if an aligned circle is present. The mechanic plays the spokes like the strings of a harp and tightens those little screw bits at the top of your spokes until the wheel spins without deviation.

Truing a wheel is not a very easy skill to learn, so even if you have the right tools lying around, taking the wheel to your friends at the shop is probably best.

Time for a tyre transplant

It takes a fairly long time, especially if you don't ride a lot, but after a while you notice that all those smart knobbles that made up your tread have gone. Your tyres are bald.

Your rear tyre wears out much faster than your front one (sometimes three times as fast), owing to the heavier load it carries. If you think your rear tyre is just wearing a bit, you can swap your tyres round to get longer use from the one pair.

If your tyres become bald, having worn away most of their tread, you start to get more and more punctures. The rubber won't offer you the same protection anymore and you might start spending a lot of time at the roadside fiddling with patches.

When you buy new tyres, ask what different types are available. If you do most of your riding on roads, you don't need mountains of tread – you roll along more freely with *slicks* (tyres with very little tread) or semi-slicks. Find out, too, about the brilliant, newer tyres which have a strip of Kevlar running all the way round beneath the rubber. While the Kevlar won't stop every puncture, it does prevent 90 per cent of them, especially from sharp little bits of glass or flint that would otherwise give you a flat. These tyres don't come cheap, but if you work out the cost of new inner tubes and add the reduction in hassle (if you're commuting, then you won't want a puncture to make you late for that meeting) they are worth every penny.

Note down the size of your tyres before you go to the shop. This information is written in relief on the side of your tyre in the form of wheel diameter multiplied by width – for example, 26 × 1.50 – or a pair of numbers, such as 622–23 or 559–40.

Squeak, rattle and clunk

If you've got any strange noises coming from your bike, you should be concerned – something could be seriously wrong. Sometimes, working out what the problem is can be simple enough, but noises have been known to baffle cyclists for very long periods of time.

Here are just a few suggestions as to where you might have a look for a particular noise:

✔ A squeak is most commonly coming from your chain. Which also means you haven't been looking after it as well as you could because the biggest cause of squeaks on bikes is an unlubricated chain. Get dripping with the lube. Other causes for a squeak are the rear dérailleur pulley wheels. Again, the cause is non-lubrication, and you should get a couple of drops of the good stuff onto your jockey wheels' moving surfaces and bearings.

✔ A rattle could be your headset (refer to the section 'Full (loose) stem ahead' earlier in this chapter), pump, bottle cage, tools or even the little circular nuts you get on Presta valves. If the rattle comes from your pump, find something you can wedge in between the pump and the frame to act as a cushion. Bottle cages might need tightening or bending so that they hold a bottle more securely. Separate your tools in your little saddle bag so that they don't jingle. Those little circular nuts – tighten them.

✔ A clunk could just be a crank repeatedly knocking against your pump if you keep it on your down tube and part of it sticks out. Move it and secure it.

✔ A creak could be a variety of hidden things. Seat posts and saddles can creak like an old staircase if they're even a little loose. Clipless pedals and shoes can make funny noises. Try cleaning them and giving your cleats just a drop of lubrication. (Careful where you walk if you do.)

We've read one story of a cyclist who lived with a creak for years. His friends laughed at him as he laboured away to track it down. He stripped his bike and rebuilt his wheels, but still couldn't identify the creak. One day it dawned on him. He took off the little spoke magnet that triggered his computer transmitter and found that its housing had been damaged. He straightened it out with pliers – and no more creak.

If you've got a noise and want it fixed, do your very best to identify where it's coming from. The guys at the bike shop can do anything. Almost anything. But they don't have time to ride your bike round and round the block.

Chapter 18

Making Checks and Adjustments: The Next Step

- -

In This Chapter

▶ Suspending disbelief (and servicing your front suspension)

▶ Looking at seating arrangements

▶ Shifting over your gears

▶ Getting braking news

▶ Changing chains

- -

*I*n this chapter, we help you take a step towards being someone who knows how to fix a bike. If you don't want to be the kind of cyclist who goes running off to the bike shop every time you need something altered or checked – or if they're just sick of the sight of you down there – we give you some good tips for getting the bike running more smoothly or more to your liking.

We cover some complex areas, such as suspension, brakes and gears. Although we show you how to make some basic adjustments, you'll still need some help if anything goes substantially wrong. You may need some tools for these jobs, but not much more than a few standard items.

Sorting the Shock Treatment

Although a slight shift has occurred over the last couple of years back towards the old utility bicycle – bikes with upright seating positions, big narrow wheels and no suspension – many bikes still have bouncing front suspension *forks* (the forks are the part of the bike that holds the front wheel). Some mountain bikes, especially expensive ones, have dual (front and rear) suspension, but this is less common.

In this section, we provide some tips on looking after your springy forks – how to keep them in good nick and working well for you.

When you purchased your bike, you should have received a manual. In fact, you should have been given two manuals: one for your bike and one for your suspension forks. A lot of the time this doesn't happen, so if you don't have yours you can go online to the forks manufacturer's website, where you should be able to download the manual for your particular forks. The manual will have specific instructions relating to your forks.

Manufacturers often recommend servicing suspension forks every two or three months. If you ride in muddy, wet conditions this advice is probably sound. If not, having a look at them that often and to check that they're functioning still makes sense. Experience suggests that in ordinary use suspension forks can go quite a long time without a great deal of attention.

Figure 18-1 shows the main parts that make up front suspension forks. Here's what you should check:

- **The boot:** The *boot* is the rubber concertina cover – if you've got one – that shields the opening where the top half of the fork slides down into the lower part. Check that the boot fits tightly and is intact because it keeps water and dirt away from that important join. You may be able to buy replacements of these for your bike, but you might find yourself asking if the shop has anything lying around that might fit.

- **The wiper seal under the boot:** The *wiper seal* is there to wipe the *stanchion* (the upper part of the suspension that slides down into the lower part, the *slider*). The seal should have a slight oily sheen and hug the stanchion. If a seal isn't gripping tightly all round, it lets in water and dirt and you'll have to have the forks looked at. Before you lift this seal make sure the stanchion and *crown* (the top bridge of the fork) are clean so that no dirt falls inside.

  The wiper seal may have a wire spring-clip around it holding it in place. Take it off and clean it. Move the seal up the stanchion. You may have to lever it up out of its home. If you do, be very careful not to slip and scratch the stanchion (you can wrap a rag around the stanchion to protect it). Inside the slider is a foam ring around the stanchion. Drop a few drops of suspension oil (not just any oil) onto this ring.

  If any dirt is present around the wiper seal, clean it and then slide it back down into position. Don't forget to put back the wire clip if one was present. Checking that these barriers are watertight and oiled helps to keep unwanted and damaging water and dirt out of your forks.

✔ **Air pressure:** If you have air suspension, you need to check periodically to see if the pressure is still correct. Air forks can keep their pressure for a long time, but seals may start to wear eventually and having the right pressure is important or they won't work. The manual for your front suspension should include a table of suggested pressures, which is dependent on your weight.

To check the air pressure of your forks and pump air into them you need a suspension pump. These pumps have a special screw fitting and a gauge. You might like to just ask the guys at the shop to do this for you if you haven't got one, as these pumps are quite expensive. The air valve is usually at the top of one of the fork legs, although you sometimes find it at the bottom.

Remove the valve cap and screw the pump onto the valve. Pump air until you get the pressure you want. If you go too high, an extra little valve should be present to let some air out without disconnecting the pump. When you're done, unscrew the pump (you'll hear a hiss, but this comes from the pump, not the valve) and replace the cap.

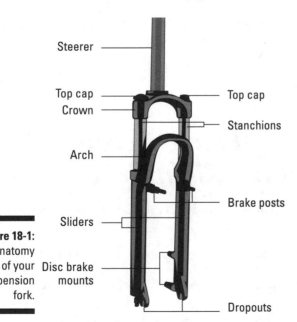

Figure 18-1:
Anatomy of your suspension fork.

Steerer

Top cap
Crown

Top cap

Stanchions

Arch

Brake posts

Sliders

Disc brake mounts

Dropouts

When you sit on your bike, about 20 per cent of the length of the stanchion should slide down into the slider. Spring forks should have a preload adjustment on top of one of the legs. This shifts the spring to adapt to how much the suspension sags when you sit on it. With air suspension you should get the right sag for your weight from the pressure recommended in the manual. If you don't know what pressure to have (and can't find out), use the following method and adjustments in pressure to get to the right setting. (You can also use this method with springs – just turn the adjuster on the fork until you get the right preload setting.)

Here's how you check how much your suspension sags:

1. **Fix a cable tie around the bottom end of the stanchion.**
2. **Sit on the bike.**
3. **Get off the bike.**
4. **Have a look at how far up the stanchion the cable tie has moved.**
5. **Make your adjustments accordingly.**

The last thing to adjust on your suspension forks is the *damping*, which is what stops you bouncing up and down like Tigger every time you hit a bump. You can make the damping loose or stiff, as you prefer. The adjusting dial is on one of the legs of the fork, either at the top or the bottom (check the manual if you're not sure).

Manoeuvring Your Throne: Getting Your Seat in Just the Right Spot

You can make three different adjustments to the seat of your bicycle, as follows:

✔ You can alter the **height** so that your leg extension to the pedal is at its most efficient so that you can reach the ground more easily or so that you find the most comfortable angle to lean forward and reach the handlebars.

✔ You can alter the **forward/back** position of the saddle. You can't move it very far, but you primarily use this adjustment to get the correct leg angle by positioning in relation to the bottom bracket. It can also help get rid of aches and pains if the distance between you and the handlebars is not quite right.

✔ You can alter the **tilt** of the saddle. A horizontal saddle is usually best, but you can alter this angle if your saddle is giving you pain in your soft tissues or if you have any prostate problems.

Here's how to alter the height of your saddle:

1. **Loosen the special bolts at the top of the seat tube.**

   You find these bolts at the top bit of the frame where you sit – where the seatpost emerges – either as a separate clamp or a 'gap' in the frame that you close and tighten with the bolts. The mechanism might have a quick release, but more commonly you need an Allen key or a spanner.

   If you haven't had your seatpost out for a while, it will be quite stiff. Even when the clamp is very loose, you might find the seatpost difficult to move. Twist it to the left and right as you try to pull it up or down. You may also have this problem if your bike features alloy seatposts in steel frames (or steel seatposts in alloy frames). A chemical reaction can take place between the two metals which means they effectively fuse together and shifting them is impossible. Applying a light film of grease (ideally anti-seize copper grease) prevents this from happening.

2. **Make adjustments.**

   If you're raising the seat, take the seatpost right out. Have a look on the post and see if you can find a line or mark showing the maximum height you can go. This line has to stay inside the seat tube, because you have to leave a minimum length of post inside the tube to keep it strong enough to support your weight and the forces you put on the frame when you ride. If your seatpost isn't long enough to raise your saddle to the height you want, take it down to the bike shop and ask them for a longer one.

   Raise or lower your saddle to solve problems of reach or discomfort in small stages. Try just one centimetre (⅜ inch) more or less and see how you go. If the change isn't enough you can always do more, but you don't want to start exercising in a radically different position.

3. **Check the new position.**

   Put the seatpost back into the seat tube at the height you want. Tighten up the bolts or quick release until they're nearly fixed. Stand behind the bike and line up the beak of your saddle with the top tube so that it faces straight ahead.

4. **Tighten everything completely.**

   Tighten up the bolts the rest of the way. A lot of force is exerted on this join, so the bolts, or quick release, must be very tight.

To move the seat back or forward or to tilt it, you need to find the bolts underneath your saddle. Older systems have a bolt running crosswise through a clamp at the top of the seatpost. Loosening the nut on this enables you to make any of these alterations in position. Newer systems either have one or two bolts rising vertically from underneath and holding small, shaped blocks together around the saddles' rails. The one-bolt set-up lets you shift the saddle back or forward and tilt in the ridged arc. The two-bolt system allows you to make your changes with just one bolt loose. This latter system is known as Micro Adjust, because it doesn't rely on the meshing of serrated surfaces for the tilt position and you can alter the angle of the saddle very finely.

Only ever make very slight adjustments to your saddle angle as just a small shifting of weight onto your handlebars can cause problems in your wrists and shoulders.

Fiddling with Your Dérailleurs

If you're having problems with your gears – for example, they're slow to change or jump – your dérailleurs might need adjusting. The principle behind dérailleurs is simpler than the mechanisms look. When you click your shifter, the cable is tightened or loosened, which moves the metal gadget sideways and pushes the chain off the ring it's on, so that it gets taken up by the next one along. The mechanism is simple in theory, but, of course, manufacturers spend millions of dollars refining these devices into delicate and precise instruments.

The rear dérailleur looks very complicated, because of the pulley wheel that hangs down. This wheel is spring-loaded and takes up any slack of the chain when the chain is on smaller *sprockets* (the individual rings of the cassette) or chainwheels.

Before you do any adjusting to this rear dérailleur, make sure it hasn't been bent out of whack. The whole rear mechanism is probably the most vulnerable part of a bicycle. If it's been knocked, or even if the bike's just been laid down on the wrong side, it may be bent in towards the wheel. If it ever makes contact with spokes, you could end up with a broken dérailleur, broken wheel and even a broken frame.

Take a look at the rear gear set-up from behind. The two little pulley wheels should be aligned vertically – they should be exactly above and beneath each other. If they're not, you might feel tempted to grab the whole thing and bend it back again, but fixing it honestly isn't that simple. Take your bike down to the shop and the mechanic will probably have to remove the entire dérailleur to get at the problem.

If your bike's quite new and you're having problems with your gears, your *limit stops* might need a tweak. Limit stops are the pair of little screws you see on both the front and back dérailleurs, and they control how far to the left and right your dérailleurs can move. (Be aware that if your gears have worked fine in the past, then adjusting these screws is very unlikely to fix the problem.)

These screws are usually marked H (high) or L (low) and you need to turn the screw that limits the dérailleur at the side of the cassette or chainwheel set where you're having trouble. For example, if you can hear your chain rubbing against the front dérailleur when it runs on the smallest rear sprocket (in the highest gear), you need to loosen the H screw on your front dérailleur.

Take note of whether any rubbing is happening in high or low gear, then have a close look to see which dérailleur is the culprit and take it from there. Bear in mind that this rubbing may well be happening because you have a bent mechanism and, although moving the limits might help, you'll have to get the bent bit straightened.

The most common adjustment needed by your gear system is called the *index* adjustment. When multiple bicycle gears were first invented, the shifting position didn't click into position. You had levers and you had to guess at the right position to move them to in order to get into a certain gear. Then along came the marvellous index system, which clicks you into the right spot – the cable is pulled to the right tension for the dérailleur to move to exactly the right position for the next gear along.

The trouble comes when, for whatever reason, the tension isn't right in the cable. The dérailleur isn't shifted to quite the right spot and you might find your gears are sluggish to change or even jump when you're not expecting them to.

Gear cables stretch over time, which affects the tension. On a new bike, or any time you have a new cable fitted, your cable might need adjusting after a few weeks of riding. The bike shop that sold you the bike or fitted the cable may well do this for nothing.

To alter the tension on your cable, find the *barrel* (the little twiddly thing that you can turn). You usually find it where the cable comes out of the shifter. If the barrel isn't there, just make your way along the cable until you find it. You can also find one where the cable meets the rear dérailleur. If more than one is present, it doesn't matter which one you use.

Just give the barrel on your cable a half twist. Without doing a fair bit more work, you won't know if your cable is too loose or too tight, so just try turning whichever way you like – but remember which way you turned it. If this adjustment makes your gears change better all the way through their range, you've probably got it right. If that half turn makes them worse, or better, but not able to switch through the whole range, try going back your half turn and carrying on for another half turn in the other direction.

Twiddling your barrel can have a pronounced and excellent effect. We've also seen riders frustrated and getting nowhere with their twiddles. If it doesn't work, go and make more friends at the bike shop.

Wiggling Your Pads until Your Brakes Work

Checking the positioning of your brake pads on your rims is something you should do frequently. After removing and replacing a wheel, your pads could have been knocked and shifted, so always have a look. Brake pads are designed so that you can set them in any position and, although altering their position is a bit fiddly, if you persevere you'll end up getting it right.

Possibly the most dangerous thing that can happen to a brake pad is for it to shift so that it rubs against the tyre (instead of your rims) whenever you squeeze your lever. This quickly damages the tyre wall and can even rip into the tyre and destroy it.

Even though the operation isn't entirely straightforward, realigning your pads is important for efficient, safe braking. When you squeeze your brake handle, the pad needs to be touching the rim of your wheel as squarely as possible, giving the maximum amount of contact. The cup-shaped spacers you get along the bolt of the pad allow you to put the pad at any angle you like, but they can be tricky to manipulate. The movement of the pad towards the rim is an arced one, so you have to guess at a position and then give it a go – and a bit of trial and error is involved in finding the perfect spot and angle.

No one knows who it's going to happen to or when, but every now and then someone gets on a bike and when they start to brake an almighty screech erupts like a steam train from hell. Heads will turn at 200 metres and that cyclist will immediately vow to get it fixed. If you've got this humiliating and shameful problem, you need to realign your brake pads.

The position your brakes should be in is called the *toe-in* position. The pad needs to be positioned so that the front end of it makes contact with your wheel rim first. This shouldn't be a sharp angle – the whole of the pad still needs to make contact with the rim as it compresses, but that front bit needs to hit the wheel first.

If your brakes are worn, you have to squeeze your lever tighter and tighter to get the same braking effect and you may eventually lose the full force of your brakes. Replacing brake pads can be as fiddly as moving them, but doing so isn't a major job and, if your current ones are getting a bit low, now's the time to get some brand spanking new ones.

If you've got cartridge pads, you don't have to remove the housing (which is the fiddly bit to align); you just have to replace the pads. Here's how you do it:

1. **Take off your wheel so that you've got good access to your brakes.**

2. **Slide the pad out of its cartridge.**

   A pin or bolt may be holding it in place.

3. **Slide in the new pad, making sure it's the right way round.**

   Don't forget to pop the pin or bolt back in, if present.

When replacing cartridge pads, only remove and replace one pad at a time, so you have the old one to use as a guide while fitting the new one.

All-in-one pads have the bolt sticking out of the back. With these, you'll have to dismantle the whole delicate brake set-up to replace the pads. Here's how:

1. **Undo the nut holding the brake set-up in place.**

   As you dismantle the collection of washers and spacers, try hard to remember what order they're in as this is how you have to put them back together.

2. **Slip in the new pad and bolt.**

3. **Replace all the washers, spacers and the nut and tighten the set-up back up.**

If you take the wheel off to replace your all-in-one brake pads, you have to wait until you put it back on before you realign the pad.

Any time you have your wheel off, have a look at the face of your brake pads. Are any little bits of grit or any other alien matter stuck into them? Anything sharp will dig a groove into your rim and weaken your wheel. Give your brake pads a wipe with a damp cloth or some soapy water if they need it. Also give your rims a good scrub so that you've got clean flat surfaces locking together to slow you down.

Having Nothing to Lose but Your Chain

Two big barriers exist to putting on a new chain. The first is your bike frame: your chain is looped inside your frame and must be broken to be removed and replaced. Second is the fear that putting on a new chain is too big a job that you should leave to the professionals. Nonsense. You're a cyclist now – show no fear and get breaking chains.

You need to take off older chains with a fancy tool called a *chain breaker*. Many different designs are available, but this bizarre-looking tool has a handle for holding, a handle for turning and some complicated bits where you carefully align the chain (see Figure 18-2).

Figure 18-2: Chain breaker in use.

A lot of newer chains come with a special kind of link, called a *master link*. With a master link, you can get your chain on and off without any special tools. If you take off an old chain, you can fix it back on with a master link and from then you won't need a chain breaker. Some new chains come with special joining pins. These pins make joining the links of the chain together with a chain breaker easier, and are supplied with clear and easy instructions.

You always need a chain breaker to shorten a new chain to the right size before fitting it to your bike.

Chains stretch after many miles of riding. This stretching isn't exactly because the links elongate. The links are all held together with rings around rivets and all of these parts wear down, allowing the links to gradually become further apart. When the chain stretches, it no longer fits the chainwheels and sprockets correctly. The chain won't sit right between the teeth of these wheels and without proper contact as it makes its way round won't pull efficiently. Eventually, the weakest link in the chain will break and the chain will fall off your bicycle.

To remove a chain with the most common type of master link:

1. **Look all round the chain until you find the link with a straight top and bottom.**

   This link will have no dip in the middle.

2. **Remove the retaining clip.**

   Point-nosed pliers are good for this.

3. **Take off the side plate.**

   This plate is underneath the retaining clip.

4. **Pull the rest of the master link out from the other side.**

To replace the master link, simply reassemble it, making sure the retaining clip is securely fastened.

When refitting any kind of master link, make sure you read the instructions carefully. If you don't fit it securely, the chain could come off and do you a terrible injury.

For older chains you need the chain breaker. First have a look at the tool. As you screw the handle in, you'll see a long prong extending towards the teeth of the thing. You need to rest your chain with these teeth between the rings of the links so that one of the pins (the small rivet-like parts that run through the centre of the rings of the chain) is aligned with the extending part of the chain breaker.

Here are the steps to getting a chain off and back on:

1. **Screw down with the chain breaker until the extending point is touching the pin.**

   Make sure you have it perfectly aligned before continuing.

2. **Start turning once more, slowly pushing the pin out.**

   If you intend to put the chain together again, don't push the pin all the way out. Pins are very hard to reinsert. When the outside plate is the only thing holding the pin, the chain should come apart.

3. **Remove your old chain.**

   When removing your old chain from the bike, watch how it is coiled through the two pulley wheels in the rear dérailleur. Remember this, because you've got to get the new chain back in again the same way.

4. **If using a new chain, trim the chain down to the right number of links.**

   To work out how many links to remove from the new chain, count the links in the old one – you need the same number. When you've trimmed down the new chain to the right number of links, hold the two chains up next to each other to see how much your old chain has stretched.

5. **Thread the chain back through the pulley assemblage, over the smallest sprocket and over the smallest chainwheel at the front.**

   Spreading the chain over the smallest sprocket and chainwheel gives you the least tension.

6. **Join the chain.**

   If you've got a master link, just snap it together to join the chain. If not, hold the chain breaker the other way round and fit in the link that has to be rejoined. This way when you screw down you push the pin back into the ring and outer plate so the chain is whole once more.

7. **Give the chain some lube and hit the black stuff.**

Part V
The Part of Tens

Enjoy an additional free Part of Tens chapter online at www.dummies.com/
extras/cyclinguk.

In this part . . .

- Benefit from some top tips on things you can do to make your cycling safer and more enjoyable and on things to be sure of not doing when you're out on two wheels.

- Discover ten brilliant bike rides from the length and breadth of the United Kingdom, rides that show off the best cycling opportunities this beautiful country has to offer.

- Cast your eyes further afield and dream about taking part in ten of the greatest rides and tours from around the world.

Chapter 19

Ten Bicycling Do's and Don'ts

· ·

In This Chapter

▶ Preparing yourself and your bike

▶ Remembering to watch and learn

▶ Being friendly, offering a helping hand and keeping your cool

▶ Looking after your bike

▶ Using your car less and your bike more

▶ Keeping cycling fun

▶ Spreading the joy of cycling

· ·

*B*icycling should be fun and it usually is, but you need to remember some things so that it can carry on giving you pleasure. By knowing which things you should do – and which you shouldn't – hopefully you won't ever think back on your ride with unpleasantness.

We wouldn't want you to look back on some chance meeting on a bike, for example, and think you could have done better. Or for you to leave your bike behind or neglect it. These thoughts are terrible, so in this chapter we provide some ideas to keep you and your bike rolling along.

Do Be Prepared

One of the worst things that can happen to you when you're out on your bike (and something that actually does happen to cyclists quite often) is to get a puncture and realise you don't have a spare tube – or a patch, or a pump. We've certainly been in this situation. Sometimes, you can find ways out of this situation – you might be close to a bike shop, you might receive charitable help from another cyclist or some other form of transport may be available. But all too often it means a long walk home.

Having a puncture without any way to fix it then and there is one of the simplest things that can go wrong and is, frankly, an easy thing to guard against. As your bicycling becomes more ambitious you may well need to pack more than a patch and a pump to be prepared for likely issues. But now you've made the decision to be a cyclist, you've taken on an attitude of more responsibility – you're the power, you're in control and getting yourself through anything that comes along is your job.

Think about your journey before you set out. What do you need? What could go wrong? If it does go wrong, what will you need then? You can't carry a workshop, but you can take all the most likely things to help you out of a predictable jam. You can be prepared. (Refer to Chapter 12 for a list of possible items to pack when touring. You can adapt this list depending on the type of riding you're doing.)

Don't Forget to Look Around

We've included this section for two very good reasons. Firstly, as a cyclist, you're vulnerable and you lessen the risks to yourself considerably if you always know what's coming at you. It really is easy to forget to look around when you shoot out into a busy junction, but don't do it: always remember in any traffic situation to keep your eyes scanning in every direction.

The second need to look around is for your learning benefit. Two main types of cyclist exist. First up are those cyclists whose heads bob and turn as they experience and learn about the world they move through. They spot things and appreciate them. They see how people live and how things are done. They take in views and note down useful facts. Secondly come the head-down riders who could cycle through the bazaars of Tunis or the Valley of the Kings and not notice a thing. Deep in thought, these cyclists stay focused on the end goal, oblivious to the outside world. We're not against any meditative benefits you might get from pedalling on and withdrawing from the world, but a bicycle is such a marvellous means of seeing what you would not otherwise see that we suggest you lift your head, come out of your shell and have a good look around.

Do Be Friendly

Once upon a time, everyone lived in little villages. They never went anywhere except maybe up a hill for a walk. If they met anyone on these minimal travels, they'd greet them and marvel that the world could contain folk they didn't know. Then people started moving to big cities and grew cold toward each other. They knew that every other face could hide treachery and murder and they shut off their fellows in a cynical human firewall.

In more modern times, people are a little more trusting, but hardly open. If you hike way out on remote trails and you encounter another soul you probably do greet them, as a kind of relic of behaviour past, but doing so is a country thing – even a remote country thing. But bicycles have taken us back (or perhaps forward) to more human times. Cyclists do greet each other. They smile, nod or wave if they can and, if in close proximity, they speak.

Cyclists are all out doing – and enjoying – the same thing and they like to acknowledge the fact. In a way, it's like they're all from the same village. So don't be stuffy – if you see another bicyclist coming the other way, do be friendly. Wave and say hello.

Do Lend a Hand

If you're stuck out on a trail or a remote country road, sitting on a bank next to a bike that won't work, and another cyclist comes along, we can almost guarantee that other rider will stop and check if you're okay. She may have that Allen key you didn't pack or even offer her spare inner tube. You'll chat and the fellow cyclist will stay with you until you're sorted.

So be prepared to do the same thing. A cyclist stopped at the roadside could either have a mechanical problem or an injury that you can't see. You don't have to be right out in the country either – if you see a cyclist in apparent distress anywhere, stop and check on him. It doesn't matter if you're not carrying any tools because that might not be what's needed.

Although most riders stop to check on other cyclists, we have heard stories of riders pedalling past fallen cyclists, even as they bled on the kerb. The idea is shocking, so make sure you're never the one they all moan about on the online forums. Instead, keep up the standards of caring for each other – you'll always feel much better that way.

Don't Lose Your Cool

You may have picked up on the fact that the roads aren't always happy places. It sometimes seems as if bicycles aren't fully welcome. Some motorists, it must be said, are even quite impatient and bad tempered. Engines do race, horns do blare and cyclists do get squeezed off the road.

We understand fully how some cyclists take this attitude as a challenge. They pick up the gauntlet and are willing to fight for the virtue of right. We even know one or two who have special tools attached to their bikes specifically for this purpose. But I'd recommend most strongly that you do not pedal down this path.

Nobody likes to be beaten and as a law-abiding cyclist on a road you're never in the wrong. But think about the motivations of aggressive behaviour – what do drivers want when they do things with their cars that they know risk your safety and cause you grief? Essentially, they want to make you feel angry or upset by exerting physical power over you. They try to bully you.

If you react strongly to the inappropriate swerve of a car that's meant to unnerve you, you give the driver exactly what he wants. You can practically hear him calling out 'Bullseye!' as he cheerfully speeds off. If, on the other hand, you wave in a friendly manner as if he's a joker, someone you know, you frustrate and upset him – he has failed and you leave him feeling the exact way he intended you to feel.

It works – try it. And apart from being one step towards a victory, you show anyone who's watching that you didn't lose your cool.

Do Leave the Car at Home

Well over half the car trips people make in the UK are over distances that you could cycle in 20 minutes or less. This amount of driving has a dreadful effect on the environment, made even worse by the fact that an engine that hasn't warmed up produces even more noxious fumes than a car on a longer journey. And the most awful thing about these effects is that car trips over such short distances are completely unnecessary.

If you take your bike instead, you'll probably get where you're going quicker, you won't do any harm at all to your environment, you'll save money and you'll take another step towards improved health and fitness. Don't think, 'I can't be bothered' – your bicycle *is* less bother.

Keep your helmet and cycling gloves by the front door, right next to your car keys. Every time you reach out, be aware that you make a decision. Watch out for excuses. Get into the habit of doing everyone – and mostly yourself – a great big favour and leave the car at home.

Don't Let Your Bike Go to Seed

It may not have cost a fortune, but your bike is still a valuable thing. It shouldn't take much looking after (although you can spend hours tending it if you want to), but you do need to do a few things regularly to make sure it carries on working properly. If you do look after it, your bike will last a very long time.

If something fell off your car, or if its engine started making odd noises, you'd get it down to the repair shop and sort it out. If you didn't, you'd risk being stranded at the roadside and having to pay a big bill to fix it. The same is true of your bicycle. If you don't do those regular checks and fix any problems that arise, you could end up just as stranded. (Refer to Chapter 17 for more on basic bike maintenance and repair.)

But looking after your bicycle is not just about saving money and staying on the road. Riding a bicycle is almost a childish pleasure: innocent fun that can bring back feelings we remember from childhood. If you step back and allow your bicycle to fall into disrepair, you're almost casting off your childhood, throwing away your innocence. Don't do it. Look after your bike.

Don't Let Cycling Become a Chore

If you look at your bike and really don't want to ride it, don't do it. People commonly need a break from the things they love. With cycling, feeling unmotivated is often because you've been doing too much and your muscles need some time off to recover fully. If this sounds familiar, you'll find all your riding isn't making you stronger and, instead, you're feeling fatigued sooner than you normally would. If you give yourself a couple of days off – or more – you'll find your performance is better than ever.

If you can't take a couple of days off, just take it easy. Cycle slowly, legs spinning, so that you're not taxing your muscles at all. Some people find this difficult and have to work very hard at not cycling fast, but if you're over-training you must pull back.

If you don't have a training problem and you just can't face getting on a bike, you've probably just been getting too much of a good thing. Don't ride when you don't feel like it, because you'll just end up putting yourself off. You should always feel great about cycling, so if it doesn't feel right one day, leave it until the next.

Do Take Your Bike on Holiday

You may like to travel light. You may be the sort of person who doesn't pack things you don't need. But if you can possibly fit in the bike, even if only an outside chance exists that you might use it, take it along. We do. If we leave all our bicycles at home, we start to miss them.

Having a bicycle with you on your holiday can bring some real highlights. You may be able to get to enticing, distant beaches, explore up a river or see far more of the hills and countryside than you would by walking. It can break up your time with an extra family activity – and one that doesn't cost anything. Cycling can help clear the cobwebs if you've relaxed too heavily the night before, or you can take it to the pub so you don't have to drive (although, of course, you still have to watch your intake of alcohol). And it gives you a chance to keep up the fitness you've achieved prior to your break.

If you've got a rack on the car, you won't lose any storage space and you can still take the kitchen sink if you're in the habit of doing so. You can always find a reason not to take a bicycle with you – and you may have someone finding reasons for you – but doing so is well worth the effort. In the past, we've both taken bikes with us on family holidays, not used them at all and still been very glad we had taken them along.

Do Spread the Word

Riding a bicycle is a great thing to have as a regular part of your life. It offers clear advantages to your health, your finances and the environment, but you can also just revel in the sheer joy of it. This may be something you've just discovered or rediscovered (or knew all along), but this factor is what makes it really special.

You can tell people about the money you're saving. You can fill them in on how you're getting into shape. You can try going on about the great good you're doing for the world. But what you really need to tell people about is all the fun they're missing: the joy of pedalling – because until they try it they won't understand. And if you go at people like a missionary, dedicated to conversion, you'll soon find you've got a happier family, a workplace full of people who arrive full of life and enjoy what they do, and friends who want to meet up and share the fun.

One of the things that has been shown about bicycles and road safety is that the more bicycles are out there, the safer riding is for each and every cyclist. Other traffic learns to make the right call and gets used to dealing with bikes on the road. So for all our sakes, tell your friends the truth – that riding a bicycle is a blast.

Chapter 20

Ten Great Rides in the United Kingdom

In This Chapter

▶ Riding the rail trails

▶ Taking on the countryside

*I*n this chapter, we talk about ten very varied rides. A couple of them – the Mawddach Trail in Wales and the Wandle Trail in London – are short, easy rides that suit the entire family. The Coast to Coast and Pennine Cycleway in Northern England are both much longer rides and are world-class trails worth taking a holiday just to visit. The Round-the-Island ride and the Chilterns Cycleway are well-signposted routes that are very popular as organised events. Sign up and you can join many other cyclists for a special day, or you can also do them any time you like and choose your perfect weather and pace combination. We've also included a couple of classic off-road rides on which you can test your skill and endurance.

All the rides we include here are rides that you could do now you have a bike. You might need to practise a bit for any of the longer ones (and you need an MTB for the off-road routes), but practise pays off, and the rides are certainly worth it. The routes we include here aren't just some of the finest bike rides in the UK – they're some of the best in the world.

The Mawddach Trail Cycleway

If you want a beautiful, tranquil ride for all the family, you'll struggle to find anything better than this. Following an old railway line in north-west Wales, the Mawddach Trail Cycleway has the Rhinog Hills on one side and the Cadair Idris massif on the other, with fantastic views everywhere along the entire ten-mile route. Unsurprisingly, this cycleway is a favourite with bikers and walkers alike.

The Mawddach trail is level, so it doesn't pose any serious physical challenges. Apart from the first part of the route at Dolgellau (where the ride starts) the surface is unsealed, but is generally good enough for you not to need a mountain bike.

The route is great for birdwatching, and the old signal box at the now unused Penmaenpool station has been converted into a bird observatory by the RSPB. All along the route you come across picnic areas, viewpoints and little nature reserves. Probably everyone's favourite bit of the ride is at the end, where it crosses the three-quarter mile long railway bridge over the mouth of the Mawddach estuary into Barmouth. But the rest of the ride is just as delightful.

Round-the-Island

Round-the-Island is a hugely popular route around the Isle of Wight. The ride is 100 kilometres (63 miles) long and takes in some of the island's best scenery, which includes views over the Solent and its scores of sailing boats, magnificent chalk cliffs and rolling countryside.

The route is circular and you can tackle it in either direction. It's well signposted, so you can even leave the map at home and follow the white bike symbols if you go clockwise or the blue bike symbols if you ride in the opposite direction. The route is fairly hilly in places, so if you don't want to do the full distance in one go, you can break it up into a more leisurely two- or three-day ride and choose from plenty of great places to stay along the way (the island is a popular holiday destination).

Many organised rides use the Round-the-Island route, so on several weekends throughout the year you see thousands of riders out to enjoy themselves. One, the Isle of Wight Randonnée, has been going since 1985. Another, the Wight Riviera Sportive, also includes a closed-road loop, making it a great way to introduce younger riders to big events. The route plays a major part in the annual Isle of Wight Cycling Festival, which involves numerous rides of varying lengths.

You find cyclists enjoying the unique charms the Isle of Wight has to offer throughout the year, though, and not just on event days. Much of the route is along the island's quiet country lanes, but it also takes in the sailing capital of the world, Cowes, as well as some lovely villages and beaches. And the route has no shortage of pubs at which to stop and recharge your batteries.

One of the great attractions of the Round-the-Island ride, which neatly bookends your ride, is the need to take a ferry there and back. Ferries go from Lymington to Yarmouth, Portsmouth to Fishbourne and Southampton to Cowes. Bikes travel free on these services.

The Round-the-Island was one of the first sportives Ben ever did. Cycling up a hill and struggling somewhat, he thought oxygen deprivation was causing hallucinations. Ahead of him was a cyclist wearing a beret and a Breton-striped top, with onions hanging over the handlebars. Ben took stock. That a Frenchman fancied taking part in this great ride certainly wasn't beyond the realms of possibility, but why did it look so wrong? It soon clicked – the guy was pedalling backwards, proof surely that Ben's body wasn't coping too well. But when back on the flat, he caught up with the apparition, which turned out to be real. The Frenchman's bike dated from the 1930s and had an ingenious two gear system where you pedal forwards for the high gear and backwards for the low gear. Even more extraordinarily, in the previous year the 70-year old rider had completed the Paris–Brest–Paris ride (see Chapter 21) on this very machine.

The South Downs Way

The South Downs Way gives mountain bike riders a chance to experience some of the finest countryside in England without having to travel too far off the beaten track. The Way links Winchester, the first capital of England, with the coastal resort of Eastbourne, and boasts some impressive history from Neolithic flint mines to Bronze Age burial mounds and Iron Age forts. And if you want expansive views, pretty villages, wildlife, some of the best pubs in the country and a varied selection of beauty spots (such as Winchester Cathedral, Ditchling Beacon, the Long Man of Wilmington and Beachy Head) you need look no further. The South Downs Way is a ride where looking around you is a definite must.

The route covers 100 miles (160 kilometres) from end to end along the top of the South Downs (now a designated National Park) following the old routes and droveways that people have been using for thousands of years. Many people are still using them today – you need to keep an eye out for walkers and horse riders too, with whom the route is equally popular.

The majority of travellers do the South Downs Way in stages, though fit cyclists can (and do) complete it in a day. If you're a real glutton for punishment, you could even get an early train out of London, ride from end to end and get another train back to London, all in a day.

Most of the route is on wide grassy or flint tracks crossing chalk downland grazed by sheep. The tracks are easy to ride in the dry, but can become very slippy and technical in the wet. The Winchester end of the downs mostly consists of rolling farmland. The central section of the West Sussex Downs are dominated by steep, often wooded scarp with dramatic views across the Weald, while the trail onwards through East Sussex towards Eastbourne goes through open grassland that runs down to sea cliffs. While no really big hills are on the route – the highest point is Butser Hill at 271 metres (889 feet) – the route undulates along its entire length so you have over 4,000 metres (13,123 feet) of climbing to do.

Coast to Coast

Coast to Coast (or C2C) claims to be the UK's most popular long-distance cycle route and it runs for 140 miles (225 kilometres) from the North Sea to the Irish Sea across the beautiful and rugged landscape of Northern England. Around 15,000 cyclists make the trip every year (with numbers increasing year-on-year) and take three to five days to do it, though some manage the whole thing in just a day.

You experience a bit of everything on this ride. The emphasis is on staying well away from traffic – the route uses cyclepaths, off-road sections and quiet country lanes, though it takes in a few short, urban miles too.

The best way to ride is from west to east, to take advantage of the prevailing wind and easier gradients, though you have nothing to stop you from doing it the other way around if you want a greater challenge. The route begins in either Whitehaven or Workington (one thing about this ride is that a number of options are available to you), in the former industrial areas of West Cumbria, before taking you on through the stunning scenery of the Lake District, on to the Eden Valley and then up onto the roof of England – the North Pennines. With the highest point of the ride being at over 2,000 feet (610 metres), some big climbs await you on the way here, but you're not in a rush so take it nice and slow and enjoy the views. The route then descends through some old lead mining villages and continues down through the Durham Dales, ending in the heartland of the industrial northeast in either Newcastle or Sunderland, whichever you prefer.

A tradition says you must dip your back wheel in the Irish Sea to mark the start of your ride, and you only finish when you do the same with your front wheel in the North Sea. Do this, and you're among thousands of other cyclists who've done just the same.

The C2C is incredibly well supported with online guides giving you all the information you need. You can find maps, accommodation suggestions, details about the sights you'll see and weather forecasts. This ride brings out the best in people and some keen riders who love the route (and who also happen to be web designers) have set up a site giving you all the up-to-date information you'll ever need. Find it at www.C2Cplaces2stay.co.uk.

The Pennine Cycleway

The Pennine Cycleway goes through some of Northern England's most beautiful counties, including Cumbria, Derbyshire and Northumberland, which means a wealth of hills and spectacular scenery awaits.

Cyclists generally consider the Pennine Cycleway a sufficiently big challenge that they split it into two. The northern section runs from Appleby and Penrith to Berwick-upon-Tweed and covers 184 miles (295 kilometres). The southern part is a shorter distance of 124 miles (198 kilometres), but can be tougher, particularly with a headwind. It runs from Holmfirth to Appleby, where it joins up with the northern section. If you want to do the whole route all the way down to Derby, you can add on another 40 miles (64 kilometres) through the beautiful Peak District.

If spectacular landscapes are what you like, the northern section has it in spades. The route takes in some of the most unspoilt countryside England has to offer. As well as the North Pennines themselves, the route goes through the Northumberland National Park and the Eden Valley, passing over 60 tourist attractions and 85 towns and villages.

The southern section offers an equally wide variety of landscapes, including a huge canal embankment, textile mills, lovely market towns, farmland and open moorland (watch out for those headwinds). One of the traffic-free sections takes you along the towpath of the Leeds and Liverpool Canal.

While only around ten per cent of the entire route is on traffic-free trails, the roads it uses are some of the quietest in the country, so you don't have to worry about battling with cars.

The Pennine Cycleway is a ride you could take weeks over if you wanted to – it would be worth it, considering everything that you can see and do along the route – and is a ride you have to consider if you really want to see what cycling in the UK has to offer.

The Chilterns Cycleway

The Chilterns Cycleway is one of only a few circular routes in the UK, which make things easy if you get to and from your rides by car. This loop totals 170 miles (274 kilometres) through the Chilterns Area of Outstanding Natural Beauty, mainly on-road, so your bike doesn't have to be especially rugged to cope. If conditions are wet, the few sections on towpaths and bridleways may not suit skinny tyres, but don't worry – on-road alternatives are there to stop you getting bogged down.

The Chilterns provide a unique landscape with some real gems of nature. You see red kites with their distinctive russet plumage and forked tails, some of the best chalk streams anywhere in the world (which are beloved of water voles and brown trout) and beech woodland carpeted with bluebells in the spring.

Many people like to do the loop at a leisurely pace, making it a one-week tour. However, you have lots of options for splitting up the ride into shorter chunks and doing it a bit at a time. The route is very well sign-posted, so you can enjoy riding without having to look at a map or consult your satnav.

The Chilterns Cycleway, however, is not a ride for novices for two reasons. Firstly, some busy sections of road on the route are impossible to avoid. You need a reasonable level of experience of riding in traffic to remain happy and safe on these sections, and avoiding riding in the rush hour along these roads is a good idea as they serve as rat-runs for commuters trying to beat the queues on the major roads in the area. Secondly, the Chilterns are hilly, with some sharp climbs and descents in places, and the route is rarely anything other than undulating.

If you're an experienced cyclist, though, don't let either of these things put you off. Most of the time the roads are peaceful and you're the only thing on them. And just as the adage about there being no such thing as bad weather, just poor clothing, holds true, so hills are only really tricky if you don't have suitable gears.

You can get hold of a useful guidebook that provides detailed information so you can prepare yourself for any potential difficulties, such as busy junctions or steep hills. Read this, and nothing will take you unawares. You can find details of how to buy the guidebook at `www.chilternsaonb.org/cycle way.html`.

The route is easily accessible from all over the country as it crosses or passes close to five major motorways. However, leaving the car at home and travelling to the route by train is also easy as numerous stations are all around the loop.

Jacob's Ladder Loop

One of the toughest mountain bike trails in the UK is the legendary Vale of Edale in the Peak District, which has a special place in the hearts of seasoned mountain bikers. The key feature is the biblically named Jacob's Ladder climb, which is a test for even the very, very best riders.

The loop is only 14 miles (22 kilometres) long, but don't be deceived. It has some lung-busting and technical climbs that only a few riders can cope with.

The ride starts fairly gently as you leave the start and finish point at Hayfield and follow bridleways toward Coldwell Clough, a steep and rocky climb that rewards you with great views of Kinder Low. The trail then follows the contour lines and rolls along the high moor, before your first descent arrives, replete with gullys and rocks. Then comes a tough climb (don't be surprised if you have to get off) and a difficult ride along the side of a hill before you see the Vale of Edale stretching out in front of you, with hills on all sides and Jacob's Ladder in the distance below the summit of Kinder Low.

The climb looms above you as you ride closer. Only a hallowed few cyclists have managed to do it without any dabs (putting your foot down). Jacob's Ladder is only 0.7 miles (1.1 kilometres) long, strewn with loose rocks and sharp turns, and goes up like . . . well, a ladder. If the technical nature of the climb doesn't get you, then the gradient tends to instead. Most cyclists struggle to even push their bike up. When you make it, you then have a relatively short and easy ride back down into Hayfield.

This ride tests the mettle of any rider, but attempting Jacob's Ladder is good fun for anyone. Lots of other trails run around Edale if you want to limber up on something a bit easier beforehand.

The Wandle Trail

For people who despair of cycling in urban areas because of the traffic and lack of nature, the Wandle Trail is a little oasis. Stretching 12 miles (19 kilometres) from Croydon in South London to the Thames in Wandsworth, the Wandle Trail is an easy meander through hidden green spaces along the banks of the Wandle River.

The story of the Wandle Trail is bound up with the fortunes of the river. Once declared one of the most polluted in England thanks to the industry along its banks, the Wandle was little more than an open sewer during the industrial revolution and for many decades afterwards. Diverted to suit the needs of heavy industry in a number of places and forgotten in tunnels and covered culverts, what was once a spectacular chalk stream brimming with trout and wildlife along its banks had become a dead, stinking wasteland.

A series of clean-ups has since worked wonders. Brown trout have returned, as have numerous other species. The Wandle River is now a veritable nature corridor reaching right into the heart of London, linking up green spaces along its path. For city dwellers, this corridor is a little bit of countryside right on the doorstep.

The Wandle Trail is a great ride to do with children. It cuts through 13 parks and goes along traffic-free cycle paths, so you can give the kids free rein. In places the trail splits – one way for cyclists, one way for walkers – so removing another potential hazard. Inevitably, a few sections exist where following the river bank is impossible, or where parks are designated bicycle-free, so you have to take to the roads. But these diversions from the river are well-marked cycle routes and you can always get off and push if the children are inexperienced.

Loads of things to see and do line the way, and of course you can just stop and marvel at the fact that you're cutting through one of the biggest and busiest capital cities in the world along a tranquil nature trail. You can enjoy views that you've never seen before, and town centres have never looked more interesting.

Vestiges of the industrial age, which nearly caused the total demise of the river, such as Victorian mills and factories are still there – now turned into offices or posh apartments. You also pass a splendid manor house that wouldn't look out of place in the middle of the countryside – which, of course, was exactly where it once would have been.

The Trail also boasts numerous pubs and other eateries along its way – you could cycle it a hundred times and choose somewhere different each time. But, as you're effectively in the country now, why not take a picnic and stop at a place like Wilderness Island and enjoy looking at the tufted ducks, darter dragonflies and kingfishers.

Causeway Coast Cycle Route

The Causeway Coast is stunning. The amazing geology of the rocks brings visitors to Northern Ireland from all over the world, and what better way to enjoy and appreciate this natural wonder than by bike.

This well-signposted route, which forms part of the National Cycle Network Route 93, runs for 23 miles (37 kilometres) along the North Atlantic coast from Castlerock to the Giant's Causeway via Coleraine. Most of the route runs on traffic-free tarmac, but it has a few road sections which aren't normally busy (except perhaps during summer weekends). On the spectacular section between Portrush and Bushmills, which is especially popular with sightseers, a footway offers an alternative path which children can use, if needs be. The route passes through the resort towns of Portrush and Portstewart so you have plenty of opportunity for refreshment and refuelling to prepare for the climbs, most of which are short though a couple between Castlerock and Coleraine and between Portrush and Bushmills take a bit longer to bag.

The great thing about having a proper surface to ride on is that you can concentrate on looking around you rather than wondering if a rock is suddenly going to appear in your path. And you definitely want to be looking around on this ride. You can take in the lovely views over the sea from Barmouth Viewpoint across the mouth of the River Bann as well as over the sandy beach at Portstewart. From here, on a clear day, you can see across to Scotland and the Mull of Kintyre.

You can stop off at Dunluce Castle, a medieval ruin perched on the edge of a basalt outcrop with dramatic steep slopes on all sides and which is connected to the mainland by a bridge. You can also visit the narrow-gauge railway which takes tourists from Bushmills along a two mile (three kilometre) coastal route to the Giant's causeway. Finally, of course, is the Giant's Causeway itself. This unique jigsaw of interlinked hexagonal rocks, created by a volcanic eruption 60 million years ago, is deservedly a World Heritage Site and a designated Area of Outstanding Natural Beauty.

For the eagle-eyed amongst you, the mention of the word *Bushmills* may have brought on an extra little frisson of excitement. The village is home to what is recognised as the oldest licensed distillery in the world. The distillery is open to visitors and for tastings. Do you need any other incentive to try this ride?

Tarka Trail

If your dream is to go on a longish ride with not a car, bus or lorry in sight, but you don't want to take to the backwaters, this trail could be the one for you. The Tarka Trail covers 30 miles (48 kilometres) between Braunton and Meeth using the old railways of North Devon. It passes through largely unspoiled countryside little changed from that which inspired the writer Henry Williamson to write his much-loved classic novel *Tarka the Otter* which was first published in 1927.

The route is one of the country's longest continuous traffic-free cycling paths and forms part of the Devon Coast-to-Coast Cycle Route. And if you find yourself completely taken with the scenery, you have the option of exploring on foot another 150 miles (240 kilometres) of trails around.

The Tarka Trail was first established in 1987 using a disused rail line between Barnstable and Bideford. Over the following years, various organisations have raised money to buy and repair sections of the railway, not least to adapt and repair bridges across the River Torridge. The Trail was formally opened by Prince Charles in 1992, though additional sections have been added as time has gone on.

You start out hugging the banks of the River Taw as the trail goes through Chivenor. At Barnstable you cross over the River Yeo via a swing bridge, before heading up the Torridge Estuary through Bideford and Great Torrington to reach Meeth at the end.

An abundance of wildlife exists along this route, taking advantage of the estuary mud flats and salt marshes, oak woodlands and numerous ponds, streams and ditches. You've no guarantee of seeing an otter, as otters are notoriously shy creatures. (While a bike is a great way of seeing most things, otters aren't one of them.) But that's hardly going to be a disappointment when you're in such wonderful, peaceful surroundings.

As you might imagine, the Tarka Trail is immensely popular. Bike hire businesses have sprung up all along the route, so you don't even have to take your own bike along to enjoy it. And Barnstable has good rail connections, so you can leave the car at home too.

Chapter 21

Ten Great Tours and Races around the World

In This Chapter

▶ Watching élite cyclists push themselves to their limits

▶ Appreciating events that might be achievable

*W*hether you want to just watch and read about amazing competitive cycling events or one day hope to be racing in one of them, something in this chapter is bound to interest you. We provide a range of both some phenomenally difficult cycling and some events you could realistically hope to compete in with a good programme of training.

The Tour de France is the most famous bicycle race of all and is certainly a tough one. Riders take on great distances and climbs that would leave most cyclists pushing, and they do it at fantastic speeds. Events such as the Simpson Desert Bike Challenge and the Iditasport Extreme attract riders tough enough to battle with conditions that threaten their very survival.

The Etape du Tour and Tour de Flanders, however, are two rides you could realistically set your sights on. Both involve a lot of climbing and can throw some pretty horrible weather at you, but once you start clocking up the miles these events become within your reach. Why not keep at it and see if you can tick off these rides one by one. You'll certainly have a hell of a time trying.

Le Tour de France: Watch and Dream

Every July the world turns its head towards France as hundreds of cyclists start on the race that takes them thousands of miles around France and often other countries as well. They roll over mountains and speed through little French villages, always saving their best until last. Every year seeing the big sprinters emerging from the pack and bolting towards the finish with unbelievable bursts of strength is a thrilling sight.

The great race has been going on for more than 100 years, with breaks for world wars, and has a different route every year. The tour is now settled at around 3,500 kilometres (2,200 miles), but has varied enormously over the years – in 1926, for example, riders fought their way through 5,745 kilometres (3,600 miles) in a little over three weeks.

Of course, with Bradley Wiggins' historic victory, everyone in the UK is now familiar with the race, which is clawing back some credibility after years of drugs scandals. Lance Armstrong, once honoured as the greatest rider the race has ever seen (with a total of seven victories to his name), is now notorious for being the most cunning of drugs cheats. No wonder that he was able to set the fastest average speed ever of 40.276 kilometres per hour (25 miles per hour). Thankfully, though, clean cyclists aren't far behind, and the record is unlikely to last forever.

The Tour de France is one of three European tours, known as the Grand Tours. The Giro d'Italia (Italy in May) and the Vuelta a España (Spain in September) are also both three-week races about 3,500 kilometres (2,200 miles) long that have varying routes around their respective countries each year. All the Tours are *stage races*, which means shorter segments throughout the competition have winners and the winner of the Tour is the cyclist who has the shortest overall time. In the Tour de France, the leader gets to wear the yellow jersey as he rides, with the overall winner getting to keep it.

The beauty of the Tour de France isn't just in the excitement of the racing. French people and visitors to France line the route almost all of the way and, as the cameras mounted on speeding motorbikes record the huge efforts of the riders, you get a vivid picture of long stretches of French communities and culture. Rural France is a beautiful place and adding a big group of the world's best cyclists makes it even more glorious.

When watching the race, at times the camerawork doesn't quite reveal how steep the hills are or how fast the riders are moving, but then with the turn of a bend the angle changes and everyone can see just how strong this cycling is. These riders put in hour after hour of immensely hard cycling.

If you're young, already fast and dedicated to putting in many hours of training, you could end up on the world's TV screens, battling for a position on the podium. Tour de France cyclists all come out of local clubs and their hard work and ambition is what gets them into this dream race with the cream of the planet's cyclists.

At the time of writing, British cycling is enjoying its greatest ever period. As well as Bradley Wiggins, Mark Cavendish has become a Tour legend with his sprinting ability. Only a brave man would bet against him becoming the winner of the largest number of tour stages in history. Chris Froome, Geraint

Thomas and a host of other young, talented British cyclists are also coming through the ranks, determined to make their mark.

If you're not quite up to vying with Bradley or Mark, you can always copy the route map of the Tour, make your way to France and cycle your way round at a more leisurely pace. Many people do, so plenty of facilities for touring cyclists appear along the way. Search online and you'll find companies that organise everything for you, and even shift your gear ahead to give you a luggage-free ride every day. The experience is wonderful, but we leave it up to you to decide whether you can subsequently say you've ridden the Tour de France.

Etape du Tour: A Taste of the Real Thing

Perhaps the best way of getting a flavour of just what riding the Tour de France involves is to enter the Etape du Tour (which means 'stage' in French). The Etape runs every year over a stage of the real tour a few days before the pro riders tackle it themselves.

In years gone by, entering without having to buy the full package tour, including accommodation and travel, was difficult for riders outside France. Together, this cost several hundred pounds, which put many off entering. The problem was that to buy the entry ticket alone involved having to have an address in France.

Thankfully, all that has now changed. Not only is organising your own travel and a place to stay now possible – which means you can do it on a budget – you now have a choice of two Etape routes. The popularity of the challenge meant it was getting very oversubscribed, so from 2011 the organisers put on Etape Acte 1 and Etape Acte 2 with thousands of riders taking part in each and a few doing both.

The Etape is the closest most cyclists ever get to experiencing the thrill of a Grand Tour, and some seriously good riders take part – including some who aren't far off the pace of the Tour itself. One of the biggest differences to other long-distance, mass-participation events is that the Etape is run over closed roads. Nothing else is quite like the feeling of sweeping down off a mountain, being able to cut corners and use the whole road. You can go so much faster, and more safely, than when you have to negotiate with traffic.

The other experience unique to the Etape is the crowds that line the route and cheer you on. You could easily be forgiven for dreaming that you're in the peloton of the Tour de France – the real thing.

Don't, for a minute, think that the Etape is an easy prospect, though. The Etape is a serious challenge that requires proper training. The routes selected are generally in the Alps and Pyrenees, so expect to do at least 5,000 metres (16,400 feet) of climbing and to cover up to 200 kilometres (124 miles), and often take in classic climbs such as the Col du Tourmalet or Mont Ventoux. And as the event takes place in July it can be very hot, which adds yet another challenge into the mix.

The Etape is great fun to watch, not least to give a boost to those riders who look as if they are struggling a bit. The Etape has a cut-off time at regular points around the route – fall behind and you get swept up by the infamous broom wagon, a bus which menacingly nips at the heels of stragglers who can't stay the pace. But make it to the end, and the thrill of riding down a wide boulevard with the finish line just ahead of you and thousands of people cheering you on makes the Etape du Tour a totally unforgettable and must-do experience for all serious cyclists.

Ironbike: Are You Tough Enough?

The name in itself – Ironbike – should give you an inkling into what this event is all about. Billing itself as the world's toughest mountain bike (MTB) *raid* (a raid is another name for a long-distance event), Ironbike is only for riders who can endure pain and discomfort for days on end.

A number of events around the world claim to be 'the toughest' of all, but what makes Ironbike a serious contender is that at the end of each day you don't have the luxury of a hotel room and restaurant; you just have your tent and a small bag of belongings. And even if that thought isn't enough to put you off, the event has a maximum of 140 entrants each year, so you might not get a place even if you want to.

The facts and figures surrounding Ironbike are daunting. It takes place over eight days in the Italian Alps, complete with a *prologue* (a short individual race against the clock, which determines who wears the leaders jersey for the first stage) and seven stages. The route covers around 700 kilometres (435 miles) and includes a whopping 22,000 metres (nearly 72,200 feet) of climbing over the most challenging terrain.

Don't think you can practise each stage and check out the route in advance, either. Those details are closely guarded secrets that are only revealed to riders on the first morning of the raid. And whilst organisers provide food and mechanical assistance at pre-arranged stops, the emphasis is very much on your being able to cope with everything that gets thrown at you. What this means is that even if you spy a hotel nearby and your loyal supporters are staying there, you've got to stick to your tent to stay in the race. The organisers do, however, provide breakfast and an evening meal which, being Italy and being cycling, always involves vast quantities of pasta.

Unsurprisingly, the Ironbike takes its toll on riders and machines and has a high dropout rate as people and equipment get broken. You need to be superfit and pretty handy at bike handling to get round, but if you manage to, you can safely say that you are among the world's élite MTBers.

The Race Across America: Coast to Coast Ultra-Marathon

In 1982, four riders started at the pier in Santa Monica, the bayside suburb of Los Angeles, and rode until they reached the Empire State Building in New York. The Race Across America – or RAAM as it is known – has been captivating the US and cyclists all round the world ever since, and now more than 250 riders take part in the event.

The Race Across America calls itself the world's toughest bicycle race. It goes from west to east, starting in Oceanside, about 60 kilometres (38 miles) north of San Diego, California, and finishing in Annapolis, Maryland. The race can be done singly or in relay teams of two, four or eight.

Relay teams are the most popular (and easier, though by no means easy) entries and teams usually take about five to seven days to complete the route. Solo riders sometimes finish in eight days, but ten is more common. The journey is over 3,000 miles, more than 4,800 kilometres, making it nearly 50 per cent longer than the Tour de France, but gets completed in less than half the time.

The ride crosses mountains, deserts, mountains, vast plains and more mountains. At the start in Oceanside the temperature is normally about 20 degrees Celsius and sunny, but within hours riders climb to San Felipe Valley at nearly 1,000 metres (3,300 feet), where the temperature is about 40 degrees Celsius. Within 24 hours from there, they tackle night temperatures below zero.

Teams don't stop. Riders spend time giving it everything they've got, then recover, then get back on the road. On long climbs, relay riders' shifts become shorter and shorter, so that they can each give a short burst and keep the speed up. In some sections, swap-over is as soon as the bike coming off the road has been loaded, the vehicle has gone ahead, pulled over and readied the next bike and rider. This can be as little as three minutes.

Now and again the riders have to sleep. Solo riders often get little more than an hour's sleep a night. Although their bodies keep on working, sometimes cyclists' minds become loose. The lack of sleep can make cyclists lose touch or hallucinate, and support crews have to keep a close eye on riders' mental states.

Fans gather and camp out at time stations along the way. Solo riders start several days before teams (so that they can all finish at roughly the same time), so waiting supporters have to stay for days to greet all the riders. This support has become a huge part of the race as competitors find it a great boost to spirits. Sometimes riders pedal into Midwest towns in darkness to find hundreds of people cheering them on.

As they close in on the east coast, the environment becomes more built up and roads become complicated. Top-level navigation skills are required of riders and support crews, all of whom suffer from severe sleep deprivation by this point. Unfortunately, at this stage riders often become lost. Reaching the ocean, however, is always a massively elating experience for all involved.

And is RAAM something that draws riders back over and over again? Gavin spoke to one cyclist from the 2007 (record-breaking) winning team who told him she'd made a pact with another team member. She'd asked him if he ever heard she'd signed up to do another one to please kill her.

Ultimate Alpine Challenge: Classic Climbs

What is it about mountains and cyclists? Where you find one, you always seem to find the other. And fortunately for those cyclists, the Alps provide everything even the most diehard mountain rider could want, and plenty of companies willingly satisfy their need for pain.

A number of Alpine challenges are run, with the Ultimate Alpine Challenge right up there with the toughest. The aim? To tackle the toughest and most iconic climbs the Alps have to offer over the space of one week.

Each climb has entered cycling folklore, and each has a history of witnessing extraordinary feats of endurance as well as misery and failure. Names such as the Col de la Colombière, Col de la Madeleine, Col du Galibier and l'Alpe d'Huez have been around from the very beginning of bike racing.

Typically riding around 125 kilometres (80 miles) per day and doing more climbing than most cyclists care to imagine, the Ultimate Alpine Challenge will either get you hooked on hills or put you off for ever. Rather cleverly, some organisers put on two routes each day, so if you aren't feeling up to it or if you're ready to tackle the Big One, you can choose the easier (relatively easier, that is) or harder route to suit your personal desire. And as you might imagine, the views are breathtaking (that's if you've got any breath left), the roads spectacular, the food wonderful and the camaraderie uplifting.

Riding in the Alps is very, very special – something which is difficult to describe, and which you can only really understand by experiencing it for yourself.

Tour of Flanders: Competing on Cobbles

Just as the uninitiated think that cycling in mountains must surely mean that you're slightly deranged, so they never understand the appeal of riding on cobbles, in Belgium, in winter. Okay, this event actually takes place at the end of March, but don't bet against there being at least a bit of sleet, a lot of rain and a howling wind.

The Tour of Flanders for pro-riders is part of the UCI (Union Cycliste Internationale, the body that promotes and controls all types of cycling, particularly at top competition level) World Tour and takes place the week-end before the equally legendary Paris-Roubaix race, which is also run over cobbles. These epics of cycle racing – known as *Monuments* in the European racing calendar – date from a time before tarmac was invented and all roads were made of stone blocks.

The surface, weather, terrain and distances involved (around 250 kilometres, that's 160 miles) in the Tour of Flanders make this race the ultimate in one-day endurance events. And the good (or bad) news is that amateurs can have a go, too. Each year, around 15,000 cyclists test themselves on the Tour de Flanders route in what's locally known as the Ronde van Vlaanderen. Around 3,000 entrants go for the full route, with the remainder going for the two shorter distances of around 140 and 80 kilometres (90 and 50 miles). Even those 80 kilometres are still a tough prospect when you know what you'll be facing.

We've already mentioned the weather. If you're lucky, you get the first taste of spring, but you're just as likely to get lashed by the tail end of winter, which makes your choice of clothing very important. In addition, the terrain is very hilly, heading through Belgian farmland to follow the ancient cobbles and avoid modern asphalt roads. The area is known for its short, sharp climbs, which sap the energy as the race goes on. Riders have around 20 of these horrors to contemplate over the full distance. These hills split the pack and make for some very exciting racing indeed.

Then comes the surface – ah, the surface. Bicycle wheels and cobbles were never designed to work together. Wet cobbles are fiendishly slippery, the gaps can trap tyres between them and the constant juddering and jarring goes right through your body. In places, the cobbled tracks are little more than a couple of metres wide and often awash with mud and puddles and littered with potholes. Thousands of people line the route, in places giving riders just a narrow corridor to get through.

Pro-riders choose bikes with a more relaxed ride, fit bigger tyres and have extra cushioning on their handlebars and nether regions. Even so, the vibration is relentless and is a test for both rider and machine. The Tour sees regular tumbles and broken equipment, which all adds to the spectacle.

Tackling conditions like these can be trying enough over just a few kilometres, but the Tour wouldn't be the classic it is without being utterly gruelling. Ride over 250 kilometres (160 miles) in these conditions and you're left in no doubt that you've just taken part in the ultimate in day racing.

Simpson Desert Bike Challenge: Satan's Velodrome

People call this event the ultimate adventure race, but the Simpson Desert Bike Challenge is a definite contender for the toughest race in the world. Over five days, riders cross nearly 600 kilometres (375 miles) of totally unforgiving desert. They pass salt lakes and ride round camels, but it's the 700 sand dunes that punish them to the verge of defeat.

The ride starts at Purni Bore, South Australia, on the western edge of the Simpson Desert. It finishes at Birdsville in Queensland – at the pub to be precise. Cyclists can lean their mountain bikes up against the posts along the veranda of the classic Birdsville Hotel. We can't think of a harder way to earn a beer.

The event is run in nine stages. On the first four days, a morning stage of 80 kilometres (50 miles) starts at 6 a.m., and then an afternoon stage, starting at 2 p.m., of 50 kilometres (31 miles) is raced. On the final day comes the last 80 kilometres into Birdsville. The first 400 kilometres (250 miles) or so is along the Rig Road. The course then switches to the Birdsville (Inside) Track all the way to the finish.

Compulsory water stops must occur every 20 kilometres (12.5 miles) during the morning and then at 15, 30 and 40 kilometres (9, 19 and 25 miles) in the afternoon. Riders have to keep up a minimum average speed of 12 kilometres (7.5 miles) per hour or they get caught by the sweep vehicle. If this happens, they get a lift to the end of the stage and a time penalty. On some stages, the sweep can pick up as many as half the riders.

Riders need to organise their own support for the event. They have to have a crew ready with shelter, food and drink after the morning stage and then shelter, washing facilities, food and a tent at the end of the day. No water is provided at the start or anywhere along the route, so rider and crew have to bring everything they need.

The sand dunes, each one an unmerciful struggle, are all in the first five stages. The gibber plains follow the dunes and form a surface of closely packed rock fragments that is never easy-going. Lastly, riders tackle the Birdsville Track, which varies with the weather: parts can be smooth, but rain disrupts the surface and clay sections can turn overnight into corridors of goo.

Often fewer than 30 cyclists take this challenge every year. Gavin talked to one rider about his experience of the Simpson Desert. He spoke of the nausea caused by the exertion in the heat and the dreadful wearing down effect, both physical and mental, of riding over dune after dune of soft sand. If you want something tough at a world-class level, here's a ride you can do in a landscape you won't find anywhere in the world but Australia.

Paris-Brest-Paris: 1,200 Kilometres, 90 Hours

Not a race, the Paris-Brest-Paris (PBP) is a *randonnée*: a long-distance, organised ride to be completed in a 90-hour time limit. Randonneurs focus on their personal best and competition is not the spirit of the day. Organisers record riders' times, of course, but everyone who takes on this major challenge is trying to get to Brest and back as fast as they can, and 90 hours is not a long time to ride 1,200 kilometres (750 miles).

The PBP has been going on for well over a century, but it only takes place every four years. It did originate as a race, but became more popular as a timed ride. In the first ever outing, just over 200 Frenchmen (only French men were allowed) started the ride. These days about 6,000 cyclists from all over the world can be expected to register.

For a long time, riders took the main N12 road from Paris to Brittany in the north-east corner of France. In 1979 the route was changed, giving cyclists the security of less busy, less dangerous roads, but still offering them the full 1,200 kilometres to ride. This route change also gave them a better view of Brittany as they pedalled past orchards and fields of artichokes.

Throughout the ride cyclists stop at stations and eat, but don't ever have time to grab more than an hour or so of sleep. As one rider later reported: 'The exhausted riders unfold a blanket and settle down against the wall or on the only floor. A Japanese rider drowses on her chair and suddenly falls. By her side, a German rider sleeps the [*sic*] head in his plate'.

Most riders leave Paris on the Sunday evening. The fast ones who have committed to a shorter ride time leave in the early hours of Monday morning. By Thursday afternoon, time's up, and everyone who has succeeded in this terrible test is back in Paris. At 5 p.m. the organisers host a cocktail reception for the tired bicyclists.

As the PBP is only held every four years and you have to qualify for it by successfully completing a number of *Audax* (long-distance) rides, you won't get many shots at this challenge. So plan it out – if you want to be a part of this amazing piece of cycling history, start training right now.

The Cape Epic: An Eight-day Race through South Africa

The Cape Epic was the first mountain bike stage race to be given UCI 2HC categorisation: a similar ranking to the Grand Tours, including the Tour de France. Cyclists can use this race to rack up points towards Olympic qualification.

The Epic is made up of a prologue and seven stages. Stages can run between 30 and 150 kilometres (19 and 94 miles), although the route and these details change every year. Thirty kilometres might sound like an easy day, but this ride aims for the steepest, rockiest pathways South Africa has to offer, and none of these days is a walk in the park. All entrants must be in teams of two and these pairs must stick with each other throughout.

Although the route is different every year, riders always see vast, open African plains, monumental mountains, deep gorges and ravines, native forests and some spectacular coastlines. Riders make their way through the rough hills and valleys 50 to 100 kilometres (31 to 62 miles) east of Cape

Town. The whole party sleep at night in tented race villages set up daily in different locations in the rugged bush.

The Cape Epic has been going for less than ten years, but in that short time its harsh but beautiful environment and punishing schedule have seen its reputation soar to one of the world's most challenging MTB races. If you fancy this one, you'd better get down to the singletrack and get some practice.

Iditasport Extreme: The Race across Snowy Alaska

Competitors in Iditasport have the choice of cycling either 563 or 1,770 kilometres (352 or 983 miles) – all across the frozen wastes of Alaska in the middle of winter. The race begins in Knik, about 70 kilometres (44 miles) from Anchorage, and follows the Iditarod Trail to McGrath for the 'short' race, then on to Nome for the full-length version.

The organisers send a snowplough through – once – along the short section of the trail in front of the ride leaders. Seven checkpoints are installed in this first stretch, where riders can eat and sleep. Two food drops also occur along this sector. After McGrath, over the next 1,200 kilometres (750 miles), just one food drop occurs and no checkpoints are in place. Riders are very much on their own.

Some ultra cyclists who have taken this challenge comment that Iditasport Extreme is not totally a bike ride, as entrants are also allowed skis and sleds, but they all do take bikes and they all use them. And nobody ever says competitors are doing anything soft. The bikes they ride are like mountain bikes, but they don't have suspension. They do have massively wide rims and very fat tyres that they use at medium-low pressure.

Riders are expected in McGrath within 10 days and Nome within 30. If they don't get there on time they aren't penalised, they just miss the party. They do get punished, however, if they're on the longer race and ask the dog sled race crews or checkpoints for any assistance. The dog sled race runs at the same time, but if riders ask for help, they lose a $750 deposit.

Over the last ten years, only 33 people have finished the full route from Knik to Nome, three of them women.

Index

About the Authors

Gavin Wright is one of Australia's leading bicycle journalists. He is well known in national cycling magazines for his features, reviews and travel articles. He has led several high-profile cycling expeditions, including a crossing of the Andes on the highest surfaced road in the world and an attempt to set the world record for cycling from sea level to high altitude. Gavin has toured unsupported on his bicycle in Indochina, Europe and the Amazon jungle. He is also a person living with type 1 diabetes and spends much time promoting exercise for other people living with the same condition.

Starting his professional career as a community worker in the troubled London boroughs in the 1980s, Gavin moved on to film school at the age of 25. He then worked as a writer and producer in community television in London before moving to Australia. Gavin worked on the Melbourne production of *Phantom of the Opera* and then changed course (again) and took up cooking. He worked as a chef and head chef in busy Melbourne CBD restaurants, but decided to take on more social hours when he started a family. Gavin took up journalism, returned to bicycling and was able to happily marry the two.

A graduate of the London Institute where he majored in Film and Photography, Gavin is also a qualified journalist from the Australian College of Journalism. He founded a bicycle users' group in Melbourne's western suburbs that is now one of the strongest in the region. He has worked for Bicycle Victoria as both a staff member and a volunteer and co-authored their 2008 book *The Bike Bible*.

Gavin Wright now lives on the Gold Coast with his wife, Julia, and his three children, Billy, Isobel and Akira. He spends many hours cycling on roads through the hills of the Gold Coast hinterland and on the hundreds of kilometres of local singletrack and fire trails.

Ben Williams has been a keen cyclist from childhood. Having a best friend next door whose father was the editor of a cycling magazine helped. Hours would be spent in his garage drooling over the line-up of shiny machines, with many an unsuccessful attempt to ride them. Just as many other kids have found, Ben found that having a bike opens a door to freedom and adventure; a chance to explore the world. What Ben's learnt now is that the same holds true for adults, too.

Biking holidays around Europe have helped Ben discover the essential ingredient for a biking holiday: mountains. Not only do you get fantastic scenery and quiet roads, but fabulous food too. Corsica and Scilly are two of the great cycling destinations and the pain of going up a hill or two justifies second helpings.

Living in London for 15 years has also shown Ben the practicalities of cycling in big, urban environments. Commuting to his job in broadcasting, shopping and taking the kids to school every day by bike is not only fun and healthy, it is also the quickest, cheapest and most reliable form of transport he's found.

Having since moved to the New Forest, cycling for Ben has become not just a great way of staying fit but a great social pastime. After all, what other sports allow you to have a proper workout while chatting with your friends for a couple of hours?

Dedications

Firstly, this book is dedicated to my beautiful, talented and discerning wife, Julia, and to my most excellent children, Billy, Isobel and Akira, for their practical, motivational and inspirational support. I hope we ride together forever.

Secondly, to two friends and cyclists: Monique Hanley and Hugh Harvey. Monique has worked hard to achieve some extraordinary feats and excel in competition. She has taken all hurdles, such as type 1 diabetes and even serious injury, as challenges and has been an inspiration to many other cyclists living with type 1 diabetes, including myself. She's much faster than me, but always a great pleasure to cycle with. Hugh has been my cycling partner on South American adventures and around Australia. We have ridden through some tough situations and had adventures the likes of which most people will never know. He's a strong cyclist, a loyal and exemplary riding companion and a very good friend.

Gavin

Authors' Acknowledgements

My thanks go to all the people working hard behind the scenes at Wiley Publishing, but my deepest gratitude goes to the editorial team: To acquisitions editor, Rebecca Crisp, for her vision and strength; to Hannah Bennett for her clarity, comprehension and incisiveness; to Laura Callow for her flair and dedication; and to Charlotte Duff for both instigating the venture and working tirelessly and thoroughly towards its completion with such energy and aplomb. I have never had the pleasure of working with a team so proficient, professional, motivated, encouraging and, frankly, charming.

My thanks also go to Ian Christie for taking the time and trouble to lend his considerable knowledge and expertise with the technical review.

For giving their time freely I would like to thank: Mark and Kylie at Nerang Mountain Bike Centre, Mary McParland at Cycling South, Monique Hanley at HypoActive, Lorisa Perebooms in New Zealand and the urbanbicyclist project (www.urbanbicyclist.org).

I would like to thank the thousands of cyclists I have shared the pleasure of the saddle with all over the world. I have tipped my helmet to all from the fastest racers to the gentlest of pedallers and every one has my respect and best wishes. In particular, although it was years ago now, I would like to thank Dave Young for putting me back on a bicycle.

Gavin

Publisher's Acknowledgements

We're proud of this book; please send us your comments at `http://dummies.custhelp.com`. For other comments, please contact our Customer Care Department within the U.S. at 877-762-2974, outside the U.S. at (001) 317-572-3993, or fax 317-572-4002.

Some of the people who helped bring this book to market include the following:

Acquisitions, Editorial, and Vertical Websites

Project Editor: Steve Edwards

Commissioning Editor: Mike Baker

Assistant Editor: Ben Kemble

Development Editor: Steve Edwards

Proofreader: Cate Miller

Production Manager: Daniel Mersey

Publisher: Miles Kendall

Cover Photos: © Maurizio Borsari/Aflo/ Jupiterimages

Composition Services

Project Coordinator: Kristie Rees

Layout and Graphics: Carrie A. Cesavice, Jennifer Creasey, Amy Hassos, Joyce Haughey

Proofreader: Melissa Cossell

Indexer: Estalita Slivoskey

FOR DUMMIES®

Making Everything Easier!™

UK editions

BUSINESS

978-1-118-34689-1

978-1-118-44349-1

978-1-119-97527-4

MUSIC

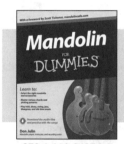

978-1-119-94276-4

978-0-470-97799-6

978-0-470-66372-1

HOBBIES

978-1-118-41156-8

978-1-119-99417-6

978-1-119-97250-1

Asperger's Syndrome For Dummies
978-0-470-66087-4

Basic Maths For Dummies
978-1-119-97452-9

**Body Language For Dummies,
2nd Edition**
978-1-119-95351-7

Boosting Self-Esteem For Dummies
978-0-470-74193-1

Business Continuity For Dummies
978-1-118-32683-1

Cricket For Dummies
978-0-470-03454-5

Diabetes For Dummies, 3rd Edition
978-0-470-97711-8

eBay For Dummies, 3rd Edition
978-1-119-94122-4

English Grammar For Dummies
978-0-470-05752-0

Flirting For Dummies
978-0-470-74259-4

IBS For Dummies
978-0-470-51737-6

ITIL For Dummies
978-1-119-95013-4

**Management For Dummies,
2nd Edition**
978-0-470-97769-9

**Managing Anxiety with CBT
For Dummies**
978-1-118-36606-6

**Neuro-linguistic Programming
For Dummies, 2nd Edition**
978-0-470-66543-5

Nutrition For Dummies, 2nd Edition
978-0-470-97276-2

Organic Gardening For Dummies
978-1-119-97706-3

FOR DUMMIES®

Making Everything Easier! ™

UK editions

SELF-HELP

978-0-470-66541-1

978-1-119-99264-6

978-0-470-66086-7

LANGUAGES

978-0-470-68815-1

978-1-119-97959-3

978-0-470-69477-0

HISTORY

978-0-470-68792-5

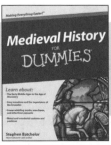

978-0-470-74783-4

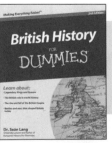

978-0-470-97819-1

Origami Kit For Dummies
978-0-470-75857-1

Overcoming Depression For Dummies
978-0-470-69430-5

Positive Psychology For Dummies
978-0-470-72136-0

PRINCE2 For Dummies, 2009 Edition
978-0-470-71025-8

Project Management For Dummies
978-0-470-71119-4

Psychology Statistics For Dummies
978-1-119-95287-9

Psychometric Tests For Dummies
978-0-470-75366-8

Renting Out Your Property For Dummies, 3rd Edition
978-1-119-97640-0

Rugby Union For Dummies, 3rd Edition
978-1-119-99092-5

Sage One For Dummies
978-1-119-95236-7

Self-Hypnosis For Dummies
978-0-470-66073-7

Storing and Preserving Garden Produce For Dummies
978-1-119-95156-8

Teaching English as a Foreign Language For Dummies
978-0-470-74576-2

Time Management For Dummies
978-0-470-77765-7

Training Your Brain For Dummies
978-0-470-97449-0

Voice and Speaking Skills For Dummies
978-1-119-94512-3

Work-Life Balance For Dummies
978-0-470-71380-8

12-47776-187x234mm

FOR DUMMIES®

Making Everything Easier! ™

COMPUTER BASICS

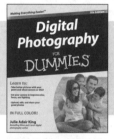

978-1-118-11533-6

978-0-470-61454-9

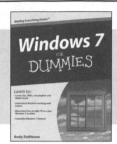

978-0-470-49743-2

DIGITAL PHOTOGRAPHY

978-1-118-09203-3

978-0-470-76878-5

978-1-118-00472-2

SCIENCE AND MATHS

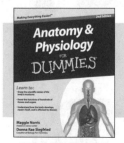

978-0-470-92326-9

978-0-470-55964-2

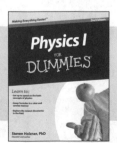

978-0-470-90324-7

Art For Dummies
978-0-7645-5104-8

Computers For Seniors For Dummies, 3rd Edition
978-1-118-11553-4

Criminology For Dummies
978-0-470-39696-4

Currency Trading For Dummies, 2nd Edition
978-0-470-01851-4

Drawing For Dummies, 2nd Edition
978-0-470-61842-4

Forensics For Dummies
978-0-7645-5580-0

French For Dummies, 2nd Edition
978-1-118-00464-7

Guitar For Dummies, 2nd Edition
978-0-7645-9904-0

Hinduism For Dummies
978-0-470-87858-3

Index Investing For Dummies
978-0-470-29406-2

Islamic Finance For Dummies
978-0-470-43069-9

Knitting For Dummies, 2nd Edition
978-0-470-28747-7

Music Theory For Dummies, 2nd Edition
978-1-118-09550-8

Office 2010 For Dummies
978-0-470-48998-7

Piano For Dummies, 2nd Edition
978-0-470-49644-2

Photoshop CS6 For Dummies
978-1-118-17457-9

Schizophrenia For Dummies
978-0-470-25927-6

WordPress For Dummies, 5th Edition
978-1-118-38318-6

12-47776–187x234mm

Think you can't learn it in a day? Think again!

The *In a Day* e-book series from *For Dummies* gives you quick and easy access to learn a new skill, brush up on a hobby, or enhance your personal or professional life — all in a day. Easy!

Available as PDF, eMobi and Kindle